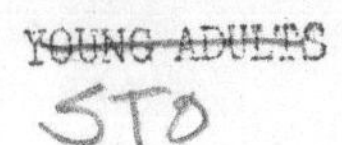
YOUNG ADULTS
STO

ALLEN COUNTY PUBLIC LIBRARY
P9-EDY-119

Silver Burdett Science Program

PHYSICAL SCIENCE
Charles R. Barman
John J. Rusch
Myron O. Schneiderwent
Wendy B. Hindin

LIFE SCIENCE
Jenne Taylor Richardson
Anne F. Harris
Oliver Crosby Sparks

EARTH SCIENCE
F. Martin Brown
Grace H. Kemper

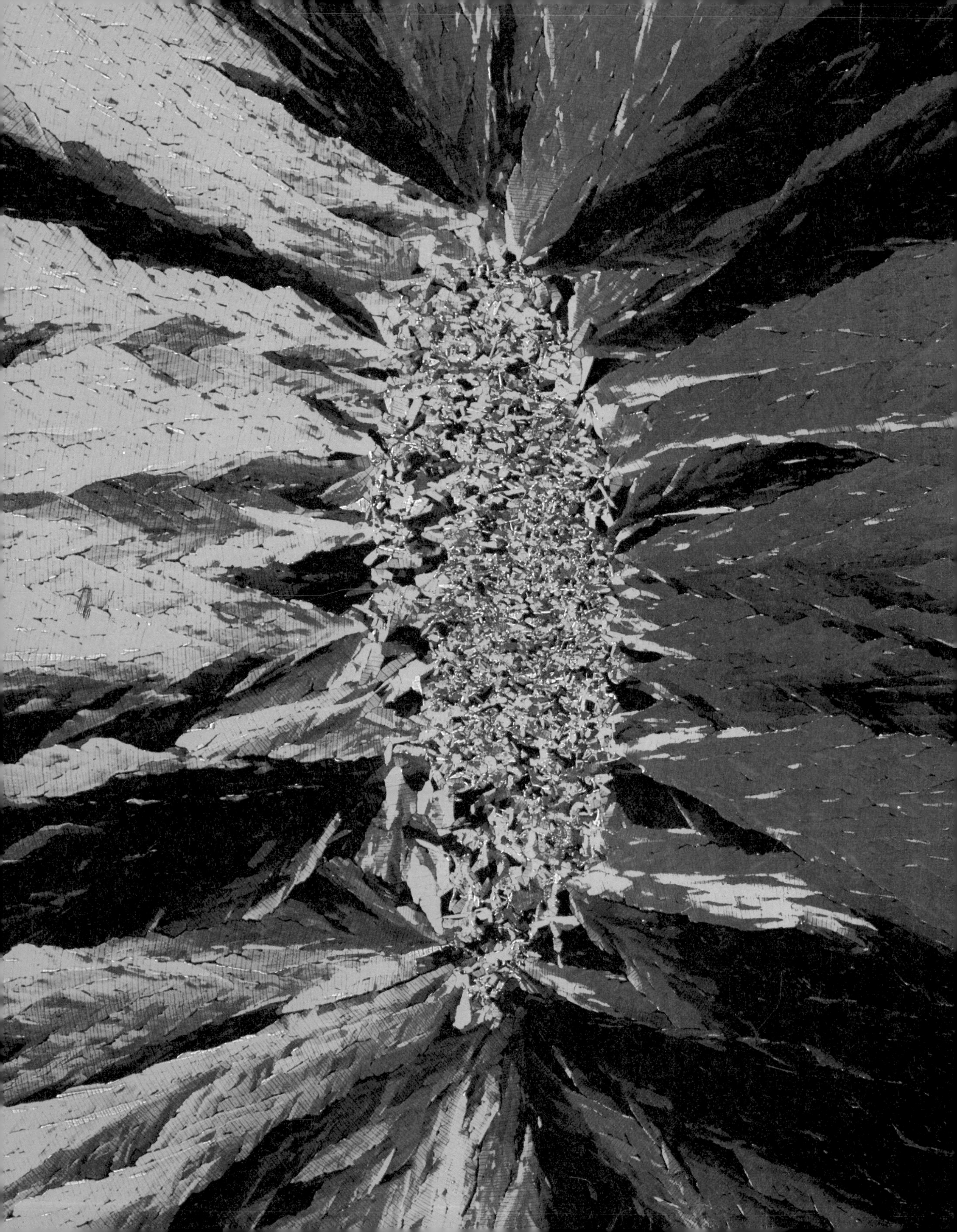

PHYSICAL SCIENCE

CHARLES R. BARMAN
Assistant Professor, Science Education
University of Wisconsin—Superior
Superior, Wisconsin

MYRON O. SCHNEIDERWENT
Associate Professor, Physics
University of Wisconsin—Superior
Superior, Wisconsin

JOHN J. RUSCH
Associate Professor, Science Education
University of Wisconsin—Superior
Superior, Wisconsin

WENDY B. HINDIN
Science Coordinator
North Shore Hebrew Academy
Great Neck, New York

Consultant and Contributor
E. LEE SPANCAKE
Chemistry Teacher, Watchung Hills Regional High School
Warren, New Jersey

SILVER BURDETT COMPANY
Morristown, New Jersey
Glenview, Illinois • Palo Alto • Dallas • Atlanta

Acknowledgments

It would be impossible to acknowledge the assistance of everyone who played a part in the development and production of this text. However, we would like to acknowledge the following people who read and criticized the program.

Critic Readers

Ann Barrette
Science Teacher
Glen Hills Middle School
Milwaukee, Wisconsin

Betty Jo Durman
Chairperson, Science Department
Constitution Hall
Johnson City, Tennessee

Jesse Harris Jr.
Director of Science and Health
Dallas Independent School District
Dallas, Texas

William Thomas
Supervisor of Science
Liberty Instructional Center
Pensacola, Florida

Gary Nakagiri
Science Specialist
San Francisco Unified School District Offices
San Francisco, California

Victor Kritz
Science Teacher
Augsburg American High School
Augsburg, West Germany

Student Readers

Cosmo Rich
Superior, Wisconsin

Kirstin Heise
Sayreville, New Jersey

ISBN 0-382-04971-3

Contents

UNIT ONE • METHODS OF SCIENCE

UNIT TWO • NATURE OF MATTER

UNIT THREE • STRUCTURE OF MATTER

UNIT FOUR • FORCES, MOTION, ENERGY

UNIT FIVE • A CHANGING WORLD

EXCURSIONS

UNIT ONE

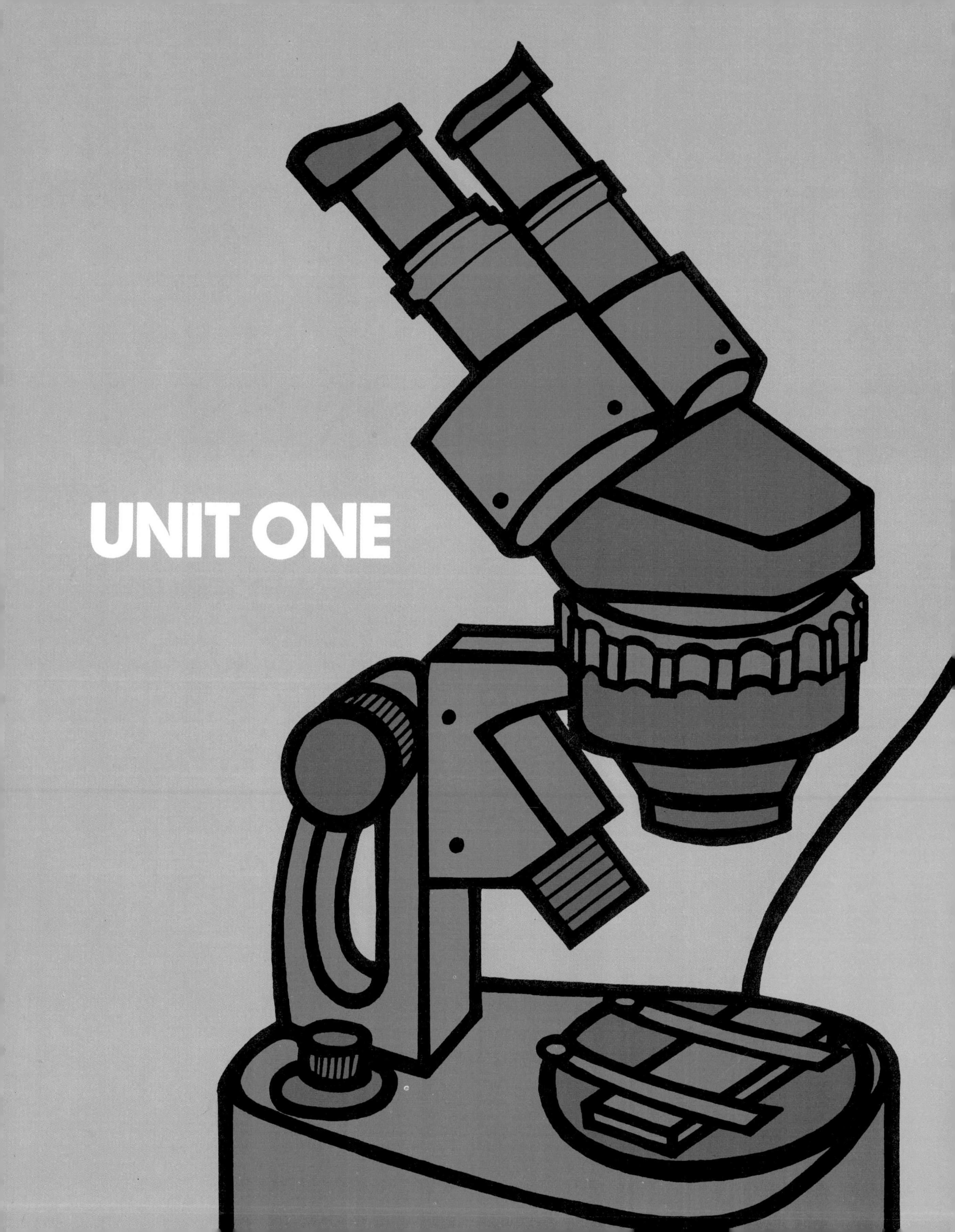

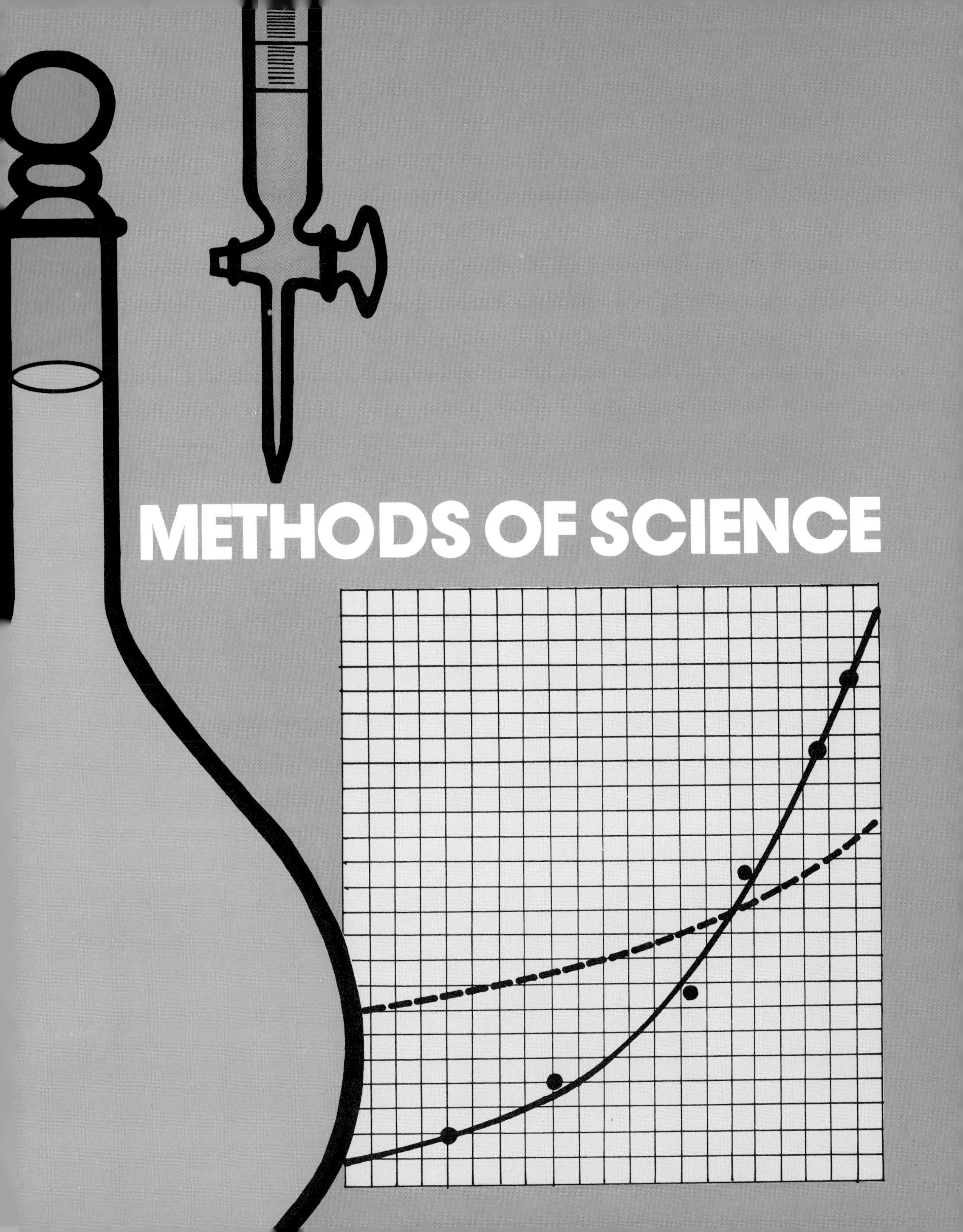

METHODS OF SCIENCE

Electronic color scanning is used to determine imperfections in this computer chip. The printed circuitry, enlarged more than 600 times, might easily be mistaken for an aerial view of city blocks in summer.

1

Describing Matter

Most people are naturally curious. They want to know about things. They especially want to know about the things around them. What is it? What does it do? How does it work? What is it made of? Curious people ask endless kinds of questions.

Science is a history of the desire to understand the world we live in. Science is also a way of thinking about things. And, it is a way of finding solutions to problems for which there would seem to be no solutions.

Science involves making observations. It involves trying to find some pattern of order, or regularity, in what has been observed. Observation of order is important in science. Science also involves trying to find explanations for what has been observed. Explanations of observations lead to predictions of what will happen in new situations under similar conditions.

Observation

There is a strange-looking object at the front of the classroom. Perhaps it was the first thing you noticed when you entered the room. You are probably wondering what the object is. Or maybe you are wondering how it is used. Maybe you are wondering why it is there and how it concerns you. If the object has made you curious, you want to know more about it.

Look at the object from a distance. List as many things as you can that describe it. You might begin with color, shape, and what the object appears to be made of. When you have completed the list, go to the object and examine it more closely. Touch it if you wish. Smell it. Listen to it. Examine the object in any way you can, but do not take it apart or lift it. When you have finished examining the object, make a new list of things that describe it. These descriptions may not agree with those in your first list. Compare the two lists. Which list, do you think, better describes the object? Why?

More detail of the tail light of this car can be observed from close up than from a distance.

In order to describe the strange-looking object, you had to observe it. Observing is something you do with your senses: sight, smell, touch, hearing, and taste. When you *see* a candle, *touch* a kitten, *smell* a flower, *taste* a hamburger, or *hear* a siren, you are making an observation. You are getting information about the object through one of your senses.

Name the five senses.

Look again at the two lists of things you used to describe the strange-looking object. Which of your senses did you use to make the first list? to make the second list? You had to rely almost entirely on your sense of sight to describe the object from a distance. If the distance was not too great, you might also have used your senses of smell and hearing. When making the second list, you were close to the object. You could still use your senses of sight, smell, and hearing. But now you could also touch the object. You could feel if it was hard, soft, dry, sticky, and so on. You might even have tried to use your sense of taste. However, *tasting things in the laboratory can be dangerous. Never taste anything unless you are told to do so by your teacher.*

EXCURSION 5
Some people claim they have a sixth sense called ESP, or extrasensory perception. This topic is discussed in Excursion 5, "ESP—Fact, or Fiction?" The Excursion includes an activity that may help you to form your own opinion about ESP.

Extending the Senses

The extent to which you can observe with your senses is limited. Sometimes you cannot observe an object directly with one or more of your senses. You may be too far away from the object to touch it or even to see it clearly. If the object makes a sound or has an odor, you also may not be able to hear it or smell it. For example, when observing the moon, you are limited to your sense of sight. However, the moon is too far away for you to see clearly the features of its surface.

Scientists are faced with the same problem. There are times when they, too, find it difficult to make

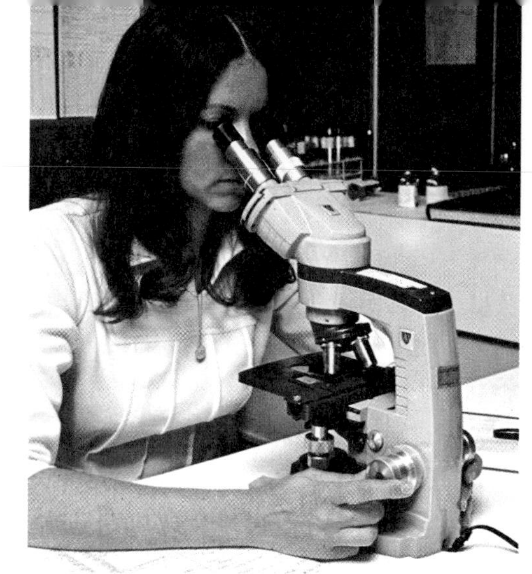

A microscope (top left) extends the sense of sight; remotely controlled mechanical arms (top right) extend the sense of touch; a radar antenna (bottom left) extends the senses of hearing and sight–it picks up radio waves that may then be displayed visually on a screen; a gas detection device (bottom right) extends the sense of smell.

certain observations. The objects they want to observe may be too small or too far away. To overcome this problem, various instruments and devices have been developed to extend the senses. A telescope, for example, extends the sense of sight. Telescopes make distant objects appear nearer than they really are. With a telescope, observations can be made of the moon that could not be made with the unaided eye. The microscope is another instrument that extends the sense of sight. Microscopes make very small objects appear larger than they really are. What other things can you think of that are used to extend the senses?

EXCURSION 6
In Excursion 6, "Telemetry," you can find out how pictures taken by satellites are transmitted to earth.

We have come to rely on many different means of extending the senses. But can we always trust our senses? Is it possible that we could be misled by what our senses tell us? Look at Figure 1–1. Which line, *A* or

B, appears longer? You may have determined that *B* is longer than *A*. In this case, your direct observation may have been inaccurate. Your eyes may have been fooled. You would have known immediately that *A* and *B* are the same length if you had measured them. Using measuring instruments is another way of extending the senses.

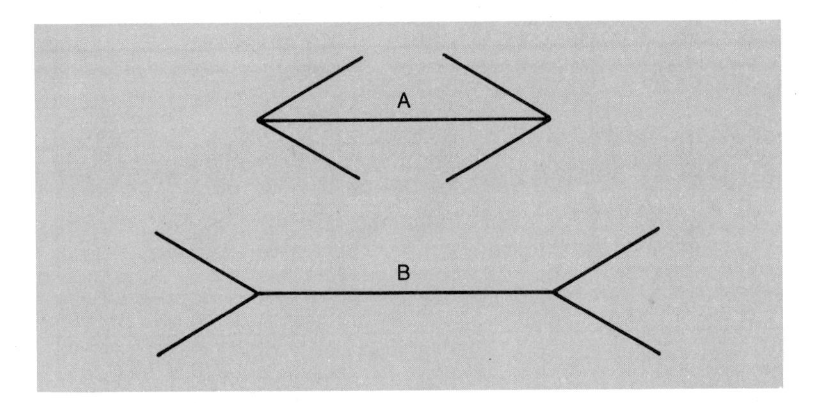

FIGURE 1–1
The apparent difference in the lengths of these arrows is an optical illusion.

Sometimes you see things that appear different from what they really are. Look at the two faces in Figure 1–2. How would you describe them? Turn your book around so that the faces are upside down. Does the way the faces now appear fit your earlier description? The way things appear often changes when they are seen from a different position.

FIGURE 1–2
The dramatic change in the way these faces are perceived depends on the position from which they are viewed.

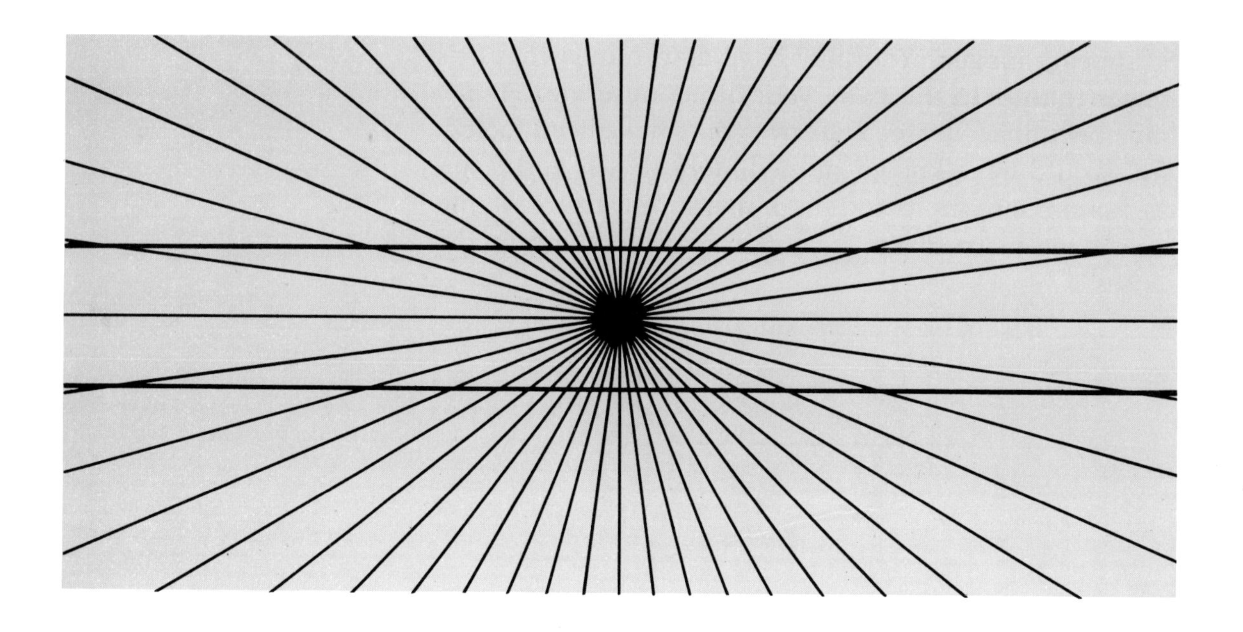

FIGURE 1–3
Visual observations sometimes are unreliable. The horizontal lines (above) are straight but appear to be bent. The ambiguous trident (below) is confusing when viewed as a three-dimensional figure but is clearly a flat pattern when viewed as a two-dimensional figure. Depth reversal is apparent in the folded card (right), which appears to project both into and out of the page.

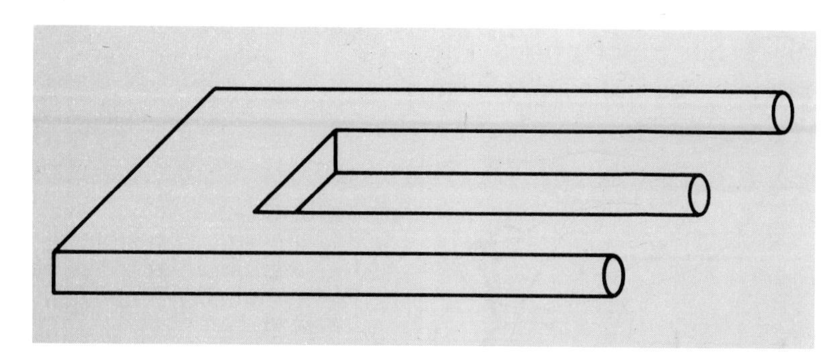

In what way are quantitative observations different from qualitative observations?

Scientists use many types of instruments to measure the things they observe. A measurement is a **quantitative** (kwon'tə tā tiv) **observation.** Describing the length of a rope in meters would be a quantitative observation. When you weigh yourself on a bathroom scale, you are making a quantitative observation of your weight. Whenever an observation is described by a number, you can be certain that it is a quantitative observation.

Some observations are not quantitative. For example, you may observe that an object is long, heavy, blue, or soft. Such observations are **qualitative** (kwol'ə tā tiv) **observations.** They describe a quality of the object, but they do not tell the actual value or amount of that quality.

Quantitative observations may be made by using instruments such as a colorimeter (top left), a serological pipette (right), or an oscilloscope (bottom left).

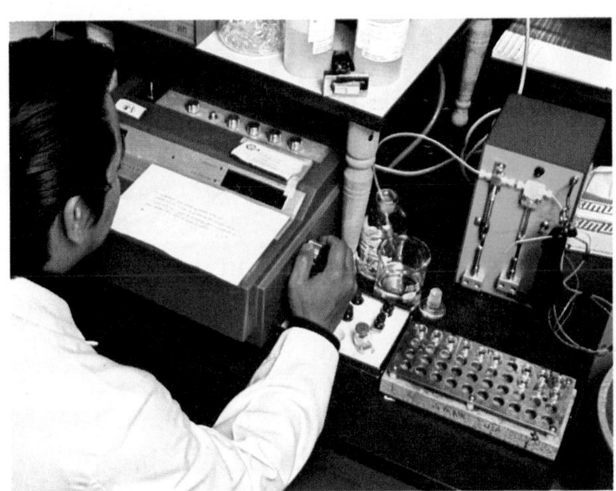

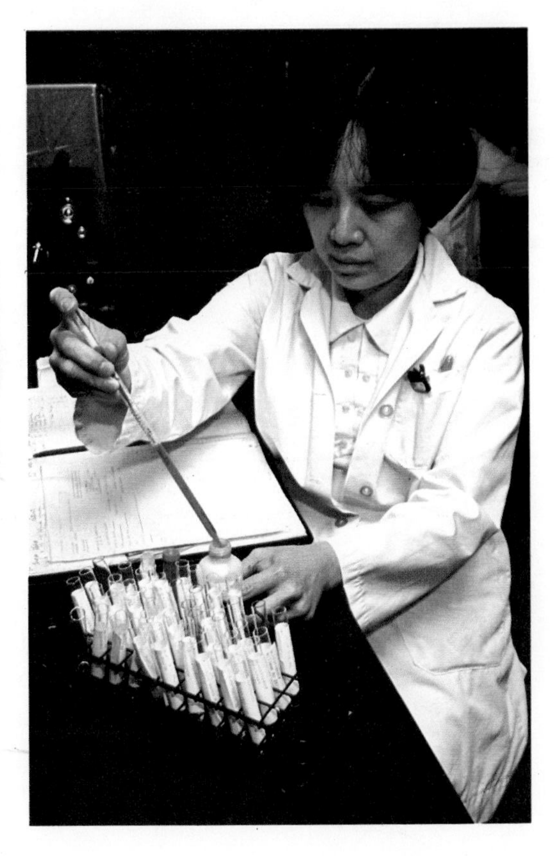

Making Inferences

What is an inference?

Being able to make good observations is important. However, you must be careful not to confuse an observation with an **inference** (in'fər əns). An inference is an interpretation of an observation. It is based on a past experience. For example, suppose you look out the window on a bright winter day and say, "It's cold outside." You are making an inference. You are inferring that it is cold based on your past experience with bright winter days. Now suppose you go outside and say, "It feels cold." "It feels cold" is an observation made with one of your senses. It is not based on your past experience with bright winter days.

Often several inferences can be based on a single observation. For example, you get up in the morning and see that the street is wet. You might infer from this observation that it rained during the night. But you might also infer that a water main broke or that a fire hydrant had been opened. What other inferences could be made from this one observation?

People infer from their observations all the time. They often do this without realizing it. Being able to infer from observations is useful in science. However, it is useful only if the inferences are not mistaken for true observations. Remember, an observation is made with one or more of the senses; an inference is an interpretation of an observation. To test an observation, ask yourself which of the senses was used to make the observation. If you can't name a specific sense, what you are calling an observation is probably not one.

In Activity 1 you will infer the contents of a can. You will make observations that are limited and based on previous experiences unrelated to the activity. When you infer from such observations, your inferences are based on indirect evidence.

Activity 1 Making Inferences

PURPOSE

To infer the contents of a can from indirect evidence

MATERIALS

Large coffee can with plastic lid
Paper
3 different items to be placed in the can

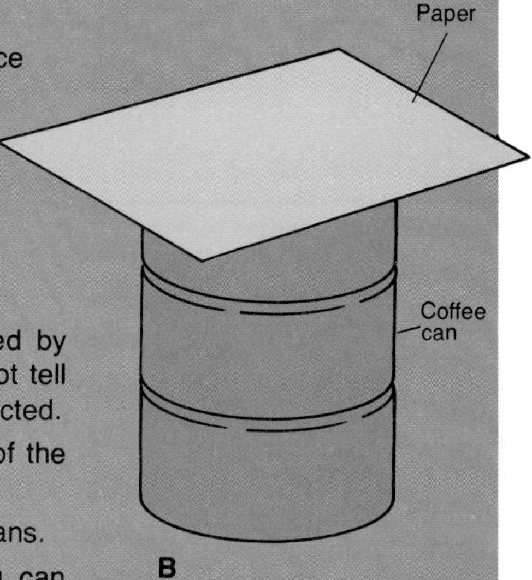

DO THIS

A. Select 3 items from the assortment supplied by your teacher. Put them in the coffee can. Do not tell other students, or let them see, the items you selected.

B. Place a sheet of paper over the open end of the can. Press the plastic lid down over the paper.

C. Write your name on the lid. Then exchange cans.

D. Using indirect evidence, list inferences you can make about the items in the can. The questions that follow may help you to organize your thinking when making inferences. Suppose the can is shaken.

- Do the items seem to slide, roll, or tumble? Does this help you to infer the shapes of the items?
- What sounds do the items make when they strike the sides of the can or each other? Does this help you to infer that the items are metallic? wooden? hard, but not metallic? soft?
- Do the items seem to move the same distance? Do they seem to strike the end of the can at the same time? Does this help you to infer how the sizes of the objects compare?

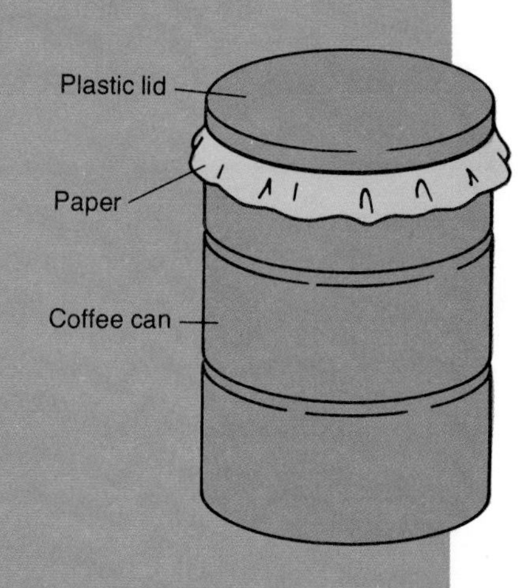

REPORT

1. What do you infer are the items in the can?

2. Open the can. How many of the inferences you made from indirect evidence were correct?

3. Why are inferences made from indirect evidence not as good as those based on direct observation?

EXCURSION 1
If you are not familiar with the metric units of length, now would be a good time to do Excursion 1, "Metric Linear Measurement."

EXCURSION 2
The concept of mass and how it is measured is discussed in Excursion 2, "Measuring Mass."

What are properties?

Properties

How do you tell materials apart? How can you point to two materials and say, This is chalk dust, that is crude oil? In some cases it is easy. The materials are so clearly different that there is no question as to which is which. In the case of chalk dust and crude oil, the chalk dust is a white, powdery solid. Crude oil is a black, thick liquid. You can tell these are different materials simply by looking at them. Suppose you had never seen these materials before. Then you might not know that one is crude oil and the other is chalk dust. But you certainly would be able to tell that they were not the same material.

The more alike materials are in physical appearance, the harder it is to tell them apart. Talcum powder looks very much like chalk dust. Baking powder also looks very much like chalk dust. If these materials were side by side, could you tell the chalk dust from the talcum powder? from the baking powder? By only looking at them, you may not be able to tell if they are the same material or different materials. What you need is more information about each material.

The features, or characteristics, that describe an object are called **properties.** Some examples of properties are color, length, width, shape, and the feel of an object. However, the properties of an object include more than a description of physical appearance. They also describe how the object behaves when it is heated, cooled, compressed, or similarly treated in a special way.

When describing an object, do not use the object's name or function as properties. Names and functions of objects are not properties. For example, *scissors* is the name given to a particular cutting instrument. *Scissors* does not describe the instrument. Similarly, the instrument is not described by saying that it is used for cutting.

The glass bowl (right) is the product of changes in the properties of sand (top left).

Activity 2 One-Property Identification

PURPOSE

To describe an item by stating one property that will identify the item from among several items

MATERIALS

Tray of assorted items

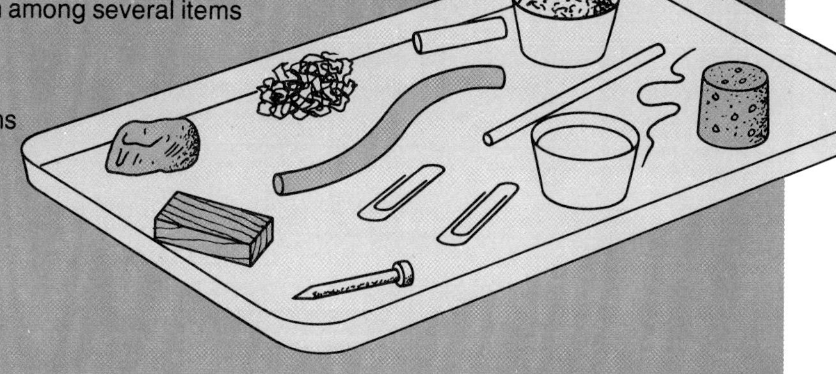

DO THIS

A. Work with a partner. Observe the items on the tray. Decide which item you want to describe. Then choose one property of the item and tell it to your partner. Your partner should try to identify the item on the basis of this one property.

B. Repeat step **A** two more times. Each time choose an item with a property different from those used previously.

C. Change roles with your partner and repeat steps **A** and **B.**

REPORT

1. How many items did your partner identify correctly? How many did you identify correctly?

2. Is it easy, or difficult, to identify an item on the basis of one property?

3. What might make identification of an item on the tray easier?

4. Name one item on the tray. Then list as many properties of the item that, you think, are necessary for it to be identified correctly.

In order to be useful, a property must be stated clearly and exactly. For example, how could you state the property of length for line *A* in Figure 1–4? You might say that the line is long. But what does long mean? How long is long? Actually line *A* is short when compared to line *B*. Suppose you measured line *A* and found its length to be 11 cm. Eleven centimeters is a quantitative observation. By measuring, the property of length for line *A* can be stated exactly. There no longer is any question as to whether the line is long or short. Line *A* is exactly 11 cm in length.

There are two kinds of properties that describe an object. The first kind are **general properties.** These are properties that may be the same for two or more objects. The second kind are **identifying properties.** Identifying properties are the specific properties that make one object different from all the other objects to which it is similar. For example, consider a golf ball and a Ping-Pong ball. Both share many of the same properties. They are small, spherical (sfer′ə kəl), and white. They are hard, shiny on the surface, and not very heavy. When dropped from a height of 1 m, they both bounce back to almost that same height. Based only on these properties, you cannot tell that the golf ball is different from the Ping-Pong ball. The properties of shape, relative size, color, and hardness are general properties that describe both balls.

However, suppose you are told that the golf ball has a diameter of 4.3 cm and a mass of 44.5 g. It also shows no apparent effect when squeezed by hand and has a surface covered with small pits. By observation and measurement, you now can tell which of the two balls is the golf ball. The diameter, mass, and pitted surface are identifying properties. They describe only the golf ball.

In Activity 3 you will work with both general and identifying properties as you try to identify one particular object in a group of similar objects.

FIGURE 1–4

A B

Activity 3 Identification Based on Several Properties

PURPOSE

To identify an object in a group of similar objects that share some of the same properties

MATERIALS

None

DO THIS

A. Look at the numbered boxes. Each box contains four symbols. Each symbol is a property of the box.

B. One of the boxes is described in this activity. You will be given the properties of that box, one property at a time. Try to identify the box after learning each new property. The first property is given in step **C.**

C. The box contains at least one circle. Try to identify the box, using this property.

D. The box contains one half-black circle. Try to identify the box, using this and the previous property.

E. The box also contains one dotted circle. Try to identify the box, using this and the previous properties.

F. The box also contains at least one square. Try to identify the box, using this and all the previous properties.

G. The box contains one clear circle. Try to identify the box, using this and all the previous properties.

REPORT

1. Which numbered box is the one described?

2. How many properties did you need to know to identify the box?

3. Are *black circle* and *half-black circle* the same property, or different properties?

4. How many different properties describe Box 11?

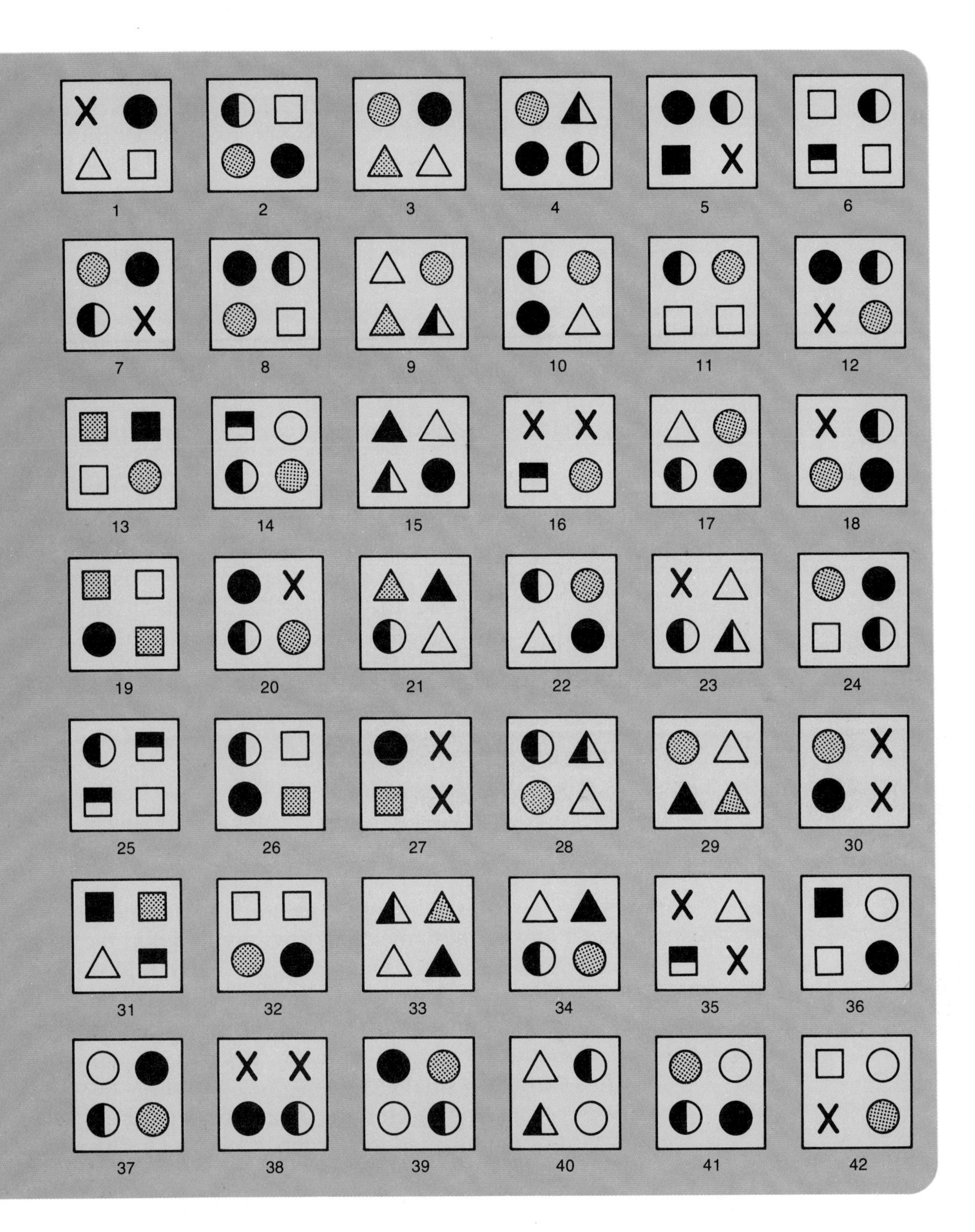
1
2
3
4
5
6
7
8
9
10
11
12
13
14
15
16
17
18
19
20
21
22
23
24
25
26
27
28
29
30
31
32
33
34
35
36
37
38
39
40
41
42

How do general properties differ from identifying properties?

Like the golf ball and the Ping-Pong ball, many boxes in Activity 3 share some of the same properties. In fact, 39 of the 42 boxes have the property *circle.* Of the 39 boxes with that property, 26 have the property *half-black circle* and 26 have the property *spotted circle.* However, only 18 boxes with the property *circle* have both *half-black circle* and *spotted circle* as properties. When you were given the first property of the box (that it contains at least one circle), you could eliminate only boxes 31, 33, and 35. When you were given the second property, you could eliminate all the boxes that did not have both properties. The more properties you were given, the more boxes you could eliminate. Finally, only one box remained that had all of the given properties.

What procedure did you follow to find the one box with all the given properties? First, you examined the properties of each box. Then you grouped, or **classified** (klas′ə fīd), the boxes. You did this on the basis of whether or not they had the properties you were given. This method of grouping objects, based on their properties, is called **classification** (klas ə fə kā′shən).

A Classification Scheme

Classification is a useful technique for organizing a large number of items. When we classify materials, we group those things that are alike in some way. For example, in a department store each department contains items of the same kind. Toys are found in the toy department, shoes in the shoe department, and so on. If you wanted to buy a hammer, you would go to the hardware department—not to the furniture department. Usually the items in each department are classified into even smaller groups. In the clothing department, each type of clothing might be a different group. Shirts might be in one group, socks in another group, and sweaters in still a different group. The clothes in each group might be further classified by size, by style, or in some other way. Into what kinds of groups are things in your home classified?

Suppose you have a pile of nails that you want to store in a cabinet with many drawers. You notice that all the nails are not the same. Some are aluminum, some are zinc-coated, and some are iron. They range in length from 0.5 cm to 9.8 cm. Some nails have a rounded head, others have a flat head. You want to sort the nails so that each different kind is in a separate drawer. To do that you would have to take into account the different properties of each nail.

Objects that are alike in some way have one or more properties in common. Some balloons, tomatoes, and fire trucks could be put into a group with stop signs. The property these things have in common is their red color. What property does a baseball, an orange, and the moon have in common?

A classification scheme for eggs includes sorting them by size and by weight.

What is binary classification?

Objects classified on the basis of a certain property may be put into one of two groups. Either the object has the property, or it does not. This type of classification is called **binary** (bī'nər ē) **classification.** For example, you could classify everyone in your class on the basis of whether they were wearing shoes with laces. Those students wearing shoes with laces would be in one group. Those wearing shoes without laces would be in a different group. If you did that, you might find the groups were not equal. There might be more students in the group with laces than in the group without laces. That wouldn't matter. Even if all the students were wearing shoes with laces, they could still be classified on the basis of that property. There simply would be no one in the without-laces group.

Suppose you wanted to classify several objects on the basis of two properties. In that case, you would first classify all the objects on the basis of one property to make two groups. Then you would classify the objects in each of those groups on the basis of the second property. If you did this, you would end with four groups. The same procedure is followed when there are three, four, or more properties to consider. No matter how many properties there are, only one property at a time is used in binary classification.

A classification scheme does not always work smoothly. Sometimes one of the properties used to classify objects may not be clearly defined. Then the classification scheme breaks down. Let us examine how this happens. We will classify dogs on the basis of hair length. In a binary classification, the dogs might be classified as long-haired, or not long-haired. Most dogs can be classified on this property. However, some dogs have hair that is neither long nor short. Where in this classification scheme does such a dog fit? Would you place the dog in the long-haired, or the not long-haired, group?

Activity 4 Binary Classification

PURPOSE

To construct and use a binary classification system

MATERIALS

Tray of assorted items

DO THIS

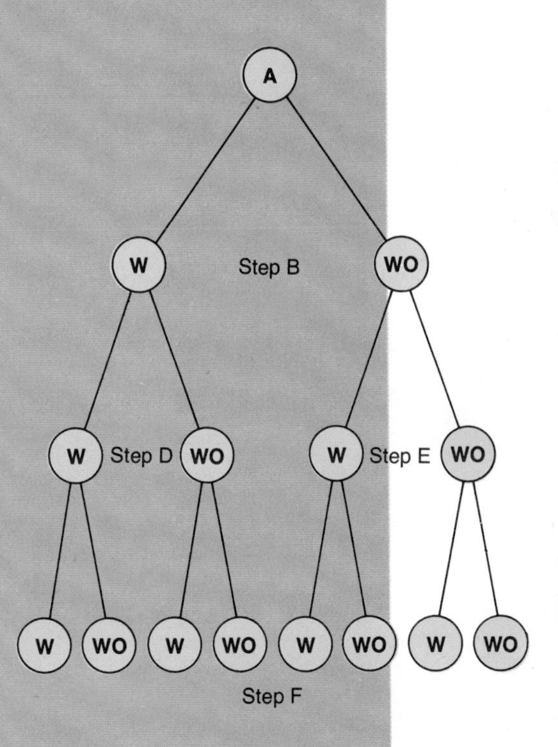

A. Study the diagram. It shows a binary classification system for items such as those on the tray. In the diagram, *A* represents all the items to be classified. *W* represents the group of items *with* a certain property. *WO* represents the group of items *without* that property. Follow the diagram as you do steps **B–F.**

B. Choose one property of an item on the tray. Place all the items with that property on the left side of the tray. Place all the items without that property on the right side.

C. Choose another property of an item on the tray. This property should be different from the one used in step **B.**

D. Work only with the items on the left side of the tray. Divide these items into two groups. One group should be the items with the property chosen in step **C.** The other group should be the items without that property.

E. Repeat step **D,** but work only with the items on the right side of the tray.

F. Choose a third property that is different from the first two. Divide the items in each group on the tray into two more groups—one with the property, and one without the property.

REPORT

1. How many properties were used to classify the items?

2. Into how many groups were you able to classify the items, using these properties?

Some objects seem either to have both qualities of a given property, or neither quality. Perhaps you have already run into that problem when classifying objects. The fact that such problems occur should remind us of the purpose of a classification system. We make up the classification system to help us organize objects. If the system breaks down, it is simply because there is more variety in objects and their properties than the system can handle. Although not perfect, classification systems are useful.

SUMMARY In order to describe something, you must observe it. Observations are made with the senses. We are aided in making observations by extending our senses through the use of various instruments. Quantitative observations involve measurement. All other observations are qualitative—they describe a quality of the observed object. When you infer, you are using past experiences to interpret an observation. Often several inferences can be based on a single observation. Those features, or characteristics, that describe an object are called properties. The general properties of an object may be the same for two or more other objects. Identifying properties are the specific properties that make one object different from all other similar objects. Classification is a useful technique for organizing a large number of items. In a classification scheme, objects are grouped on the basis of their properties. Grouping objects on the basis of whether or not they have a certain property is called binary classification.

SCIENCE WORDS

quantitative observation
qualitative observation
inference
properties
general properties
identifying properties
classification
binary classification

REVIEW QUESTIONS

Complete the following by choosing the correct answer.

1. The features, or characteristics, that describe an object are called (a) observations. (b) inferences. (c) properties. (d) a classification scheme.
2. Using one's senses to get information about an object is called (a) measuring. (b) inferring. (c) binary classification. (d) observing.
3. In a binary-classification system, the number of properties needed to classify objects into 16 different groups is (a) 2. (b) 4. (c) 8. (d) 16.
4. Which of the following is not one of your senses? (a) sight (b) smell (c) touch (d) sour taste

Mark each statement true (T) or false (F).

1. ______ An inference is an interpretation of an observation.
2. ______ Grouping materials that are alike in some way is called classification.
3. ______ The property *knife* describes a cutting instrument.
4. ______ A measurement is a quantitative observation.

APPLYING WHAT YOU LEARNED

Observation is important in science. A good observer should be able to solve the following puzzle.

Step A The words below are shown as they appear in a dictionary. Copy the words exactly as they are shown, but in the correct alphabetical order.

or•gan–grind•er	jack–in–the–box	mole•hill
rub•ber•like	right–hand•ed	mis•un•der•stand

Step B Number the words 1–6, starting with the first word.
Step C Use the numerical order of the words to interpret the meaning of the chart to the right. If you are a careful observer, you can now fill in the puzzle boxes with letters that spell out a message.

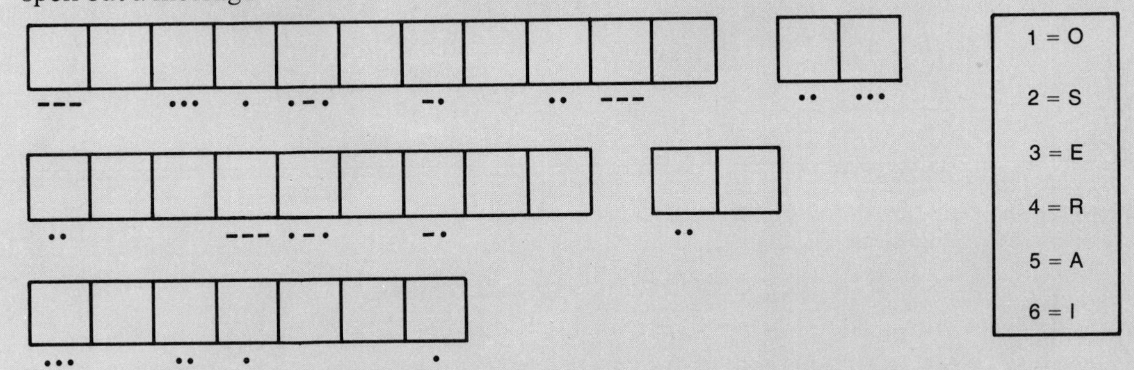

DÉFENSE DE FUMER
EXIT
MOLD
TRED
PNCH

Engineers can design tire treads with the aid of a computer. A light pencil is used to make design changes that the computer immediately analyzes.

2

Working with Data

What do you do when you have a problem to solve? If the problem is a homework assignment, you probably discuss it with other students, exchanging ideas and information. You may try to get more information about the problem from books in the library. You and your classmates may even work together to find a solution to the problem.

Scientists work in much the same way, sharing ideas and helping each other. They read about the work of other scientists who are trying to solve the same or similar problems. They report the research they have done and the results of their investigations.

There are many ways to sort out and summarize important information. Several methods of presenting such information accurately and in a meaningful way are discussed in this chapter.

Reporting Data

What are data?

The information that you work with to solve a problem is called **data** (dā′tə). In many cases data are measurements, but data can also be other kinds of observations. Collecting data is important, but being able to use data is equally important.

Suppose data were collected on the number of days each year that the temperature was above 38°C. The following record of these data is for a 10-year period.

> The temperature was above 38°C on 1 day in 1969. In 1970 and 1971, there were 4 days when the temperature was above 38°C. There were temperatures above 38°C on 5 days in 1972. The temperature was above 38°C on 2 days in 1973, and on 10 days in 1974. In 1975, there were 3 days when the temperature was above 38°C. A temperature above 38°C was recorded on 7 days in 1976. There were 10 days in 1977 and 13 days in 1978 when the temperature was above 38°C.

This data record contains the essential information, but it is hard to read and to interpret. The form in which the data are recorded makes it difficult to find information quickly. For example, in what years was the temperature above 38°C on 10 days? To find that information, you must read the data record from beginning to end. The data record would be easier to use if the data were organized differently.

There are many ways to organize data. One way is to record the data in a **data table,** such as Table 2–1. It shows the same temperature data used previously.

TABLE 2–1 • Days per Year with a Temperature Above 38°C

YEAR	1969	1970	1971	1972	1973	1974	1975	1976	1977	1978
DAYS	1	4	4	5	2	10	3	7	10	13

Notice how uncluttered and simple the data appear. The title of the table describes the kind of information collected. The rows and columns contain the specific data. Information is easy to read and ready to use without having to search for it.

What is the purpose of a data table?

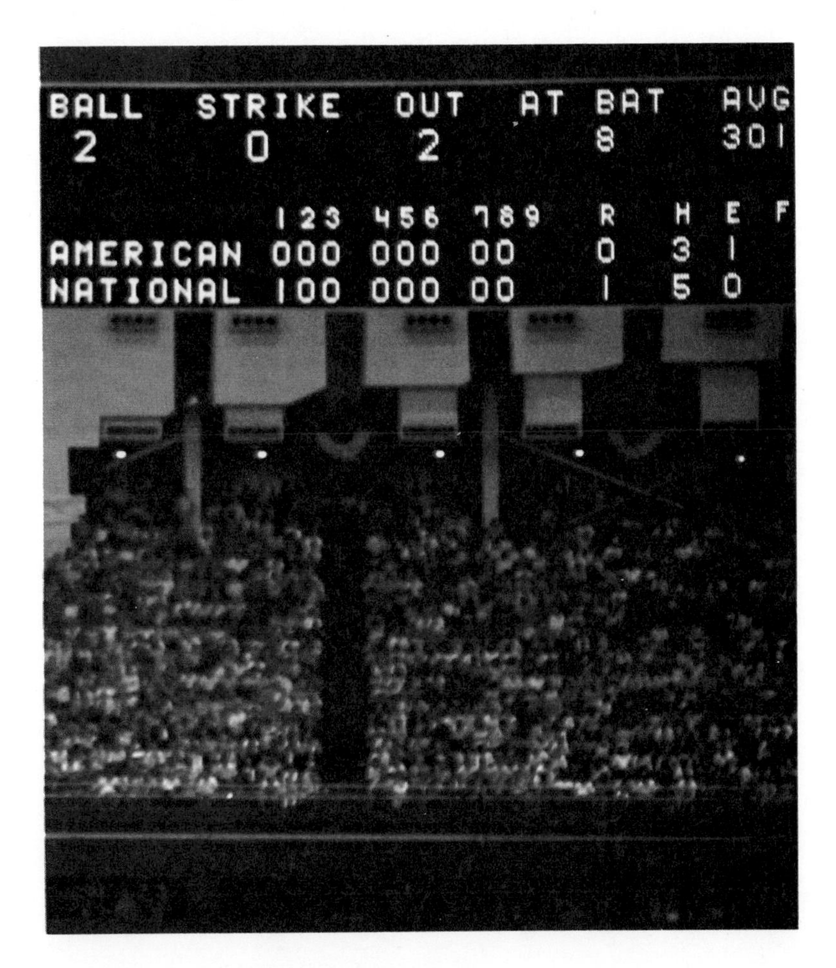

Data tables may have many different forms depending on the data to be organized.

Bar Graphs

Organizing data in a table makes the data easier to use. However, the data may still be unclear, or hard to understand. In those cases, data are often reported on a **graph** (graf). A graph is a picture of data. It shows how one variable changes in relationship to the way one or more other variables change. The data are shown in a special way, making them easier to interpret.

What is a graph?

One type of graph is the **bar graph,** or **histogram** (his′tə gram). On a bar graph, straight lines, or bars, are used to present a picture of the data. On some bar graphs, the bars run up and down. These graphs are called **vertical** (vėr′tə kəl) bar graphs. Figure 2–1 is a vertical bar graph of the data in Table 2–1. The same data can be shown on a **horizontal** (hôr ə zon′təl) bar graph.

FIGURE 2–1

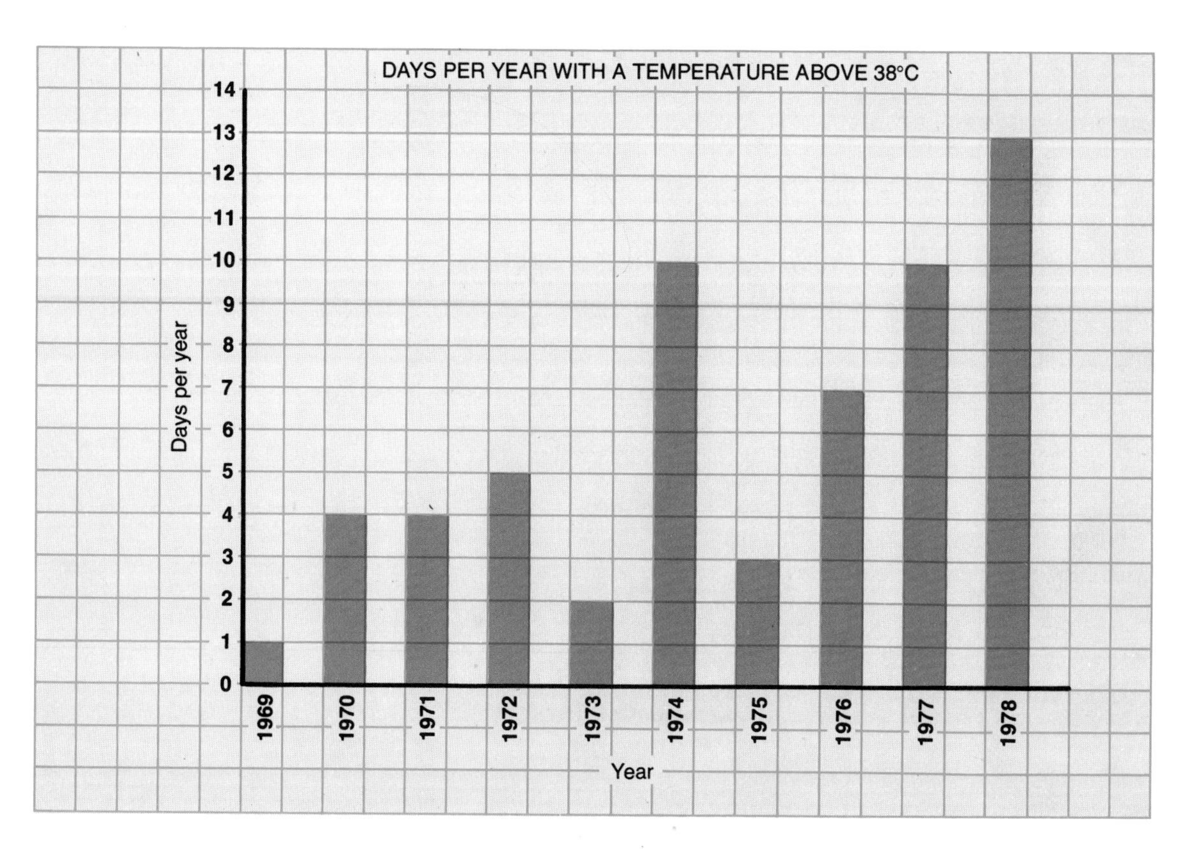

A bar graph is a way of showing a set of data so that comparisons can be made quickly. The lengths of the bars show the relationship between two variables. Information about one variable is given on the vertical scale. Information about the second variable is given on the horizontal scale. Study the bar graph in Figure 2–1. You can easily see on how many days the temperature was above 38°C each year. You can also see at a glance how the number of days varied from year to year. There is another advantage to graphing data. If there is a pattern to the data, it is evident immediately.

Grouping Data

Why should data be grouped?

Another way to organize data is by **grouping.** This method is used to organize numerical data that will be reported on a bar graph. Suppose data were collected concerning the masses of twenty pieces of metal. **Mass** is the amount of matter in an object. The masses are listed below in the order in which they were measured.

20.0 g	23.8 g	33.4 g	21.4 g
25.3 g	30.1 g	37.8 g	24.9 g
21.5 g	28.6 g	37.1 g	35.0 g
40.3 g	21.6 g	24.2 g	23.9 g
31.7 g	30.0 g	32.3 g	36.1 g

These data are difficult to work with in this form. It would be better if these data were ordered numerically, as follows.

20.0 g	23.9 g	30.0 g	35.0 g
21.4 g	24.2 g	30.1 g	36.1 g
21.5 g	24.9 g	31.7 g	37.1 g
21.6 g	25.3 g	32.3 g	37.8 g
23.8 g	28.6 g	33.4 g	40.3 g

Numerically ordering the data, three things are obvious. First, the pieces of metal range in mass from 20.0 g to 40.3 g. Second, the mass of each piece of metal is different. Third, some masses vary from other masses by only 0.1 g. If a bar graph were made of these data, the graph would have twenty bars. The mass of each piece of metal would be shown by one bar. To show the masses accurately, each unit of the scale for mass would be 0.1 g. Part of that scale is shown in Figure 2–2. The scale would have to be more than six times longer to show 40.3 g. Using a scale of that size would make the graph unwieldy. Also, such a graph would have no real purpose. The same information presented on the graph could be gotten just as easily from the numerically ordered data.

FIGURE 2–2

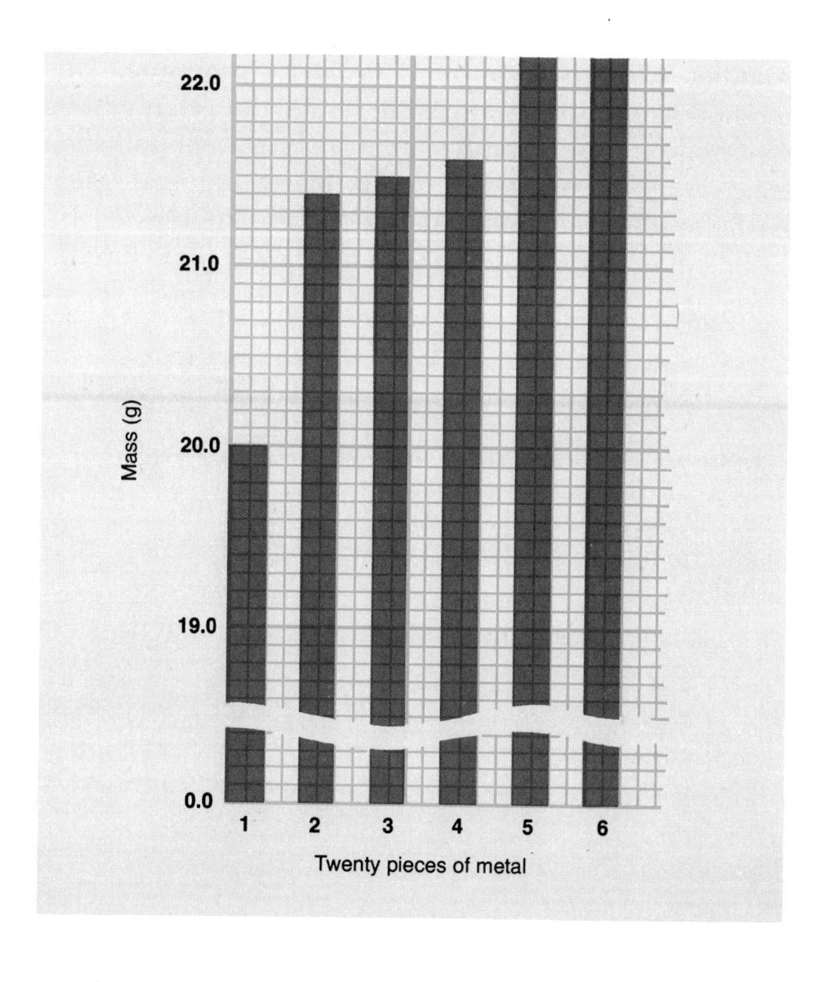

Changing the units of the scale for mass to 1.0 g would reduce the size of the graph. Figure 2–3 shows some of the data graphed to that scale. Notice that the tenths of a gram must now be estimated. The graph cannot be read as quickly or as accurately as when the units were 0.1 g.

FIGURE 2–3

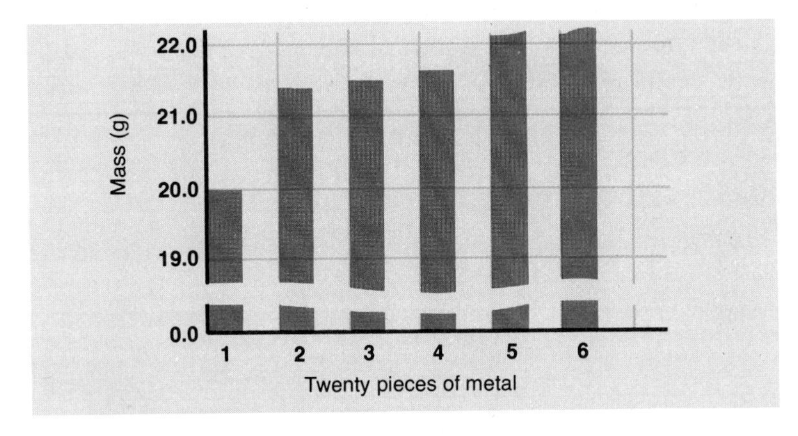

What can you do with these data to construct a useful and accurate graph? In this case, it might be better to show how many pieces of metal have a mass that falls within certain narrow limits. This can be done by grouping the data so that each bar of the graph represents a range of masses. For example, the data might be grouped as in Table 2–2. The range of the masses in each group is 3 g. A bar graph of the grouped

TABLE 2–2 • Grouped Mass Data for Twenty Pieces of Metal

MASS (g)	PIECES OF METAL
20.0–22.9	4
23.0–25.9	5
26.0–28.9	1
29.0–31.9	3
32.0–34.9	2
35.0–37.9	4
38.0–40.9	1

data is shown in Figure 2–4. Grouping makes the data to be graphed more manageable and results in a graph that is both useful and accurate.

FIGURE 2–4

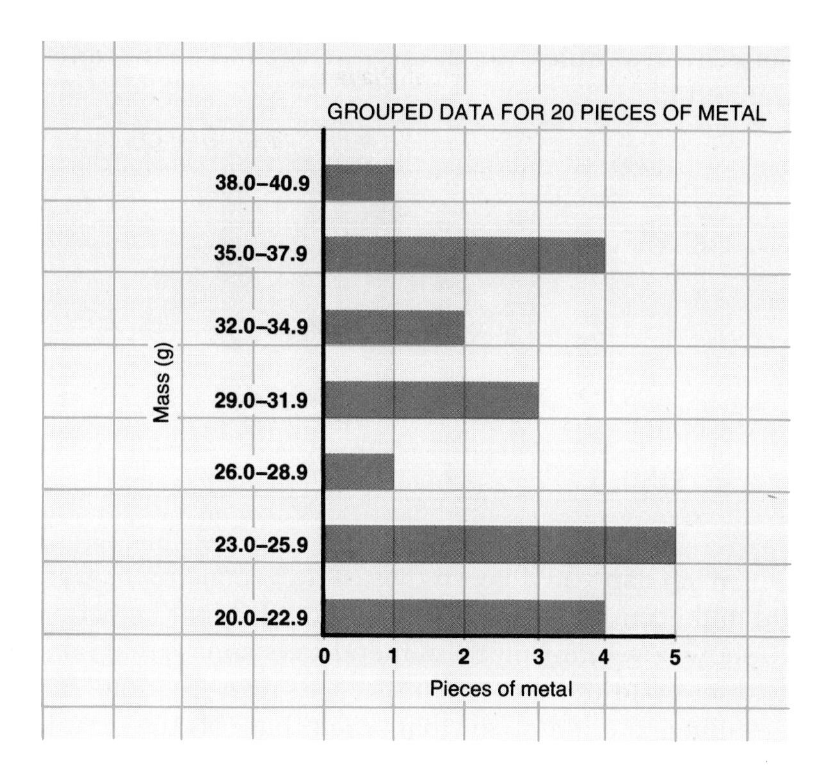

Rounding Numbers

Table 2–3 shows the weights of some members of a basketball team. Suppose you were asked to graph these data on a bar graph. It is easier to graph whole numbers than decimal numbers. These decimals can be **rounded** to whole numbers. The weights of the basketball players were measured to a tenth of a kilogram (kg). To round the decimal numbers to whole numbers, look at the number in the tenths place. If this number is less than 5, it is dropped. If it is 5 or more, the number before the decimal point is increased by one. Table 2–4 shows the measured weights and the rounded off weights of the basketball players.

TABLE 2–3 • Weights of Basketball Players

PLAYER NUMBER	WEIGHT (kg)
1	69.7
2	70.6
3	71.5
4	71.8
5	73.3
6	74.2

TABLE 2–4 • Rounded Off Weights of Basketball Players

MEASURED VALUE (kg)	ROUNDED OFF VALUE (kg)
69.7	70
70.6	71
71.5	72
71.8	72
73.3	73
74.2	74

Suppose you had data of measurements made to the nearest hundredths of a gram (g). The rules for rounding off to the nearest tenth are the same as those for whole numbers. If the number in the hundredths place is less than 5, it is dropped. If it is 5 or more, the number in the tenths place is increased by one. The way this is done is shown in Table 2–5.

TABLE 2–5 • Rounding Off to the Nearest Tenth

MEASURED VALUE (g)	ROUNDED OFF VALUE (g)
34.57	34.6
35.51	35.5
48.78	48.8

The rules for rounding off numbers are the same no matter how many decimal places there are. The following examples show how this is done. To round off to the nearest hundredth

24.573 is rounded off to 24.57
46.991 is rounded off to 46.99
37.819 is rounded off to 37.82

To round off to the nearest thousandth

12.4312 is rounded off to 12.431
90.6683 is rounded off to 90.668
56.1229 is rounded off to 56.123

In this course you may sometimes work with numbers with many decimal places. Generally these numbers should be rounded off to the nearest thousandth, or three decimal places.

Line Graphs

What is a number line on a graph called?

Which value is the horizontal coordinate; the vertical coordinate?

Another kind of graph used to report data is the **line graph.** You have probably seen line graphs in newspapers, magazines, or other text books. Line graphs are drawn on a rectangular grid. Number lines are drawn at right angles, or perpendicular, to each other. Two of these number lines intersect at zero. Each of these intersecting lines is called an **axis** (ak′sis). The horizontal line is called the ***X* axis.** The vertical line is called the ***Y* axis.** The relationship between two variables is shown by points on the axes. To locate a point on the grid, the *X* value and *Y* value must be given. These *X* and *Y* values are called **coordinates** (kō ôr′də nits). The *X* value is the **horizontal coordinate.** The *Y* value is the **vertical coordinate.** The coordinates of the point of intersection of the axes are (0,0). Figure 2–5 shows two points, *A* and *B*. The coordinates of these two points are written as follows: *A* (5,2) and *B* (3,6). When writing coordinates, the *X* value is always written before the *Y* value. The following example may help you to understand the use of coordinates.

Suppose Figure 2–6 is a map of your town. One house on each street is shown. A student lives in each house. To visit friends after school, you would need directions from school to each friend's house. To get to Fred's house, you must go 4 blocks over and 4 blocks up. To get to Ann's house you must go 0 blocks over and 3 blocks up. Since the streets are laid out in a grid, an easy way to give directions is by coordinates. The number of blocks *over* is the ***X*** coordinate. The number of blocks *up* is the ***Y*** coordinate. School is point (0,0). The coordinate for Lynn's house are (3,4). The coordinates for Terry's house are (2,2). What are the coordinates of the food store? What are the coordinates of Eva's house? Activity 5 will give you more practice in working with coordinates.

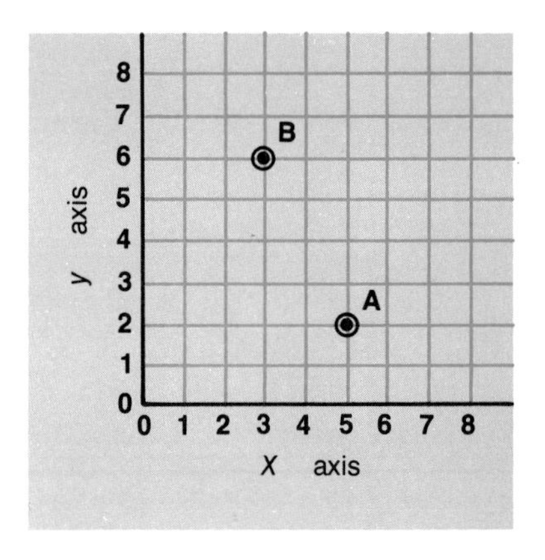

FIGURE 2–5

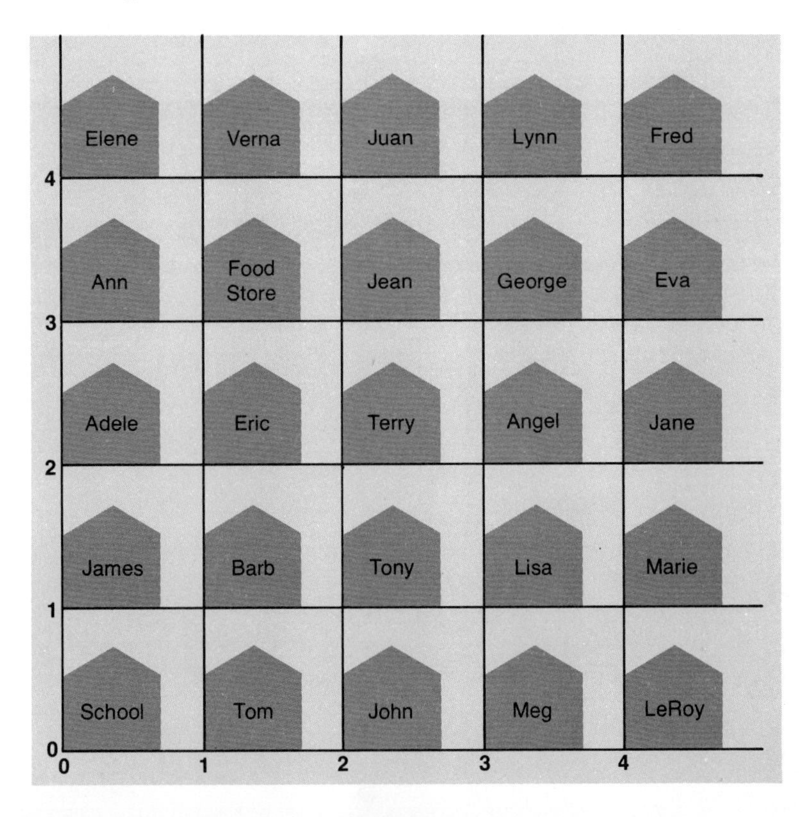

FIGURE 2–6

Activity 5 Using Coordinates

PURPOSE

To describe the location of words in a puzzle by using coordinates

MATERIALS

None

DO THIS

A. Copy the puzzle.

B. Using the word list in report question 1, locate the words in the puzzle. The words may be spelled in any direction. As you find a word, circle it.

REPORT

1. Write the coordinates for these words.

a. coordinates	**i.** property	**q.** classification
b. observation	**j.** sense	**r.** solid
c. temperature	**k.** conductor	**s.** Celsius
d. centimeter	**l.** liquid	**t.** decimal
e. thermometer	**m.** volume	**u.** class
f. space	**n.** mass	**v.** metric
g. histogram	**o.** inference	**w.** graph
h. science	**p.** measure	**x.** gram

2. How is the knowledge of coordinates useful in solving this puzzle?

Further Activities

Find out how coordinates are used in the following activities: map reading, surveying, navigating, and map making. Report your findings to the class.

16	C	O	O	R	D	I	N	A	T	E	S	S	R	M	A	Q	T
15	L	C	L	V	C	N	Z	D	B	L	C	R	S	I	J	A	H
14	A	E	L	I	A	F	E	D	E	C	I	M	A	L	R	B	E
13	S	N	B	E	F	E	S	P	A	C	E	A	E	U	Z	Y	R
12	S	T	U	B	E	R	T	I	N	O	N	S	L	T	M	N	M
11	I	I	G	F	M	E	S	S	A	L	C	S	L	E	E	P	O
10	F	M	S	L	E	N	D	H	A	M	E	I	K	P	C	R	M
9	I	E	W	E	A	C	V	O	L	U	M	E	S	O	E	D	E
8	C	T	O	B	S	E	R	V	A	T	I	O	N	L	L	R	T
7	A	E	C	Q	U	I	R	M	T	Z	V	D	E	O	S	C	E
6	T	R	O	U	R	I	S	A	V	L	U	I	E	Q	I	E	R
5	I	S	M	A	E	Z	G	R	A	C	I	E	S	N	U	N	C
4	O	Z	E	H	P	A	R	G	T	T	R	G	N	Z	S	I	V
3	N	A	T	W	X	V	C	O	E	Y	T	R	E	P	O	R	P
2	T	B	R	T	P	I	R	R	E	S	P	L	S	O	L	I	D
1	P	L	I	Q	U	I	D	S	H	I	S	T	O	G	R	A	M
0	W	Z	C	L	U	E	R	U	T	A	R	E	P	M	E	T	W
	0	1	2	3	4	5	6	7	8	9	10	11	12	13	14	15	16

Line graphs can be very useful in reporting data. Information such as production in industry, taxes, salaries, students' grades, population, and athletic records can all be displayed on line graphs. But the information is of value only if it is accurately interpreted. Figure 2–7 is a graph of a person's height from birth to age 60. From the graph you can obtain certain information about this person's growth. The line indicates that growth increased for only the first 20 years. At that point the line levels off, indicating no further growth.

FIGURE 2–7

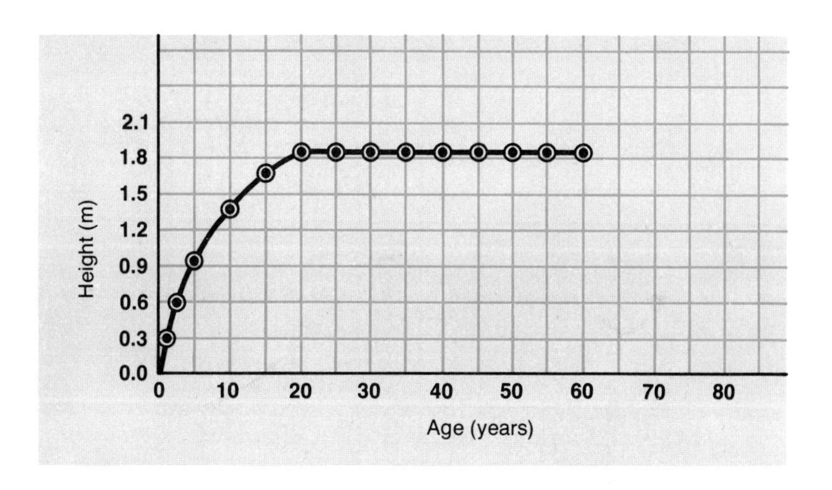

The graph also allows certain assumptions and predictions to be made. For example, what would you estimate the person's height was at age 12? Predicting or estimating data between known points on a graph is called **interpolation** (in tėr pə lā'shən). What would you suppose the person's height was at age 70? To predict information beyond known points on a graph is called **extrapolation** (ek strap ə lā'shən). There is no data on this graph beyond age 60. Therefore the prediction based on interpolation is probably more accurate than that based on extrapolation.

What is interpolation?

What is extrapolation?

Figure 2–8 shows the data gathered from an experiment. A scientist wanted to determine how much of a

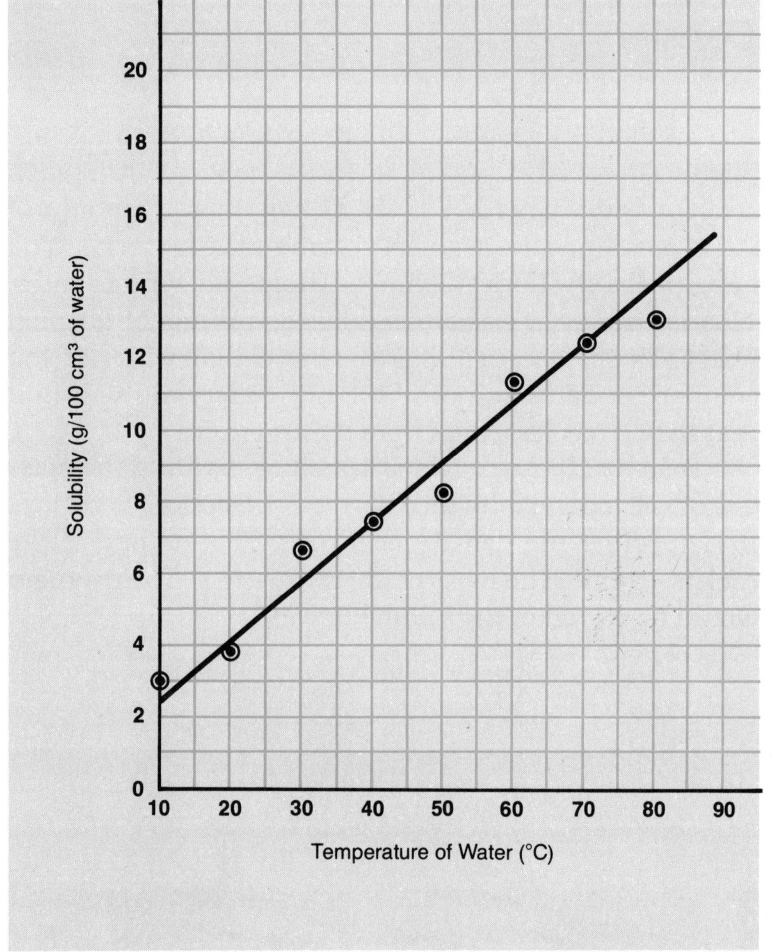

FIGURE 2–8

EXCURSION 3
Techniques for measuring the volume of liquids and solids are discussed in Excursion 3, "Measuring Volume."

EXCURSION 4
The Celsius temperature scale is discussed in Excursion 4, "Measuring Temperature."

substance dissolved in water as the temperature of the water was increased. Notice that the points on the graph are almost, but not quite, in a straight line. The line on the graph does not go through all the points. Half the points are on one side of the line, while the other half of the points are on the other side of the line. This line is called the **best fit line.** Since half the points are on either side of the line, it is believed that any errors that may have been made in measurement would be cancelled out.

What is the best fit line?

Density

What is density?

What is the formula for determining density?

The methods of grouping and recording data can be applied to the study of many scientific concepts. One such concept is **density** (den′sə tē). Density is the amount of mass contained in a given volume of a material. You have probably noticed that oil floats on top of water. This is true even if there is a larger volume of oil than water. This is because oil is less dense than water. If you compare equal volumes of oil and water, you will find that the oil has less mass than the water.

Density (D) can be determined by dividing the mass (m) of the material by the volume (v). Suppose you want to determine the density of a rock. The volume of the rock is 10 cm³. The mass of the rock is 15 g. The problem would be solved in the following way.

$$D = \frac{m}{v}$$

$$= \frac{15\ \text{g}}{10\ \text{cm}^3}$$

$$= 1.5\ \text{g/cm}^3$$

When this ship is loaded with cargo, its density will be increased and it will float lower in the water.

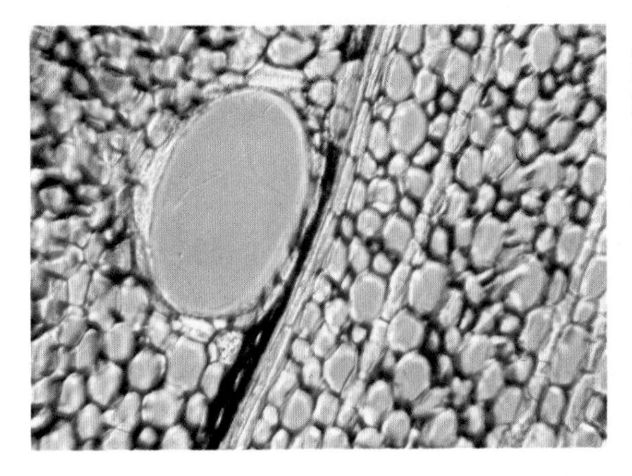

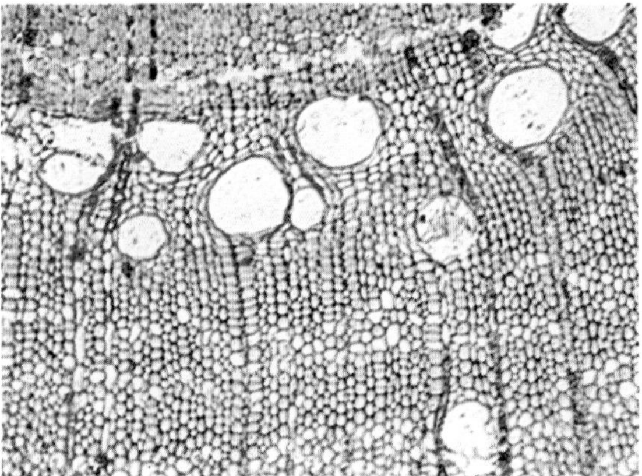

Air trapped in the large cells of balsa wood (left) makes it less dense than oak wood (right).

Density is a property that can be used to identify materials or to compare two different objects or substances. However, to compare two liquids or two gases the property of **specific** (spi sif′ik) **gravity** is often used. Specific gravity is the ratio of the density of the material compared with the density of a standard. The standard of comparison for liquids is usually water. For gases, the standard is usually air. Specific gravity is usually more convenient and easier to measure than density.

SUMMARY Scientists acquire a great deal of information in the course of their work. This information is called data. To be of most value to the scientist, data should be organized and accurately recorded. Grouping data makes it easier to work with. Rounding off numbers is another way to make data more manageable. Graphs are used to record data. Bar graphs, or histograms, and line graphs are used to record many kinds of data. Coordinates are used to locate points on a graph. Additional information may be obtained from a graph by interpolation and extrapolation. The best fit line connects some but not all points on a graph. An equal number of points are on either side of the line. Density and specific gravity are used to identify and compare different materials or substances. Specific gravity is usually easier to measure than density.

SCIENCE WORDS

data
data table
graph
bar graph
histogram
vertical
horizontal
grouping
mass
rounding off
line graph
axis
coordinates
horizontal coordinate
vertical coordinate
interpolation
extrapolation
best fit line
density
specific gravity

REVIEW QUESTIONS

Fill in the blanks with the correct terms.

1. The X and Y values used to locate a point on a graph are called ____________.
2. ____________ is information with which you work to solve a problem.
3. A ____________ is a picture of data that shows the relationship of variables.
4. The ratio of the density of a material compared to the density of a standard is called ____________ ____________.
5. Predicting data between known points on a graph is called ____________.

Mark each statement true (T) or false (F).

1. ______ Another name for line graph is histogram.
2. ______ A number line on a graph is called an axis.
3. ______ Coordinates are used to locate points on a graph.
4. ______ Predicting data beyond known points on a graph is called interpolation.
5. ______ The amount of mass contained in a given volume of material is called density.

APPLYING WHAT YOU LEARNED

1. Order the following data numerically. 28.6 g, 35.0 g, 37.8 g, 23.8 g, 40.3 g, 32.3 g, 21.6 g, 37.1 g, 20.0 g, 24.2 g.
2. Round off the following numbers to the nearest tenth. 73.89, 62.33, 12.37, 55.55, 41.14.
3. The average daily temperature was recorded for a one-week period in Anytown, U.S.A. Make a bar graph of the following data. Day 1, 26.3°C; day 2, 26.7°C; day 3, 26.1°C; day 4, 25.9°C; day 5, 25.6°C; day 6, 23.6°C; day 7, 26.3°C.
4. The weight of a laboratory animal was recorded over a ten-week period. The data is shown in the following table. Make a line graph of the data.

Weekly Weight of a Laboratory Animal

WEEK	1	2	3	4	5	6	7	8	9	10
WEIGHT (kg)	1.3	1.8	1.9	2.6	2.8	3.1	3.4	3.9	4.4	4.6

5. An object has a volume of 10.5 cm^3 and a mass of 32.6 g. What is the density of the material? Round off your answer to the nearest thousandth.

UNIT REVIEW

1. List three advantages of using the metric system of measurement in the United States. List three difficulties that may be involved in changing from the English system to the metric system.
2. Keep a list of the number and kinds of measurements you make in one day. What units of measurement did you use?
3. List five adults you know very well. Make a list of things that each of these people might measure or observe during one day on their job. Check your list with each person. Ask them to explain what units of measurement and the type of tools they use in their work.
4. Suppose you wanted to determine the number of BBs needed to fill an odd-shaped glass container. Explain how you could do this without counting all the BBs one by one.
5. Suppose you wanted to determine the thickness of an ordinary piece of paper. How could this be done using only a metric ruler?
6. Choose six different items found in the grocery store. Record all measurements of weight (mass) and volume for each. Classify the packaged materials by (a) the English system of measure; (b) the metric system of measure; (c) both systems. Why are the different units used?
7. Determine the mass of a chalk mark one meter long. Explain the method you used in solving this problem.
8. The units of measurement of length, mass, volume, temperature, and time are determined by comparison with a standard. Use the library to find out what these standards are and how they were developed. Be sure to use only the metric system.
9. Make a list of all the observations and inferences you made today. Explain each item.

Careers

Do you like to ask questions about the way different substances behave? Do you ever wonder why changes in nature take place during the year? If you are interested in questions such as these, then you possess an important quality needed by every scientist. This quality is curiosity. Scientists look for explanations for the changes and actions that they see around them. For this reason a scientist is a kind of detective. A biologist is a scientific detective who investigates the nature of life. A physical scientist is a detective in search of explanations about the nature of matter. Chemists and physicists are types of physical scientists. Since matter is very complex, there are many different kinds of chemists and physicists.

You probably realize that laboratory work is usually part of your science course. Many scientists do most of their actual work in laboratories. Some investigators may be involved in measuring as many of the properties of matter as possible. Other investigators may be determining how substances react with each other. Scientists analyze the data and observations that have been collected. They try to use the data to improve their ideas about the nature of matter. Investigators who make measurements, collect data, and make observations are usually called experimental scientists. Some scientists do very little work in the laboratory investigating the properties of matter. Instead, using data collected by many experimental scientists, these people develop theories about the nature of matter. These people are theoretical scientists.

What is required to become an investigator of matter? To be an experimental or a theoretical scientist, a college education with a major in a physical science is the minimum requirement. Those scientists actually involved in planning, supervising, and analyzing the experiments usually have a master's and a doctoral degree.

There are many jobs in science that do not require a college education. Lab technicians usually have several months of training in a technical school. Lab technicians often get on-the-job training when they begin their employment. The technician usually handles routine laboratory work using proven scientific methods. This person may gather data and make observations during an experiment. Since the lab technician does much of the laboratory work, scientists have more time to devise experiments and study the data.

Other types of jobs available in science require various amounts of education beyond high school. Two-year colleges award associate degrees that may qualify a person for laboratory work. Ask your teacher or guidance counselor for more information about careers in science.

Lab technicians may become highly skilled specialists in specific aspects of scientific work.

Research

Scientists are always looking for better ways to measure the properties of matter. In this course you are using the metric system in taking your measurements. Perhaps you do not realize that this system would be useless if one particular thing happened. What could make the entire metric system useless? The answer is the loss of the standards on which the system is based. A standard is some constant that forms the basis for a scale of measurement.

In the past many different items were used as standards for systems of measurement. The distance from the tip of the king's nose to the tip of his outstretched finger was called a *yard.* The length of his foot was defined as a *foot.* The length of three barley corns laid end to end was called an *inch.* These units of measurement are still used in everyday life. They are part of the English system of measurement. However, the old standards proved useless because they were not constant. Kings die. A new king may have a longer arm or a shorter foot. Barley corns vary in size and also decay. Instead of kings and barley corns, metal bars have become the official standards of length for the English system. These bars are housed in the Bureau of Standards.

In the late 1700s a committee of people in France devised a new system of measurement. They wanted to have some constant feature of nature as the standard unit of length. The committee decided to use the earth itself. The standard unit of length was called a *meter.* The meter was defined as 1/10 000 000 of the distance from the equator to the North Pole along a line through Paris, France. That distance had to be permanently recorded so that it could be used as the standard. To do this, the committee made a bar of a special mixture of two metals, Pt *[platinum]* and Ir *[iridium]*. (The bar was formed into an X shape for additional strength. Remember, the standard must be durable.) Two scratches were made along the surface of the bar. The distance between the scratches was equal in length to one meter. When those scratches were made, the metric system was born. Most countries obtained copies of this bar to serve as a convenient standard for their own use. The original bar is still kept in a vault at the International Bureau of Weights and Measures outside Paris.

Scientists continued to search for a standard that could not be destroyed and could be more available to all scientists. In 1960 an international committee accepted a new method for measuring the length of a meter. The meter was defined as 1 650 763.73 times the wavelength of the orange-red spectral line of a particular isotope of krypton. Scientists feel that this is the most durable and accurately reproducible standard known today.

Standards of time and temperature are used to measure the durability of many products.

UNIT TWO

NATURE OF MATTER

Water is shown here in three forms—the solid state, the liquid state, and the gaseous state.

Matter Changes in Form

All things change in form. People, animals, and plants change in form as they grow and develop. Nonliving things also change in form. You can observe many of these changes in the physical world around you. For example, you probably have noticed that a slice of bread becomes hard and dry when left exposed to air. It no longer is the soft, moist material it once was. Some changes in form of materials take place quickly, while other changes occur more slowly. If you break a dish, it changes in form quickly. When you fry an egg or burn a candle, the changes in form are more gradual.

In this chapter you will explore some changes in form that occur in materials. You will also develop some models to help explain how those changes might have occurred.

Activity 6 Changes in Water and Wax

PURPOSE

To identify and describe changes in water and wax

MATERIALS

Heat source
Matches
150-mL beaker
Ice cube
1 cm^3 paraffin wax
Aluminum foil (5cm × 5cm)
Metric ruler
Tripod
Wire gauze
Asbestos gloves
Safety goggles

DO THIS

A. Set up the heat source, tripod, wire gauze, and beaker as shown. Put an ice cube in the beaker. **CAUTION:** *Be sure you are wearing safety goggles.* Then light the heat source.

B. Observe the ice cube carefully. Record all the changes that take place in the form of the ice cube.

C. Shut off the heat source. Put on asbestos gloves and remove the beaker from the tripod. Place the beaker out of the way to cool.

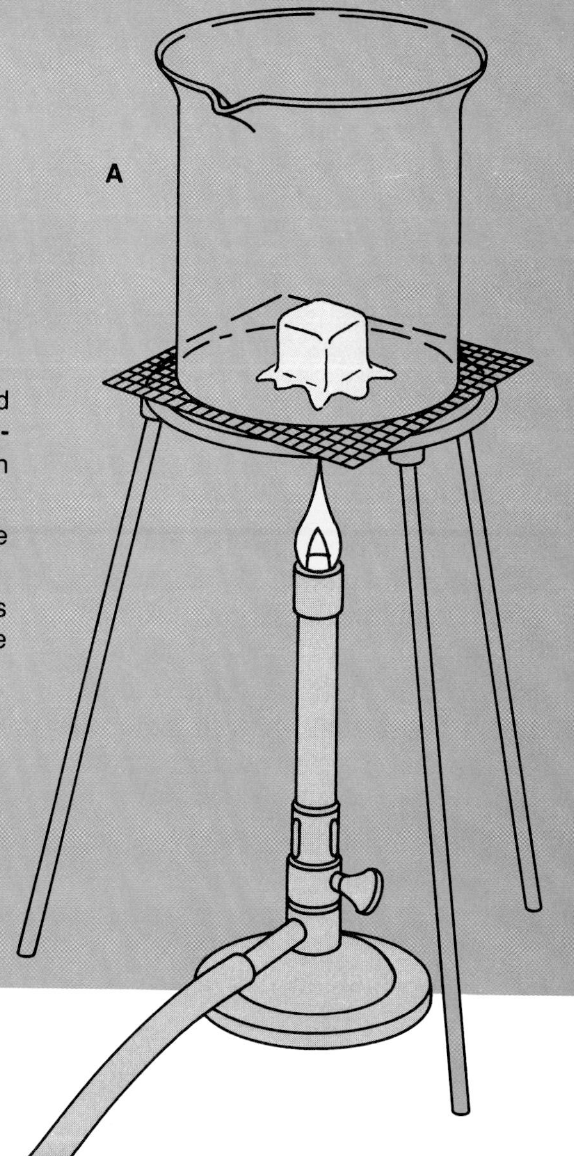

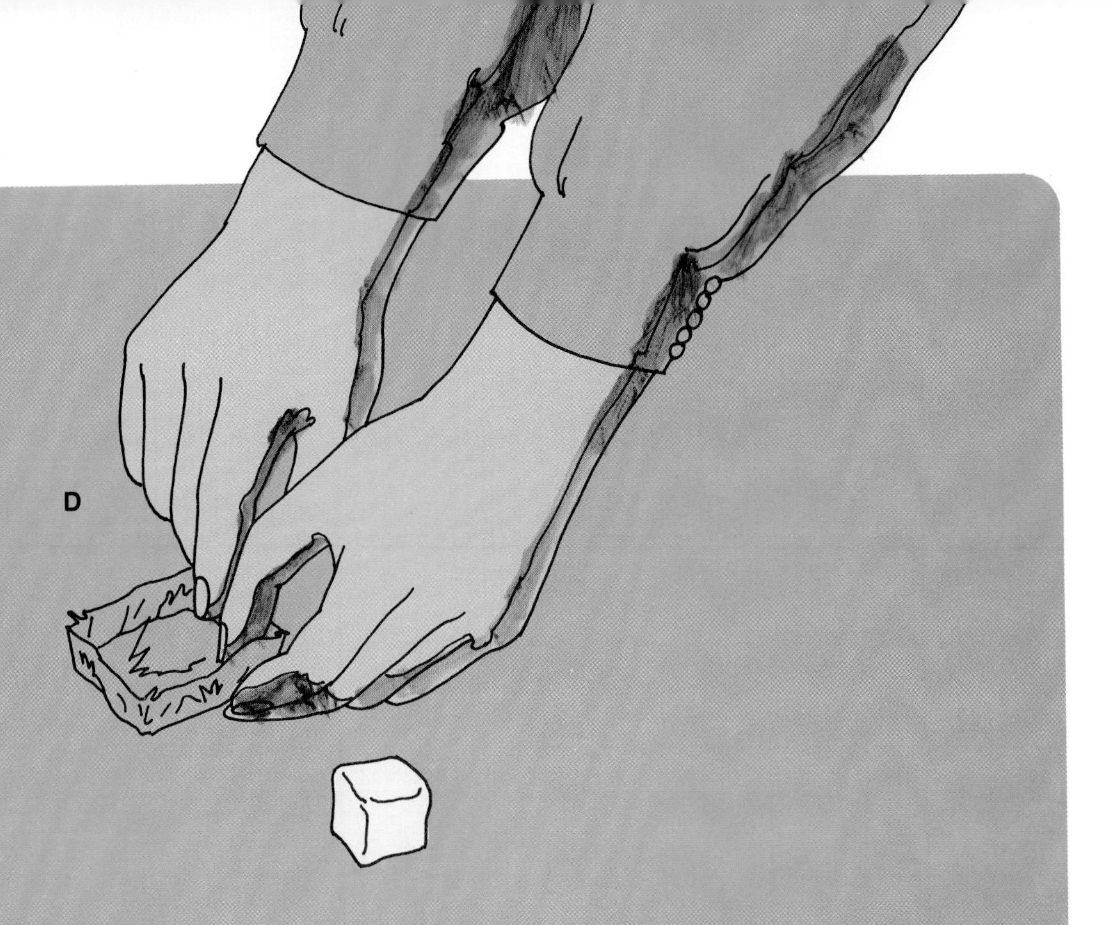

D. Shape the aluminum foil into a shallow pan by bending up the edges.

E. Put the cube of paraffin wax in the pan and place the pan on the tripod. **CAUTION:** *Be sure you are wearing safety goggles.* Then light the heat source.

F. Observe the paraffin wax carefully for a few minutes. Record all the changes that take place in the form of the paraffin wax.

G. Shut off the heat source. Observe the paraffin wax as it cools. Record the changes that take place. Then remove the foil pan from the tripod.

REPORT

1. How did the ice cube change in form?

2. How did the paraffin wax change in form?

3. How did the two materials differ in the way they changed form?

4. After cooling, how was the form of each material different from its original form?

Activity 7 Changes in Wood

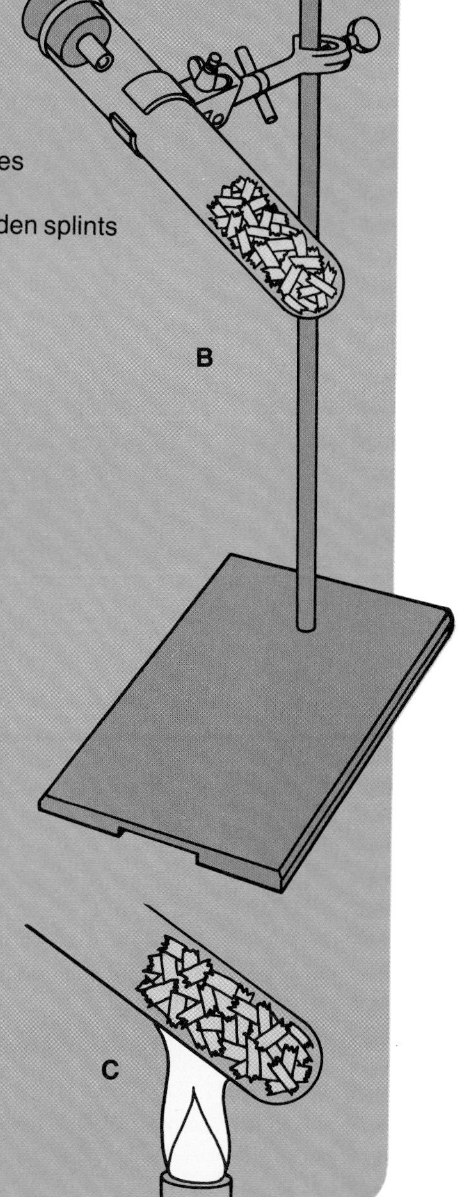

PURPOSE

To investigate changes in wood

MATERIALS

Ring stand with clamp for test tube
Pyrex test tube (16 mm × 150 mm)
1-hole rubber stopper to fit the test tube (with glass tubing inserted)
Heat source
Safety goggles
Matches
Several wooden splints

DO THIS

A. Fill the test tube about one-fourth with small pieces of wooden splints.

B. Push the rubber stopper firmly into the test tube. Then clamp the test tube to the ring stand as shown. Be sure that the test tube is slanted.

C. CAUTION: *Be sure you are wearing safety goggles.* Then light the heat source. Heat the lower one-fourth of the test tube for about 10 minutes. Observe and record the changes that take place in the wood.

D. Watch for some material to escape from the end of the glass tubing. Strike a match and try to ignite the material. Describe the material and what happened when you tried to ignite it.

E. Shut off the heat source. Let everything cool completely before disassembling the apparatus and cleaning up.

REPORT

1. Describe all the ways the wood changed.

2. What do you infer was the material that escaped from the end of the glass tubing?

3. Compare the changes in the wood with the changes in the ice cube and in the paraffin wax in Activity 6.

4. Explain why and how you think these changes in the form of the three materials took place.

Melting Points and Boiling Points

When matter changes from a solid into a liquid, it melts. Ice cream, ice cubes, and paraffin wax are familiar examples of materials that melt. Many other materials, such as plastics and metals, also melt when heated. However, different materials melt at different temperatures. The temperature at which a material changes from a solid into a liquid is called its **melting point**. Under ordinary conditions, the melting point of a material is always the same. It is a constant physical property of the material and can be used as a means of identifying or classifying it.

At what temperature does a material melt?

Whenever the temperature of a material falls below its melting point, the material changes back to the solid state. The material is said to freeze, or **solidify** (sə lid′ə fī). If the material is a pure substance, its freezing point and melting point are the same temperature.

Molten metal, at a temperature above its melting point, is poured into molds called ingots. When the metal solidifies again, it will have the shape of the ingot.

Gallium, a silver-white metal, melts at 29.78°C—a temperature below that of the human body.

Why are the boiling point and melting point of a material called physical constants?

Name two processes that are not dependent on a boiling point to bring about a change in state between liquids and gases.

In Activity 6 you heated an ice cube until it melted. If you heated it long enough, perhaps the water began to boil. Many materials that melt can be heated further until they change from a liquid into a gas. The temperature at which a liquid changes into a gas is called the **boiling point**. The boiling point of material is also a physical constant. That means, under ordinary conditions, the boiling point of the material is always the same. Boiling points, like melting points, can be used to identify or classify materials. Water has a melting point of 0°C and a boiling point of 100°C. In certain circumstances, those temperatures may vary. However, no other material has that particular melting point and boiling point. The properties of melting point and boiling point are different for different materials.

Some changes in the state of a material do not involve its melting point or its boiling point. For example, after a rain the puddles dry up. Similarly, water left in an open container will change from a liquid into a gas without boiling. Each day there will be less water in the container until there is none left. This change from a liquid into a gas, without boiling, is called **evaporation**. The water in the container evaporated, or changed into a gas from its liquid state, without being heated to the boiling point.

Perhaps you have observed that on a warm day a glass containing a cold drink soon becomes covered with little drops of water. That happens when water in the **gaseous** (gas′ē əs) state changes into the liquid state, even though it is not at the boiling point. This change from a gaseous state to a liquid state below the boiling point is called **condensation**. Water in the gaseous state exists in the air as water vapor. Other examples of condensation are the fogging of a bathroom mirror after a hot shower and the formation of dew on grass.

In Activity 7 you explained how and why you thought the changes in the wax, water, and wood took

Water vapor in the air condenses to form fog (left). The salt in salt water comes out of solution as the water evaporates from these salt beds in the Canary Islands (right).

place. Those changes were brought about by energy in the form of heat. The concepts of melting point, boiling point, and evaporation might have helped to explain the changes. Certainly the concepts of melting point and boiling point would have helped to describe the changes in the forms of the ice cube and the wax. However, did the wood melt or boil? As you observed, the wood changed in a number of ways. But it did not react like the ice cube or the wax. The changes in the form of the wood could not be described as melting or boiling. This must mean that the concepts of melting point and boiling point do not work for all materials that are heated. The wood did not evaporate or condense as it was heated and cooled. There must be an additional explanation for what happened when the wood was heated and changed in form.

Using Models

When we use concepts such as melting point, boiling point, evaporation, and condensation, we are using **models.** These models are explanations of how we think a particular change takes place. But what actually happens when something melts or boils? What takes place when something evaporates or condenses? Scientists are not satisfied with simply using words to label certain changes. They want to know exactly what is happening when a change takes place. However, it is often impossible to make direct observations of what is taking place. Then scientists make up models that might help them understand what is happening. Models are very useful for this purpose.

What is a model?

Some models are scale models. Perhaps you have built or worked with scale models of cars and airplanes. Architects (är′kə tekts) often construct scale models of a building they are designing. Such models give them a better understanding of how the building will look and function when their plans are completed. A map is a scale model of a part of the earth's surface. The floor plan of a room is a scale model. It might be used to show how furniture could be arranged or how much carpeting would be needed to cover the floor.

There are other kinds of models besides scale models. Engineers use mathematical models to design a bridge. These models often appear as formulas. By using mathematical models to design a bridge, engineers can determine beforehand if it will be structurally sound. Both mathematical and scale models are used to design airplanes. The mathematical models help the engineers determine that the plane will fly properly. The scale models are placed in wind tunnels to determine how certain wing and body shapes affect the flow of air around the airplane.

Computers are useful tools in the making of models. Information about a bridge, an airplane, or even a community can be put into a computer. Then the computer is programmed to build a model showing what will happen when certain changes take place. These models are usually mathematical models and are useful in solving certain kinds of problems.

Models serve many purposes. An architect (bottom right) develops a model that can be used by other people (top) to visualize how the house under construction will appear. The three-dimensional computer display (bottom left) is a model of radio sources from celestial space.

Scientists' models are usually mental models. Their models are ideas about how they think materials that cannot be observed directly might behave under certain conditions. How can you be sure a made-up model is correct? To prove whether or not a mental model is true, scientists set up experiments in which they make predictions. They reason that if their mental model is correct, certain things should happen to a material when it is changed in some way. For example, if you had a mental model that *all metals* melt when heated, you would heat various metals to determine whether or not they actually do melt. If all the different metals you tested did melt when heated, you would feel confident that your mental model was useful. If you had a mental model that *all materials* melt when heated, you would find that your model was useful for some materials, but not for others. You would then develop another model that might be more useful in explaining the behavior of all materials. In each case, you used a mental model to make a prediction about the behavior of certain materials under certain conditions. These predictions are not guesses. They are always based on some mental model of how nature operates. In Activity 8 you will make and test some mental models.

Interaction of Materials

Materials can be changed in a number of ways. Scientists believe that changes in materials are always caused by something that interacts with them. If you drop a beaker and it breaks, the beaker's change in form is the result of several interactions. You interact with the beaker, which interacts with the force of gravity. When the beaker comes in contact and interacts with the hard surface of the floor, it breaks. When you open a book, you are interacting with it. When you ride a

Activity 8 Mental Models

PURPOSE

To develop mental models and then make predictions

MATERIALS

Gameboard

A special note The gameboard consists of a puzzle composed of words, pictures, and symbols that make up a sentence related to science. The puzzle is covered by cards printed with letters. There are two letters of each kind, but on different cards. Over the lettered cards there is another series of cards that are numbered. Now read the entire activity.

DO THIS

A. The game is played by each player taking a turn until the puzzle is solved.

B. The first player calls out any two numbers on the gameboard. Those numbers are removed, exposing the letters underneath. If the letters match, they also are removed to reveal part of the puzzle.

C. The procedure in step **B** is repeated by each player, in turn, until all the puzzle is revealed or the puzzle is solved.

D. The objective of the game is to develop mental models of the puzzle sentence as each new part of the puzzle is revealed. You can test your mental models at any time by predicting what the puzzle sentence says. However, you are allowed to make only two predictions. Therefore, make sure that your mental model is a good one before making a prediction.

E. The first player who states the sentence correctly (even if all of it has not been revealed) wins the game.

REPORT

1. Describe how your mental models changed as each new part of the puzzle was revealed.

2. What did the puzzle sentence say?

bicycle or turn on a television set you are interacting with those objects. Interactions in which materials come in physical contact with each other might be called touching interactions. Touching interactions usually result in some change in one or more of the interacting materials. In some cases, the change might be in the position of the materials. In other cases, such as that of the beaker, it might be a change in form. Occasionally, a touching interaction might cause a change in the energy a material has. That type of change occurs when you hit a tennis ball or kick a soccer ball.

Name two kinds of interactions.

Sometimes interactions between objects take place without the objects actually touching. If two magnets are brought close to each other, there is a push or pull between them. The two magnets are interacting at a distance. A falling object interacts at a distance with the earth by responding to the force of gravity. When you heated the ice cube and the paraffin, energy in the form of heat was not in direct contact with either of the materials. In both cases, however, there was an interaction at a distance. You know the interaction took place because both materials melted.

Hitting a tennis ball with a racket is a touching interaction. It causes a change in position of both the ball and the racket.

The effect of gravity on these sky divers is an example of interaction at a distance.

Interaction at a distance and touching interactions both cause change. Yet, changes in the form of materials are not all alike. The model of a material having a melting point was useful in describing the changes that occurred in the ice and the paraffin. However, the models of melting point and boiling point were not useful in explaining the changes that took place in the wood. One way to explain these differences is to examine the materials after they changed. Although the physical forms of the ice cube and the paraffin were changed when they melted, the materials themselves did not change. The water from the melted ice cube remained water. However, if the water were cooled to its freezing point it would again become ice. The paraffin, after it had cooled, again became a solid. However, it had a new shape. When a beaker breaks, its physical form changes, but all the pieces are still glass. Changes that result in a different physical shape or form of a material, but not in the material itself, are called **physical changes**. What other physical changes can you think of?

Define *physical change*.

When you heated the wood, a different kind of change took place. It resulted in materials that did not recombine into wood upon cooling. New and different materials were formed. Whenever interactions change materials into new and different materials, a **chemical change** has taken place. A chemical change usually includes physical changes. After heating, the physical properties of the wood were quite different. But more important, the *materials* of the wood were different. The original solid wood changed into a solid black material; a liquid, brownish material; and a gaseous material that burned. The process that changed the wood is called **destructive distillation** (dis tə lā'shən). The original wood was destroyed by the heating process, but new materials with different properties were produced.

Rusting and burning are familiar examples of chemical change. Chemical changes are also important to living things. Food, water, and air undergo chemical changes to form the cells and tissues of our bodies.

The observation of physical and chemical changes helps scientists to understand the behavior of materials. But what really happens in a physical or chemical change? What actually happens when a material changes state? What actually occurs when a liquid evaporates or a gas condenses? In the following chapters, you will become familiar with some of the models that are used to help answer these questions.

The deterioration of this column of the Erechtheum, a Greek ruin, is the result of chemical changes caused by air pollution.

SCIENCE WORDS

melting point
solidify
boiling point
evaporation
gaseous
condensation
models
physical change
chemical change
destructive
distillation

SUMMARY All materials can change in form. One very common kind of change is a change of state. Matter normally exists as a solid, liquid, or gas. A change from one state to another involves a change in the temperature of the material. The concepts of boiling point and melting point are mental models used to help explain the changes in state of materials. Physical and chemical changes in materials are the result of interactions. A change in the position, energy, or shape of a material, but not in the material itself, is a physical change. Chemical changes result in the formation of new materials with different properties.

REVIEW QUESTIONS

Match the term in Column A with the correct definition in Column B.

A

1. Mental model___
2. Evaporation___
3. Touching interaction___
4. Destructive distillation___
5. Condensation___

B

a. A process by which wood is changed physically and chemically to form new materials
b. An idea of how something that cannot be observed directly might behave under certain conditions
c. A change from the liquid state into the gaseous state at a temperature below the boiling point
d. Physical contact between two materials that usually result in their being changed
e. A change from the gaseous state into the liquid state at a temperature below the boiling point

Mark each statement true (T) or false (F).

1. ______ The breaking of a beaker is a chemical change.
2. ______ If a material is a pure substance, its freezing point and melting point are the same temperature.
3. ______ A change in the state of a material requires a change in temperature.
4. ______ Models are always physical representations of an idea.
5. ______ Rusting is an example of a chemical change.

Complete the following by choosing the correct answers.

1. The push or pull between two magnets is an example of
(a) a physical change. (b) a touching interaction. (c) a chemical change. (d) interaction at a distance.
2. Which of the following is a chemical change?
(a) water freezing (b) wood burning (c) glass breaking (d) wax melting
3. Kicking a soccer ball is an example of
(a) a mental model. (b) a touching interaction. (c) a chemical change. (d) interaction at a distance.
4. A falling object reacting to the force of gravity is an example of
(a) a physical change. (b) a touching interaction. (c) a chemical change. (d) interaction at a distance.
5. Maps, scale drawings, and floor plans are examples of
(a) models. (b) changes. (c) interactions. (d) reactions.

There is no apparent motion in the Golden Gate Bridge. But the bridge is actually made of particles that are in constant motion.

4

Particles in Motion

What really happens in a physical or chemical change? What actually takes place when a material changes state? These questions, and others posed in the last chapter, also puzzled the ancient Greek philosophers. More than 2500 years ago, they developed models to explain the way materials behave. Some believed that all matter is composed of tiny particles that are held together in some way.

In this chapter you will explore some models that have been developed more recently to explain the way materials behave. These models will help you understand the changes that occurred in the materials you have already observed.

Particle Model of Matter

The ancient Greeks studied the physical world. Some proposed that all materials could be broken apart into smaller and smaller pieces. Finally, it would be impossible to break the materials into still smaller pieces. They believed that these pieces were the smallest particles of any material that could exist. This model is known as the **particle theory of matter.** It is possible to break materials into successively smaller pieces until the smallest piece can barely be seen. Only in the last few hundred years have scientists realized how small the particles of matter really are. Today, they are certain that the smallest particle that can be seen with the best microscope is composed of billions of still smaller particles!

What is the particle theory of matter?

Air is one kind of matter. In Activity 9 you will study the behavior of air. After completing the activity try to explain your observations, using the particle model. For a better explanation of your observations it will be necessary to build another model.

Aristotle and Plato were among the most famous Greek philosophers. They are shown at the center of this old woodcut at the School of Athens.

Activity 9 Studying the Behavior of Air

PURPOSE

To investigate how the volume of air changes in a closed system

MATERIALS

250-mL flask
Heat source
Tripod
Wire gauze
Balloon
Safety goggles
Matches

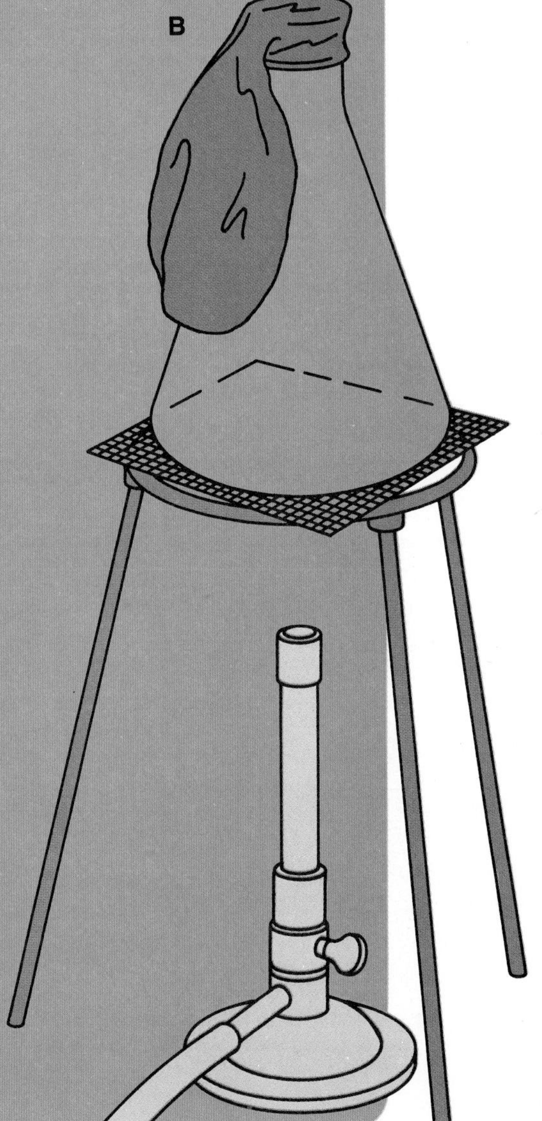

DO THIS

A. Stretch the open end of the balloon over the mouth of the flask.

B. Set up the tripod, wire gauze, and flask as shown. **CAUTION:** *Be sure you are wearing safety goggles.* Then light the heat source and place it under the flask.

C. Heat the flask gently for a few minutes. Observe any changes that take place in the closed flask-balloon system.

D. Turn off the heat source. Observe any changes that take place in the closed flask-balloon system as it cools.

E. Let everything cool completely before disassembling the apparatus and cleaning up.

REPORT

1. What changes occurred as the system was heated?
2. What changes occurred as the system cooled?
3. What was inside the closed flask-balloon system?
4. How did the material inside the system change?
5. What do you think caused those changes?

The Kinetic Particle Model

What is the kinetic theory of matter?

The particles that make up all materials are in constant motion. This model is known as the **kinetic** (ki net'ik) **theory of matter.** The word *kinetic* comes from *kine,* the Greek word-prefix, which means "motion." It takes energy to move materials. When you ride a bicycle, you use muscular energy. If you wish to go faster, you must pedal harder to supply more energy. The more energy you supply, the faster you will move. It also takes energy to move even the smallest particles. The kinetic theory of matter states that the more energy supplied to particles of matter, the faster they will move. By using both the kinetic and particle theories of matter, the behavior of the balloon in Activity 9 can be explained.

Dust particles can be seen in this beam of light. The particles seem to be in a random and constant motion. The dust particles get their energy from collisions with one another.

EXCURSION 11

Some science terms may seem unfamiliar and difficult. In Excursion 11, "The Language of Science," you can study root words that will help you determine the meaning of these terms.

When kernels of popcorn are heated they acquire kinetic energy and move around as they pop. In a similar manner, the particles in matter that is heated acquire additional kinetic energy and move faster.

What caused the balloon to inflate in Activity 9?

When energy, in the form of heat, was supplied to the flask-balloon system, an interaction at a distance occurred. The heat energy interacted with the flask and heated the air inside. As the air particles gained energy, they moved faster. This increased motion caused them to push harder against both the walls of the flask and the balloon. Since the balloon is more flexible than the flask, the faster moving air particles caused the balloon to expand.

The ideas of the particle and kinetic models are combined into one model known as the **kinetic particle theory.** You may still be unsure of how these models work. In the next activity, you will construct a physical model of these mental models. The physical model that you develop may help you to understand some of the changes you observed in Activity 6.

Explain what happens when a solid melts.

Particles move faster when energy is added to them. In Activity 6, heat energy was applied to an ice cube and to paraffin wax, which were solid materials. The heat caused the particles to move faster until the materials changed into liquids. If a liquid is given even more energy, the particles will move still faster and the liquid will change into a gas.

Activity 10 Modeling Particle Motion

PURPOSE

To develop a model of particle motion

MATERIALS

Plastic pill vial with snap-top lid
BB shot

DO THIS

A. Place enough BBs in the plastic vial to just cover the bottom. The BBs should be only one layer deep. Then snap the lid on the vial.

B. Make a drawing of the BBs as they are arranged in the vial.

C. Hold the vial by the ends with your thumb and index finger. Tip the vial slowly back and forth. Make a series of drawings to show how the BBs moved.

D. Hold the vial as in step **C** and shake it rapidly back and forth. Make drawings to show how the BBs moved.

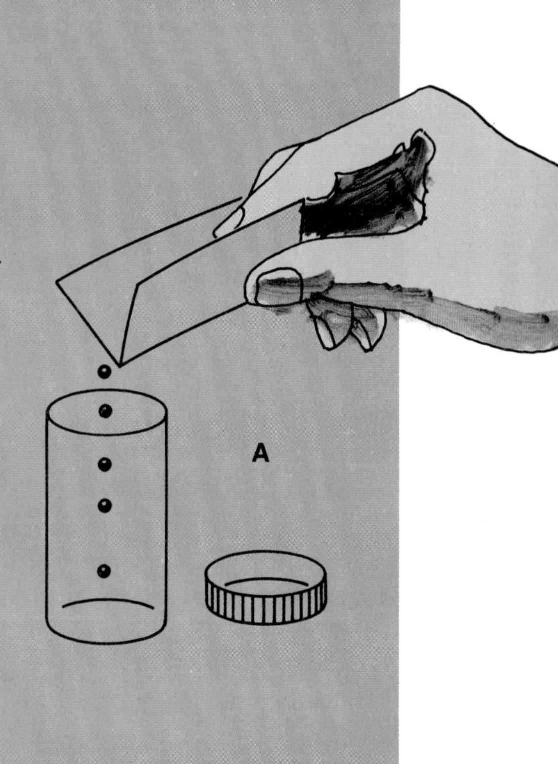

REPORT

1. What do the BBs represent in this model of particle motion?

2. In steps **C** and **D,** what did you give the BBs that they did not have before?

3. If the BBs correspond to the air particles in Activity 9, to what does the motion of your hand correspond?

4. Which of the drawings (step **B,** step **C,** or step **D**) is the most accurate model of the behavior of the air in Activity 9?

5. Refer to the record of your observations in Activity 6. Which of the drawings (step **B,** step **C,** or step **D**) is most like the properties of the ice cube and the solid paraffin before they were heated?

6. Which of the drawings (step **B,** step **C,** or step **D**) most accurately represents the properties of the melted ice cube and the melted paraffin in Activity 6?

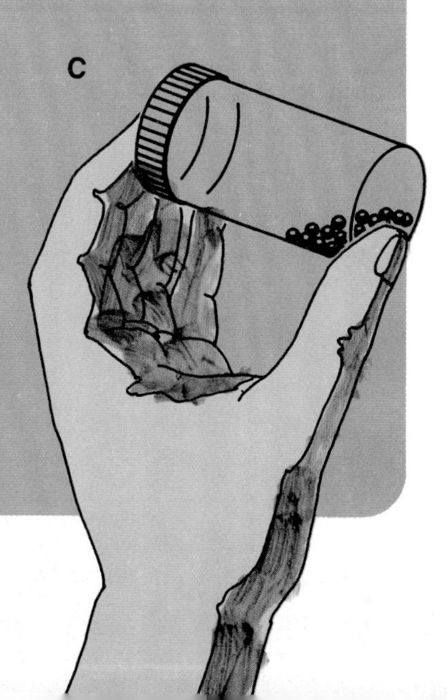

There is physical evidence that a change of state takes place when this glass tube is heated. The color change, a yellow-orange, is typical of sodium, an ingredient of the glass. The bent glass tube is the result of heating and bending the glass.

It is important to remember that models are similar to, but not exactly like, the object they describe. While the BB model developed in Activity 10 is similar to what happens when matter changes state, it is not exact. Because the particles of matter are very small, no one has ever seen them. However, it is believed that it is the behavior of these particles that causes the changes in materials.

In Chapter 3, you studied the processes of evaporation and condensation. The kinetic particle model can now be used to explain these processes. When a liquid evaporates, particles near the surface are moving so rapidly that they escape into the surrounding air. This implies that all the particles in a material are not always moving at the same rate of speed. In Activity 10, when you shook the BBs rapidly, not all of them had the same amount of energy all the time. Some BBs bounced against the sides of the vial, while others flew directly into one another. Some were hit by others and moved even faster than they did before they were hit. You may have observed a similar situation when watching a

Describe what happens when a liquid evaporates.

The cue ball transfers energy to the billiard balls. Collisions between other billiard balls result in additional transfer of energy.

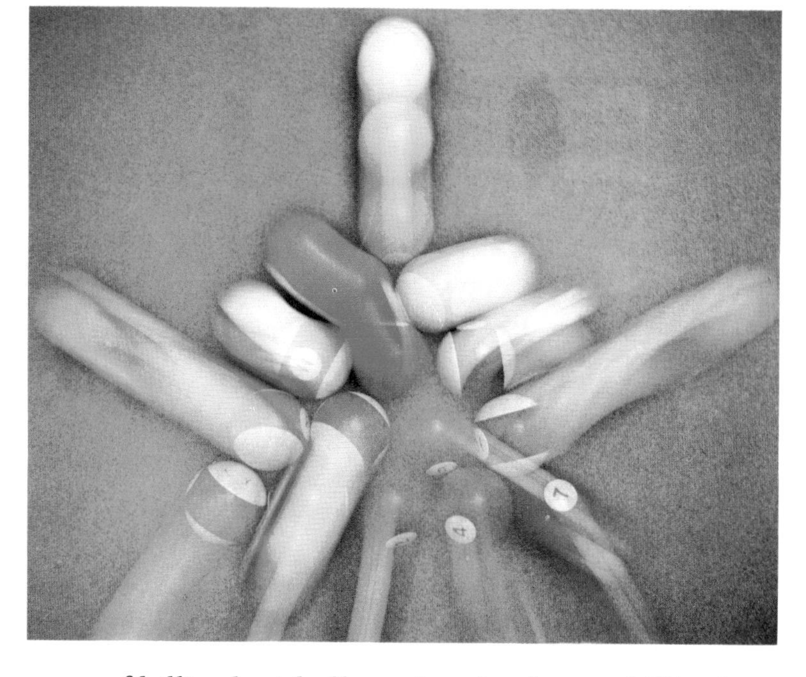

Dew drops, formed on these blades of grass, condensed from water vapor in the air. The particles making up the dew drops are moving much slower than they were as water vapor.

game of billiards. A ball moving slowly on a billiard table might be hit by a faster moving ball. This physical interaction gives extra energy to the slower moving ball. In a liquid, the particles are moving and colliding. These collisions may supply just enough extra energy to cause particles to leave the surface and become water vapor.

The process of condensation also involves the motion of particles. When two BBs collide, they both lose energy and travel slower. On a billiard table, a ball slows down each time it hits the sides of the table or another ball. In a similar way, particles of water vapor in the air may strike an object and lose energy to it. When these particles lose energy, they move slower. Some particles move so slowly that they stick to the object they strike. A cool object absorbs enough energy from the gaseous water particles to cause them to condense. When the number of particles is great enough, droplets of liquid water are formed.

Equilibrium

Water in a closed container will still evaporate and condense. How can the kinetic particle model be used to explain this fact? Particles evaporate from the surface of the water into the air in the container. Some of the particles of water vapor collide with the sides or top of the container. Particles also collide with other particles in the air and with the surface of the water. When these particles collide, some of them lose enough energy to slow down and condense. Since both processes are occurring at the same time, a balance should eventually be reached. For every water particle that evaporates a corresponding particle condenses. The rate of evaporation equals the rate of condensation. This condition is called **equilibrium** (ē kwə lib′rē əm). Equilibrium is another word for balance. Because there is a balance between two processes that involve action and motion, the condition is more precisely called **dynamic** (dī nam′ik) **equilibrium.**

What is dynamic equilibrium?

These high wire performers must maintain their balance, or equilibrium, to avoid falling.

Activity 11 Expansion of a Liquid

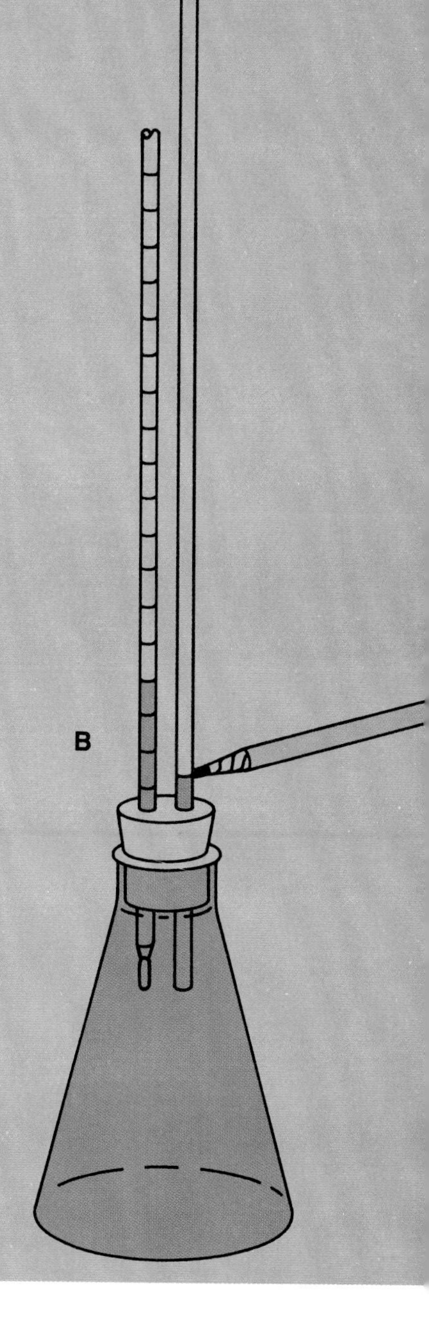

PURPOSE

To investigate how water behaves when heated

MATERIALS

250-mL flask
Tripod
Wire gauze
Rubber stopper to fit the flask (with a thermometer and a 60-cm glass tube inserted)
Food coloring
Water
Grease pencil
Meterstick
Safety goggles
Heat source

DO THIS

A. Fill the flask almost to the top with water to which food coloring has been added.

B. Push the rubber stopper firmly into the flask. Some of the colored water will rise in the glass tube. Mark the water level on the glass tube with the grease pencil.

C. Read the thermometer and record the temperature of the water.

D. Stand the flask on the tripod. **CAUTION:** *Be sure you are wearing safety goggles.* Then light the heat source and gently heat the water for 5 minutes. Every 30 seconds, mark the water level on the glass tube and record the temperature.

E. Turn off the heat source. Then measure the distance from the rubber stopper to each grease mark. Record these data.

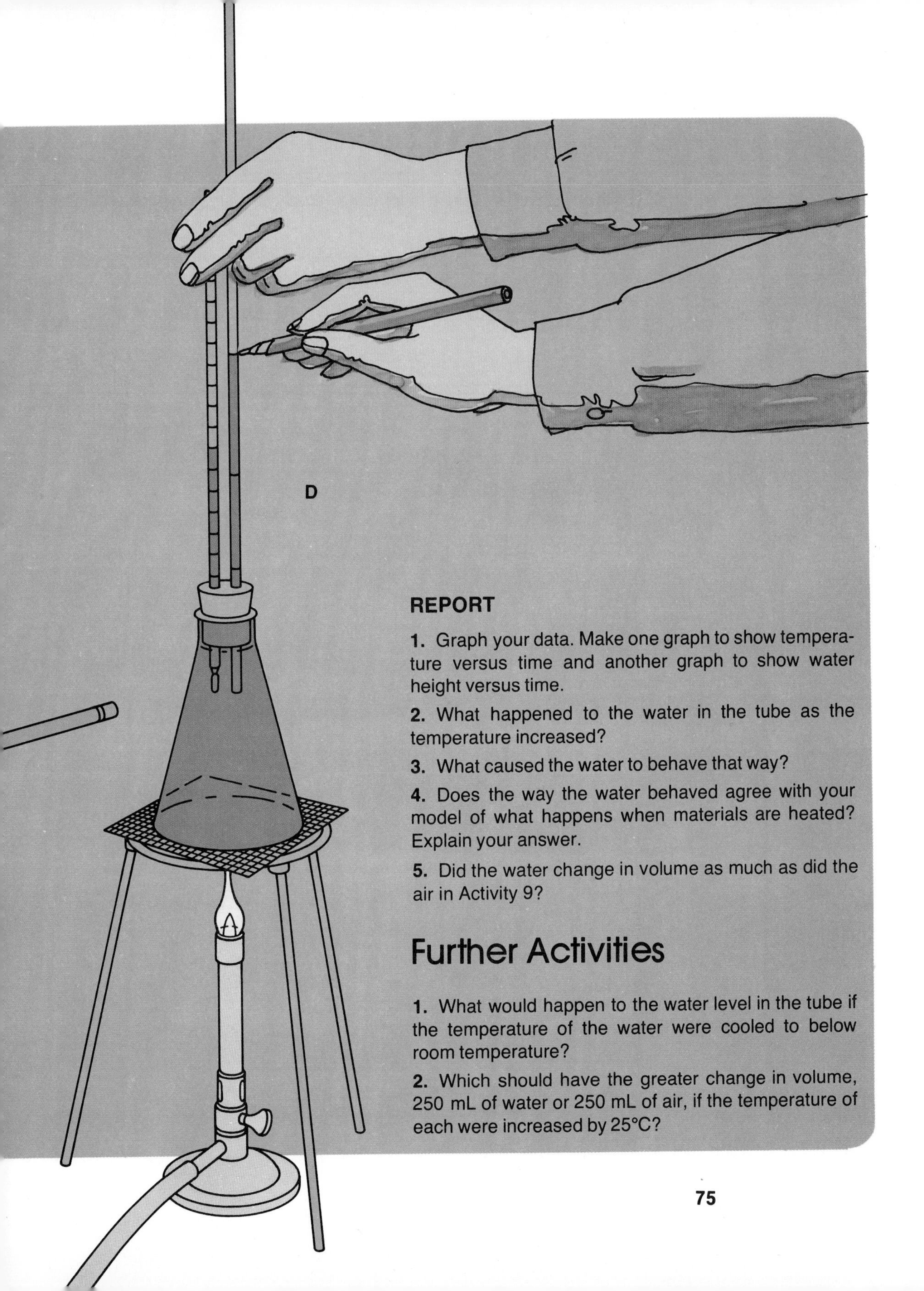

REPORT

1. Graph your data. Make one graph to show temperature versus time and another graph to show water height versus time.

2. What happened to the water in the tube as the temperature increased?

3. What caused the water to behave that way?

4. Does the way the water behaved agree with your model of what happens when materials are heated? Explain your answer.

5. Did the water change in volume as much as did the air in Activity 9?

Further Activities

1. What would happen to the water level in the tube if the temperature of the water were cooled to below room temperature?

2. Which should have the greater change in volume, 250 mL of water or 250 mL of air, if the temperature of each were increased by 25°C?

You have seen how the kinetic particle model can be used to explain the changes in form of materials. In the last activity, you discovered more about this kinetic model.

The kinetic particle model has been used to investigate and explain the behavior of liquids and gases. But how does this model help to explain the behavior of solids? The BB model represented particles in a solid as being at rest. Is this physical model a good one for explaining the behavior of solids?

Some Properties of Solids

When the temperature of a liquid falls below its melting point, the liquid begins to solidify. The particles of the material pack together in an orderly fashion. This is similar to the action of BBs as they are poured into a container. There are forces that attract the particles to one another. These same forces attract the particles in liquids and gases, but not to the same extent. The way the particles pack is determined by their shapes and sizes. The packing together of billions of particles causes most solid materials to form into special shapes called **crystals** (kris′təls). Almost all solid materials have their own unique crystal form. Sugar and salt are familiar **crystalline** (kris′tə lin) materials. Examine salt and sugar crystals under a microscope or with a hand lens. Describe the appearance of the crystals.

What are crystal forms?

You may have noticed metal strips extending across the roadway of a bridge. Perhaps you have learned that a metal jar lid can be removed more easily if it is first held under hot water. Both situations give some clues about the behavior of solids. In an experiment conducted to investigate this behavior, a 70-cm iron bar was heated from 0°C to 200°C. After each increase of 25°, the length of the bar was carefully measured. The bar became longer as the temperature increased. It expanded a total of 1 cm. This experiment proves that particles in a solid are moving also. As a solid gains energy, its particles begin to move faster. This motion caused the bar to become longer.

The fact that solids expand when they are heated is of concern to architects and engineers. When large bridges or buildings are constructed, **expansion joints** must be installed. A steel bridge will expand on a hot day and contract on a cold day. The 70-cm bar expanded only 1 cm while being heated. However, a bridge 70 m long might expand and contract as much as 50 cm between summer and winter. The expansion joints on a bridge allow for this expansion and contraction. Otherwise, the bridge would buckle on a hot day and pull away from the pavement on a cold day.

These crystals are formed from different solids. Each has its unique crystal form. A crystal of sodium salt of saccharin (top left), recrystalized from water; sulfur crystals and molten sulfur enlarged 50 times (top right); crystals of uranium alloy (bottom left); crystals of triphenyl methane (bottom right).

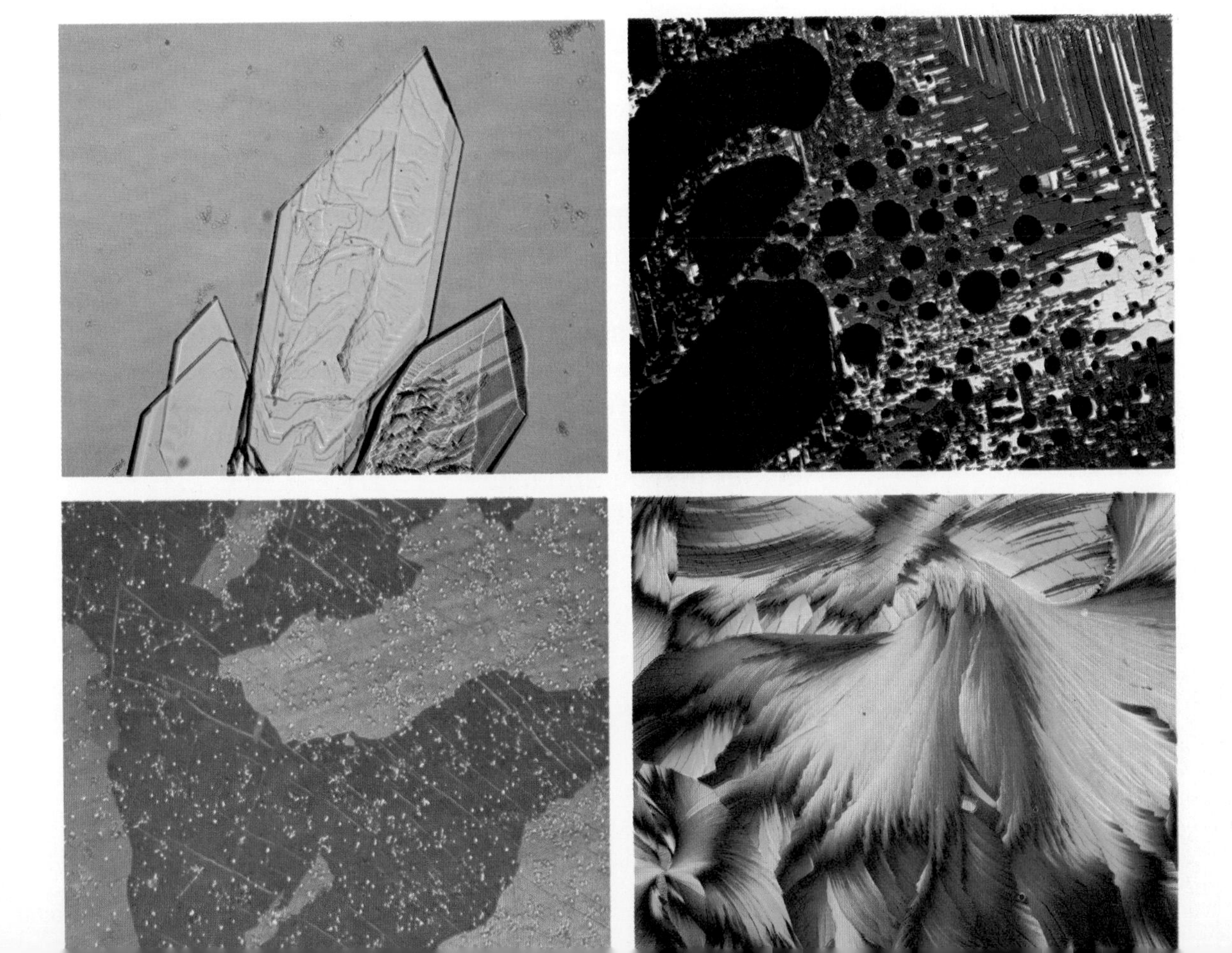

An expansion joint, such as this, allows for expansion and contraction due to changes in temperature. The number of expansion joints on a bridge depends on the length of the bridge.

Buildings made of steel, aluminum, and glass, must be designed to allow for expansion of the walls. Walls facing south will expand more than those facing north because the sun's energy strikes the south-facing walls more directly. The expansion of solids is also important in machines that have parts which become hot and are in contact with one another. Piston rings in an automobile engine are an example. They allow for expansion of the metal pistons and cylinders as the engine becomes hot.

If the particles of a solid are in motion, why doesn't the solid melt? The kinetic particle model cannot answer that question.

Solids have particles that pack together in orderly patterns producing solid, rigid crystals. Most solids can expand when energy is added to them and contract when energy is taken away. The best model that has been developed to explain this behavior is one that describes different kinds of particle motion.

Types of Particle Motion

In the gaseous state of matter, the motion of particles is mainly **translational** (trans lā′shə nəl) **motion.** The particles have enough energy to overcome the forces that attract them to each other. They can move in any direction. However, some particles may also have **rotational** (rō tā′shə nəl) **motion** and **vibrational** (vī brā′shə nəl) **motion.** When the particles lose energy, they lose their translational motion and clump together. This results in gaseous matter becoming a liquid. In a liquid, the particles still move around one another. In addition, they vibrate. The particles in a liquid have rotational motion and vibrational motion. When the particles organize to form crystals in solids, they can no longer rotate about one another. They have only vibrational motion. This vibrational motion can be increased or decreased by adding or removing energy.

Name the three types of particle motion.

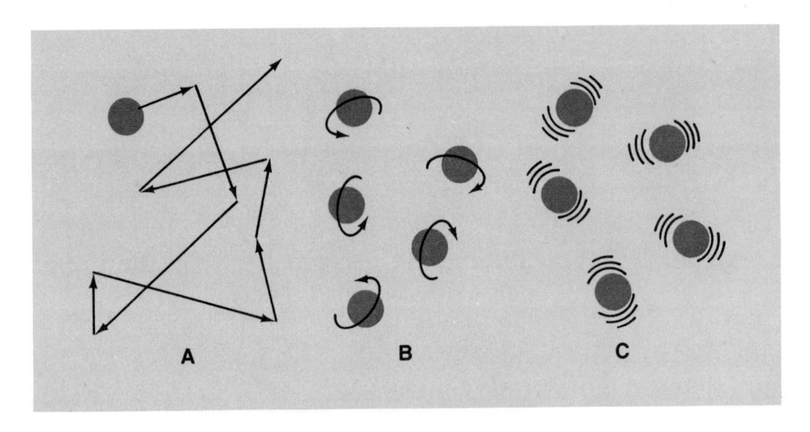

FIGURE 4–1
The three types of particle motion are shown here. **A** *demonstrates translational motion,* **B** *rotational motion, and* **C** *vibrational motion.*

You have learned that a change in state or a change in particle motion requires the addition or removal of heat energy. When materials are heated and change state, their temperature, which is a measure of heat intensity, increases. This indicates that heat energy is actually the motion of particles. The energy of motion

Energy is transferred from the fire to the pan and from the pan to the fish.

that all particles have is sensed by humans as heat. This relationship between materials and energy is an important one. Heat is the connecting link.

The kinetic particle model has been useful in explaining the change of state of materials and the motion of particles. However, it has not been useful in explaining what happened to the wood that was heated in Activity 7. The kinetic particle model can explain other physical interactions. You will explore some of these interactions in the next chapter.

SCIENCE WORDS

particle theory of matter
kinetic theory of matter
kinetic particle theory
equilibrium
dynamic equilibrium
crystals
crystalline
expansion joints
translational motion
rotational motion
vibrational motion

SUMMARY All materials are made of very small particles. These particles are billions of times smaller than those that can be seen with the best microscopes. These particles are in constant motion. When energy is added, particles move faster and materials expand. When energy is removed, particles slow down and materials contract.

Particles can have three types of motion. Particles in solids have only vibrational motion. In liquids, particles have both vibrational and rotational motions. Particles in gases are physically separated from one another and can move in any direction. This motion is called translational motion. The energy that causes particles to move faster is heat energy. Heat is actually the motion of particles of matter.

REVIEW QUESTIONS

Mark each statement true (T) or false (F).

1. ______ The smallest particles of a material can be seen with a microscope.
2. ______ The word *kinetic* comes from a word meaning "motion."
3. ______ As energy is added to a material, the particles move slower.
4. ______ Almost all solids have a unique crystal form.
5. ______ The particles of a solid are always in motion.

Fill in the blanks with the correct terms.

1. In the gaseous state, the motion of particles is mainly ____________ motion.
2. A balance between two processes that involve action and motion is called ____________ ____________.
3. When a liquid ____________, its particles escape from the surface.
4. ____________ occurs when particles of water vapor stick to cool objects.
5. The motion of particles in a solid is called ____________ motion.
6. The packing together of billions of particles causes solid materials to form special shapes called ____________.
7. The two types of motion that particles in a liquid have are ____________ and ____________ motion.
8. ____________ energy is actually the motion of particles.
9. The way particles in a solid pack together is determined by both their ____________ and ____________.

Match the term in Column A with the correct definition in Column B.

A

1. Expansion joints ___
2. Ancient Greek philosophers ___
3. Kinetic particle theory ___
4. Equilibrium ___
5. Temperature ___

B

a. Used to explain changes of state of materials and the motion of particles
b. Allow for expansion and contraction of bridges due to temperature changes
c. The number of water particles evaporating equals the number of particles condensing
d. Measure of heat intensity
e. First to propose particle theory of matter

APPLYING WHAT YOU LEARNED

1. Look up examples of dynamic equilibrium other than the one given in this chapter.
2. Suggest some ways of demonstrating that heat energy is actually the motion of particles.

The pigments in these paints can be mixed to obtain different colors. The result is a mixture.

5

Special Interactions

Most people like to experiment with things around them. Many children, for instance, like to mix favorite foods to try to produce an even better taste. However, combinations such as ketchup on ice cream and powdered orange juice in hot chocolate do not usually work out as expected. But sometimes such experiments are successful. Peanut butter and jelly, hot dogs with mustard, and apple pie with cheese are mixtures of unlikely foods that did work out.

Mixing things is one method scientists use to investigate the nature of materials. In previous chapters you mixed energy with materials. You have some useful models for explaining what happens to materials when energy is added to or taken away from them. In this chapter you will investigate mixing interactions of a different kind.

Activity 12 Mixtures

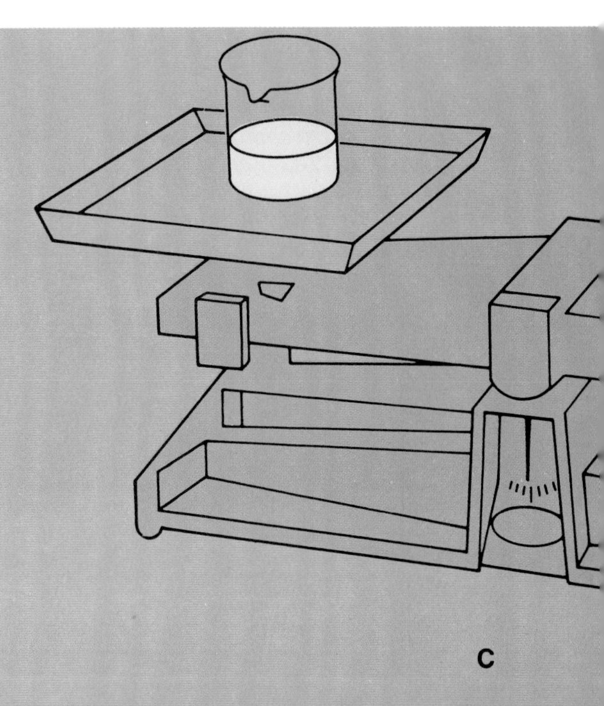

PURPOSE

To study the properties of mixtures

MATERIALS

Iron filings
NaCl [*sodium chloride*]
White sand
$NaNO_3$ [*sodium nitrate*]
Several 150-mL beakers
Magnet
Graduate
Balance and mass set
Spoon
Stirring rod
Funnel
Funnel support
Filter paper
Water
Ice water

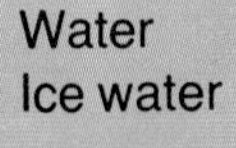

DO THIS

A. Make four or more *different* mixtures of iron filings, NaCl, white sand, and $NaNO_3$. The mixtures may contain two, three, or all four materials. Use one spoonful of material per mixture. Stir each mixture thoroughly. Record the materials used to make each mixture in a table like Table 1.

TABLE 1 • Mixtures

MATERIALS IN MIXTURE	METHOD OF SEPARATION

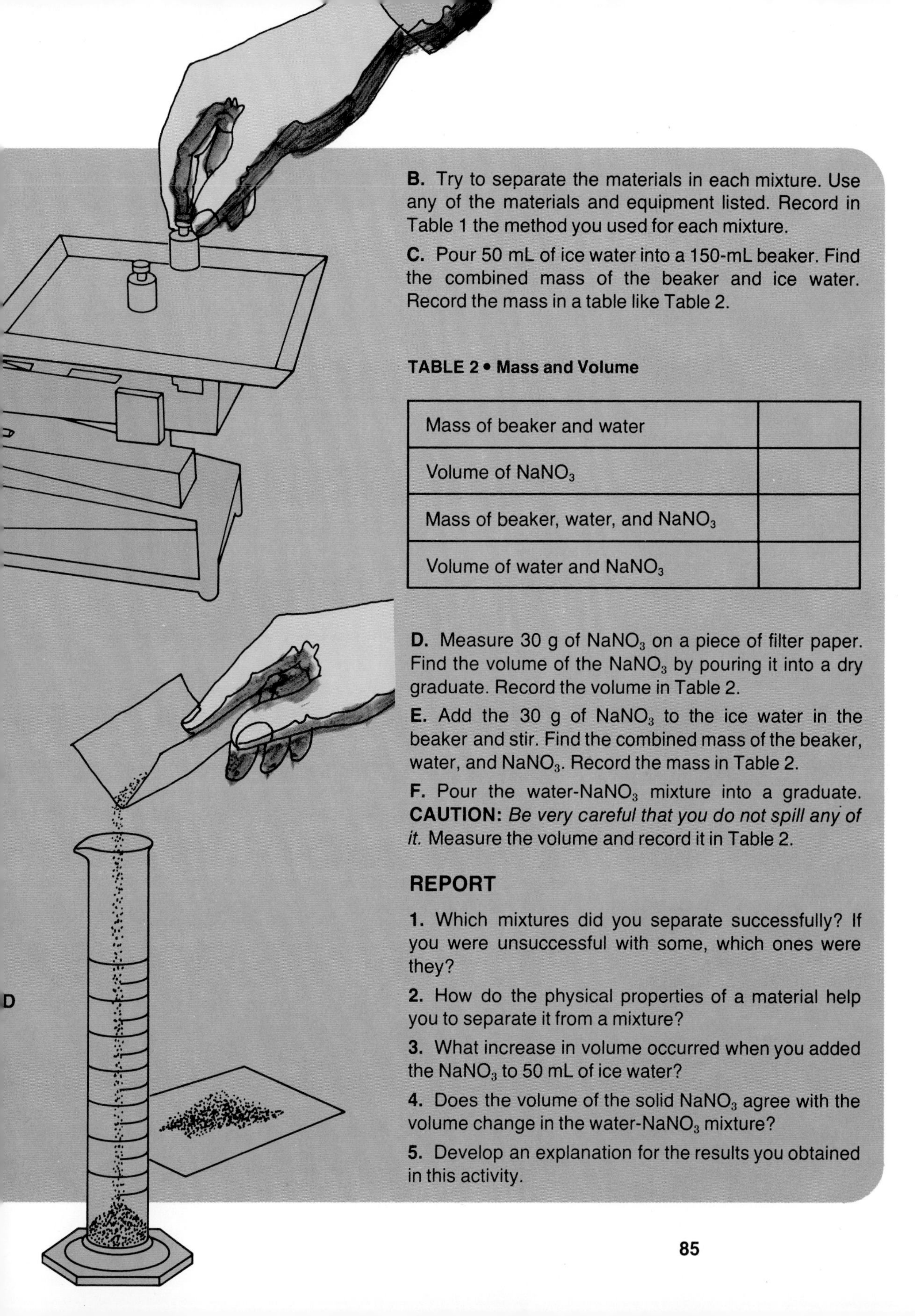

B. Try to separate the materials in each mixture. Use any of the materials and equipment listed. Record in Table 1 the method you used for each mixture.

C. Pour 50 mL of ice water into a 150-mL beaker. Find the combined mass of the beaker and ice water. Record the mass in a table like Table 2.

TABLE 2 • Mass and Volume

Mass of beaker and water	
Volume of $NaNO_3$	
Mass of beaker, water, and $NaNO_3$	
Volume of water and $NaNO_3$	

D. Measure 30 g of $NaNO_3$ on a piece of filter paper. Find the volume of the $NaNO_3$ by pouring it into a dry graduate. Record the volume in Table 2.

E. Add the 30 g of $NaNO_3$ to the ice water in the beaker and stir. Find the combined mass of the beaker, water, and $NaNO_3$. Record the mass in Table 2.

F. Pour the water-$NaNO_3$ mixture into a graduate. **CAUTION:** *Be very careful that you do not spill any of it.* Measure the volume and record it in Table 2.

REPORT

1. Which mixtures did you separate successfully? If you were unsuccessful with some, which ones were they?

2. How do the physical properties of a material help you to separate it from a mixture?

3. What increase in volume occurred when you added the $NaNO_3$ to 50 mL of ice water?

4. Does the volume of the solid $NaNO_3$ agree with the volume change in the water-$NaNO_3$ mixture?

5. Develop an explanation for the results you obtained in this activity.

Mixtures

How can iron filings be separated from sand?

Mixtures (miks'chərs) result from the physical interaction of two or more materials. In Activity 12 you made mixtures of solid materials. After mixing, you could still distinguish the different materials in the mixtures. Materials that have been mixed can be separated out of the mixture by various physical methods. By using a magnet, you could easily separate the iron filings from the other materials with which they were mixed. Interacting with a magnet is a physical property of iron filings. The other materials do not have this property. Sometimes the particles in solid mixtures can be separated by size, using a screen. This method is often used by earth scientists to separate sand grains. If you added water to any of the mixtures of solids, you found that some materials interact with water and dissolve. Other materials do not. This is another method of separating mixtures of solids. You may have found that some of the solids were more difficult to separate than were others. The more similar the physical properties of materials in a mixture, the more difficult it is to separate the materials.

Both of these pictures show heterogeneous mixtures. Soil (bottom left) is not often thought of as a mixture. The components of the concrete (bottom right) are sand, cement, and gravel.

You may have been surprised at how much $NaNO_3$ [*sodium nitrate*] dissolved in ice water. When the $NaNO_3$ dissolved, there was no change in its mass. This fact is important. It is called the **law of conservation of matter.** This law states that under ordinary conditions, matter cannot be destroyed. All matter has mass. That the mass of the $NaNO_3$ did not change is evidence supporting the law of conservation of matter.

After the $NaNO_3$ dissolved in the ice water, you were not able to see it. The ice water appeared to be clear. The $NaNO_3$ mixed so thoroughly in the water because it broke apart into tiny invisible particles. This is an example of a **homogeneous** (hō mə jē′nē əs) **mixture.** The mixture is the same throughout. Salt or sugar dissolved in water are other examples of homogeneous mixtures. The solid mixtures you made earlier in Activity 12 were not always the same throughout. The original materials could still be distinguished. These mixtures are called **heterogeneous** (het ər ə jē′nē əs) **mixtures.** Peas and carrots and fudge ripple ice cream are examples of heterogeneous mixtures.

Homogeneous mixtures, such as this one of $KMnO_4$ and water, are the same throughout. You cannot distinguish between the particles of the $KMnO_4$ and the water.

What does the law of conservation of matter state?

You may be concerned that the volume of the solid $NaNO_3$ did not agree with the volume change of the mixture. It appears that the $NaNO_3$ lost volume but not mass. It is difficult to explain what happens to the solid $NaNO_3$ when it dissolves in water. Based on the kinetic particle model, it would appear that the solid $NaNO_3$ particles pick up energy from the water and change into a liquid. But how can this be when the $NaNO_3$ was at room temperature and it dissolved in ice water? What actually happens to the $NaNO_3$? To explain this, it is necessary to explain also why the combined volume of the water and the $NaNO_3$ does not equal their separate volumes. One must either account for the lost volume or be skeptical of the law of conservation of matter. The problem can be solved by building another model to expand on the kinetic particle theory.

Activity 13 A Model for Dissolving

TABLE 1 • Mixture Volume Data

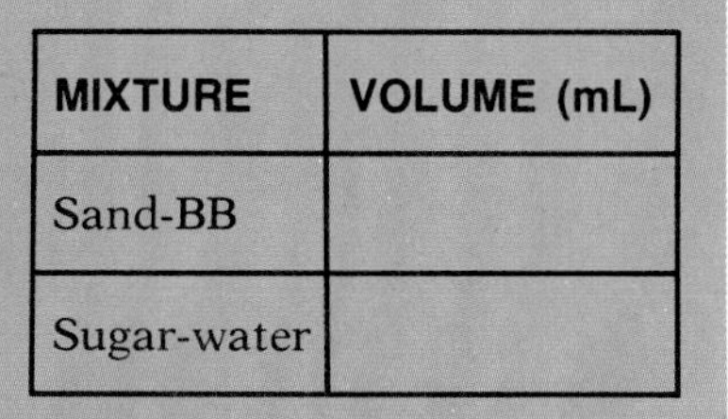

MIXTURE	VOLUME (mL)
Sand-BB	
Sugar-water	

PURPOSE

To expand the kinetic particle theory to account for the dissolving of $NaNO_3$ in water

MATERIALS

2 50-mL beakers
2 25-mL graduates
2 spoons
Fine sand
BBs
Sheet of paper
$C_{12}H_{22}O_{11}$ [*sugar*]
Water
Stirring rod

DO THIS

A. Measure 10 mL of sand with a graduate. Then pour the sand into a 50-mL beaker.

B. Measure 10 mL of BBs with the graduate and pour them into the beaker containing the sand. Stir to mix the sand and BBs thoroughly.

C. Roll a sheet of paper to form a cone funnel. Use the cone funnel to pour the sand-BB mixture into the graduate. Measure the volume of the mixture. Record the volume in a table like Table 1.

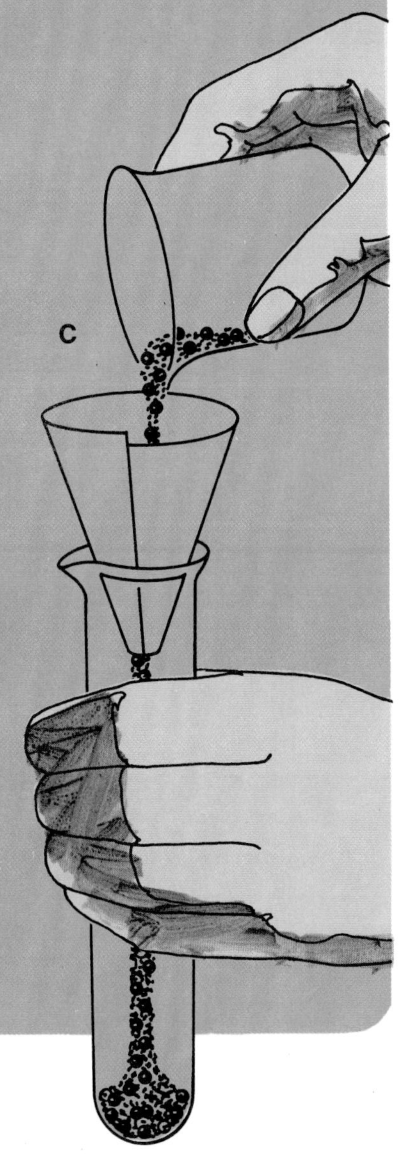

D. Use a second graduate to measure 5 mL of sugar. Pour the sugar into a clean 50-mL beaker.

E. Measure 15 mL of water and pour it into the beaker containing the sugar. Stir until the sugar dissolves.

F. Carefully pour the sugar-water mixture into the graduate. Measure the volume and record it in Table 1.

REPORT

1. Explain why 10 mL of sand and 10 mL of BBs do not amount to 20 mL of sand-BB mixture.

2. Explain why 5 mL of sugar and 15 mL of water do not amount to 20 mL of sugar-water mixture.

A lava flow is an example of a heterogeneous mixture. Even in a molten state, different particles can be distinguished.

In Activity 13 you built a model for dissolving. You were probably able to develop a good explanation of how the $NaNO_3$ particles behaved in the water.

The forces that hold the particles of $NaNO_3$ together are very weak, and the crystals of $NaNO_3$ break apart quite easily in water. There also is evidence that the individual particles of $NaNO_3$ break apart in the water. This breakdown will be discussed in more detail in later chapters. The kinetic particle model can be used to help explain what happens when a solid dissolves in a liquid. The solid particles that break down fit into spaces between the particles of the liquid. The sand-BB model showed that the spaces between the BBs were large enough to hold many sand grains. In the last activity, the BBs were to the water particles as the sand was to the sugar. This type of model is sometimes referred to as an **analogy** (ə nal′ə jē).

Solutions

Homogeneous mixtures are called **solutions** (sə lü′shənz). There are two parts to a solution. The material that dissolves is called the **solute** (sol′yüt). The material into which the solute dissolves is called the **solvent** (sol′vənt). In the sodium nitrate-water mixture, water was the solvent and $NaNO_3$ was the solute. Water is often referred to as the *universal solvent* because so many materials will dissolve in it. There are many different kinds of solutions. Solution can take place between solids and liquids, liquids and liquids, liquids and gases, and even between two solids or between solids and gases.

Why is water called the universal solvent?

There are some cases in which mixtures of materials appear to be solutions but are not. John Tyndall, a physicist (fiz′ə sist), found that when a beam of light is directed through a true solution, it will be bent, or diffracted. However, it will pass through the solution as a beam. When a beam of light is passed through a mixture

Oil (bottom left) is shown in solution and not in solution. The oil and water do not form a solution. The oil and benzene do form a solution. The benzene is the solvent. A water and sugar solution is sometimes used in intravenous feeding (bottom right).

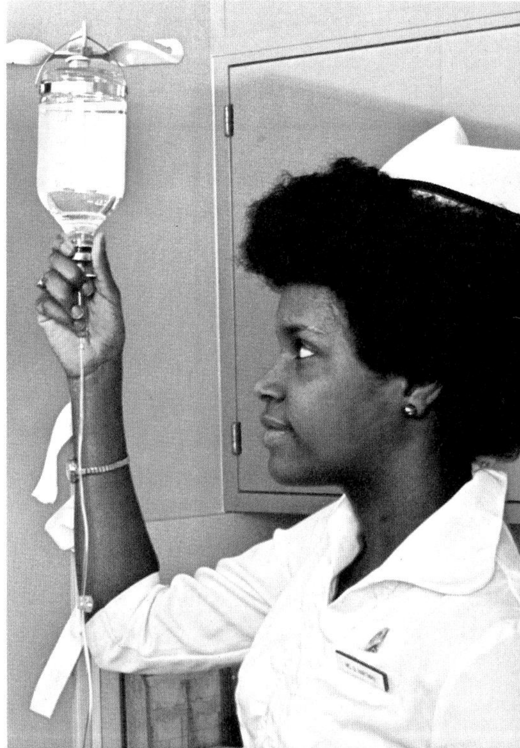

that is not a true solution, the light beam will be scattered. This scattering of the light beam is called the **Tyndall** (tin′dəl) **effect.** Mixtures showing the Tyndall effect are called **colloids** (kol′oids). A colloid consists of tiny suspended particles of one material distributed evenly in another material. There are many different kinds of colloidal systems. Gelatin is an example of a solid-in-liquid colloid. Milk is an example of a liquid-in-liquid colloid. Liquid-in-liquid colloids are called **emulsions** (i mul′shəns). Shaving cream and whipped cream are examples of gas-in-liquid colloids. They are known as **foams.** Fog is an example of a liquid-in-gas colloid. Liquid-in-gas colloids are common in various spray-can products. They are known as **aerosols** (ãr′ə sols).

Shaving cream is a gas-in-liquid colloid. In this type of colloid there is more liquid than gas.

Brownian Movement

Solid particles in a colloidal system may remain suspended indefinitely. They are bumped around by collisions with other particles in the system. Have you ever observed smoke or dust particles in the air in bright light? You can actually see the movement of these tiny solid particles. They move in random, zigzag paths. This random motion of the suspended particles is called **Brownian** (brou′nē ən) **movement.**

Brownian movement also occurs in solid-in-liquid colloidal systems. Therefore, Brownian movement supports the kinetic particle model of matter. The model has now been expanded to explain the apparent loss of volume when a solid dissolves in a liquid. In the next activity, you will again test the kinetic particle model. The kinetic model indicates that the particles of a material move faster as they are given more heat energy. How would an increase in temperature affect the amount of solid that will dissolve in a liquid?

FIGURE 5–1
This is a plotted path of a particle in a colloid. The plotted path demonstrates Brownian movement.

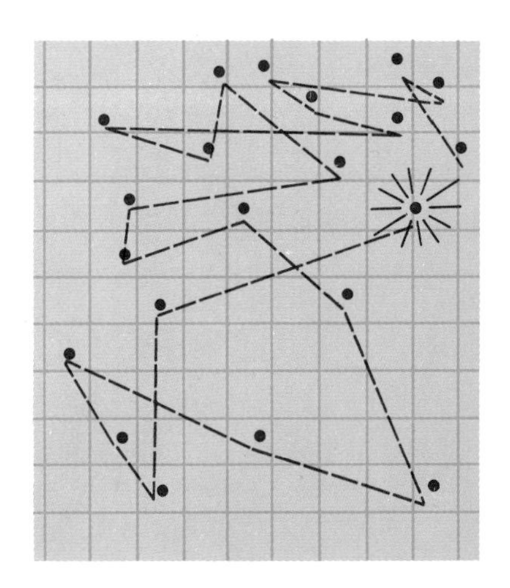

Activity 14 Heating Solutions

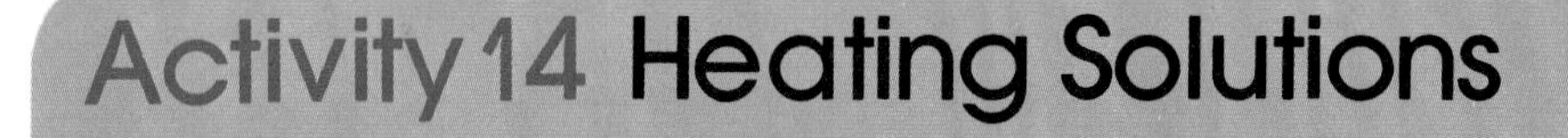

B

PURPOSE

To determine how heating a solution affects solubility

MATERIALS

Heat source
Matches
$NaNO_3$ [*sodium nitrate*]
150-mL beaker
Tripod
Wire gauze
Water
Balance and mass set
Celsius thermometer
Safety goggles
Graduate
Asbestos gloves
Stirring rod
Spoon

DO THIS

A. Pour 50 mL of water into a 150-mL beaker. Then determine the combined mass of the beaker and water. Record the mass in a table like Table 1.

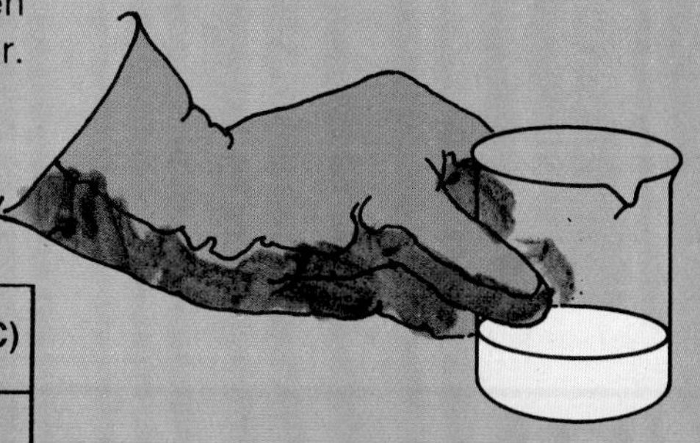

TABLE 1 • Heat and Solutions

Combined mass of the beaker and water ______.

STEP	TOTAL MASS OF $NaNO_3$ IN SOLUTION (g)	TEMPERATURE (°C)
B		
D		40
E		60

B. Measure the temperature of the water and record it in the table.

Stir constantly while adding $NaNO_3$ to the water a little at a time until no more will dissolve. **CAUTION:** *Do not use the thermometer as a stirring rod.* Determine the mass of the $NaNO_3$ that dissolved. Record this data in the table.

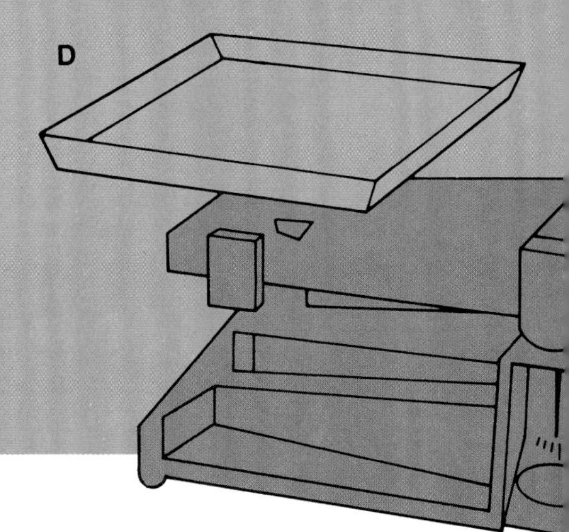

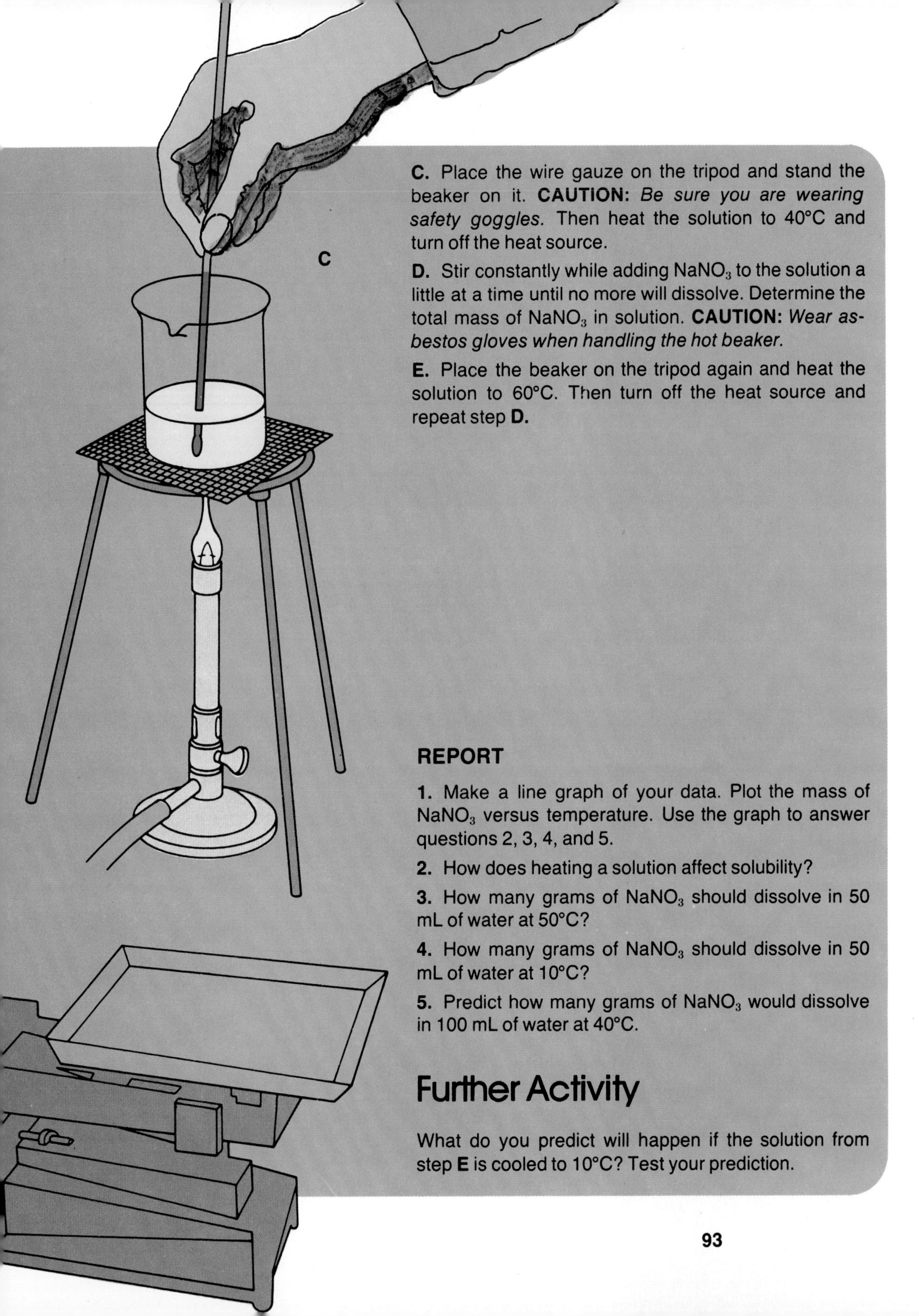

C. Place the wire gauze on the tripod and stand the beaker on it. **CAUTION:** *Be sure you are wearing safety goggles.* Then heat the solution to 40°C and turn off the heat source.

D. Stir constantly while adding $NaNO_3$ to the solution a little at a time until no more will dissolve. Determine the total mass of $NaNO_3$ in solution. **CAUTION:** *Wear asbestos gloves when handling the hot beaker.*

E. Place the beaker on the tripod again and heat the solution to 60°C. Then turn off the heat source and repeat step **D.**

REPORT

1. Make a line graph of your data. Plot the mass of $NaNO_3$ versus temperature. Use the graph to answer questions 2, 3, 4, and 5.

2. How does heating a solution affect solubility?

3. How many grams of $NaNO_3$ should dissolve in 50 mL of water at 50°C?

4. How many grams of $NaNO_3$ should dissolve in 50 mL of water at 10°C?

5. Predict how many grams of $NaNO_3$ would dissolve in 100 mL of water at 40°C.

Further Activity

What do you predict will happen if the solution from step **E** is cooled to 10°C? Test your prediction.

The addition of heat energy to a solvent increases the amount of solid that will dissolve in it. According to the particle model of matter, the particles of a material move faster as more heat energy is applied. This increased particle motion causes the material to expand. As expansion occurs, the particles move farther apart. This increases the distance between each particle and allows more particles of a solute to fit between the particles of the solvent.

Saturated Solutions

What is a saturated solution?

You mixed $NaNO_3$ with water until no more $NaNO_3$ could be added without some remaining as a solid. What you made is called a **saturated** (sach′ə rā tid) **solution.** A saturated solution is one in which the amount of solute takes up all the available spaces between the particles of the solvent. If any more solute ($NaNO_3$) is added at that temperature, there will be no room for it, and it will not go into solution. The temperature of the solution is a critical factor. As the temperature increases, there is more room for solute in the solution. Therefore, the temperature of a solution will determine the amount of solute that can be dissolved. Temperature is a **variable** (văr′ē ə bəl) **property.** It influences the solubility of a material. Another variable in the formation of a solution is the amount of solvent present. The larger the amount of solvent, the larger the amount of solute that can be dissolved. In the last activity you controlled both these variables. Each solution was made using the same volume of solvent. Temperature was controlled by dissolving $NaNO_3$ only at certain temperatures. Although these two variables were controlled, you did not control the amount of $NaNO_3$ that would dissolve. The amount of $NaNO_3$ that would dissolve in 50 mL of water at a certain temperature was an **uncontrolled** (un kən trōld′), or **responding variable.** Scientists conduct most experiments in this way. They try to control all but one of the variables that might influence an experiment. In this way, they can determine which variable caused a change to occur.

Based on the kinetic particle model, the particles in a saturated solution should slow down when the solution is cooled. The distance between particles in the solution would become smaller. When there is less room between the particles of the solvent, there is less room for the particles of the solute. Some of the particles of solute will begin to change back into the solid state. Crystals that form fall to the bottom of the container.

When soda is poured from a bottle into a glass, the gas in the solution forms bubbles. These bubbles of gas eventually escape from the solution.

To form crystals, the solute must have some solid material upon which to build its orderly pattern of particles. Under certain conditions it is possible to cool a saturated solution carefully so that none of the solute begins to come out of solution. Suppose the solution does not have any solid particles on which the solute particles can begin to grow crystals. The solution will then actually hold more solute than it should be able to hold at that temperature. Such a solution is known as a **supersaturated** (sü pər sach′ə rāt id) **solution.**

What is a supersaturated solution?

A saturated solution that has some undissolved solute in it is in dynamic equilibrium. In this situation particles of solute are continuously leaving the crystal of the solute and going into solution. At the same time solute particles are crystallizing out of solution onto the crystals in the container. An unsaturated solution and a supersaturated solution are not in equilibrium. In an unsaturated solution, the rate of dissolving is much faster than the rate of crystallization. In a supersaturated solution, any disturbance will cause crystallization to exceed the rate of dissolving. Once the supersaturated solution has crystallized and reached its saturation point, this solution will be in equilibrium.

Activity 15 New Dissolving Process?

PURPOSE

To determine if chemical as well as physical changes take place in the dissolving process

MATERIALS

Test tube
Stirring rod
$CuCl$ [*copper(I) chloride*]
Graduate
Water
Thin aluminum foil
Balance and mass set
Filter paper
Spoon
Watch or clock

DO THIS

A. Dissolve 6 g of $CuCl$ crystals in 20 mL of water in a test tube. Observe the dissolving process closely.

B. Loosely roll a 2 cm × 2 cm piece of aluminum foil. Push the foil into the $CuCl$ solution with the stirring rod.

C. Observe closely the changes that take place in the solution for the next five minutes.

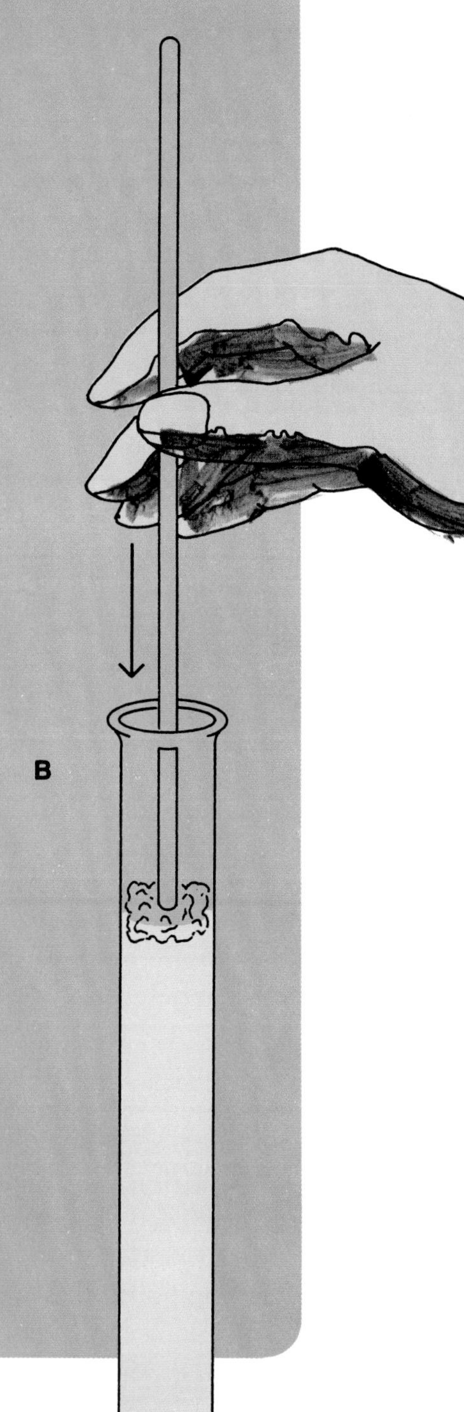

REPORT

1. What changes did you observe in the $CuCl$ solution when the aluminum foil was added?

2. What changes did you observe in the aluminum foil?

3. Is there evidence that a physical interaction took place?

4. Is there evidence that a chemical interaction took place?

5. What evidence is there that the aluminum went into solution?

6. What evidence is there that the aluminum did not go into solution?

7. Do you believe that what happened to the aluminum foil is an example of a solid dissolving in a liquid? Why or why not?

In Activity 14 many changes took place. You may have noticed color changes, bubbles, and the formation of a reddish-brown solid. The CuCl [*copper(I) chloride*] dissolved in the water, forming a solution. The Al [*aluminum*] appeared to dissolve, but another solid material was produced. In addition, some gaseous material was generated. Because these materials were produced, you cannot say that the aluminum became part of the solution. A solution consists only of a solute and a solvent. It does not produce other kinds of new materials. In the activity the conditions for physical interaction were satisfied by the changes that took place. The conditions for chemical interaction were also satisfied because new materials with new properties were formed. The interaction of the aluminum with the copper(I) chloride is an example of a chemical change.

The kinetic particle model has been quite useful in explaining a variety of physical interactions. However, it has not been useful in explaining chemical interactions. Many important and interesting changes that take place every day are chemical interactions.

SUMMARY Mixtures are the result of the physical interaction of two or more materials. Any combination of materials in the solid, liquid, or gaseous state can form a mixture. Mixtures follow the law of conservation of matter.

A solution is a special kind of homogeneous mixture in which the particles of the materials break down into their smallest components. Solutions are possible among any combination of states of matter, although solid-liquid solutions are quite common. A solution is composed of a solvent in which a solute dissolves. The amount of solute in solution determines whether a solution is unsaturated, saturated, or supersaturated. A number of variables control the amount of solute that will dissolve in a solvent. They are the type of solvent, the type of solute, the volume of solvent, and the temperature of the solution.

SCIENCE WORDS

mixture
law of conservation of matter
homogeneous mixture
heterogeneous mixture
solutions
solute
solvent
Tyndall effect
colloids
emulsions
foams
aerosols
Brownian movement
saturated solution
variable property
uncontrolled variable
responding variable
supersaturated solution

REVIEW QUESTIONS

Fill in the blanks with the correct terms.

1. In a solution, the material that *dissolves* is called the ____________.
2. A saturated solution in which there is undissolved solute is in ____________________ ____________.
3. ____________ result from the physical interaction of two or more materials.
4. Homogeneous mixtures are called ____________.
5. The material *into which* another material dissolves is called the ____________.

Mark each statement true (T) or false (F).

1. _____ Increasing the temperature of a solution increases the amount of solid that will dissolve in it.
2. _____ A physical interaction is one from which new materials with different properties result.
3. _____ Fudge ripple ice cream is a heterogeneous mixture.
4. _____ Water is known as the universal solvent.
5. _____ When a solution is cooled, particles slow down.

Complete the following by choosing the correct answer.

1. A solution in which the solute takes up all the available spaces is
   (a) unsaturated. (b) saturated. (c) supersaturated. (d) suspended.
2. Shaving cream and whipped cream are examples of
   (a) foams. (b) emulsions. (c) aerosols. (d) solutions.
3. Changing the temperature throughout the course of an experiment is an example of
   (a) a control. (b) a variable. (c) a model. (d) a solution.
4. When a solution is cooled, the distance between the particles
   (a) increases. (b) stays the same. (c) decreases. (d) varies.
5. Colloids can be identified by
   (a) Brownian movement. (b) the Tyndall effect. (c) the law of conservation of matter. (d) the kinetic particle theory.

APPLYING WHAT YOU LEARNED

1. Using the kinetic particle theory, describe how a solution is formed.
2. Explain how temperature affects the formation of solutions.

UNIT REVIEW

1. Place an object in a shoe box or similar container. Don't let anyone else see what the object is. Close and seal the container. Let several other students take the container and study it in as many ways as they wish. They may not open the container. Ask them to describe and diagram what they infer is inside the container. How close to the actual size and shape did they guess? Have other students repeat the procedure with other objects. What senses are used in this procedure? In what ways is this problem related to the problems faced by a scientist?
2. List five examples of a physical change and five examples of a chemical change. Do not include those mentioned in the text. Which list was more difficult to complete? Why do you suppose you had trouble?
3. Explain why your body feels cool when you first come out of water on a hot day. Why might it feel even cooler if the wind is blowing? How would you compare this cooling effect with putting rubbing alcohol on your skin? Use the concepts of energy, particle motion, and particle interactions in your explanation.
4. List five solutions you can find around the house. Try to determine the solute and solvent for each. What is the most common solvent used?
5. You have learned that particles are in constant motion. Give examples to prove this other than those given in the text.

Careers

The synthetic materials that many of us wear, the plastics found in items around the home, and many substances helpful in fighting disease are frequently the result of work done by chemists. A chemist investigates the properties and composition of matter. A chemist also studies the laws that govern the behavior of elements and compounds.

More than half of all chemists work in research and development (R&D). Basic research has many practical uses. For example, the study of how small molecules unite to form larger ones has given us plastics and synthetic rubber. This process is called *polymerization.*

In R&D, new products are created and existing products are improved. For instance, a chemist might be given a description of a material needed for a particular job. The description would include a list of the properties needed in the material. If a substance already exists that has the necessary properties or similar ones, it is studied to determine if it can be used. The substance might have to be modified before it is usable. However, if no such material exists, the chemist, using experimental methods, searches until a substance fitting the description is prepared. If you like to perform experiments and work with your hands, chemistry might be the field for you. A bachelor's degree with a major in chemistry is sufficient for most beginning jobs in chemistry.

There are many other fields in chemistry that might be of interest to you. Analytical chemists determine the types and quantities of ingredients found in various substances. They might be considered chemical detectives. Organic chemists study the compounds of carbon. These are the most complex compounds that can exist. Synthetic fabrics are produced as a result of work done by organic chemists. Inorganic chemists study the compounds formed from elements other than carbon. These scientists may develop compounds used in solid-state technology. Physical chemists study energy effects that accompany changes in matter. Physical chemists will probably play an important role in supplying the energy needs of the world's people in the future.

A beginning chemist with a bachelor's degree will do routine lab work and help senior research scientists with their projects. A master's or doctor's degree is needed to actually perform basic research and original types of experimentation. The student of chemistry must be interested in mathematics and enjoy studying science. Have you ever thought about becoming a chemist? There are many sources you can use for further information. Start with your teacher and the guidance department.

Chemical analysis of materials and products is important in maintaining quality control.

Research

Throughout history many different materials have been used to make clothing. Humans have used the skins of various animals to provide warm clothing when needed. Fibers formed by plants and by silkworms have also been important natural materials for making clothing. Such natural materials as cotton, linen, and silk have been used by humans for centuries. However, as population increased, the need for fibers also increased. Chemists first began producing synthetic fibers only in this century. Today scientists have given us many kinds of synthetic fibers. These synthetic fibers can be used along with natural fibers in clothes. In some cases synthetic fibers have completely replaced natural fibers in clothing.

Examples of synthetic products made from plant substances are rayon and cellulose acetate. Rayon is usually produced from the cellulose of spruce or other softwoods. Short cotton fibers are also used to make rayon. Some cellulose is used to prepare cellophane.

Other synthetics are formed as a result of polymerization. Nylon, acrylic, and polyester fibers are examples of such materials. The basic raw materials for making nylon are obtained from crude oil or coal. Two different substances, adipic acid and hexamethylenediamine, are needed. The molecules of these substances are attached to one another chemically to form long chains called *polymers.* The polymers are formed into filaments by forcing the material through small openings in spinnerets. Stretching the filaments causes the individual molecules in the polymer to line up and become stronger and very elastic. These qualities are especially useful and desirable in making stockings and durable clothing.

People want their clothing to be beautiful as well as durable. Part of the beauty is in the color and the design of a fabric. Chemists are continually searching for new dyes to use with fabrics. These dyes must be colorful and yet not fade or discolor.

Polymer chemists are also seeking a fabric that will never need cleaning. This fabric will, instead, repel dirt. In addition, a great deal of research is being done to find a fabric that is fireproof. Race car drivers now wear a fire-resistant suit made from a material called Nomex. If you are interested in fabric research, perhaps you see a place for yourself in the scientific future.

To be assured that a new product meets specifications, it is subjected to a variety of tests.

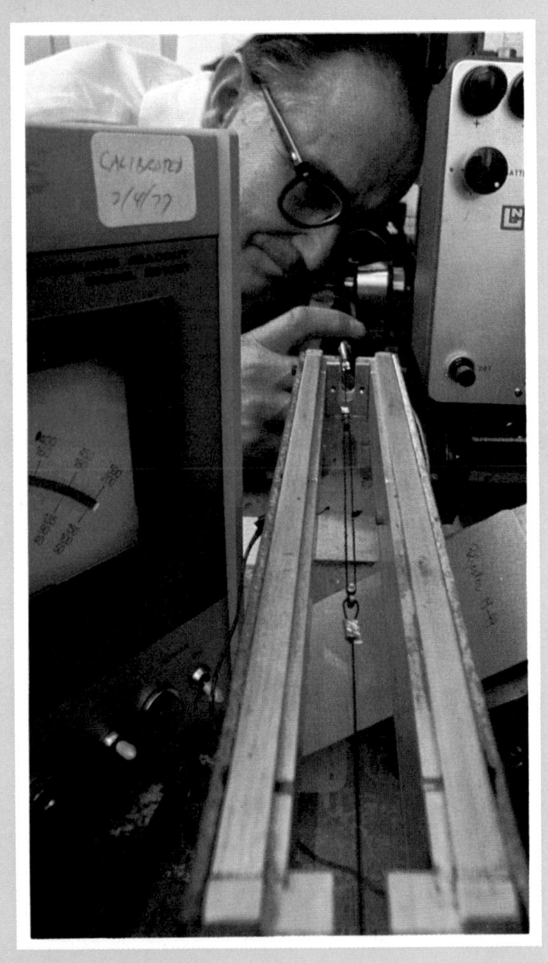

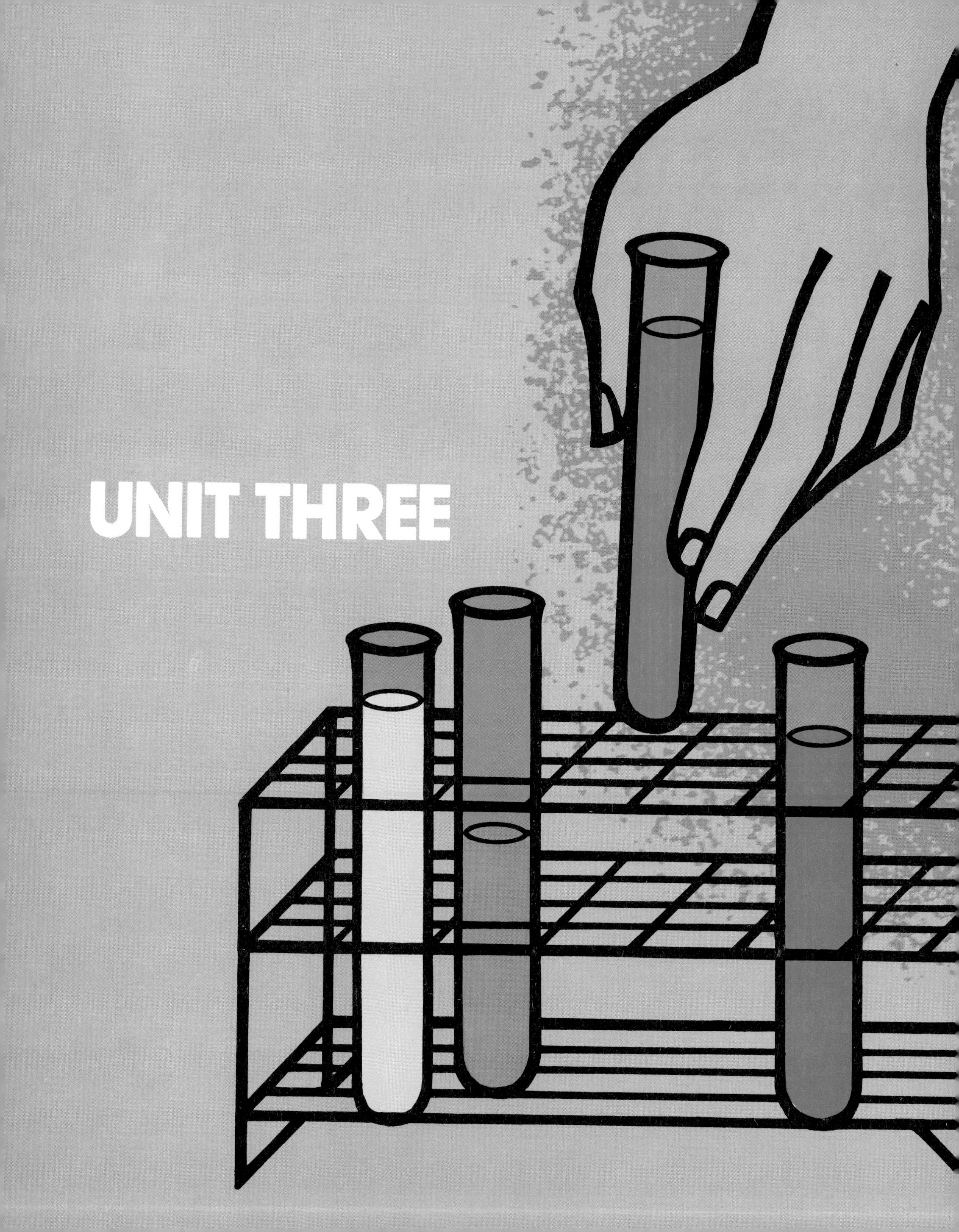

UNIT THREE

STRUCTURE OF MATTER

N50DE

Helium-filled balloons have many uses. Balloons, such as this one, have been used in attempts to cross the Atlantic Ocean from North America.

A Better Particle Model

In the last unit you explored chemical and physical interactions. You developed a kinetic particle model to explain the behavior of different materials. However, you found that the kinetic particle model could not be used to explain all the chemical interactions you observed. To better explain chemical interactions, you must use what you already know about the nature of matter and build a better model.

A Review of Matter

You have discovered the following facts about matter.

1. Matter is made of extremely tiny particles.
2. The particles of matter are constantly moving.
3. Matter can exist in different states depending on the energy of the particles.
4. The tiny particles in a solid appear to pack in an orderly arrangement. They form crystals having distinctive shapes.
5. The particles of matter appear to have spaces between them.
6. The particles of matter cannot be created or destroyed by chemical or physical interactions.

Your knowledge of particles of matter is the result of evidence you collected. You obtained that evidence by conducting investigations and building models. Then you tested the models to find if they agreed with your observations. Based on this knowledge, there are also some inferences that can be made about matter.

1. There must be different kinds of particles of matter. We are aware of many different kinds of materials. It seems logical therefore that all the particles that make up these materials must be different in some ways.
2. The different kinds of particles of matter must have different physical properties.
3. The particles of matter must be capable of combining with one another in some way. This, too, seems logical. There is evidence that new materials with new properties result from chemical interactions.
4. The energy required to cause a chemical interaction depends on the type of particles involved in the interaction. You have seen what happens when wood and water are heated with the same heat

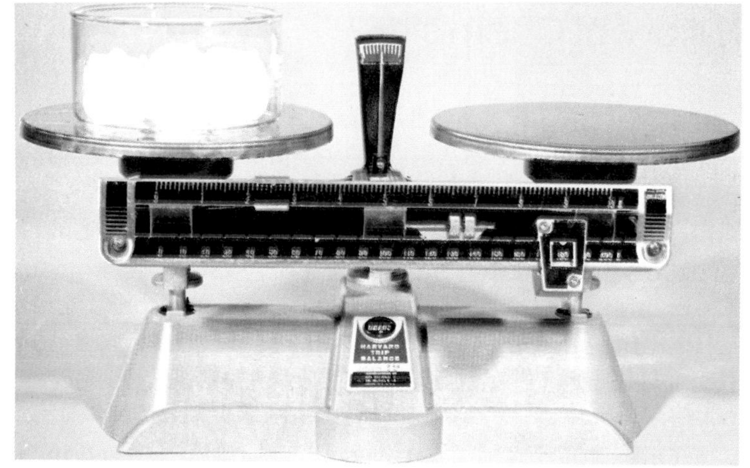

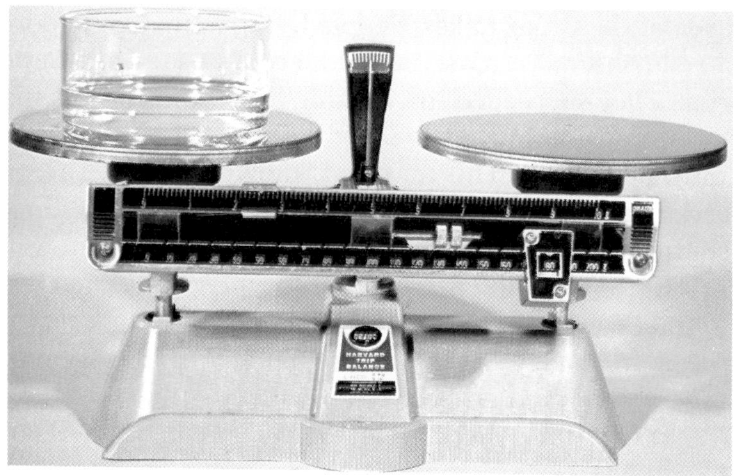

These photographs illustrate the law of conservation of matter. The change in state of a given quantity of solid water (top) to liquid water (bottom) results in no change in the mass of the water.

source. The water changes state but remains water. The wood, however, goes through a chemical change. New materials are formed. This happens because the different particles of material in water and wood behave differently.

A better particle model must be able to explain all these observations and inferences. A better model should also allow you to predict how chemical interactions might occur. It should pose new questions to investigate concerning the chemical nature of matter.

History of Chemistry

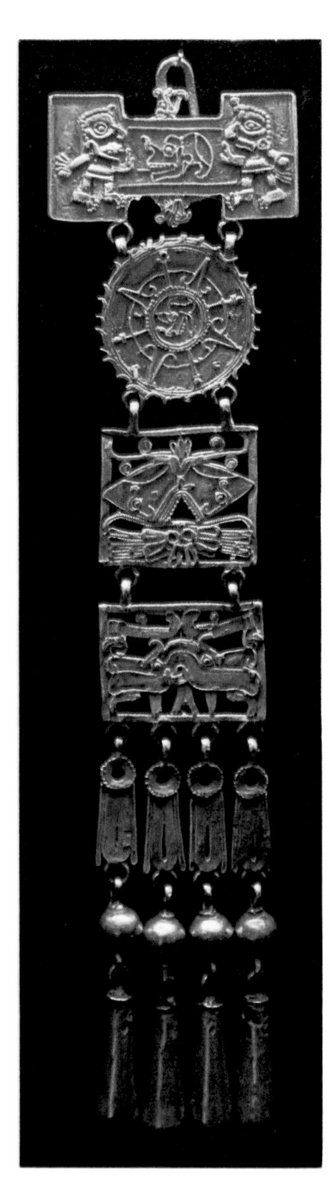

Gold has been known and sought after for centuries. Alchemists tried to change metals, such as lead, into gold.

The early Greeks were the first to propose the idea that particles of matter are very tiny. They called these particles **atoms.** Although they had never seen them, the Greeks proposed that these particles could not be broken into smaller particles. For over two thousand years after the Greek proposals, people experimented with different types of materials to try to change them in some way. The experiments were not always successful.

One experiment that was successful occurred in the area of the Great Lakes. People living in that area found a reddish-brown material in the rocks near Lake Superior. They succeeded in breaking loose some of this material and found that it could be pounded and shaped into spearheads. This material, known today as Cu [*copper*], was highly valued. Unlike bone or rock, it did not shatter when the spearheads were sharpened.

In the Middle East and Europe, people learned how to make new materials by heating certain kinds of rocks. In history the terms *Bronze Age* and *Iron Age* refer to societies that discovered those metals.

During the Middle Ages, kings directed magicians to change certain materials into more precious materials. Records show that a group called **alchemists** (al'kəmists) tried for fourteen hundred years to change different kinds of metals into Au [*gold*]. They were unsuccessful.

In the 1700s some important discoveries were made. Some people thought that certain materials could not be broken down into other more elemental materials. These people relied on experimentation rather than magic. The French scientist Antoine Lavoisier conducted careful experiments. He found a number of materials that could not be broken down into

Alchemists studied ways to prolong life, sought a universal cure for disease, and tried to change base metals into gold. Alchemy was a chemical science as well as a speculative philosophy.

simpler materials. He referred to them as **elements**, or elemental substances. In 1789 Lavoisier published a list of thirty-three elements. Twenty-six of these are still listed as elements today.

Two of the elements named by Lavoisier were *soufre* (sulfur) and *fer* (iron). In Activity 16 you will investigate these elements.

Shown here, from left to right, are the elements lead, copper, and magnesium (top row); sulfur, zinc, and phosphorus (bottom row).

Activity 16 Soufre et Fer

PURPOSE

To investigate the nature of chemical interactions

MATERIALS

Powdered sulfur
Iron filings
Test tube
Buret clamp
Ring stand
Heat source
Matches
Asbestos gloves
Beaker
Magnet
Forceps
Safety goggles
Balance and mass set
Stirring rod
3 pieces of filter paper
Cold water

DO THIS

A. Measure 10 g of iron filings on a piece of filter paper.

B. Observe the appearance of the filings. Move a magnet along the undersurface of the filter paper. Observe any interaction between the iron filings and the magnet. Record all your observations in a table like Table 1. Then transfer the filings to a test tube.

C. Measure 6 g of powdered sulfur on a clean piece of filter paper. Observe the appearance of the sulfur. Test the sulfur with the magnet. Record your observations in the table.

D. Add the sulfur to the iron filings in the test tube. Mix the two materials with the stirring rod. Describe the appearance of the mixture.

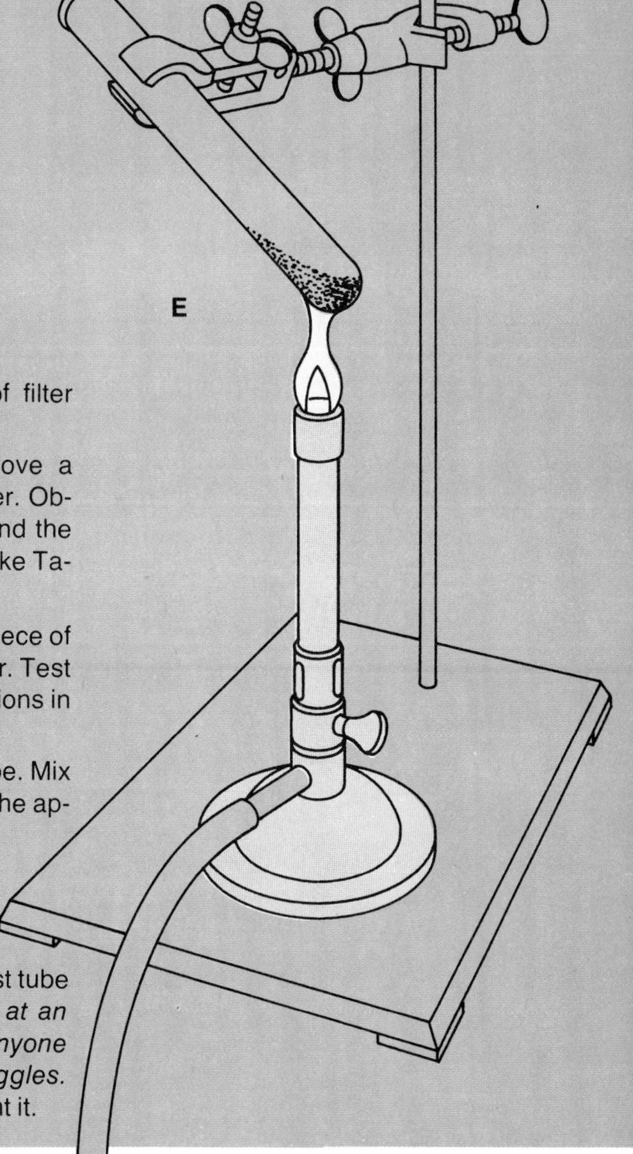

E. Assemble the ring stand, buret clamp, and test tube as shown. **CAUTION:** *Be sure the test tube is at an angle and the open end is pointed away from anyone nearby. Also be sure you are wearing safety goggles.* Place the heat source under the test tube and light it.

TABLE 1 • Chemical Interactions

MATERIAL	OBSERVATIONS
Iron filings	
Sulfur	
Iron-sulfur mixture	
Iron-sulfur (during heating)	
Iron-sulfur (after heating)	

G

F. Observe the iron-sulfur mixture as it is being heated. Continue heating until no more changes seem to occur. Record your observations.

G. CAUTION: *Put on asbestos gloves.* Remove from the ring stand the clamp with the hot test tube still attached. Break the tube by plunging it into a beaker of cold water.

H. Use forceps to remove the iron-sulfur material from the broken glass. Place the material on a piece of filter paper. Observe it carefully. Also test it with a magnet. Record your observations.

REPORT

1. How did the properties of the iron filings differ from those of the sulfur?

2. How did the properties of the iron-sulfur material after heating differ from the properties of the original iron-sulfur mixture?

3. What evidence is there of a physical change in the iron-sulfur material?

4. What evidence is there of a chemical change in the iron-sulfur material?

Lavoisier, using a device called a "pelican," boiled water for 101 days to prove that the transmutation of elements was impossible.

Compounds and Law of Definite Composition

Lavoisier spent a great deal of time attempting to break down materials into their simplest elemental substances. In Activity 16 you combined two elemental substances. You combined S [*sulfur*] and Fe [*iron*] to form a chemical combination of two elements. Chemical combinations are new materials that result from chemical interaction. The new material has properties that are different from those of the original materials. When two or more elements combine chemically to form a material with new properties, the new material is called a **compound**. Once a compound has been formed, the individual elements can no longer be identified. Another chemical action is necessary to separate them.

Scientists experimented with elements by making compounds. They found that elements in a chemical reaction behave in predictable ways. For example, when different quantities of iron and sulfur were combined, sometimes some of the sulfur did not react. Other times there was some iron that did not react. By experimenting with various quantities, it was determined that in order for the reaction to be complete

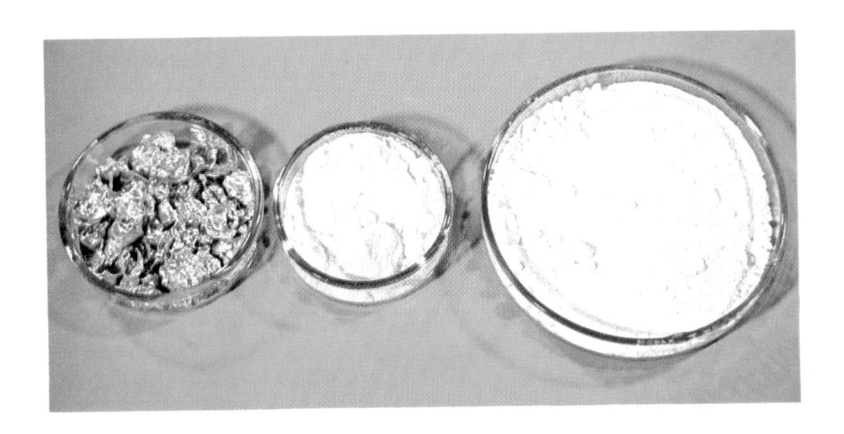

This picture illustrates the law of definite composition. If exactly 32.65 g of zinc is combined chemically with exactly 16.03 g of sulfur, the product is 48.68 g of zinc sulfide. No elemental zinc or sulfur remains.

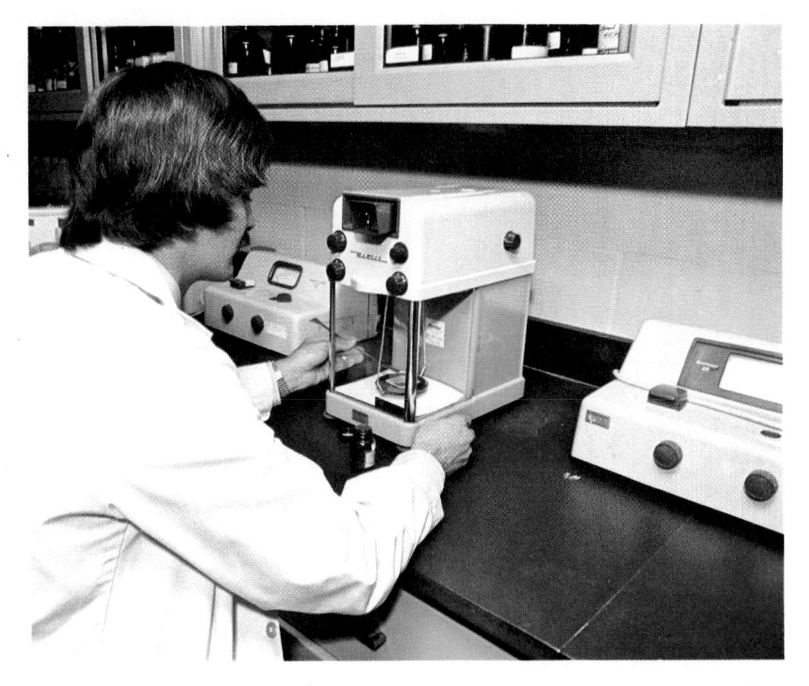

This technician is using a Metler balance to make extremely accurate mass measurements. A balance of this type is used for quantitative analysis.

the amounts of sulfur and iron must be constant. It takes 55.85 g of iron to completely react with 32.06 g of sulfur. To determine the mathematical ratio of this reaction, divide 55.85 g by 32.06 g. This shows that for every 1 g of sulfur to react completely, 1.742 g of iron is needed. This mathematical relationship for sulfur and iron is a constant. If 10 g of sulfur is to react completely with iron, 17.42 g of iron is needed. In a similar way, 65.37 g of Zn [*zinc*] combines with 32.06 g of sulfur.

All elements that combine to form compounds do so in a certain proportion. This proportion is always the same for each specific compound. These findings led scientists to formulate the **law of definite composition.** The law states that the elements in a compound always combine in definite mass proportions. In other words, the masses of the various elements that make up a compound are always related to each other in the same way. The composition of the masses of elements that react to form a compound is always the same.

What is the law of definite composition?

The idea that chemical compounds always have a definite composition by mass interested an English school teacher named John Dalton. Dalton was familiar with the Greek ideas about atoms. He reasoned that the law of definite composition must be related to the mass of different atoms.

Dalton's Atomic Theory

Dalton used the information that had been collected about compounds according to the law of definite composition to determine the masses of different atoms. He gave the lightest element known an atomic mass of 1.00. This element was H [*hydrogen*]. He then used the known information about compounds to determine the atomic masses of other elements. In all cases he based his findings on the assigned mass of 1.00 for hydrogen.

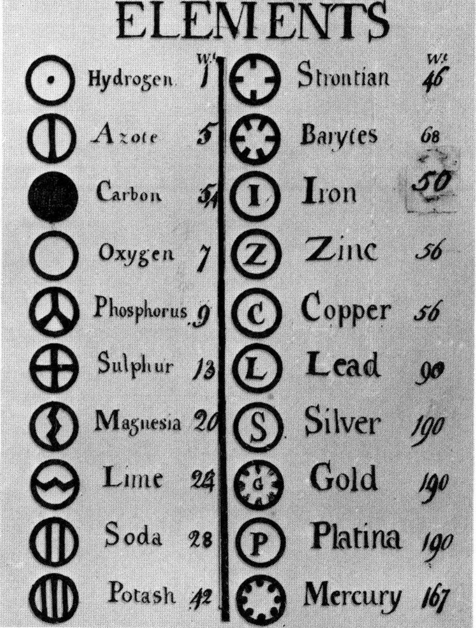

John Dalton was the first scientist to determine that different elements had different atomic masses. However, his lecture diagram shows that sometimes he gave the same atomic mass for different elements. Compare his symbols and atomic masses with those in the periodic table at the back of this book.

In 1805 Dalton published the first atomic theory. His theory was based on the original ideas of the Greeks. He also used the many experiments that he and other scientists had conducted on elements and compounds. Dalton did not know if one atom of each element combined to form a compound. He also did not know if two atoms of one element combined with one atom of another element. He guessed how they would combine. He assumed that one compound could be made from two different elements. This compound would be made up of one atom of one element and one atom of the other. He also assumed that two compounds with different properties could be made from the same two elements. Dalton stated that one compound would be made of one atom of each element. The other compound would be made of one atom of one element and two atoms of the other. He stated this according to mass proportions that had been derived by experimentation. This model worked well for some compounds but not for others. Dalton did not have all the experimental evidence he needed to test his model. Nevertheless, his work was very important and led to further experimentation by other scientists.

Who published the first atomic theory?

Atomic Model of Matter

Dalton's idea of using an atomic mass of 1.00 for a base resulted in the atomic masses for other elements. It was discovered later that using an atomic mass of 16.00 for the element O [*oxygen*] worked better as a base. The atomic masses of the other elements could be determined more accurately. Recently an atomic mass of 12 for one kind of C [*carbon*] atom was made the base. The atomic masses of all the elements are determined using this base.

The atomic mass of the uranium in this ore sample is about 238 times greater than the atomic mass of the hydrogen used to inflate this balloon.

Scientists continued to investigate the chemical nature of materials. They questioned why some atoms had greater atomic masses than others. They also wondered how atoms stuck together to form compounds. They wondered why some combined more easily than others. These kinds of questions caused a great deal of interest in the new science known as chemistry. During the 1800s many important discoveries about the nature of chemical interactions were made. One important discovery was that atoms are *not* the smallest unit of material. In Activity 17 you will investigate another property of matter that helped lead to this important discovery. This discovery set the stage for the development of a new model for the atom.

Activity 17 Making Electricity

PURPOSE

To explore the nature of charged particles

MATERIALS

Plastic comb
Paper

DO THIS

A. Tear a sheet of paper into at least 10 small pieces. Each piece should be less than 5 mm on a side.

B. Comb your hair for about 5 seconds. Then hold the comb near the pieces of paper. Record your observations.

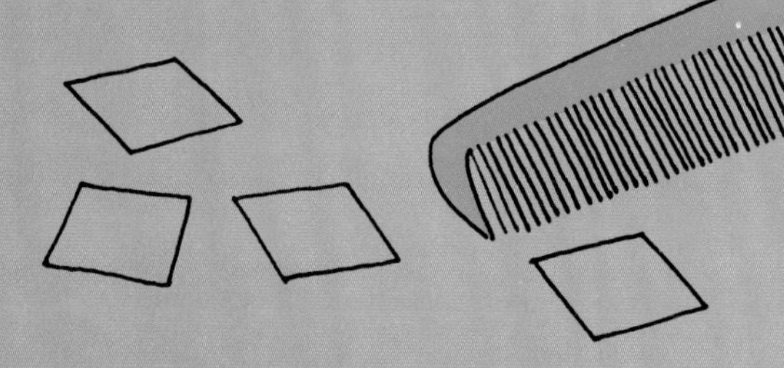

C. Repeat steps **A** and **B**, but this time rub your hand over the comb before holding it near the pieces of paper. Record your observations.

REPORT

1. In steps **A** and **B**, what evidence is there of an interaction?

2. What evidence is there, if any, of an invisible force acting? Explain what you think is occurring.

3. In step **C**, how does rubbing your hand over the comb influence the interactions?

4. On the basis of your observations in step **C**, what changes can you make in your explanation of what you think is occurring?

The idea that there are charged particles on atoms was a revolutionary step forward in understanding chemistry. There was evidence indicating that something happened during a physical interaction. It seemed that electrically charged particles of matter could be rubbed off one material and transferred to another. Evidence also indicated that something happened when a solute and solvent interacted to form a solution. Charged particles were produced that would conduct an electrical current. Without the interaction that formed the solution, neither the solute nor the solvent would conduct electricity. In Activity 18 you will explore how this kind of electricity is related to solutions. Similar experiments led scientists to make some additions to their atomic model of matter. These additions were

1. Atoms have negatively charged particles that are called **electrons** (i lek′trons).
2. The electrons are smaller than the atoms.
3. When some solutes dissolve in some solvents, charged particles are involved in the physical change.
4. Compounds and elements do not appear to have an electrical charge unless physically acted upon by other materials. Therefore atoms must have other charged particles that make them electrically neutral. The negative electrical charges of an atom must be exactly balanced by some positive charges in the atom.

Experiments showed that solids could have negatively charged electrons added to or removed from them. Scientists believed that the electrons were particles. They reasoned that they could determine the mass of a material that had no charge, rub some electrons off, and then determine the new mass. In this way they hoped to obtain some idea of the mass of electrons. Such experiments failed to show any change in mass. This led scientists to believe that electrons were probably much smaller particles than atoms. Since the electrons could be moved around easily, they were also probably on the outside of atoms. This inference led to another inference that the positively charged particles of atoms were much heavier than electrons. Scientists inferred that these heavier particles were located in the interior of the atom. New ideas and techniques had to be developed before scientists were able to build a good model for the parts of an atom. In Chapter 9 you will learn more about these ideas and techniques.

Static electricity produced by a Van de Graaff generator is evidence of the existence of charged atomic particles. The negatively charged particles–electrons–can be transferred from one material to another as shown by the hair-raising experience of this student.

Activity 18 Electricity and Solutions

PURPOSE

To determine if solutions can conduct electricity

MATERIALS

Magnesium ribbon
Thin brass strip
2 pieces of insulated copper wire
Liquid bleach
Graduate
50-mL beaker
Miniature screw-base bulb
Bulb holder
Steel wool

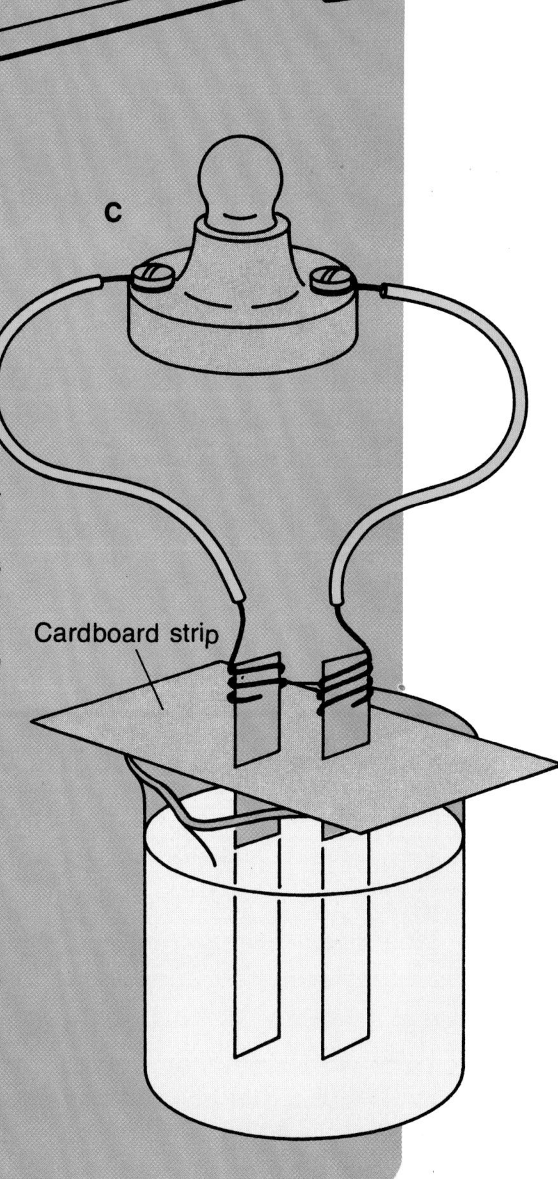

DO THIS

A. Clean a brass strip and a piece of magnesium ribbon with steel wool.

B. Strip back the insulation about 4 cm from the ends of 2 pieces of copper wire. Then wrap 3–4 turns of wire securely around one end of each metal strip. Attach the free end of each wire to a different terminal on the bulb holder.

C. Fill a beaker with 40 mL of liquid bleach. Lower the free ends of the brass and magnesium strips into the bleach. Keep the two metals from touching each other.

D. Allow time for the system to interact. Then record your observations.

REPORT

1. What evidence was there of an interaction in the system?

2. What physical changes occurred in the brass and magnesium strips?

3. What physical changes occurred in the liquid bleach?

Today we have a fairly good model of the atom. No one has ever actually seen an atom. However, there are different atomic models. These models are useful in predicting the behavior of atoms. One which will be used in the next chapters, is shown in Figure 6–1.

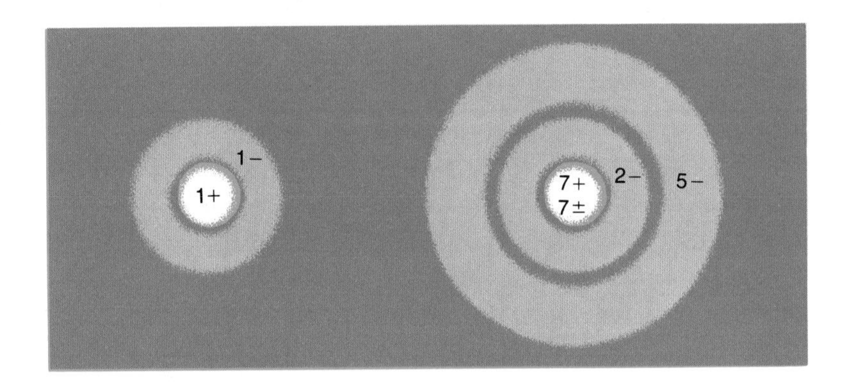

FIGURE 6–1
These models show the atomic structure of the elements hydrogen and nitrogen.

Structure of an Atom

What are the three basic particles in atoms?

As Figure 6–1 shows, an atom is composed of three basic particles. These are electrons, **protons** (prō'tons), and **neutrons** (nü'trons). Each electron has one negative electrical charge, which is indicated by the symbol (−). Electrons have more than 1800 times less mass than protons or neutrons. Electrons move very rapidly around the interior portion of the atom. This interior portion is called the **nucleus** (nü'klē əs). Some electrons move in a region very close to the nucleus. Others move around in a region that is farther away.

What is the interior portion of the atom called?

The nucleus of the atom is made up of protons and neutrons. Protons have much more mass than electrons. Each proton has one positive electrical charge, which is indicated by the symbol (+). A neutron has slightly more mass than a proton. Neutrons have no electrical charge and are electrically neutral. Neutrons are indicated by the symbol (±).

EXCURSION 12
You can learn more about the composition and organization of elements in Excursion 12, "Exploring the Periodic Table."

You learned that elements are materials composed of only one kind of atom. This means that each element must have its own special kind of atom. The simplest atom is the one John Dalton first identified as the simplest. It is the element hydrogen. A hydrogen atom is composed of only two particles. Hydrogen has a proton at the center and an electron that moves in a region around the proton. Since hydrogen is composed of the fewest particles, it is not surprising that it is also the lightest of the elements.

The next simplest atom is He [*helium*]. Helium is composed of two protons and two neutrons in the nucleus. Two electrons move in a region around the nucleus. Helium is the second lightest of the elements. Both hydrogen and helium exist as gases under normal conditions. Both are lighter than air. Hydrogen and helium are often used to fill balloons and lighter-than-air craft.

Oxygen, sulfur, iron, and C [*carbon*] are common elements. A carbon atom is composed of 6 protons, 6 neutrons, and 6 electrons. Oxygen is composed of 8 protons, 8 neutrons, and 8 electrons. Sulfur is composed of 16 protons, 16 neutrons, and 16 electrons. Iron is composed of 26 protons, 30 neutrons, and 26 electrons. As you can see, the number of neutrons is usually close to the number of protons but may not be the same. The number of protons that an atom has determines what kind of atom is it. All oxygen atoms have 8 protons. All iron atoms have 26 protons. The number of protons in an atom of an element is called the **atomic number** of that element. Each element has a different atomic number.

What is the atomic number of an element?

The number of electrons that an atom has should always equal its number of protons. Therefore when the negative charges of the electrons are added, they should equal the positive charges of the protons. However, most atoms can lose or gain electrical charges. Under normal conditions, an atom should have a total charge of 0. This means that an atom should be electrically neutral. If an atom is not neutral it is called an **ion** (ī′ən). When an atom is an ion, its chemical properties are different. For example, an atom of iron can lose 2 electrons to its surroundings. When these 2 electrons are lost, the iron has 26 positive charges in the nucleus. However, it has only 24 negative charges outside the nucleus. The total electrical charge on this iron ion is 26 positive charges and 24 negative charges. This results in a +2 electrical charge on the iron(II) ion [Fe^{+2}]. Iron can also be made to lose 3 electrons. Its charge as an iron(III) ion [Fe^{+3}] is then +3.

Other atoms can become ions by gaining extra electrons from their surroundings. Oxygen can gain 2 electrons and become an oxide ion [O^{-2}]. The previously neutral oxygen atom then has 8 protons and 10 electrons. This results in an electrical charge of −2. The names of negative ions of elements end in the suffix *-ide*.

FIGURE 6–2
This diagram illustrates the difference between a neutral atom and its ion.

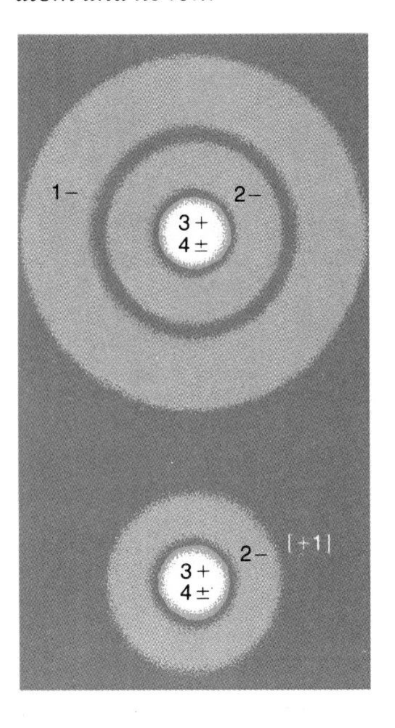

Atomic Mass and Mass Number

Atomic masses for all the elements were determined by using as a base an atomic mass of 12 for one kind of carbon. However, by adding the protons and neutrons in the nucleus, a value close to the atomic mass can be obtained. The sum of the protons and neutrons is called the **mass number**. For example, most sulfur atoms have 16 protons and 16 neutrons in the nucleus. Therefore they have a mass number of 32. A few sulfur atoms have 17 neutrons in the nucleus. These atoms have a mass number of 33 (16 protons + 17 neutrons). A few sulfur atoms also have 18 neutrons which gives them a mass number of 34. These differences in the number of neutrons in atoms of sulfur do not change the chemical properties of sulfur.

How is mass number determined?

FIGURE 6–3
These are isotopes of the element hydrogen.

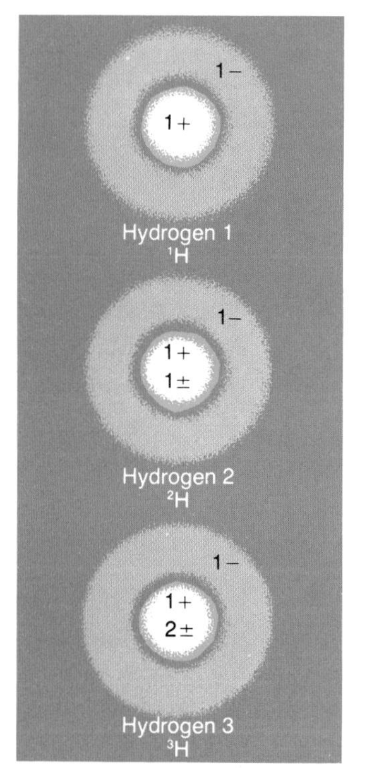

Atoms of the same element with different mass numbers are called **isotopes** (ī′sə tōps). The difference between isotopes of an element is shown by how they are written. One method uses the name of the element followed by the mass number. For example, carbon 12 is the isotope of carbon with the mass number 12. Carbon 14 is the isotope with the mass number 14. Isotopes may also be written using the mass number and the chemical symbol for the element. The mass number is written as a superscript preceding the chemical symbol. Written this way carbon 12 would be ^{12}C and carbon 14 would be ^{14}C. Similarly, sulfur 32 would be written ^{32}S.

Isotopes are important in reactions that occur in the nucleus of atoms. In Chapter 9 you will learn more about isotopes.

SUMMARY All materials are composed of atoms. A material composed of only one kind of atom is called an element. When two or more elements combine chemically, they form a compound. Compounds always have physical and chemical properties that are different from those of the original elements. When elements combine to form compounds, they always follow the law of definite composition.

John Dalton developed the first atomic theory, which provided a model of how atoms differed in mass and size and how they combined. Scientists experimenting after Dalton found that atoms were actually composed of even smaller particles. Negatively charged electrons, positively charged protons, and neutrons with no charge are the basic particles of which atoms are composed.

Each element has its own unique atomic number. The atomic number is the number of protons in the nucleus of an atom of that element. The atomic mass of an element is a determination based on the atomic mass of carbon 12. The mass number of an atom is found by adding the number of protons and neutrons in the nucleus.

SCIENCE WORDS

atoms
alchemists
elements
compound
law of definite composition
electrons
nucleus
protons
neutrons
atomic number
ion
mass number
isotopes

REVIEW QUESTIONS

Mark each statement true (T) or false (F).

1. ______ Atoms are the smallest units of material.
2. ______ In the formation of certain solutions, charged particles that conduct electrical current are produced.
3. ______ Elements are materials composed of only one kind of atom.
4. ______ Hydrogen is the heaviest element.
5. ______ Most atoms can be made to gain or lose electrons.

Match the term in Column A with the correct answer in Column B

A	B
1. Isotope ___	a. First to propose the atomic theory
2. Electron ___	b. Atomic particle that has no electrical charge
3. Dalton ___	c. Atoms of an element that have different mass numbers
4. Lavoisier ___	d. Negatively charged atomic particle
5. Neutron ___	e. Discovered twenty-six elements

Fill in the blanks with the correct terms.

1. The ______________ tried to change different kinds of metals into gold.
2. A ______________ is the chemical combination of two or more elements in which the individual elements can no longer be identified.
3. The particles that move around the nucleus of atoms are the ______________.
4. ______________ is the simplest element.
5. The law of ______________ ______________ states that elements of a compound always occur in definite mass proportions.

APPLYING WHAT YOU LEARNED

1. Briefly describe the history of chemistry from the early Greeks through Lavoisier.
2. Describe John Dalton's contribution to the knowledge of matter.
3. How does Dalton's atomic theory explain the structure of matter?
4. Describe what is meant by the law of definite composition and give an example.

This line worker is held to the utility pole by a safety belt. The safety belt acts like the force that bonds molecules to one another.

7

How Chemicals Combine

The atomic model developed in the last chapter is incomplete. There is still much to be learned about it. Scientists continue to explore the nature of the atom and its behavior in chemical reactions. In this chapter you will study some ways in which chemicals react. Adding new ideas to the atomic model will help explain how atoms interact in a chemical reaction.

Using Chemical Symbols

What is a chemical equation?

Whenever materials interact chemically, new materials are formed. The new materials have new properties. In the last chapter you caused Fe [*iron*] and S [*sulfur*] to interact. A new compound was formed. This new compound did not have the properties of either iron or sulfur. Scientists use a chemical equation to describe this interaction. A chemical equation is like a sentence. It is a statement that shows what happens when a chemical reaction takes place. The iron and sulfur reaction can be written as follows.

iron plus sulfur when heated produces iron sulfide

Chemists work with many different chemical reactions. Describing them by writing chemical equations in words can be time-consuming. Suppose chemists from many countries wanted to communicate their work to each other. Chemical equations written in words would have to be translated into the various languages. Translations can sometimes cause mistakes in understanding.

To solve these problems, chemists have developed their own language. Chemists all over the world have agreed to use certain symbols to represent different kinds of atoms and their interactions. You have seen some of these symbols in previous chapters. Perhaps you have wondered what they mean.

Chemical symbols are the international shorthand of chemistry. Each element has been given its own symbol. The symbols of some common elements are shown in Table 7–1. Chemists also use symbols to show other parts of a chemical reaction. A plus sign (+) is used to indicate that chemicals are added to each other in a chemical reaction. An arrow (→) is used to indicate the formation of a new material or materials. The equa-

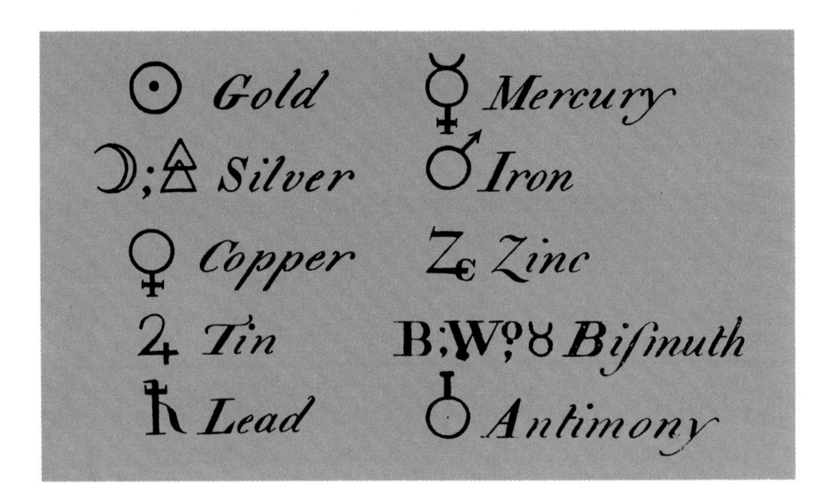

The medieval alchemists had their own symbols for the elements. Shown here are some of those early symbols.

tion for the iron and sulfur reaction can be written using these symbols and the chemical symbols in Table 7–1.

$$Fe + S \rightarrow FeS$$

There are other symbols in the language of chemistry. For example, ↑ represents a gas. The addition of heat is represented by Δ. Heat energy, when added to the iron

TABLE 7–1 • Common Elements and Their Symbols

ELEMENT	SYMBOL	ELEMENT	SYMBOL
Hydrogen	H	Potassium	K
Helium	He	Calcium	Ca
Carbon	C	Manganese	Mn
Nitrogen	N	Iron	Fe
Oxygen	O	Cobalt	Co
Fluorine	F	Nickel	Ni
Neon	Ne	Copper	Cu
Sodium	Na	Zinc	Zn
Magnesium	Mg	Silver	Ag
Aluminum	Al	Iodine	I
Silicon	Si	Tungsten	W
Phosphorus	P	Gold	Au
Sulfur	S	Mercury	Hg
Chlorine	Cl	Lead	Pb

and sulfur, caused a chemical reaction. The following equation describes that reaction.

$$\mathrm{Fe} + \mathrm{S} \xrightarrow{\Delta} \mathrm{FeS}$$

(iron) (plus) (sulfur) (when heated produces) [*iron(II) sulfide*]

You have learned that a compound is formed by the interaction of two or more elements. As in a chemical formula, the compound can be written using the symbols of the elements. Iron(II) sulfide is a compound having iron and sulfur combined chemically. The chemical formula for iron(II) sulfide is the combination of the chemical symbols for iron and sulfur written together. When sulfur combines with another element chemically, the new compound is called a **sulfide** (sul'fid). The suffix *-ide* is added to many elements that combine. There are *oxides, chlorides, bromides,* and *fluorides.* You will learn more about the procedures for naming compounds later.

The periodic table of elements is universal. Scientists from all over the world can use the table.

Compounds are always composed of two or more elements, but they may appear quite different. The blue-green compound is $NiSO_4$ [nickle sulfate]; the dark blue compound is $Cu(NO_3)_2$ [copper(II) nitrate]; the orange compound is $K_2Cr_2O_7$ [potassium dichromate]; the rust-colored compound is Fe_2O_3 [iron oxide].

Some compounds have simple chemical formulas such as FeS. Other compounds have more complicated formulas. The chemical formula for water is H_2O. What does this formula mean? Notice that a subscript number follows the symbol for hydrogen. This indicates that two atoms of hydrogen are combined with one atom of oxygen. This combination of atoms forms the simplest unit of the compound water. This unit is called a **molecule** (mol′ə kyül). A molecule is the simplest unit of a compound that can exist and still have the chemical properties of that compound. Other examples of common chemical formulas are CO_2 [*carbon dioxide*] and $NaHCO_3$ [*sodium bicarbonate*], or baking soda. The chemical formula CO_2 shows that a molecule of carbon dioxide is made up of one atom of carbon and two atoms of oxygen. However, CO [*carbon monoxide*] has only one atom of oxygen. A molecule of sodium bicarbonate is made up of one atom of Na [*sodium*], one atom of H [*hydrogen*], one atom of C [*carbon*], and three atoms of O [*oxygen*]. In the next activity you will apply your knowledge of chemical symbols to chemical reactions.

What is a molecule?

Activity 19 Chemical Reactions

PURPOSE

To investigate a chemical reaction between lead(II) nitrate and sodium iodide

MATERIALS

$Pb(NO_3)_2$ [*lead(II) nitrate*] solution
NaI [*sodium iodide*] solution
2 test tubes
Test tube rack
Graduate
Filter paper
$Pb(NO_3)_2$ crystals
NaI crystals

DO THIS

A. Measure 15 mL of $Pb(NO_3)_2$ solution and pour it into a test tube. Wash the graduate. Then measure 15 mL of NaI solution and add it to the $Pb(NO_3)_2$. Observe and record what happens.

B. Pour a few crystals of $Pb(NO_3)_2$ onto a piece of filter paper. Examine the crystals.

C. Pour a few crystals of NaI onto a piece of filter paper. Examine the crystals.

D. Without using water, mix the crystals of $Pb(NO_3)_2$ and NaI in a test tube. Record your observations.

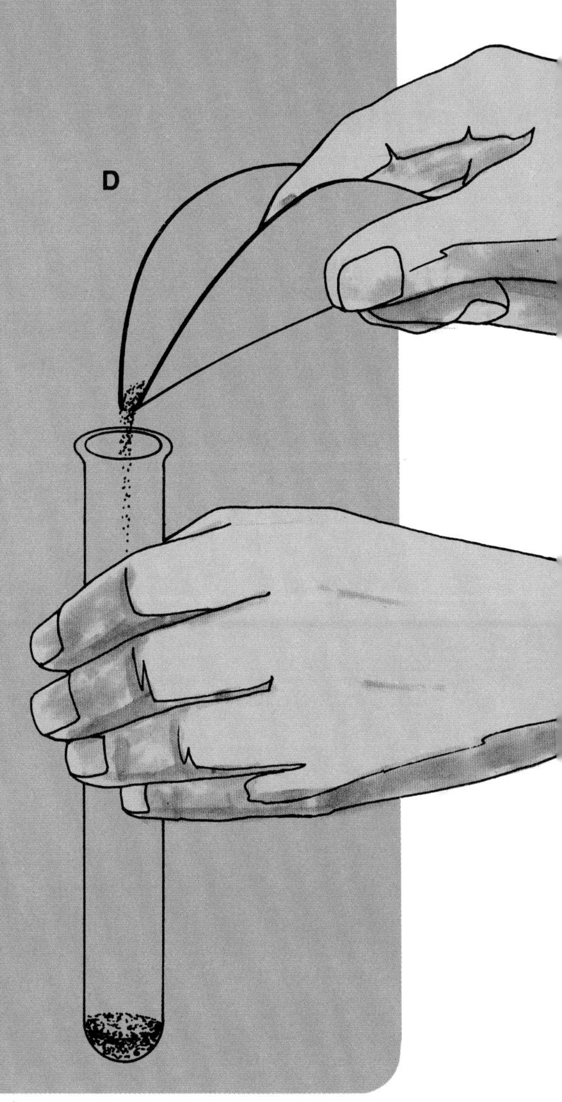

REPORT

1. What evidence was there of a chemical reaction between the two solutions?

2. What evidence was there of a chemical reaction when the crystals were mixed?

3. Write a word equation for what you think happened when the solutions were mixed.

4. Write a word equation for what you think happened when the crystals were mixed.

5. Using chemical symbols, write equations for what you think happened to both the solutions and the crystals when they were mixed.

Chemical Word Equations

You may have found it difficult to write an equation describing the exact results of the chemical reaction between $Pb(NO_3)_2$ [*lead(II) nitrate*] and NaI [*sodium iodide*]. This kind of chemical reaction was different from those you have worked with before. There is evidence that a chemical interaction took place because new products were formed. To help you understand this reaction, some new ideas about chemical interactions will have to be developed. Recall the law of conservation of matter. This law states that materials cannot be created or destroyed by chemical or physical interactions. The law can now be understood in a more accurate way. New atoms cannot be made by a chemical or physical interaction. A chemical reaction may change compounds and their properties. However, the number and kinds of atoms remain the same. This means that a chemical equation must balance. Earlier a word equation was written to describe the reaction of iron and sulfur. This equation was a balanced word equation. Iron plus sulfur produced iron(II) sulfide. The original atoms of iron and sulfur are called **reactants** (rē ak′tənts). Iron(II) sulfide, the material formed in the reaction, is called the **product.** No new kinds of atoms were produced in the reaction. None of the original iron or sulfur atoms disappeared. They simply combined to form molecules of a new compound. The new compound has properties different from either iron or sulfur. In all chemical reactions the law of conservation of matter demands that the reactants and the products must be equal.

This same idea applies to the reaction of lead(II) nitrate with sodium iodide. How would the equation for this reaction be written? Start by writing the reactants.

lead(II) nitrate plus sodium iodide

When sodium chloride reacts in solution with silver nitrate, the product is silver chloride. The silver chloride is an insoluble salt that precipitates out of solution.

What do these two compounds produce? To balance this equation make sure that the same words are used on the product side and the reactant side. A chemical reaction took place. Therefore, the products and reactants cannot be the same. To write the products, the words must be rearranged to describe what took place. The most logical way to do this is to switch the lead with the sodium. You will learn the reason for doing that later in this chapter. By switching the words a chemical change is indicated. The products can now be written to complete the balanced equation.

lead(II) nitrate plus sodium iodide produces
sodium nitrate plus lead(II) iodide

Chemical Symbol Equations

You have written the word equation for the lead(II) nitrate–sodium iodide reaction. The next step is to develop the chemical symbol equation. The simple chemical formula for sodium iodide is NaI. This means that a molecule of sodium iodide is composed of one atom of Na [*sodium*] and one atom of I [*iodine*]. The lead(II) nitrate is more complicated. $Pb(NO_3)_2$ [*lead(II) nitrate*] has one atom of Pb [*lead*]. But how many other atoms are there? The N [*nitrogen*] and O [*oxygen*] are combined as a group. The formula for this group is NO_3. It is called a nitrate group. It is made up of one atom of nitrogen and three atoms of oxygen. The nitrate group is enclosed in parentheses. The group acts as a single atom might in a chemical reaction. The subscript 2 indicates that there are two nitrate groups. Since there are two nitrate groups on the reactant side, there must be two nitrate groups on the product side of the equation. A balanced chemical equation can now be written.

$$Pb(NO_3)_2 + NaI \rightarrow Na(NO_3)_2 + PbI$$

This chemical symbol equation shows the same thing as the chemical word equation. It is more useful because it shows the different kinds of atoms involved in the reaction. However, there is still a problem with the chemical symbol equation as it is written. There are the same number of lead, sodium, iodine, nitrogen, and oxygen atoms on either side of the equation. Therefore the reactants equal the products. But how many molecules of lead(II) nitrate and sodium iodide react? It may be that one molecule of lead(II) nitrate reacts with one molecule of sodium iodide. It is also possible that one lead(II) nitrate molecule reacts with more than one sodium iodide molecule. To find a way to solve this problem, a better explanation of how atoms actually combine is needed.

Photosynthesis is a complex chemical reaction. Green plants use solar energy to produce sugar. The chemical reaction is shown by the following equation.

$$\underset{\text{(carbon dioxide)}}{6CO_2} + \underset{\text{(water)}}{6H_2O} \xrightarrow{\text{(solar energy)}} \underset{\text{(sugar)}}{C_6H_{12}O_6} + \underset{\text{(oxygen)}}{6O_2}$$

Electron Models

What are the energy levels of the atom?

In Chapter 6 you studied the particles that make up an atom. You learned that electrons move rapidly around the outside of the atom. You also learned that there are a number of different models of the atom. These models can help explain certain atomic behavior. One model of the atom describes the arrangement of electrons around the nucleus as a series of **shells.** Think of these shells as **energy levels.** There is room for only a certain number of electrons in each energy level. Another model of the atom describes the arrangement of electrons around the nucleus as being cloudlike. Both the shell model and the cloud model have advantages and disadvantages. The shell model is useful in understanding how atoms combine or bond together. The shell model will be used to help you understand chemical reactions.

Electrons fill in around an atom to make it electrically neutral. They can fit only into certain shells around the nucleus. These shells can be compared to the shell around a walnut. The nutmeat inside the walnut

The songs on this long-playing record are separated by distinct space. These songs can be thought of as electrons arranged around the nucleus of an atom. The electrons, like the songs, occupy only a given area.

shell is like the nucleus. The electrons form a series of increasingly larger shells around the nucleus. The farther they are from the nucleus, the larger the shells become. this series of shells is illustrated in Figure 7–1.

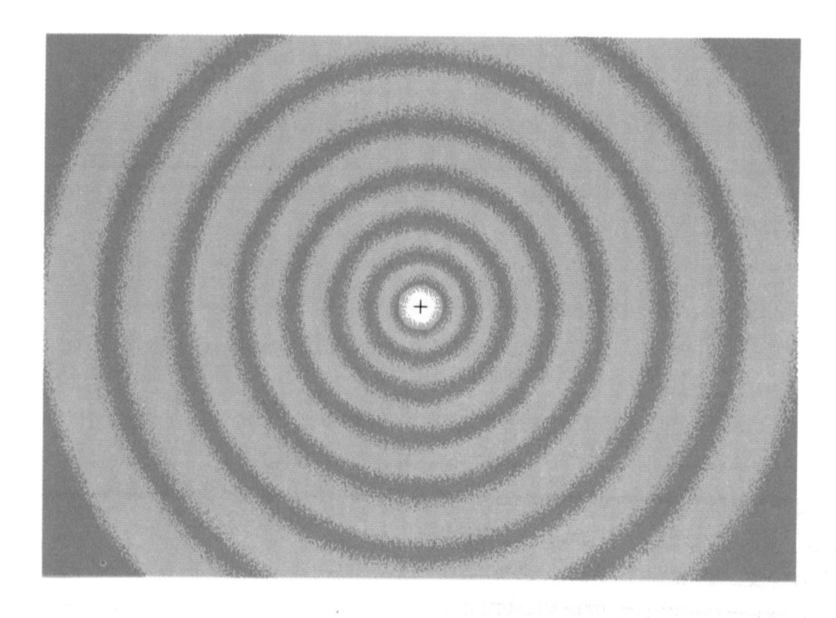

FIGURE 7–1

Remember, only a certain number of electrons can fit in each shell. There are a total of seven shells into which the electrons of even the largest atoms will fit. Of course, small atoms do not have enough electrons to fill all these shells. The number of electrons that can fit into the first four shells is shown in Table 7–2.

TABLE 7–2 • Electron Shells

SHELL NUMBER	ELECTRONS PARTIALLY FILLING SHELL, IN GROUPS	ELECTRONS TOTALLY FILLING SHELL
1	2	2
2	2 + 6	8
3	2 + 6 + 10	18
4	2 + 6 + 10 + 14	32

The first shell around an atom can hold no more than 2 electrons. For example, the hydrogen atom, which has an atomic number of 1, has only 1 electron circling around the hydrogen nucleus. This 1 electron will fit into the first shell. He [*helium*], with an atomic number of 2, has 2 electrons circling its nucleus. These 2 electrons will completely fill the first shell of the helium atom. The Li [*lithium*] atom has an atomic number of 3. Only 2 of the 3 electrons necessary to make lithium electrically neutral will fit into the first shell. The third electron must fit into the second shell. No electrons can fit into any of the higher-numbered shells until the lower-numbered shells are completely filled.

Figure 7–2 shows the electron shells of a Na [*sodium*] atom and a Cl [*chlorine*] atom. The sodium and the chlorine atoms each have three shells containing electrons. Sodium has an atomic number of 11. This means that a neutral sodium atom must have 11 electrons. Two electrons completely fill the first shell. Eight electrons completely fill the second shell. Therefore the eleventh electron must exist alone in the third shell.

FIGURE 7–2

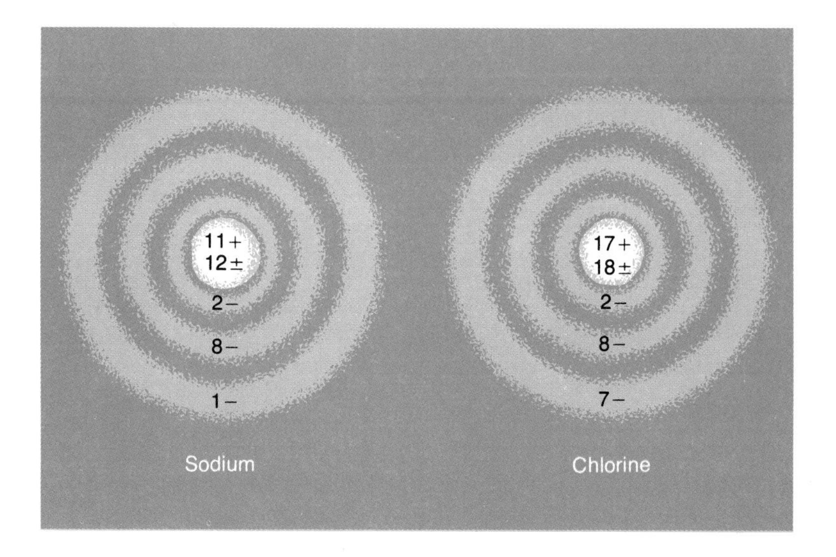

TUNGSTEN LAMP (CONTINUOUS SPECTRUM)

ATOMIC HYDROGEN

SODIUM

As electrons change energy levels, energy in the form of visible light may be emitted. Shown here are the bright line emission spectra of atomic hydrogen and sodium.

Chlorine has an atomic number of 17. Electrons completely fill both its first and second shells. There are 7 electrons in its third shell. The shells describe the energy relationships of electrons in atoms. When its outer shell is filled, it is very difficult to chemically change an atom. There is a strong tendency for an atom to gain or lose electrons so that its outer shell will have the maximum number of electrons.

Ions

Sodium atoms have a tendency to lose the single electron in their outer shells. When they do, they become ions. A sodium atom that has lost an electron becomes a sodium ion [Na^{+1}]. In a sodium ion there are 11 positive charges from the nucleus and 10 negative charges from the remaining electrons. The total charge on the sodium ion is +1. Ions with positive electrical charges are called **cations** (kat'ī ənz). Cations are produced only when atoms lose electrons. Chlorine atoms fill their outer shells in a different way. They pick up another electron. The chloride ion [Cl^{-1}] has 17 positive charges from the protons in the nucleus. It has 18 negative charges from the electrons that fill all the

What is a cation?

What is an anion?

shells. Therefore, the total charge on the chloride ion is −1. Ions with negative electrical charges are called **anions** (an′ī ənz). Anions are produced only when electrons are gained.

You learned that a chlorine atom picks up an electron to fill its outer shell. It must pick up the electron from its surroundings. What would happen if sodium and chlorine were put together in the same environment? The sodium could lose its outer electron to the chlorine. This loss and gain of an electron would result in both the atoms becoming ions. The end result would be a combination or **bond** between the two ions. This bond is known as an **ionic** (ī on′ik) **bond.** An ionic bond forms when an electron from the outer shell of one atom is transferred to the outer shell of the atom with which it is bonding. NaCl [*sodium chloride*] is an ionic compound. It is composed of sodium and chlorine ions that are held together by ionic bonds. The compound sodium chloride is familiar to you as table salt.

The aurora borealis, or northern lights, is a common phenomenon in the Northern Hemisphere. This phenomenon is possibly caused by charged particles from the sun ionizing molecules and atoms in the ionosphere.

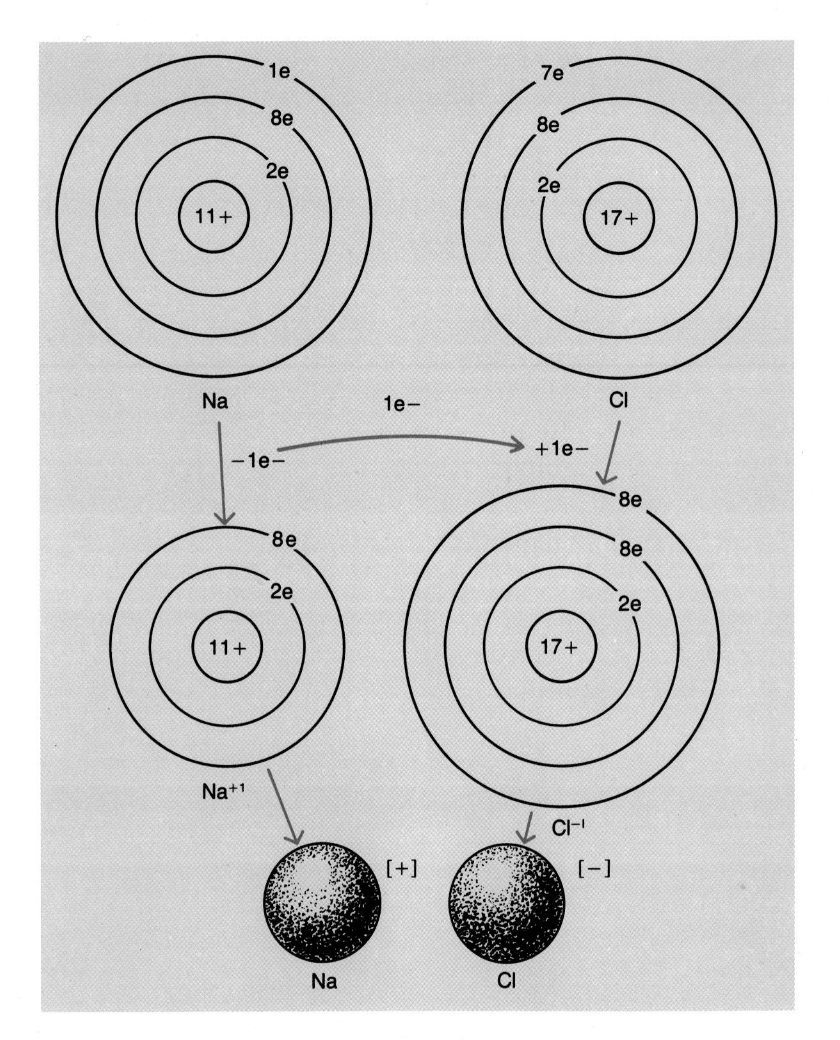

FIGURE 7–3

A sodium atom transfers an electron to the chlorine atom in this ionic bond. The result of this bond is common salt, NaCl.

Ionic compounds are very soluble in water. An ionic compound that acts as a solute will easily dissolve in water. You can test the ionic bonding theory. You can dissolve an ionic compound in water and determine whether or not there are charged particles in the water. If an ionic compound dissolves in water, it breaks apart into ions. This produces charged particles in the solution. In the next activity you will investigate a number of solutions to determine if their solutes are ionic compounds.

Activity 20 Classifying Compounds

PURPOSE

To determine if certain compounds are ionic

MATERIALS

Volt-ohm milliammeter
2 copper wire electrodes
Distilled water
13 50-mL beakers
Saturated water solutions of

- $NaCl$ [*sodium chloride*]
- NaI [*sodium iodide*]
- $NaNO_3$ [*sodium nitrate*]
- $Pb(NO_3)_2$ [*lead(II) nitrate*]
- $C_{12}H_{22}O_{11}$ [*sugar*]
- CH_3OH [*alcohol*]
- KCl [*potassium chloride*]
- KNO_3 [*potassium nitrate*]
- $CuCl$ [*copper(I) chloride*]
- $CuSO_4$ [*copper(II) sulfate*]
- Na_2CO_3 [*sodium carbonate*]
- $CaCO_3$ [*calcium carbonate*]
- $PbSO_4$ [*lead(II) sulfate*]

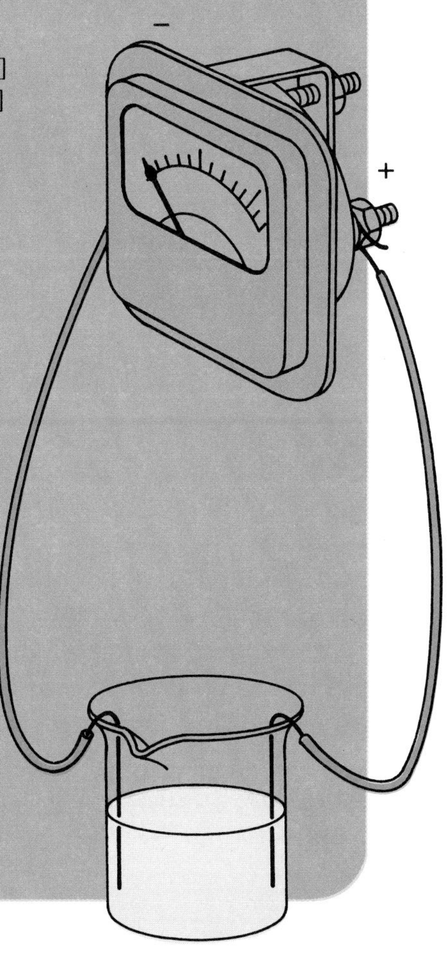

DO THIS

A. Follow your teacher's instructions for operating the volt-ohm milliammeter. The volt-ohm milliammeter measures electrical resistance rather than conductivity. Therefore the more ionic the solution, the less the resistance the instrument will register.

B. Test each solution to determine how well it conducts electricity. Be sure the two electrodes are the same distance apart each time. **CAUTION:** *After testing each solution, clean the electrodes in distilled water.* Record which solutions conduct electricity and which do not.

C. After each ionic compound you identify, write the name of the cation and the anion for that compound.

REPORT

1. Did the ionic compounds have any common chemical properties. Explain your answer.

2. Which compounds do not appear to be ionic?

You probably observed that some of the compounds you tested did not appear to be ionic. If a compound is not ionic, how can its atoms be held together? An example of a compound that is not ionic is carbon dioxide. The formula CO_2 indicates that two oxygen atoms are combined with one carbon atom in each molecule of carbon dioxide. Oxygen has an atomic number of 8. Its first shell is filled with 2 electrons. Its second shell contains 6 electrons. Oxygen needs 2 more electrons to fill its outer shell. It could lose the 6 outer electrons. Then the first shell would be the outer shell and it would be filled. However, a great deal of energy is required to remove 6 electrons. It is easier for oxygen to pick up 2 electrons to fill its outer shell. Carbon has an atomic number of 6. There are 2 electrons in the first shell and 4 in the second. To fill its outer shell, carbon would have to gain or lose 4 electrons. In the formation of carbon dioxide, the oxygen atoms do not completely gain electrons. The carbon atom does not give up its electrons completely to the oxygen atoms. Instead, the carbon atom will *share* its electrons with the oxygen atoms. The two oxygen atoms combine with the carbon atom to form a compound that is not easily broken apart. The kind of bond in which electrons are shared is called a **covalent** (kō vā′lənt) **bond.** Because of its ability to form covalent bonds, carbon can combine with many other atoms. The study of carbon compounds is known as **organic** (ôr gan′ik) **chemistry.**

What is a covalent bond?

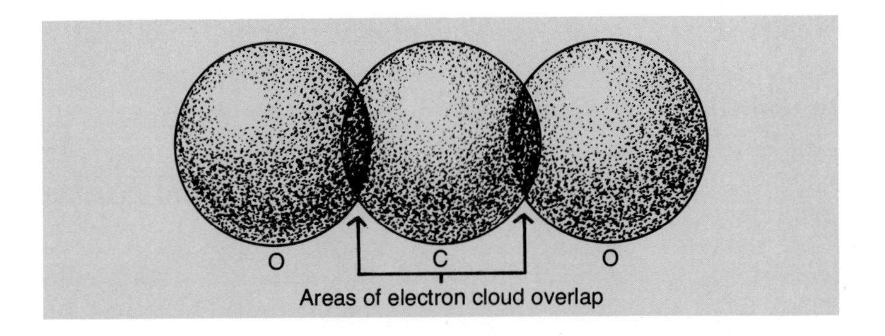

FIGURE 7–4

Carbon has the ability to form covalent bonds with many other atoms. The items shown here illustrate the diversity of carbon compounds.

Earlier you investigated the chemical reaction between lead nitrate and sodium iodide. The NO_3^{-1}, or nitrate group, behaves as an individual atom might in a chemical reaction. Actually, the nitrate group is bonded together by covalent bonds. There is a sharing of electron pairs between the oxygen and nitrogen atoms. This group of bonded atoms can have completely filled outer shells if only 1 electron is added. When this group gains an additional electron, the group has a total electrical charge of −1. This means that NO_3^{-1} is really an anion. Remember, the nitrate group interacts with other atoms or groups of atoms as though it were a single unit. Because of this it is given a special name. It is called a **radical** (rad′ə kəl). There are several groups of atoms that will pick up extra electrons and act as a chemical unit. Negatively charged radicals may combine with cations to form new compounds. A list of

What is a radical?

these radicals, their names and electrical charges, is found in Table 7–3. One of the common radicals in the list is not negatively charged. This is the ammonium (ə mō′nē əm) radical [NH_4^{+1}]. It behaves like a cation. The ammonium radical combines with anions to form compounds.

TABLE 7–3 • Common Radicals

NAME	SYMBOL	NAME	SYMBOL
Ammonium	$(NH_4)^{+1}$	Nitrate	$(NO_3)^{-1}$
Bicarbonate	$(HCO_3)^{-1}$	Nitrite	$(NO_2)^{-1}$
Bisulfate	$(HSO_4)^{-1}$	Phosphate	$(PO_4)^{-3}$
Carbonate	$(CO_3)^{-2}$	Sulfate	$(SO_4)^{-2}$
Hydroxyl	$(OH)^{-1}$	Sulfite	$(SO_3)^{-2}$

Predicting the Behavior of Atoms

The electron shell model has been useful in helping you to understand the nature of ions and radicals. It has also helped in understanding what takes place when an ionic compound dissolves in water. There are some general ideas that can be applied to atoms, using the electron shell model. These ideas will help you to predict the behavior of many atoms.

1. If an atom has less than 4 electrons in its outer shell, it will lose electrons to make a filled outer shell.
2. If an atom has more than 4 electrons in its outer shell, it will gain electrons to make a filled outer shell.
3. Atoms with exactly 4 electrons in their outer shells may either gain or lose 4 electrons. However, they usually form covalent bonds and share electrons.

4. Atoms that have filled outer shells do not gain or lose electrons easily.
5. Atoms must bond together in some way to form a compound.
6. The total number of electrical charges in a compound must equal zero.
7. The electrons in the outer shells of atoms have almost complete influence over the chemical properties of those atoms.

The first four ideas best apply to elements having atomic numbers from 1 to 20. They also apply to a number of other selected atoms. A better model will be developed in the next chapter.

The atoms of inert gases, such as neon, argon, and krypton, have completely filled outer shells. They ordinarily do not enter into chemical reactions. The inert gases often are used in neon signs and glow in a characteristic color when energy is applied.

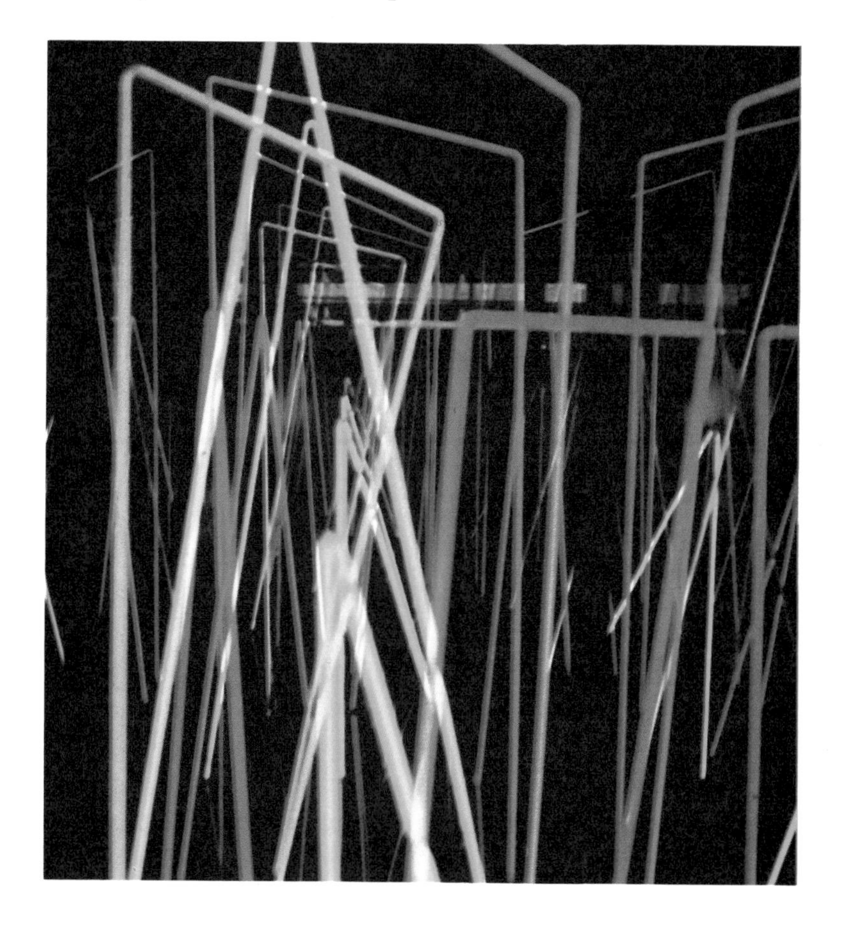

The equation describing the lead(II) nitrate–sodium iodide reaction posed a problem. That problem was to determine how many molecules of each reactant were involved in the reaction. The equation for the reaction is as follows.

$$Pb(NO_3)_2 + NaI \rightarrow Na(NO_3)_2 + PbI$$

The same number of atoms are present in the products as in the reactants. However, care must be taken to make sure that the formulas of the products are electrically neutral. To balance the equation write the reactants and products as if they were individual ions. Both reactants were probably ionized since they both dissolved in water. An ion is usually indicated by a superscript number. This shows the number and kind of charge it has. The nitrate radical has 1 negative charge. It is always written NO_3^{-1}. In the above equation there are two nitrate radicals combined with one lead ion. Therefore the lead ion must have 2 positive charges in order to form an electrically neutral compound. The lead ion is written as Pb^{+2}. One sodium ion combines with one iodide ion. The sodium ion has a charge of +1, therefore the iodide ion must have a charge of −1. These ions are written as Na^{+1} and I^{-1}. Now the equation can be written as follows.

$$Pb^{+2} + 2NO_3^{-1} + Na^{+1} + I^{-1} \rightarrow Na^{+1} + 2NO_3^{-1} + Pb^{+2} + I^{-1}$$

Add the electrical charges on each side of the equation. The reactant side is atomically and electrically balanced. On the product side, however, two sodium ions are needed to balance against the two nitrate radicals. Also, two iodide ions are needed to balance against the lead ion. When two NaI units react with one $Pb(NO_3)_2$ unit the equation will balance. The balanced equation may be written as follows.

$$Pb(NO_3)_2 + 2NaI \rightarrow 2NaNO_3 + PbI_2$$

Part of the Viking I spacecraft can be seen here on Mars. It was sent there to analyze samples of Martian soil. The analysis of soil samples could determine if there were forms of life on Mars.

Additional information can be added to the equation to make it even more understandable.

Symbols can be used to indicate the solid, liquid, or gaseous state of reactants and products. Lowercase letters after each compound indicate whether it is a solid (*s*), a liquid (*l*), or a gas (*g*). The symbol (*aq*) shows that a compound is in a water solution. This symbol stands for *aqueous,* the Greek word for *water.* All these symbols are placed in parentheses.

The final equation with all this information can now be written as follows.

$$Pb(NO_3)_2(aq) + 2NaI(aq) \rightarrow 2NaNO_3(aq) + PbI_2(s)$$

The last equation indicates that the lead(II) iodide is a solid. You observed that the chemical reaction between lead(II) nitrate and sodium iodide resulted in the formation of a solid substance. This new material was evidence that a reaction took place. Sometimes solids form out of chemical interactions of liquids or gases. This solid is called a **precipitate** (pri sip′ə tāt).

Metallic Bonding

Most of the chemical compounds that have been discussed thus far are formed by ionic or covalent bonding. Some bonds are strongly ionic, such as in sodium chloride. Others are strongly covalent, as in carbon dioxide. Some bonds are neither ionic nor covalent but are intermediate between the two. The models of these bonds are used primarily to simplify the concept of atomic bonding.

There are other kinds of chemical bonds. One, the **hydrogen bond,** will be examined more closely in the next chapter. Another kind of bond is very common and is important. It is called the **metallic** (mə tal′ik) **bond.** Metals might be described as a family of elements.

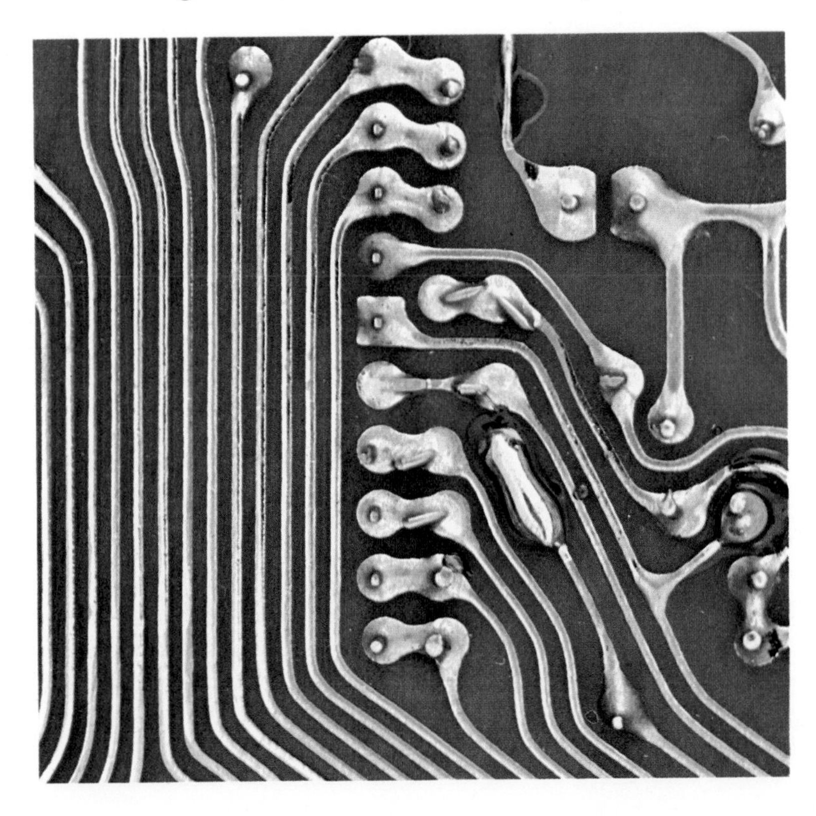

Copper and silver are two metals that can be easily drawn into electrical wire. The unique metallic bonding in metals makes them good conductors of electricity.

Atoms of all metals are alike in that they can give up electrons from their outer shells. Metal atoms can combine to form solid crystals. When this happens the electrons can move freely from one atom to the next in the metallic crystals. Because of this unique metallic bond, metals are excellent conductors of electricity. The metallic bond also allows solid solutions of different metals to be melted together. **Alloys** (al′oiz), which have different properties than the original metals had, are formed in this way. The study of the chemistry of metallic bonds and the properties of metals and alloys is called **metallurgy** (met′ə lėr jē). This science has produced metallic materials used in the manufacture of special machines.

What is metallurgy?

In the next chapter you will examine other families of elements and find new ways to classify elements.

SCIENCE WORDS

alloys
sulfide
molecule
reactants
product
shells
energy levels
cations
anions
bond
ionic bond
covalent bond
organic chemistry
radical
precipitate
hydrogen bond
metallic bond
metallurgy

SUMMARY Atoms can combine chemically to form compounds. The smallest unit of a chemical compound is called a molecule. Chemists identify elements by using symbols. These symbols are unique for every kind of atom. When compounds or elements interact, they conform to the law of conservation of matter. This means that the reactants and products of a chemical reaction must be equal.

The formulas for compounds are expressed using chemical symbols. A chemical reaction can be described by writing a chemical equation. A chemical equation must be balanced.

The electron shell model of the atom is useful to help us understand how chemicals interact. This model states that only a certain number of electrons can fit in any shell. Atoms have a tendency to completely fill their outer shells.

When one atom contributes electrons to another atom in a compound, the atoms are joined by an ionic bond. Many compounds with ionic bonds dissolve easily in water. When compounds ionize in water, the solution will conduct an electric current. Some atoms bond by sharing electrons in covalent bonds.

REVIEW QUESTIONS

Fill in the blanks with the correct terms.

1. In a chemical reaction the starting materials are called ____________.
2. ____________ bonds are formed when electrons are transferred from the outer shell of one atom to the outer shell of another atom.
3. The bond that forms between the atoms in metals is called a ____________ bond.
4. The study of carbon compounds is called ____________ chemistry.
5. The bond that forms when electrons are shared between atoms is called a ____________ bond.

Mark each statement true (T) or false (F).

1. _____ Atoms having filled outer shells do not gain or lose electrons easily.
2. _____ Atoms must bond together in some way to form compounds.
3. _____ In a balanced equation the reactants and products are equal.
4. _____ Scientists all over the world use the same language of chemical symbols.
5. _____ Metals are poor conductors of electricity.

Match the term in Column A with the correct answer in Column B.

A	B
1. Precipitate ___	a. A group of atoms that reacts as a single unit
2. Molecule ___	b. A positive ion
3. Radical ___	c. A solid substance that forms from a chemical reaction in a liquid or a gas
4. Cation ___	d. The smallest unit of a compound that can exist and still have the chemical properties of that compound
5. Alloy ___	e. Substance formed when different metals are melted together

APPLYING WHAT YOU LEARNED

1. For each of the following elements, describe in which energy level, or shell, the electrons would be found. The atomic number of each element is given. Ca [*calcium*] 20, Be [*beryllium*] 4, Si [*silicon*] 14, Ar [*argon*] 18, N [*nitrogen*] 7.
2. Using the five elements listed above, describe what must happen for each atom to have a filled outer shell.

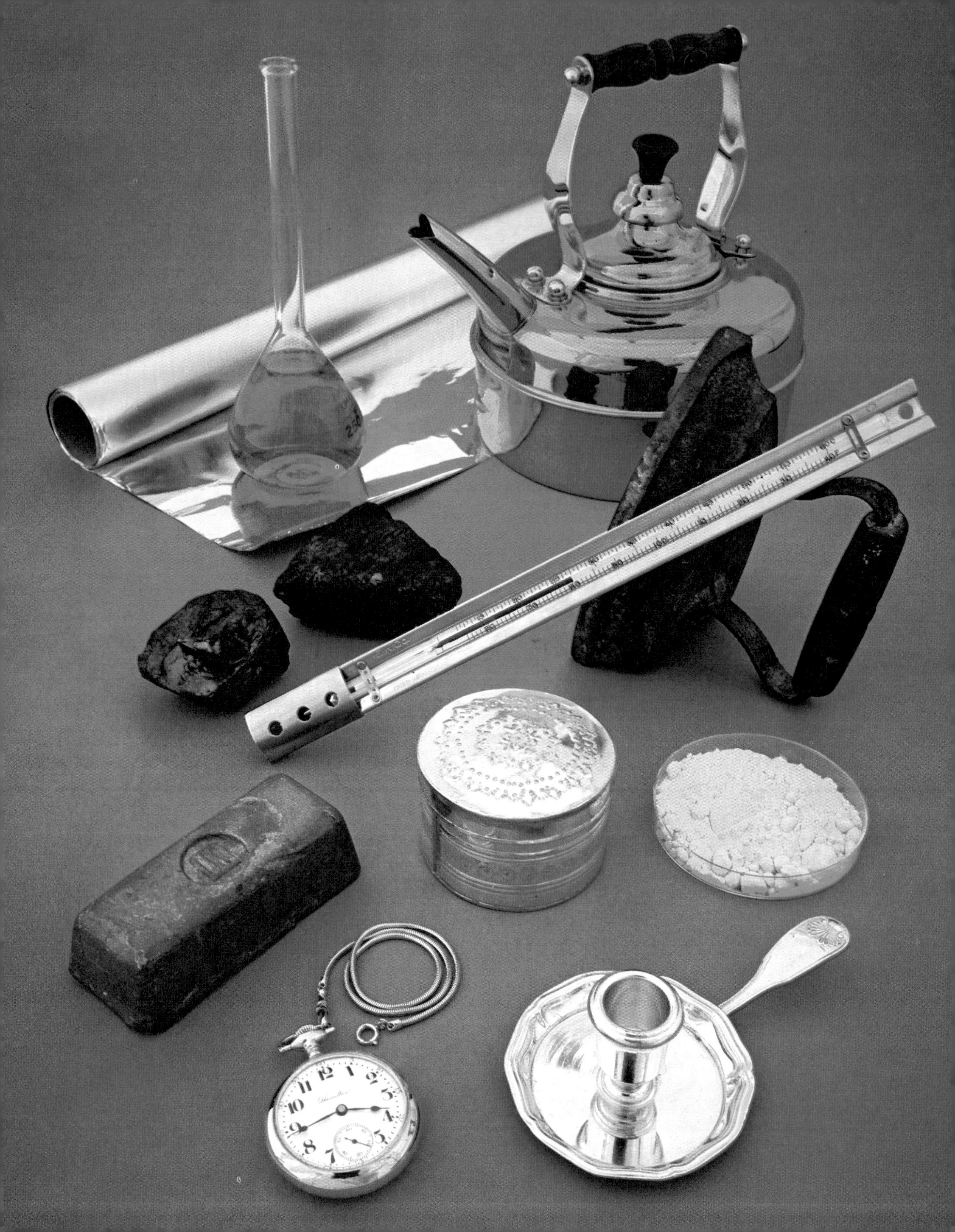

All of these materials contain some element or combination of elements. Some of the elements are metallic, others are nonmetallic.

8

Classification Systems for Chemistry

Many atoms have similar properties. For example, all metals conduct electricity. All metals lose electrons easily. Metals also have similar physical properties. Most have a silvery metallike appearance. Many can be hammered or drawn into wires without breaking. Scientists have used these similarities of metals to classify elements. Elements are classified as metals or nonmetals. This is an example of binary classification.

Chemical reactions can also be classified. This classification system can be useful in understanding how different kinds of chemical reactions take place. Many chemical compounds also display similar properties. Both chemical compounds and chemical elements can be classified. This helps in understanding their behavior and in making predictions about their reaction with other compounds or elements. In this chapter you will investigate some of these classification systems.

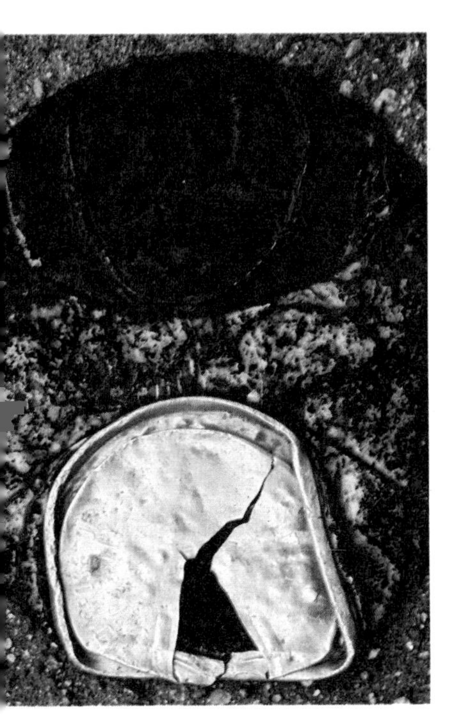

Oxygen combines easily with iron forming the rust on this can. The aluminum does not readily combine with oxygen.

What is the name of the reaction that involves breaking apart a compound?

Classifying Chemical Reactions

There are many different types of chemical reactions. The chemical reactions you have investigated and will investigate this year can be classified into four different groups. They are (1) Synthesis, (2) Decomposition, (3) Single replacement, (4) Double replacement.

In a **synthesis** (sin'thə sis) **reaction** two elements or compounds are chemically combined. This combination forms a new compound. If the two reactants are symbolized by the letters A and B, the reaction will look like this.

$$A + B \rightarrow AB$$

When you combined iron and sulfur to produce iron (II) sulfide, you were conducting a synthesis reaction.

$$Fe(s) + S(s) \rightarrow FeS(s)$$

A **decomposition reaction** involves breaking a compound apart into two new compounds or elements. Suppose the compound being broken down is symbolized by AB. The reaction will look like this.

$$AB \rightarrow A + B$$

The compound H_2O [*water*] can be broken down. This is done by applying electrical energy to the elements hydrogen and oxygen.

$$2H_2O(l) \xrightarrow{\text{electricity}} 2H_2(g) + O_2(g)$$

In a **single replacement reaction**, an element and a compound may react to form a new compound and a new element. Suppose the element is symbolized by C and the compound by AB. The reaction will look like this.

$$C + AB \rightarrow CB + A$$

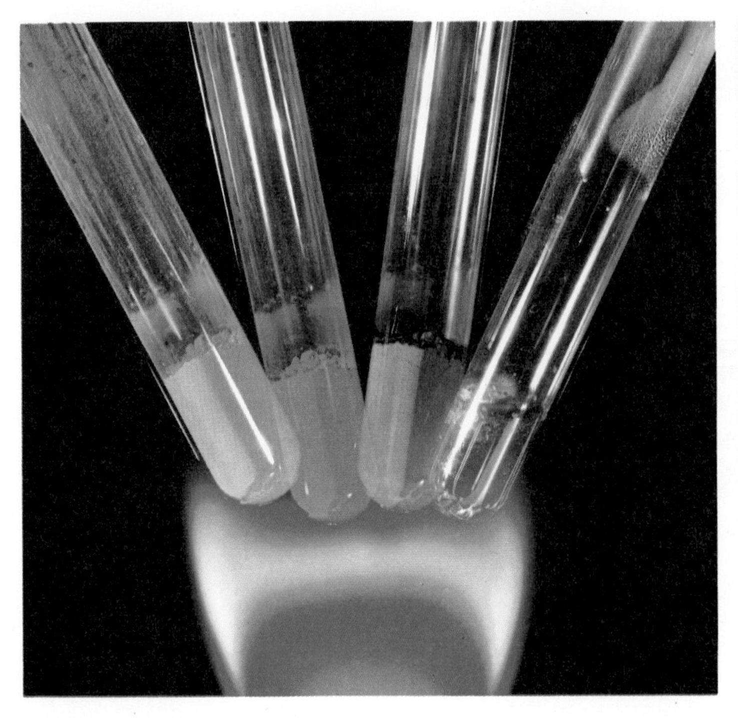

The decomposition of mercuric oxide (left) results in elemental mercury. Oxygen gas is given off in this process. In the single replacement reaction (right) zinc and sulfuric acid react to form zinc sulfate and hydrogen gas.

When you reacted Al [*aluminum*] with copper(I) chloride, you produced a single replacement reaction. The reaction looks like this.

$$Al(s) + 3CuCl(aq) \rightarrow AlCl_3(aq) + Cu(s)$$

A **double replacement reaction** takes place when two compounds react to form two new compounds. Suppose the two compounds are symbolized by AB and CD. The reaction will look like this.

$$AB + CD \rightarrow AD + CB$$

When you added lead(II) nitrate to sodium iodide, you produced a double replacement reaction. The formula equation for this reaction looks like this.

$$Pb(NO_3)_2\,(aq) + 2NaI(aq) \rightarrow PbI_2(s) + 2NaNO_3(aq)$$

In the next activity you will produce and classify a number of chemical reactions.

Activity 21 Classifying Chemical Reactions

PURPOSE

To investigate and classify chemical reactions

MATERIALS

Safety goggles
Solutions of:
  $NaOH$ [*sodium hydroxide*]
  $FeCl_3$ [*iron (III) chloride*]
  $CuSO_4$ [*copper sulfate*]
Magnesium ribbon
Zinc metal strip
$C_{12}H_{22}O_{11}$ [*sugar*]
Heat source
Matches
Forceps
2 test tubes
Test tube clamp
Graduate
150-mL beaker

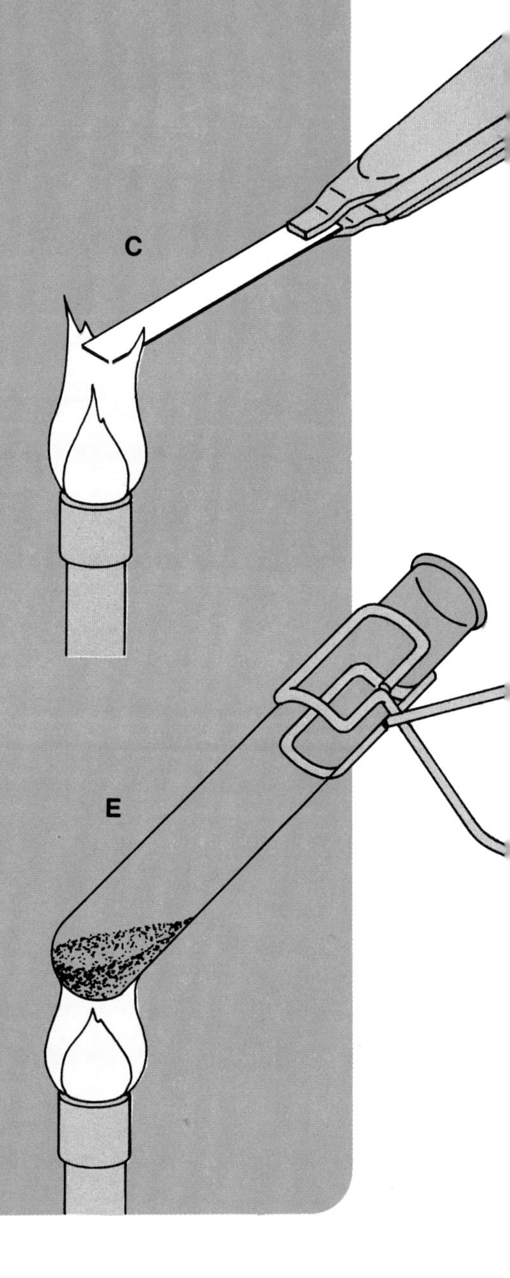

DO THIS

A. CAUTION: *Put on safety goggles. Wear them throughout this activity.*

B. Mix 10 mL of $NaOH$ solution and 10 mL of $FeCl_3$ solution in a test tube. Record what happens.

C. Using forceps, hold a 4-cm strip of magnesium ribbon in the flame of the heat source. **CAUTION:** *Do not look directly at the reaction.* Record your observations.

D. Place a zinc metal strip into a 150-mL beaker half-filled with $CuSO_4$ solution. Record what happens.

E. Heat 20 g of sugar in a test tube for 5 minutes. Observe and record what happens.

REPORT

1. What evidence is there that a chemical reaction took place in steps **B, C, D,** and **E**?

2. Write word and chemical equations that describe each of the four reactions.

3. Classify each reaction as synthesis, decomposition, single replacement, or double replacement. Give a reason for classifying each reaction as you did.

You now have a general idea of some basic types of chemical reactions. There are other kinds of reactions. However, many reactions can be classified using this system. Groups of chemical compounds can also be classified in this manner.

What is an oxide?

Compounds in which an element combines with oxygen are called **oxides**. Compounds in which elements combine with sulfur are called **sulfides** (sul′fīdz). Radical groups will combine with other elements or compounds. They also have families that can be grouped together in a classification scheme. There are several other important families of compounds in chemistry. These compounds are unique in the way they interact with other materials. They are called **acids** (as′idz) and **bases** (bā′siz).

The lead oxide in this photo is orange in color. The lead sulfide is grayish in color. Both of these compounds are a result of chemical reactions.

The Water Molecule

In Chapter 6 you found that certain materials will ionize when they dissolve in water. Water is a very special chemical compound that helps ionization take place. When materials ionize they break apart into electrically charged atoms called ions. The ions have either positive or negative electrical charges. Most chemical reactions involve ionic or covalent bonding. Some ions are usually involved in these reactions. Water molecules are special because of the way they can bond to each other. In a water molecule, the two hydrogen atoms are bonded to the oxygen atom by covalent bonds (Figure 8–1). The single electron of each hydrogen atom forms part of one covalent bond. Since covalent bonds involve sharing electrons between atoms, the oxygen atom supplies two electrons to form the bonds. Each oxygen atom has 8 electrons. Two of the electrons are in the completely filled first shell. Six electrons partially fill the outer shell. Four of these outer shell electrons are paired with each other and cannot form bonds.

FIGURE 8–1

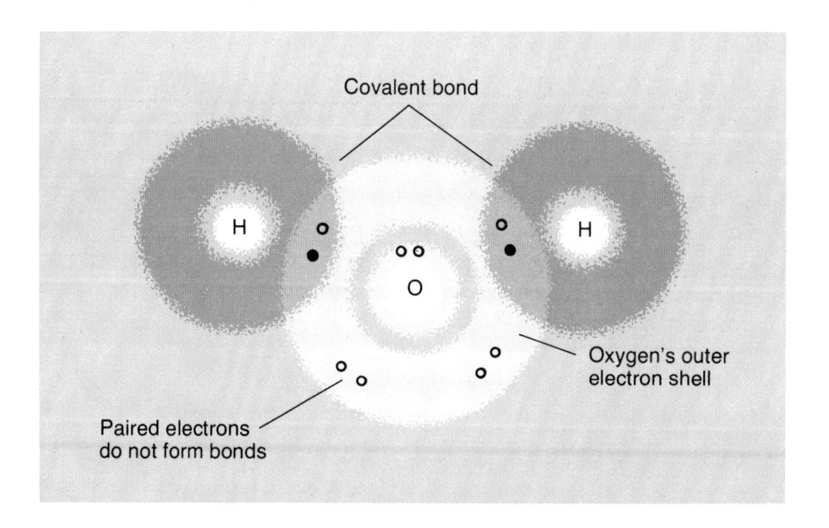

However, two of these electrons are unpaired. This means that they can form covalent bonds with the electrons from the hydrogen atoms. Each covalent bond is formed by pairing an electron from a hydrogen atom with an electron from the oxygen atom.

The electrons forming the covalent bonds of a water molecule are not shared equally by the hydrogen and oxygen atoms. The oxygen atom attracts the shared electrons more strongly than the hydrogen atoms. This

means that the electrons are closer to the oxygen atom than to the hydrogen atoms. Since electrons carry negative charges, the oxygen atom acquires a negative charge. The hydrogen atoms each have a positively charged proton in the nucleus. Because the electrons have been pulled away from the hydrogen atoms, the hydrogen atoms have a positive charge. This means that the electrical charges on a water molecule are not evenly distributed. The water molecule has a **negative pole** in the area of the oxygen atom and **two positive** poles in the areas of the hydrogen atoms. For this reason, water is a **dipolar** (two-poled) molecule.

Water's unique properties make it the most important compound needed for life on the earth. One of the states in which water exists on the earth is water vapor, as in these clouds.

What is a dipolar molecule?

Water molecules are very poor conductors of electricity. This is because the covalent bonds between the hydrogen atoms and the oxygen atom are very strong. However, molecular collisions between water molecules sometimes result in the ionization of a water molecule. When this happens, the ionized particles are a H^{+1} [*hydrogen ion*] and a OH^{-1} [*hydroxide ion*]. The hydrogen ion is actually a single proton with its single positive charge. The single proton will be quickly attracted to the negatively charged side of another water molecule. They will combine to form a H_3O^{+1} [*hydronium ion*]. About one water molecule in 500 million will naturally ionize to form a hydronium ion and a hydroxide ion. There is a name given to the special bond between the proton and the negative side of a water dipole that forms a hydronium ion. This special bond is known as a **hydrogen bond**.

Acids and Bases

What are acids?

When some compounds are dissolved in water, the number of hydronium ions increases in the solution. These compounds are called acids. When an acid reacts with water, it gives hydrogen ions to the water molecules. These form hydronium ions. Since a hydrogen ion is simply a proton, acids are often called **proton donors.** An example of a compound that is a proton donor is HCl [*hydrogen chloride*]. When hydrogen chloride (a gas) combines with water, the following reaction takes place.

$$HCl(g) + H_2O(l) \rightarrow H_3O^{+1}(aq) + Cl^{-1}(aq)$$

Hydrogen chloride combined with water is called **hydrochloric acid.** Another proton donor compound is H_2SO_4 [*hydrogen sulfate*]. When it is combined with water, it produces the following reaction.

$$H_2SO_4(aq) + H_2O(l) \rightarrow HSO_4^{-1}(aq) + H_3O^{+1}(aq)$$

This is a very common acid called **sulfuric acid.**

Some compounds have a special property. This property enables them to become acids. These compounds can free a hydrogen ion (a proton) from the compound to form a hydronium ion in water. Table 8–1 in-

Ants produce formic acid. The acid is one of many produced in nature.

dicates a number of compounds that are acids. In most chemical reactions acids are in a water solution.

What is a base?

Some compounds will combine with water to form hydroxide ions. These compounds are called bases. When a base reacts with water, it combines with water molecules to form OH^{-1}. One way a base can be formed is by having a compound with a single oxygen atom react with water. For example, when sodium oxide combines with water, the following reaction takes place.

$$Na_2O(s) + H_2O(l) \rightarrow 2Na^{+1}(aq) + 2OH^{-1}(aq)$$

TABLE 8–1 • Acids

NAME	FORMULA
Nitric	HNO_3
Carbonic	H_2CO_3
Phosphoric	H_3PO_4
Acetic	$HC_2H_3O_2$

Sodium hydroxide is the most important commercial base used in the United States.

Another way in which a base may be formed is by having NH_3 [*ammonia gas*] react with water.

$$NH_3(g) + H_2O(l) \rightarrow NH_4^{+1}(aq) + OH^{-1}(aq)$$

The ammonia gas accepts, or takes away, a hydrogen proton forming an ammonium ion [NH_4^{+1}] with 1 positive charge. The bond between the nitrogen atom and the hydrogen ion (or proton) is another hydrogen bond. Bases form hydroxide ions by taking protons away from water molecules. They are known as **proton acceptors**. Table 8–2 indicates a number of compounds that are bases. Bases are usually in a water solution when they are used in most chemical reactions.

TABLE 8–2 • Bases

NAME	FORMULA
Sodium hydroxide	$NaOH$
Ammonium hydroxide	NH_4OH
Potassium hydroxide	KOH
Calcium hydroxide	$Ca(OH)_2$

Some acids can produce more hydronium ions when they combine with water than can others. Some bases also produce more hydroxide ions. Acids and bases that produce many hydronium or hydroxide ions are **strong acids** and **strong bases**. Acids and bases that do not produce as many hydronium or hydroxide ions are **weak acids** and **weak bases.** The number of hydronium or hydroxide ions in an acid or a base determines the **concentration** (kon sən trā′shən) of the solution. A high concentration of hydronium ions means the acid is strong. A low concentration of hydroxide ions means the base is weak.

Acid-Base Indicators

You can measure the concentration of an acid or a base by using an **acid-base indicator** (in′də ka tər). Indicators are organic chemical compounds. These compounds combine with either hydronium or hydroxide ions in a solution. The indicators display different colors when they combine with hydronium or hydroxide ions. When there are more hydronium ions present, the indicator units combine with the hydronium ions and form a compound of a certain color. When there are more hydroxide ions present, the indicator units combine with them to form a compound of a different color. There are many kinds of acid-base indicators. They can be used for acids and bases of different concentrations.

One of the most widely used indicators is called universal indicator paper. It is a paper strip with indicator chemicals in it. This paper can show the concentration of hydronium ions and hydroxide ions present. All acids and bases contain both hydronium ions and hydroxide ions at the same time. Scientists have measured the actual concentrations of these ions.

This student is performing a titration. Titration is used to determine the strength or concentration of an acid or a base.

They have devised a scale for expressing the relative concentrations of both kinds of ions. This scale ranges from 0 to 14. It is called **pH**. The pH of a solution indicates whether the solution has a high concentration of hydronium ions relative to the hydroxide ions. It also indicates a high concentration of hydroxide ions relative to hydronium ions. When a solution has an equal number of hydroxide ions and hydronium ions it is **neutral** (nü'trəl). Figure 8–2 shows how the pH scale works.

What is the pH scale?

FIGURE 8–2

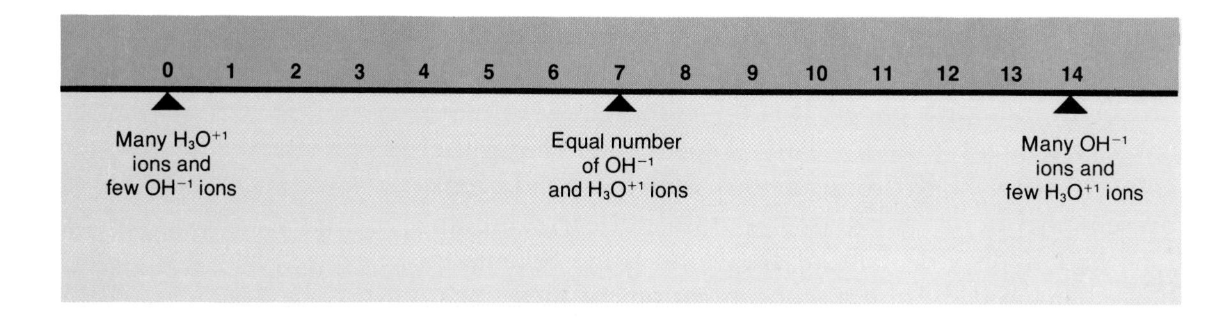

Pure water has as many hydroxide ions as hydronium ions. Therefore, in any reaction the two ions cancel each other's actions. Water is neutral. Pure water has a pH of 7.0. In the next activity you will explore the acid-base properties of some common chemical compounds. You will use universal indicator paper in your investigation.

As you will see, acids and bases are common materials. They can be part of many different chemical reactions and changes. Your body contains solutions that are acidic and basic. Television commercials mention that acid in the stomach causes indigestion. Scientists have measured the pH of contents of the human stomach under normal conditions. They found the pH to be about 1.6. This tells us that the stomach normally has a very acidic environment. The term *acid indigestion* indicates a very high hydronium ion concentration in the stomach. The acidic condition of the human stomach is essential. This condition helps the stomach break down food chemically.

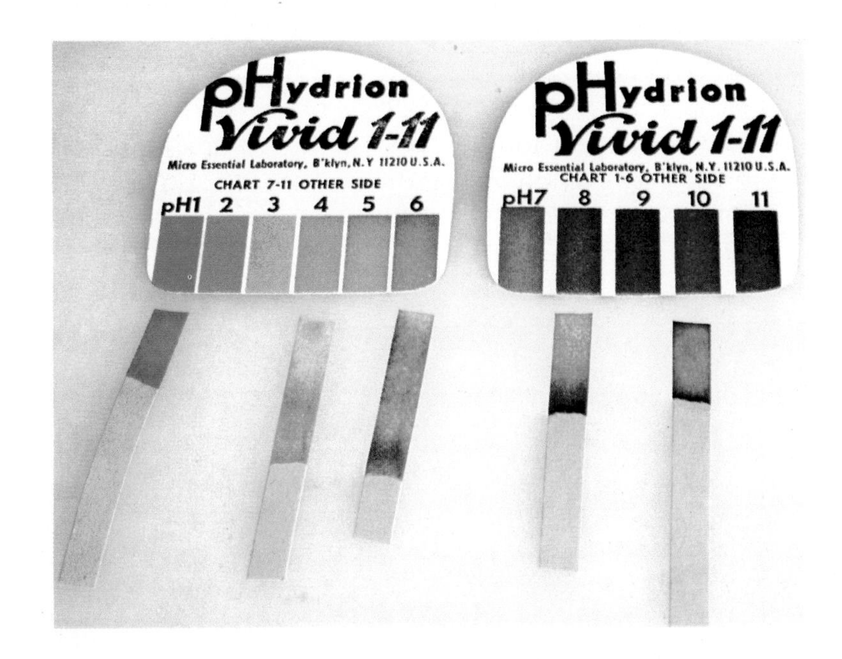

The strength of an acid or base can be determined with pH paper. The scale on the left shows acid concentration. The scale on the right shows base concentration. The pH 7 indicates a neutral solution.

Activity 22 Common Acids and Bases

PURPOSE

To determine which of several common materials are acids, which are bases, and which are neutral

MATERIALS

Universal indicator paper
Safety goggles
Each of the following, in dropper bottles

Bleach	Hydrogen chloride solution
Ammonia solution	Hydrogen sulfate solution
Vinegar	Sodium bicarbonate solution
Lemon juice	Tap water
Grapefruit juice	Distilled water
Tomato juice	Sodium hydroxide solution
Cola soft drink	Potassium hydroxide solution
Lemon-lime soft drink	Iron(III) hydroxide solution
Milk of magnesia	Sodium chloride solution

DO THIS

A. CAUTION: *Put on safety goggles. Wear them throughout this activity.*

B. Put a drop of hydrogen chloride solution on a 3-cm strip of universal indicator paper. Match any color change in the paper with the color key on the indicator paper holder. In a table like Table 1, record the name of the material and its pH.

TABLE 1 • pH of Some Common Materials

MATERIAL	pH	ACIDIC, BASIC, OR NEUTRAL

C. Repeat step **B** with each of the other materials.

REPORT

1. After each material in Table 1, indicate if it is acidic, basic, or neutral.

2. Is a material an acid or a base when it has ions? What is the evidence for your answer?

3. What evidence do you have that people eat acids and bases?

4. Are the acids and bases that people eat strong, or weak?

5. Of the materials tested, which should have the highest concentration of hydroxide ions?

6. Of the materials tested, which should have the highest concentration of hydronium ions?

Neutralization

Antacid tablets are sometimes taken by people having acid indigestion. Commercials claim that these tablets will neutralize the acid in the stomach and relieve indigestion. In the next activity you will investigate a way in which acids are neutralized.

When acids and bases react with each other, the reaction involves hydroxide and hydronium ions. For example, in the reaction NaOH + HCl, the following formula expressing the reaction can be written.

$$Na^{+1}(aq) + OH^{-1}(aq) + H_3O^{+1}(aq) + Cl^{-1}(aq) \rightarrow 2H_2O(l) + Na^{+1}(aq) + Cl^{-1}(aq)$$

In this reaction the hydronium and hydroxide ions combine to form two molecules of water. The sodium and chloride ions are not really part of the reaction. They remain ions throughout. They are called **spectator ions**. If sodium hydroxide and hydrochloric acid react, the resulting products are water, sodium ions, and chloride ions. This is the way all acids and bases usually interact. It can be written this way.

Acid + base → water + salt

If all the hydronium and hydroxide ions react completely, the sodium and chloride ions will be left in a water solution. If the water in this solution evaporates, common sodium chloride crystals will remain. In Activity 23 you will observe a chemical reaction between an acid and a base. It will be a neutralization reaction. The hydronium and hydroxide ions will be neutralized. A word formula for the reaction could be written this way.

Vinegar (an acid) + sodium bicarbonate (a base) →
water + sodium acetate (a salt) + ?

Activity 23 Neutralizing an Acid

PURPOSE

To investigate the neutralization of an acid

MATERIALS

Vinegar
$NaHCO_3$ [*sodium bicarbonate*]
Water
2 150-mL beakers
Universal indicator paper
Graduate
Spoon
Stirring rod
Safety goggles

DO THIS

A. Pour 50 mL of water into a 150-mL beaker. Add sodium bicarbonate, a little at a time, until no more will dissolve. Stir the solution after each addition of sodium bicarbonate.

B. CAUTION: *Put on safety goggles.* Pour 25 mL of vinegar into a 150-mL beaker.

C. Use universal indicator paper to measure the pH of each solution. Record these values.

D. Measure 10 mL of sodium bicarbonate solution and add it to the vinegar. Stir. Record your observations. Then test and record the pH of the vinegar solution.

E. Repeat step **D** until all the sodium bicarbonate solution has been used. **CAUTION:** *Be careful that none of the undissolved sodium bicarbonate is added to the vinegar.*

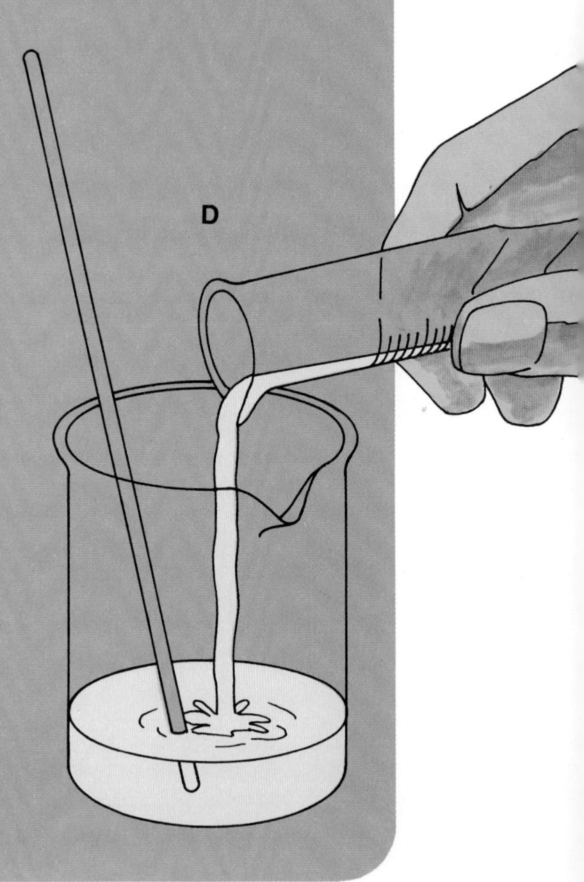

REPORT

1. Construct a line graph. Graph pH of the vinegar versus the total amount of sodium bicarbonate added, in 10-mL increments. How did the pH change?

2. What evidence was there of a chemical reaction?

3. Did the vinegar–sodium bicarbonate solution become neutral? If not, extrapolate from your graph how much additional sodium bicarbonate would be needed.

Activity 24 Seltzer Tablets and pH

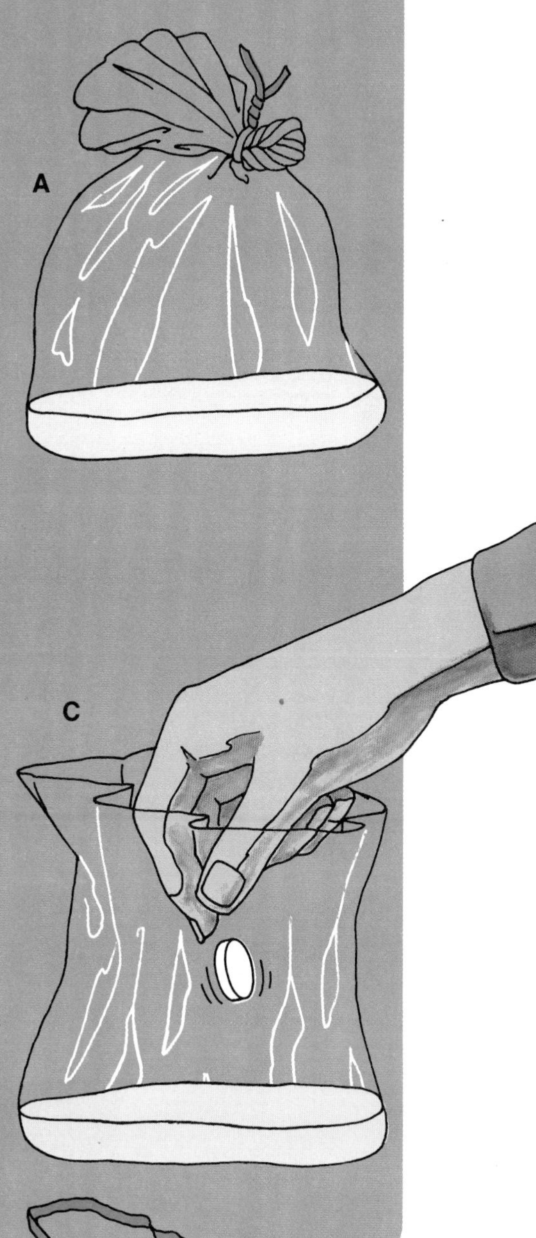

PURPOSE

To investigate the relationship between seltzer tablets and pH

MATERIALS

Seltzer tablet	Water
Graduate	Balance and mass set
1-L plastic bag with twist tie	Universal indicator paper

DO THIS

A. Fill the plastic bag with 20mL of water. Measure the pH of the water with universal indicator paper and record it. Then seal the bag with the twist tie.

B. Place the bag and a seltzer tablet on the left pan of the balance. Measure and record their combined mass.

C. Open the bag. Put the seltzer tablet in the bag and quickly reseal it. Observe and record what happens.

D. When the reaction is complete, measure and record the mass of the bag and its contents.

E. Open the bag. Measure and record the pH of the solution.

REPORT

1. Compare the water–seltzer tablet reaction with the vinegar–sodium bicarbonate reaction.

2. How did the combined mass of the bag, water, and seltzer tablet before the reaction compare with their mass after the reaction? Explain your answer.

3. How did the pH of the water change after the reaction?

4. Predict what chemicals were involved in the reaction?

5. How can you test your prediction?

In Activity 23, the reaction showed that a gas was given off when the two chemicals interacted. To find out what this gas was, look at the chemical formula.

$$2HCH_3COO(aq) + 2NaHCO_3(s) \rightarrow H_2O(l) + 2Na^{+1}(aq) + 2CH_3OO^{-1}(aq) + 2CO_2(g)$$

Carbon dioxide is a gas under normal conditions. It fizzed or bubbled into the atmosphere in this reaction.

The pH of the acid did not change much as the baking soda solution was added. It is possible that a point was reached where no more bubbles formed. However, the pH remained acidic. Both sodium bicarbonate and acetic acid are weak compounds. This means that they do not produce as many hydronium or hydroxide ions as strong acids or bases. They do not ionize as much as strong acids or bases. Some acetic acid molecules and sodium bicarbonate molecules do not ionize.

The two molecules of acetic acid and sodium bicarbonate ionize only slightly. They can always supply more hydronium or hydroxide ions after the chemical reaction has taken place. Weak acids and bases ionize slightly. These acids and bases can be used to keep the pH of a solution fairly constant. They form **buffer solutions**.

Blood contains natural buffers to keep the pH fairly constant. Buffers, such as seltzer, are taken to neutralize stomach acid.

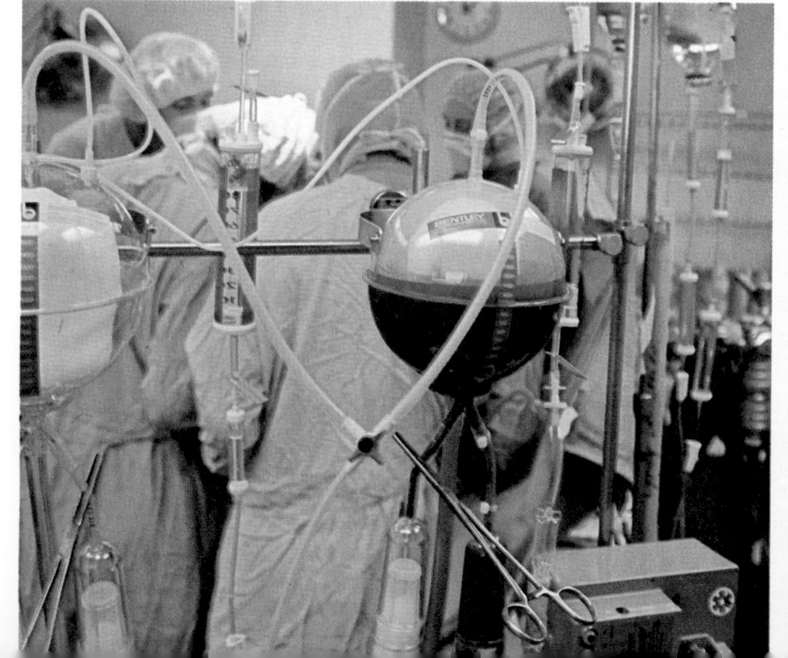

EXCURSION 9
You can learn more about the chemistry of matter in Excursion 9, "Qualitative Analysis."

In Activity 24, the seltzer tablet reacted in water. This reaction was similar to the sodium bicarbonate and acetic acid reaction. In fact, the seltzer tablet is a mixture of compounds. Two of the compounds are sodium bicarbonate and $C_6H_8O_7$ [*citric acid*]. Citric acid can exist easily as a solid. It dissolves in water to form a weak acid. What do you suppose was the chemical reaction between the compounds in the seltzer tablet? What gas do you suppose formed? What do you suppose would happen to the pH of the resulting solution as you added more acid or base?

The Periodic Table

Dmitri Mendeleev. The modern periodic table, although it has been modified, is still similar to Mendeleev's original table.

It is obvious that there are similarities among many compounds, reactions, and elements. The similarities are used by chemists to organize their thinking about families or groups of elements, reactions, and compounds. A good classification scheme helps them to make predictions about how chemical interactions may proceed. It can also help to predict what the properties of the products of reactions may be like. By the 1860s about sixty-three chemical elements had been discovered. Some chemists tried to organize or classify them. A classification system would help explain their chemical behavior in reactions. It would also help explain physical properties.

Dmitri Mendeleev, a Russian chemist, and Julius Lothar Meyer, a German chemist, worked on the classification of chemical elements. They discovered that certain properties seemed to appear periodically when elements were grouped by their atomic masses. For example, elements with atomic masses of 7, 23, 39, 85, and 133 were all metals. These metals reacted vigorously with water to form bases. The elements with the next closest atomic masses that were heavier (9, 24, 40, 87, and 137) were also metals. These metals reacted with water to form bases, also. However, the reactions were less vigorous. The elements with the next closest atomic masses that were lighter (4, 20, 39, 83, and 131) did not react with anything. They were gases.

Much of the work of these chemists took place before all the natural elements were discovered. They worked without good models of atoms. However, the classification tables developed by Mendeleev and others proved to be very helpful in explaining and predicting chemical reactions. In these tables the elements were grouped in rows and columns. They were grouped according to their atomic masses and the periodic changes that occurred in their chemical properties. The table was known as a **periodic** (pir ē od'ik) **table.**

FIGURE 8–3
This is a simplified version of a modern periodic table. The different families, groups, and series are colored for easy identification.

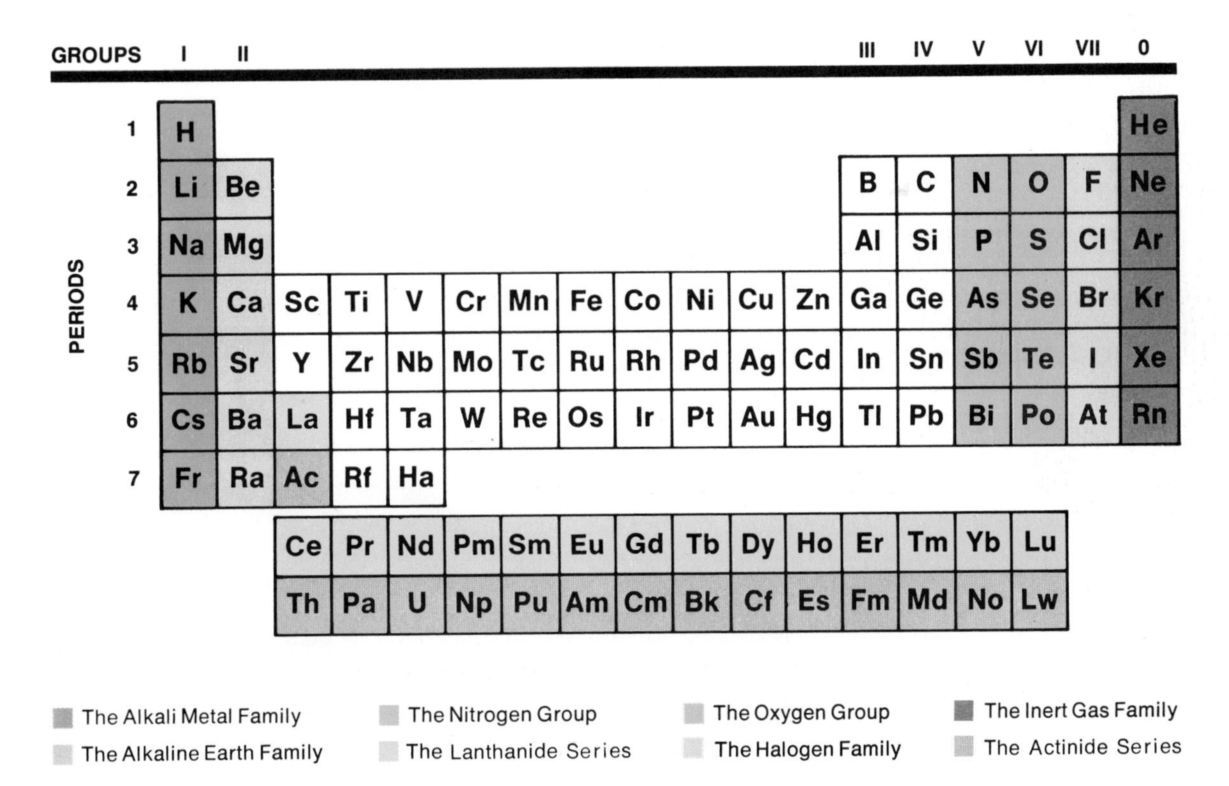

What is the periodic law?

A modern periodic table was organized that grouped elements on the basis of their atomic numbers. This table was developed after scientists had atomic models for the proton, electron, and neutron. Figure 8–3 shows a simplified diagram of a modern periodic table. When elements are grouped in this manner, there is a periodic repetition of their chemical and physical properties. This idea is known as the **periodic law.** Each box in the table represents a different element. O [*oxygen*] is near the upper right portion of the table. The element to the left of oxygen in that row is N [*nitrogen*]. The element to the right of oxygen is F [*fluorine*]. The atomic number of oxygen is 8. The atomic number of nitrogen is 7. What is the atomic number of fluorine? What is the atomic number of Ne [*neon*]?

EXCURSION 12
You can learn more about the composition and organization of elements in Excursion 12, "Exploring the Periodic Table."

The periodic chemical and physical properties of the elements can be found by reading down the columns of elements. For example, Li [*lithium*], Na [*sodium*], K [*potassium*], Rb [*rubidium*], Cs [*cesium*], and Fr [*francium*] are in the left column of the table. All these elements are members of the same chemical family known as the **alkali** (al′kə lī) **metals.** They have similar

These are representative of the halogen family. Reading from left to right they are calcium fluoride, chlorine, iodine, and bromine.

chemical and physical properties. Other elements with similar chemical and physical properties are grouped in other columns.

The center portion of the periodic table is grouped differently. The center groups of elements are known as **transition** (tran zish′ən) **elements.** Included in this section are two series of elements that also act as families. They are called the **lanthanide** (lan′thə nīd) series and the **actinide** (ak′tə nīd) series. These series were named after their first element, La [*lanthium*] and Ac [*actinium*], respectively.

FIGURE 8–4

GROUPS / PERIODS	I	II											III	IV	V	VI	VII	0
1	H																	He
2	Li	Be											B	C	N	O	F	Ne
3	Na	Mg											Al	Si	P	S	Cl	Ar
4	K	Ca	Sc	Ti	V	Cr	Mn	Fe	Co	Ni	Cu	Zn	Ga	Ge	As	Se	Br	Kr
5	Rb	Sr	Y	Zr	Nb	Mo	Tc	Ru	Rh	Pd	Ag	Cd	In	Sn	Sb	Te	I	Xe
6	Cs	Ba	La	Hf	Ta	W	Re	Os	Ir	Pt	Au	Hg	Tl	Pb	Bi	Po	At	Rn
7	Fr	Ra	Ac	Rf	Ha													
			Ce	Pr	Nd	Pm	Sm	Eu	Gd	Tb	Dy	Ho	Er	Tm	Yb	Lu		
			Th	Pa	U	Np	Pu	Am	Cm	Bk	Cf	Es	Fm	Md	No	Lw		

■ Transition Elements

The eight main groups (columns) are made up of elements having the same number of electrons in their outer shells. For example, in group II, Be [*beryllium*], Mg [*magnesium*], Ca [*calcium*], Sr [*strontium*], Ba [*barium*], and Ra [*radium*] all have two electrons in their outer shells. As a result, these elements have similar properties. The elements are organized in the table to show these similarities.

There is much more to be learned about the periodic table. There are many more uses for it.

SCIENCE WORDS

synthesis reaction
decomposition reaction
single replacement reaction
double replacement reaction
oxides
sulfides
acids
bases
poles
dipolar
hydrogen bond
proton donors
hydrochloric acid
sulfuric acid
proton acceptors
pH
neutral
strong acids
strong bases
weak acids
weak bases
concentration
acid-base indicator
spectator ions
buffer solutions
periodic table
periodic law
alkali metals
transition elements
lanthanide series
actinide series

SUMMARY Chemical reactions can be classified in many different ways. Chemical compounds can also be grouped together in families. Acids and bases are two families of chemicals that are very important in chemistry. Acids are compounds that produce many hydronium ions. Bases are usually formed when a metallic oxide dissolves in water and accepts a proton from its surroundings.

When an acid reacts with a base, a salt and water are always produced. When acids partially ionize in water, they are said to be weak. When they ionize a great deal, they are said to be strong. This same idea applies to bases.

The chemical elements have been organized in a table called the periodic table. They are grouped according to their atomic number and the periodic repetition of their chemical properties. The periodic table is extremely useful to chemists in explaining the behavior of elements in chemical reactions.

REVIEW QUESTIONS

Complete the following by choosing the correct answer.

1. C + AB → CB + A is an example of what type of reaction?
   (a) synthesis (b) decomposition (c) single replacement (d) double replacement
2. AB + CD → AD + CB is an example of what type of reaction?
   (a) synthesis (b) decomposition (c) single replacement (d) double replacement
3. One end of the water molecule is negatively charged, while the other end is positively charged. Therefore the water molecule is said to be
   (a) stable. (b) covalent. (c) dipolar. (d) an indicator.
4. A solution with a high concentration of hydronium ions is
   (a) a base. (b) an acid. (c) neutral. (d) dipolar.
5. AB → A + B is an example of what type of reaction?
   (a) synthesis (b) decomposition (c) single replacement (d) double replacement

Match the term in Column A with the correct answer in Column B.

A	B
1. Indicator ___	a. A solution that has equal numbers of hydroxide and hydronium ions
2. Synthesis reaction ___	b. Used to measure the concentration of an acid or base
3. Base ___	c. Two elements chemically combined to form a new compound
4. Buffer ___	d. Weak acids and bases that are used to keep the pH fairly constant
5. Neutral ___	e. A solution that has a high concentration of hydroxide ions

Mark each statement true (T) or false (F).

1. ______ Compounds in which an element combines with oxygen are called oxides.
2. ______ The contents of the human stomach are normally very acidic.
3. ______ Acids are called proton acceptors.
4. ______ Acetic acid is a very strong acid.
5. ______ Water is a good conductor of electricity.

APPLYING WHAT YOU LEARNED

1. Look up information about the dipolar nature of water. What special features does the water molecule have because it is dipolar?
2. Using a chemistry book, look up an example of each of the following reactions: decomposition, synthesis, single replacement, double replacement.

Radioactive isotopes are used in making some industrial measurements. Here, high intensity gamma radiation is used to measure the thickness of rolled steel.

The Atomic Nucleus

As you learned in Chapter 4, the early Greeks studied the physical world. They explored the nature of matter, and they suggested the particle theory. They even questioned the existence of atoms. Later you learned that John Dalton proposed an atomic theory.

Today scientists believe in the existence of the atom. They also believe that the atom contains a nucleus. The study of the nucleus and how it behaves is important in developing an understanding of the physical world. In this chapter you will learn about this small, but very powerful, part of the atom.

Radioactivity

What is radioactivity?

Who discovered X rays?

Radioactivity (rā dē ō ak tiv′ə tē) is the giving off of particles and rays from the nucleus of the atom. Radioactivity was discovered in the late nineteenth century by Henri Becquerel (bek rel′), a French scientist. He was trying to determine whether any element gives off **X rays.** Earlier Wilhelm Roentgen (rent′gen) had discovered X rays when he bombarded a copper target with electrons. The X rays could be detected by using a photographic plate. When a plate was exposed to X rays and developed, it showed a certain amount of exposure to light. Roentgen also found that a new kind of picture could be taken using X rays. If a hand, for example, were placed between the source of the X rays and a photographic plate, a picture of the bones in the hand could be obtained.

This discovery inspired other scientists. Roentgen had been able to produce X rays in the laboratory. Becquerel wondered if he could find a natural source of X rays. He knew that X rays would expose a photographic plate. He therefore placed different materials on wrapped photographic plates. After a period of time, he developed the plates. Most of them showed no exposure. There was one element, however, that caused a plate to be exposed. That element was U [*uranium*]. This discovery led Becquerel to other discoveries. He found that other elements give off rays similar to X rays. Two such elements are Th [*thorium*] and Ac [*actinium*].

Marie and Pierre Curie (kyůr′ē), using the property of radioactivity, discovered two new elements, Po [*polonium*] and Ra [*radium*]. The radioactivity of these two elements was different from X rays. It was caused by the breakdown of an atomic nucleus. There appeared to be three kinds of radiation coming from these elements. The radiation could be identified by passing it between the poles of a magnet. Two rays were deflected by the magnet. The third ray was not.

It was found that **gamma** (gam′ə) **rays** were not at all affected by the magnet. Gamma rays come naturally from the nucleus of the atom. They are similar to X rays, but they are more penetrating. **Beta** (bā′tə) **rays** were most affected by the magnet. Beta rays were found to consist of negative particles identical in charge and mass to the electron. **Alpha** (al′fə) **rays** were found to be positively charged particles. Alpha particles are helium ions [He^{+2}], made up of two protons and two neutrons. Alpha particles are less affected by the magnetic field than are beta particles.

Lise Meitner was a physicist who published the first report on uranium fission. Wilhelm Roentgen produced and identified X rays in his laboratory.

Half-life

What is half-life?

The amount of radioactivity present in a sample of material changes as time passes. Each time a nucleus gives off a radioactive particle the element changes. Uranium is one of the many radioactive elements. When a uranium nucleus gives off an alpha particle, a thorium nucleus remains. This process is known as **radioactive decay.** The amount of uranium remaining can be graphed against time. The period of time necessary for half of the atoms of a radioactive substance to decay into another element is called its **half-life.** Uranium has a half-life of 4.5 billion years. Each radioactive element has its own unique half-life. Radium has a half-life of 1620 years. Some elements have half-lives of less than a second. You will learn more about half-life in Activities 25 and 26.

Badges, such as this one, are worn by people who work in a radioactive environment. The badges can be broken down and the film developed to determine the amount of exposure to radiation.

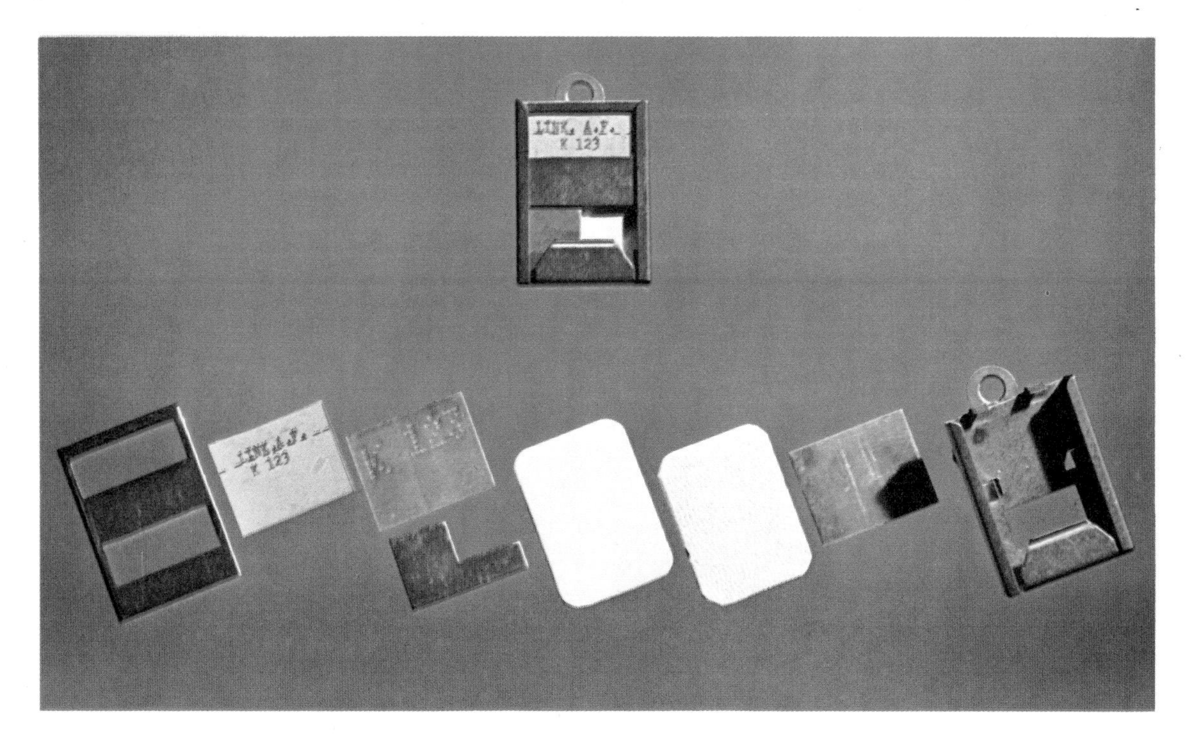

Activity 25 Half-life

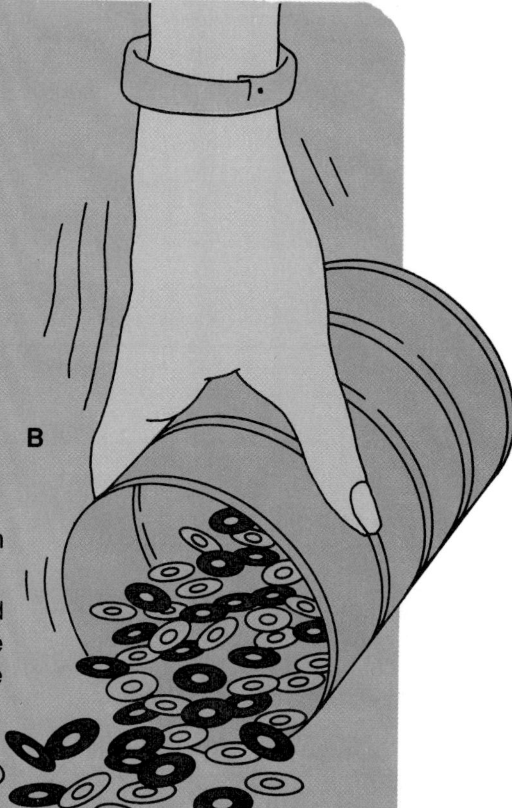

PURPOSE

To demonstrate the principle of half-life

MATERIALS

100 washers painted black on one side
Large coffee can with plastic lid

DO THIS

A. Place the washers in the coffee can and snap on the lid.

B. Shake the can vigorously. Then remove the lid and pour out the washers. Record in a table like Table 1 the number of washers that come up black. Put those washers to one side.

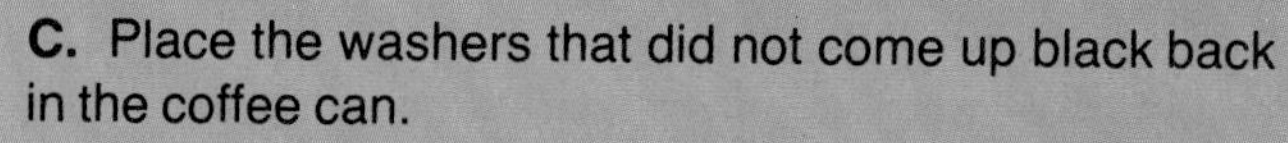

C. Place the washers that did not come up black back in the coffee can.

D. Repeat steps **B** and **C** until all the washers have come up black.

REPORT

1. Make a graph of your data. Plot the number of trials on the vertical axis and the number of black washers per trial on the horizontal axis.

2. Consider each trial as a unit of time and the washers as atoms of a radioactive element. If the washers coming up black indicate decay to a stable form, what would be the half-life of the element?

TABLE 1 • Washer Data

TRIALS	NUMBER OF BLACK WASHERS
1	
2	
3	
4	
5	

Activity 26 Voltage Charging

PURPOSE

To determine charging half-life

MATERIALS

50-microfarad capacitor
6-megohm resistor
Dry cell (D type)
Battery holder
5 connecting wires
Clock with a second hand
Voltmeter

DO THIS

A. Connect the circuit as shown, except for the dry cell. You will need to keep track of the time as soon as the dry cell is connected.

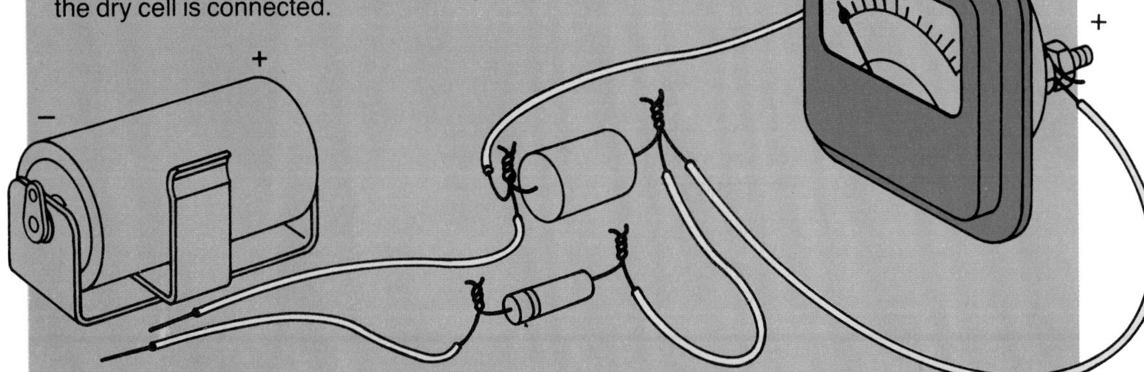

B. Design a table in which to record the data you will collect. Then connect the dry cell. Record the voltage at 30-second intervals for 10 minutes. Assume that the voltage at 0 seconds is zero.

C. Disconnect the circuit but leave the apparatus set up for the next activity.

REPORT

1. Construct a graph of voltage versus time. Plot time on the horizontal axis.

2. What is the charging half-life?

Measuring Radiation

Several methods are used to detect or measure amounts of radiation. The **Geiger** (gī′gər) **counter** is probably the most common method in use today. The Geiger counter consists of a tube filled with a gas. There is a wire in the center of the tube and a window in one end of the tube. The window is made of a material that allows radioactive particles or rays to pass through. Radioactive particles collide with the particles of the gas in the tube. This causes the gas to ionize by losing electrons. This ionization charges the central wire. The charge is registered on the counter. The number of counts in a period of time is a measure of the radioactivity of the material. The Geiger counter is usually used to detect beta and gamma rays.

A **cloud chamber** is used to measure the paths made by radioactive particles. It is made of a transparent material. Inside the chamber there is a vapor of alcohol or water. Radioactive particles moving through the vapor cause the formation of vapor trails. The paths of the particles can be studied by using electric and magnetic forces around the particles.

Geiger counters are used to measure levels of radiation. The radiation levels can be determined by the number of counts over a given period of time.

A **bubble chamber** is also used to study the paths made by radioactive particles. It is similar to the cloud chamber. However, it is more complicated. The bubble chamber is made from transparent materials. The chamber is filled with liquid hydrogen at a temperature near its boiling point. A particle moving through the liquid causes bubbles to form. These bubbles can be photographed and the path of the particles can be studied.

Name four devices used to measure radioactivity.

Another instrument used to measure radiation is the **scintillation** (sin tə lā'shən) **counter.** Some materials give off light when they are struck by radiation. This property is called **fluorescence** (flü ə res'əns). The scintillation counter determines the amount of radia-

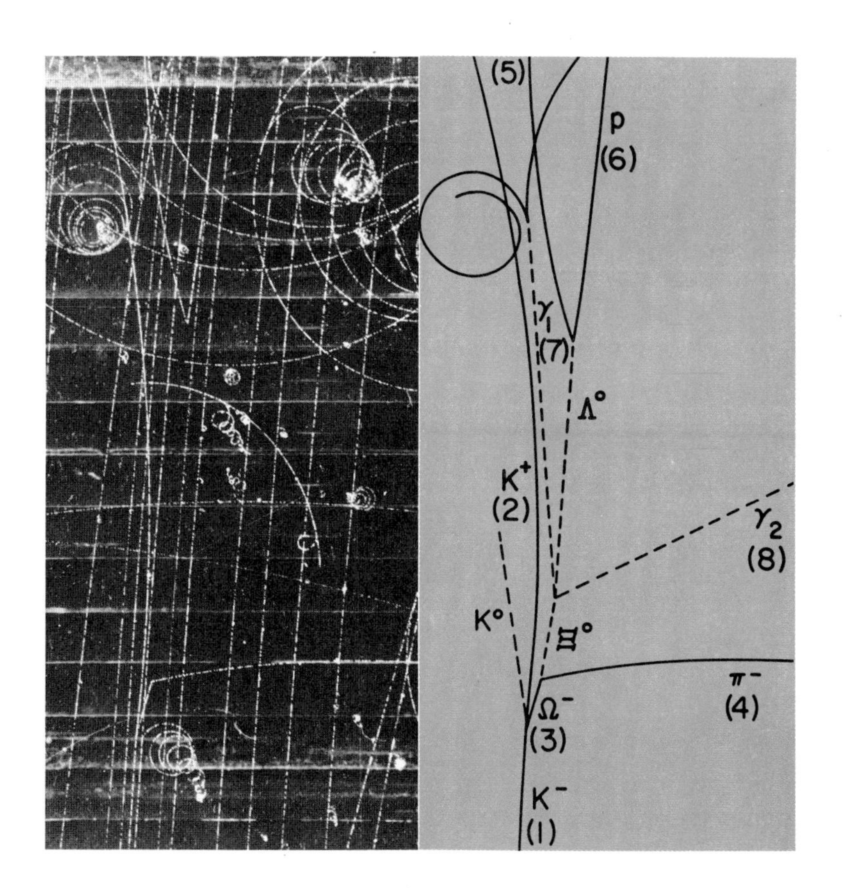

The photograph (left) shows the paths made by various subatomic particles in a bubble chamber. The sketch (right) identifies by symbols the paths made by different particles. Path (3), made by a negative omega meson is symbolized by Ω^-. The existence of this particle was predicted by physicists and confirmed by experiments with the bubble chamber.

tion by measuring the fluorescence of the material. The scintillation counter is more sensitive than the Geiger counter. It is used to measure low levels of radiation.

Radioactive Series

There are several radioactive elements that decay into other radioactive elements. These elements decay in a series until a stable element is finally produced. One example is the decay of uranium 238 to lead 206. The following is another example of radioactive decay.

^{238}U emits an alpha particle to form ^{234}Th
^{234}Th emits a beta particle to form ^{234}Pa [*protactinium*]
^{234}Pa emits a beta particle to form ^{234}U

You will investigate another type of decay in Activity 27.

Use of Radioactive Elements

Radioactive elements are sometimes called **radio-isotopes.** They are used as **tracers** in many scientific investigations. Tracers are used to follow and identify certain biological, chemical, and physical processes. Chemists use radioisotopes to determine how ions move from solution to solution. Earth scientists use radio-isotopes to trace ocean currents or to measure the speed of underground water flow. Nutrient uptake and release of carbon dioxide in plants is measured by biologists, using radioactive tracers. Radioisotopes are also used in genetics. Radiation can alter the genetic code of plants and animals. This alteration produces offspring with characteristics that are different from those of their parents.

Activity 27 Voltage Decay

PURPOSE

To investigate voltage decay from discharging

MATERIALS

50-microfarad capacitor
6-megohm resistor
Dry cell (D type)
Battery holder
5 connecting wires
Clock with a second hand
Voltmeter

DO THIS

A. Reconnect the circuit used in Activity 26. Charge the capacitor for 15 minutes.

B. Design a table in which to record voltage and time. Then disconnect the dry cell. Start timing as you hook up the circuit as shown. The voltage at 0 seconds should be about 1.5 volts.

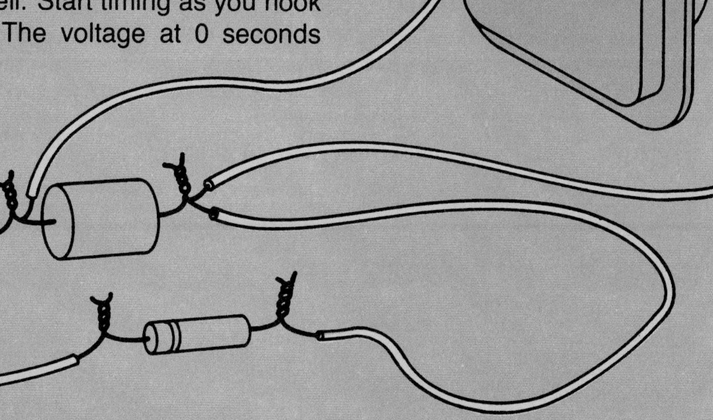

C. Record the voltage at 30-second intervals for 10 minutes.

REPORT

1. Construct a graph of voltage versus time. Plot time on the horizontal axis.

2. What is the discharging half-life?

Radioisotopes also have applications in the field of medicine. Radioactive iodine, for example, is used to diagnose and treat diseases of the thyroid gland. X rays and gamma rays are used to treat certain types of cancer. Gamma rays from Co [*cobalt*] are focused inside the body at the point where the cancerous tissue is located. If the treatment is successful the cancerous tissue will be destroyed. However, gamma rays may also destroy healthy tissue.

What source of radiation is used in the treatment of cancer?

Engineers use radioactive isotopes to investigate moving parts in machines. A small amount of a radioisotope is added to the part to be studied. Different oils can be used as lubricants. After the machine has been run, the amount of radiation present in each oil is measured. The measurement is an indication of how effective the lubricant is. By using radioactive isotopes, engineers can study how parts of machines wear.

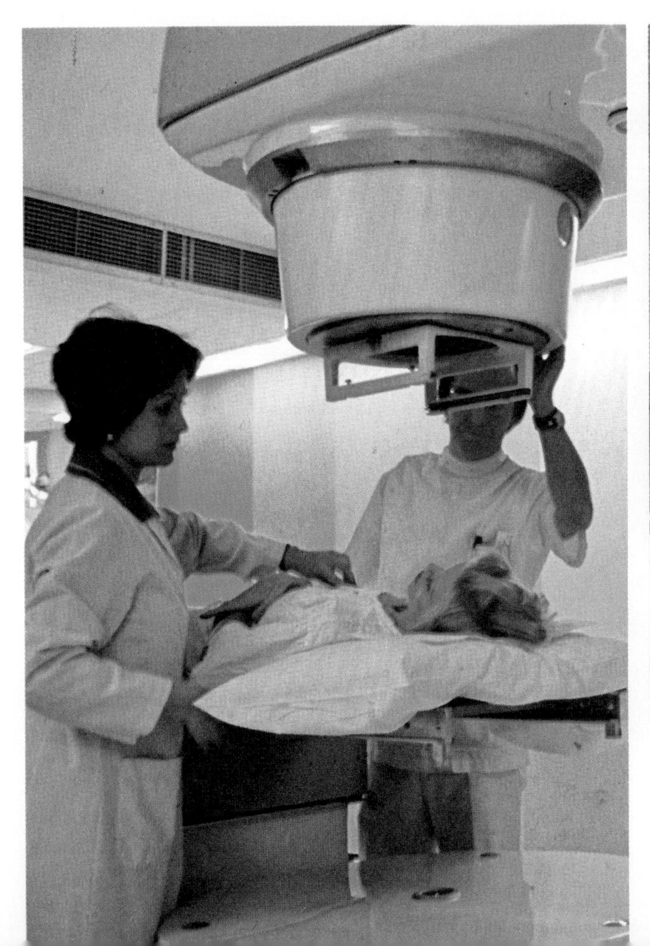

Various kinds of radiation in controlled amounts are used in the treatment of certain illnesses (left). X rays and radioactive isotopes are used to detect flaws in structural joints and parts of machinery (right).

Carbon Dating

An interesting and useful application of radioactivity is carbon dating. The age of a material can be determined by measuring the amount of ^{14}C present. Carbon 12 is the more common isotope of carbon. It is not radioactive. Carbon 14 is radioactive. It has a half-life of 5770 years. Carbon 14 is produced when a neutron strikes a nitrogen atom and is captured by it. Immediately a proton is emitted from the nucleus. This results in the nitrogen nucleus becoming a carbon 14 nucleus.

The age of this ancient tiger skull can be determined by carbon dating. Using only a small amount of material, scientists can determine age fairly accurately by this dating process.

The key to carbon 14 dating is the assumption that the rate of carbon 14 production in the past was the same as it is now. That assumption is not strictly true. However, it is close enough to allow accurate dating of very old materials. The concept is simple. If carbon 14 is

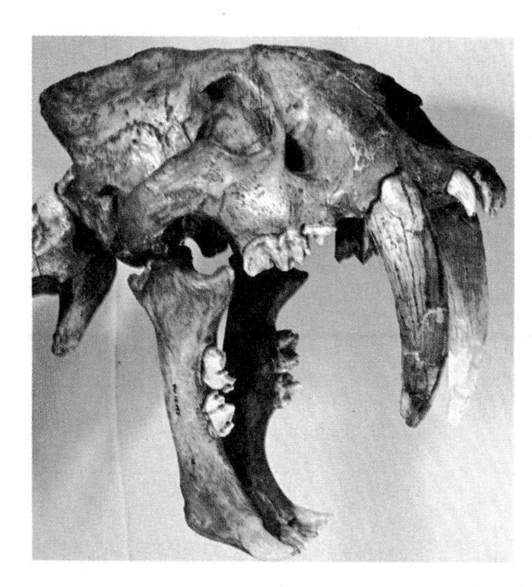

produced at a constant rate, a certain percentage of the carbon in a plant or animal must be carbon 14. As soon as the plant or animal dies it stops taking in carbon, and the amount of ^{14}C begins to decrease. To determine the age of an old wooden wheel, a small sample of wood from the wheel would be taken. The ratio of ^{14}C to ^{12}C in the sample would be determined. This method can be used to date objects several thousand years old.

Uranium Dating

What advantage does uranium dating have over carbon dating?

The uranium method of dating is used when carbon dating is not possible or practical. The uranium method is used to determine the age of rocks that are hundreds of millions of years old. This is also done by ratios. Uranium 238 decays, after several steps, into lead 206. Uranium 235 decays into lead 207. The most common isotope of lead is lead 208. The age of rocks can be determined by using ratios of uranium 235 to lead 207 and uranium 238 to lead 206. This method has been used to date rocks that are 4.6 billion years old.

SUMMARY Alpha, beta, and gamma rays are the most common forms of radioactivity. Alpha rays (positive particles) are helium ions. Beta rays (negative particles) are identical to high-speed electrons. Gamma rays are like X rays but are much more penetrating.

All radioactive elements decay into other elements. The period of time necessary for half of a radioactive material to decay into another element is called its half-life. Some elements, such as uranium, decay into a series of radioactive elements, each decaying in turn, usually to lead.

Radioisotopes have many uses in the fields of medicine, biology, chemistry, and physics. Tracing, treating cancer, and genetic experiments are some of the many uses of radioisotopes.

SCIENCE WORDS

radioactivity
Henri Becquerel
Wilhelm Roentgen
gamma rays
beta rays
alpha rays
radioactive decay
half-life
Geiger counter
cloud chamber
bubble chamber
scintillation counter
fluorescence
radioisotopes
tracers

REVIEW QUESTIONS

Fill in the blanks with the correct terms.

1. The three types of radiation are ____________, ____________, and ____________ rays.
2. Marie and Pierre Curie discovered the elements ____________ and ____________.
3. The period of time necessary for half of the atoms of a radioactive substance to decay into another element is called its ____________.
4. Two radioactive elements that are used to determine the age of materials are ____________ and ____________.
5. The type of radiation that is identical to a high-speed electron is ____________ rays.
6. ____________ ____________ radiation is actually a helium ion.

Mark each statement true (T) or false (F).

1. _____ Gamma rays are less penetrating than X rays.
2. _____ A cloud chamber is used to measure the paths made by radioactive particles.
3. _____ Gamma rays are not affected by magnets.
4. _____ Radioactive elements decay into other elements.
5. _____ Carbon 14 can be used to date rocks 4.6 billion years old.

APPLYING WHAT YOU LEARNED

1. Describe the various uses of radioactive materials in medicine, biology, chemistry, and physics.
2. In the library look up some information about how Marie and Pierre Curie discovered radium.
3. Look up some of the harmful effects of radiation on plants and animals.

UNIT REVIEW

1. Originally the elements were arranged in order of increasing atomic masses. Today they are arranged according to their assigned atomic numbers. Study the first ninety-two elements listed in the periodic table. In which cases do the masses not increase with the order of the atomic numbers? Explain why this is so.
2. Which letter is used most often as the first letter of a chemical symbol? In what way is the symbol a part of the actual name of the element? How are the symbols derived for the unusual cases?
3. Identify each of the following reactions as synthesis, decomposition, single replacement, or double replacement. Write each equation on a sheet of paper and balance the number of atoms.
   - **a.** $Na(s) + O_2(g) \longrightarrow Na_2O(s)$
   - **b.** $Zn(s) + HCl(aq) \longrightarrow ZnCl_2(aq) + H_2(g)$
   - **c.** $CuSO_4(aq) + KOH(aq) \longrightarrow Cu(OH)_2(aq) + K_2SO_4(aq)$
   - **d.** $C_6H_{12}O_6(s) \longrightarrow C(s) + H_2O(l)$
   - **e.** $H_2SO_4(aq) + NaCl(s) \longrightarrow HCl(g) + Na_2SO_4(aq)$
   - **f.** $KClO_3(s) \longrightarrow KCl(s) + O_2(g)$
   - **g.** $H_2O_2(aq) \longrightarrow H_2O(l) + O_2(g)$
4. Copy the following table and fill in the missing information.

ELEMENT'S NAME	ELEMENT'S SYMBOL	NUMBER OF			ATOMIC MASS	ATOMIC NUMBER
		PROTONS	NEUTRONS	ELECTRONS		
	P					
		20				
				35		
						48
	Au					
tungsten						
		50				
oxygen						

Careers

When a scientific discovery is announced, we usually hear of one or perhaps a few people involved in the discovery. Actually, however, most scientific discoveries involve a much larger group of people. The person or persons who receive the credit probably did much of the original thinking on the project. However, other scientists, technicians, librarians, lawyers, and even students were most likely involved in the actual research.

Most discoveries are the result of extensive experiments carried out by many scientists. Lab technicians with technical-school training or even simply on-the-job training do much of the routine laboratory work. These technicians are also involved in the testing programs that verify results. Sometimes technicians work directly with a senior scientist in designing experiments or determining what new equipment might be needed for a project. Other technicians and specialists are needed to maintain and repair the many types of scientific equipment being used.

Outside the laboratory, librarians search the literature for reports about research related to a project. These people usually have a master's degree in library science and an undergraduate degree in a scientific field.

Once enough data is gathered, specialists are needed to program a computer to analyze the information. Most testing accumulates large amounts of data. This data is easier to handle with the aid of a computer. Although many programmers and computer operators are taught by the company they work for, many are college graduates with a major, or specialization, in the scientific field being studied.

Patent lawyers check all related patents to be sure the discovery is original. These attorneys are college graduates who also have a law degree. Most of the time a patent lawyer will have a good background in a scientific field. These lawyers are vital to the protection of the rights of a scientist whose ideas led to a discovery.

If a discovery has an immediate, practical application, such as a new medical product, it will be put into full-scale production. This task falls to the engineers. An engineer has a college education and usually a graduate degree. Technicians with a high-school education are usually involved in the production process.

After a successful product is available, the marketing group takes over. Advertising and sales are the responsibility of this group. If you like meeting people and traveling, you might consider scientific marketing as a job.

There are many other types of jobs associated with a new discovery. If you want to be part of this type of work, try to get involved with science now.

The work of a computer programmer is important in the collection, storage, and analysis of data.

Research

Roger Billings of Provo, Utah, has created the Billings Energy Corporation. Billings feels that the use of hydrogen as a fuel is one possible answer to our future energy needs. At this time the United States is using about 90 billion (9×10^{10}) cubic meters of hydrogen annually. Most of this hydrogen is produced from natural gas. Billings believes that hydrogen can be obtained from our most abundant fossil fuel—coal. He suggests converting the coal to hydrogen rather than gasoline. The conversion of coal to hydrogen rather than gasoline appears to be more efficient, according to current technology.

There are some good reasons for using hydrogen as a fuel. It can replace other fuels now in use. Natural gas could be replaced by hydrogen, with only minor difficulties. The hydrogen gas could be transported through existing natural-gas lines. Automobiles could be designed to use hydrogen for fuel. Hydrogen would not cause the severe pollution produced by current internal-combustion engine fuels. Hydrogen burns in an oxygen environment to form water vapor, which is returned to the atmosphere. According to Billings, an engine fueled by hydrogen produces only about 0.5 percent of the oxides of nitrogen found in normal engine exhaust.

Scientists have known of hydrogen's potential as a fuel for nearly a century. However, technology has moved slowly in using hydrogen as a possible new fuel source. This is due to some of the problems connected with the use of hydrogen. One problem is the question of storage safety. Perhaps you know about the German airship *Hindenburg,* which used hydrogen gas for buoyancy. The *Hindenburg* was destroyed in a flaming tragedy caused when the hydrogen ignited. The fire hazard of hydrogen is always present. Today, however, hydrogen can be stored in a rather safe powdered form. This is accomplished by the use of compounds called *metal hydrides,* which act as hydrogen sponges. The metal hydride absorbs the hydrogen, stores it, and releases it when properly heated. These sponges have an indefinite lifetime. Such metal hydrides are currently being used by the Public Service Electric and Gas Company of New Jersey to store energy. Hydrogen is generated by electrolysis and stored during low demand periods. It is then released to help produce electricity during peak periods. The Billings Energy Corporation is using a similar metal hydride to store hydrogen in automobiles converted to hydrogen fuel use.

The idea of using hydrogen as a fuel came to Roger Billings in the ninth grade. His science teacher did a demonstration of the reaction of hydrogen and oxygen to produce water plus energy. Keep your eyes and ears open for information that may start you on your scientific way.

The discovery of hydrogen sponges aided in the development of hydrogen as a safe fuel.

UNIT FOUR

FORCES, MOTION, ENERGY

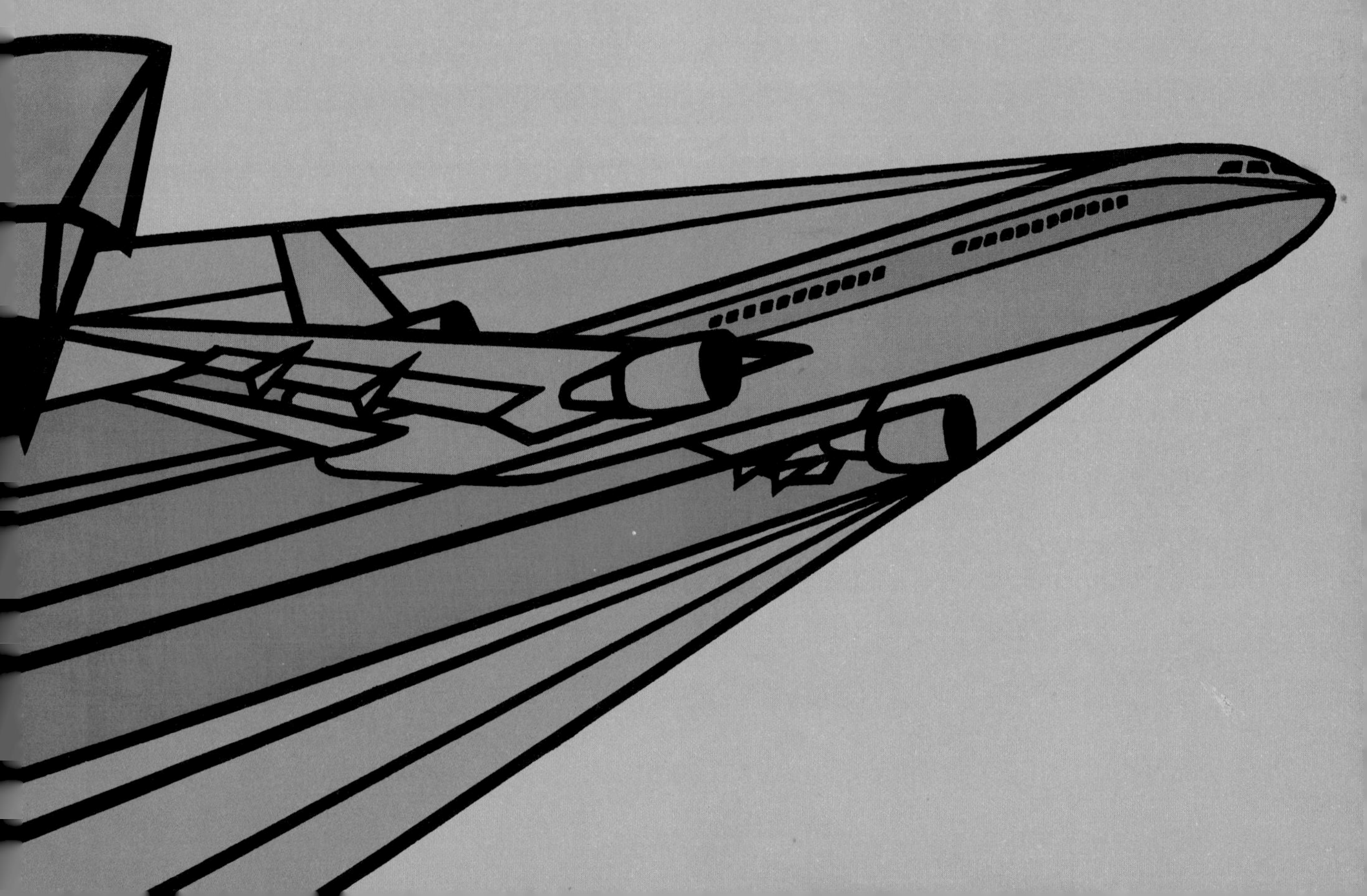

A watch is a system. The gears are parts of this system. They work together in making the system function.

10

Systems Can Be Analyzed

You have been working with **systems** all your life. But what are systems? Systems are groups of objects that work together. One example of a system is a dry cell, a bulb, wires, and a battery holder. These are connected together so that the bulb lights.

Systems can be composed of any number of objects. People make up their own systems out of useful objects. Some systems are very large. The universe is such a system. Your classroom is also a large system. If the system is too large, it is difficult to keep track of all the objects in the system. It is easier to analyze a system when it is composed of a small number of objects.

Force and Friction

What is a force?

A **force** is something that can make things move. When you drag an object across a table you are using a force. However, things do not always move when a force is applied. If you push on a brick wall it will not move.

Forces are measured by how much they can move things. The stretching of a piece of metal is one way to measure force. A spring scale measures force in this way. Force is measured in units called **newtons** (nü'tənz). A newton (N) is determined by the degree to which a piece of metal, such as a spring scale, is bent or stretched.

Forces are pushes and pulls. In a football game forces act against each other.

Sometimes friction is useful. To move this car in the snow, some friction is necessary.

When objects are in contact or are moving across each other there is a force between them. This contact force is called **friction** (frik'shən). Friction is a force that opposes motion between two objects in contact. Sometimes two objects are in contact but are not moving. The friction between them is **static friction**. When one object is moving across another the friction is called **sliding friction**. The force of sliding friction is usually less than the force of static friction. The amount of friction between two surfaces depends on several things. The weight at the surfaces in contact is important. The greater the weight, the greater the friction. The kinds of surfaces in contact also affect the force of friction. The smoother the surfaces, the less friction there is. Sometimes friction can be reduced by placing a lubricating material between the contacting surfaces. This is why oil is used to lubricate moving parts in many machines.

What is friction?

How can friction be reduced?

Activity 28 Friction in a Force System

PURPOSE

To determine the force needed to overcome friction in a simple force system

MATERIALS

5 wooden blocks of the same size, one with an eye hook attached
String
Spring scale, calibrated in newtons

DO THIS

A. Prepare a data table like Table 1.

B. Tie one end of the string to the eye hook in the block. Tie the other end to the hook on the spring scale.

C. Use the spring scale to pull the block at a steady speed across the floor. Be sure to pull parallel to the floor. Read the spring scale while the block is in motion. Record the reading in Table 1.

D. Repeat step **C** using 2, 3, 4, and 5 stacked blocks.

TABLE 1 • Force Measurements

NUMBER OF BLOCKS	FORCE (N)
1	
2	
3	
4	
5	

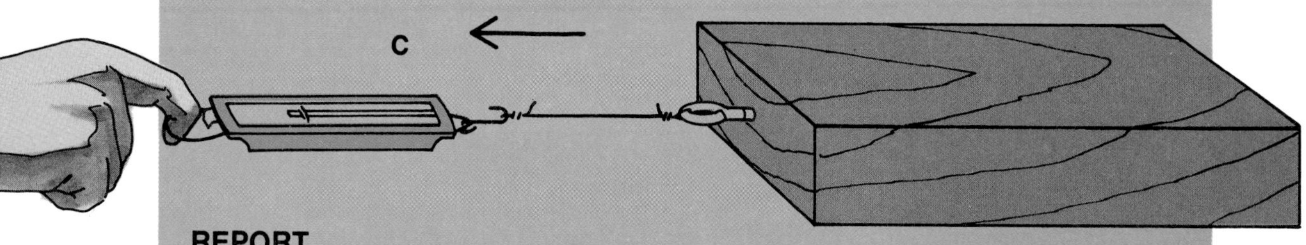

REPORT

1. Graph your data.

2. How does the force needed to move the blocks change as the number of blocks increases?

3. Predict from your graph how much force would be needed to move 6 blocks across the floor.

Activity 29 Force and Mass

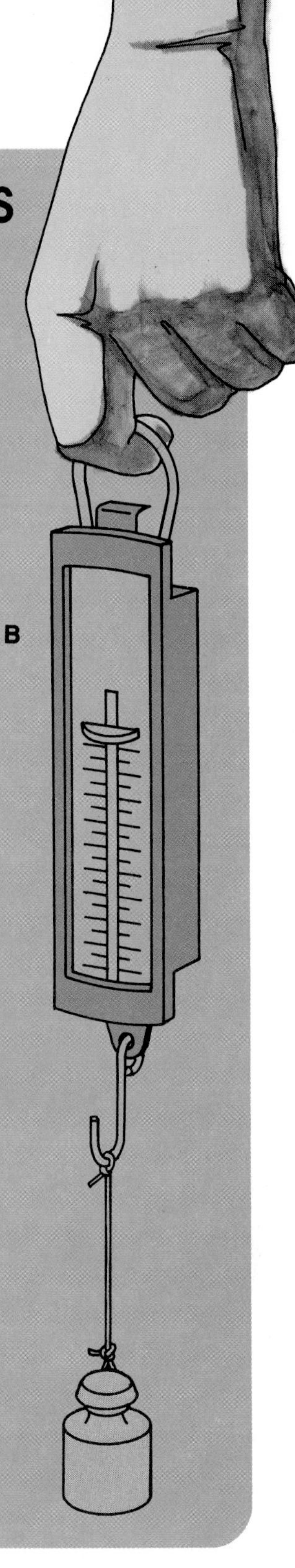

PURPOSE

To determine how force is related to mass

MATERIALS

Spring scale, calibrated in newtons
Set of metric masses
String

DO THIS

A. Prepare a data table like Table 1.

TABLE 1 • Force (Weight) Measurements

MASS	WEIGHT (N)
50 g	
100 g	
200 g	
1000 g	

B. Using a spring scale, measure and record the weight of each mass listed in Table 1. Hang the masses from the spring scale with string.

REPORT

1. List the components, or parts, of the weighing system.

2. Construct a line graph of your data. Plot weight along the vertical axis and mass along the horizontal axis.

Force and Mass

You are probably familiar with measuring the amount of an object by its **mass**. This measure is expressed in grams or kilograms. Some type of balance (not a spring scale) is used to determine the mass of an object.

Many different balances are used in making scientific measurements. This balance is called a triple beam balance.

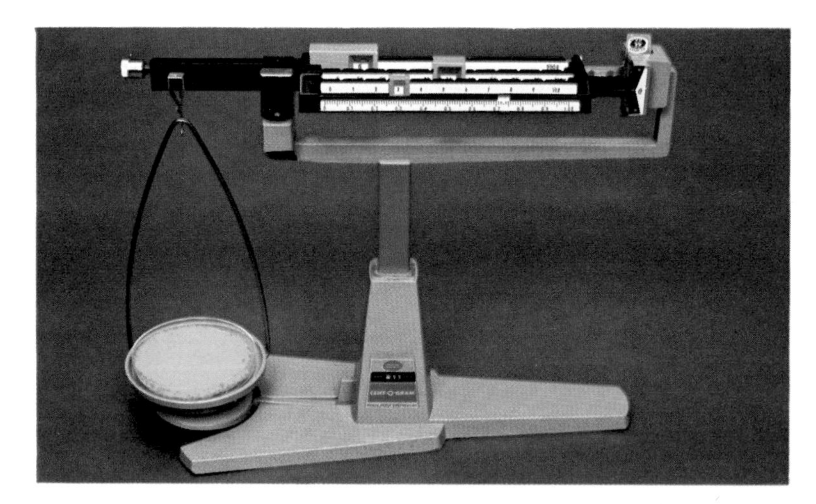

The mass of the astronaut is the same on the moon as on the earth. However, the moon's gravitational force is only about 0.17 of what the gravitational force is on the earth. Therefore the astronaut's weight on the moon is only about 0.17 as much as it is on the earth.

Mass and force are different. Mass is related to the amount of material in an object. Force is a push or a pull. An object with a larger mass needs a large force to move it.

Suppose you are holding an object in your hand. If it feels light it has a small amount of mass. If the object feels heavy it has a large amount of mass.

The feeling of heaviness is due to the force of gravity. This force is called **weight**. Weight is measured by an instrument that measures force. It seems that force and mass are related in some way. You investigated that relationship in Activities 28 and 29.

In Activity 29 you probably found that 1 kg weighs 9.8 N. Due to the earth's gravitational field, this is true to the nearest tenth of a newton any place on the earth's surface.

Systems Can Help Get Things Done

Certain workers are frequently faced with the problem of lifting heavy crates or packages. Suppose a worker has to move a 1200 N crate the height of 1 m into a truck. The problem is solved when a ramp is used to help move the crate up into the truck. Using a ramp seems to make things easier to lift. What are the components of the ramp system? You will investigate this system in Activity 30.

What does the word *easier* really mean? Does it mean "the amount of force needed" or "the distance the cart moves"? Suppose it means "the amount of force." Then it is *easier* to move the cart by pulling it up the ramp. But if *easier* refers to the distance moved, it is *easier* to lift the cart straight up.

Moving stairs are systems that help get work done. These stairs are types of ramps.

Activity 30 Using a Ramp

PURPOSE

To compare the force needed to lift an object straight up with the force needed to move the object up a ramp

MATERIALS

Board, about 1 m in length
Spring scale, calibrated in newtons
Cart
Meterstick
String

DO THIS

A. Attach the cart to the spring scale with string. Measure and record the force needed to lift the cart straight up.

B. Make a ramp by propping one end of the board as shown. Elevate the propped end of the board about 30 cm.

C. Place the cart at the lower end of the ramp. Pull the cart up the ramp with the spring scale. Pull parallel to the ramp and at a steady speed. Measure and record the force needed to move the cart.

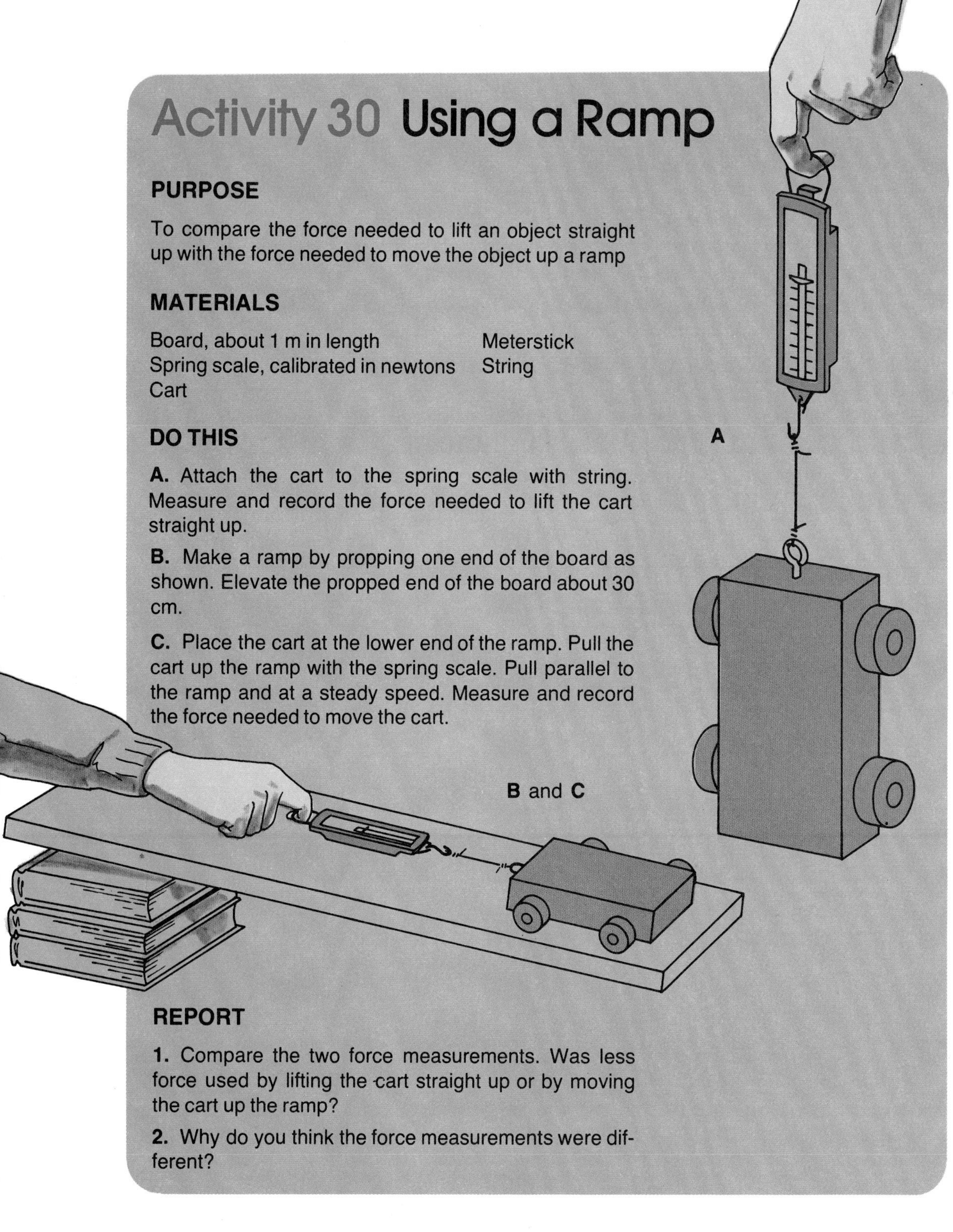

REPORT

1. Compare the two force measurements. Was less force used by lifting the cart straight up or by moving the cart up the ramp?

2. Why do you think the force measurements were different?

Work

When a force is used to move an object a certain distance, **work** is being done. The amount of work (W) being done can be determined by multiplying the force (F) used by the distance (d) the object is moved. In other words, work equals force times distance.

What is work?

Suppose the cart in Activity 30 weighed 2.5 N. It was lifted 0.3 m. How much work was done?

Work equals force times distance
$W = F \times d$
$W = 2.5 \text{ N} \times 0.3 \text{ m}$
$W = 0.75$ newton meters

Notice that newtons are multiplied by meters. The unit of work is the newton meter (N·m). How much work would be done in lifting the cart the height of the ramp? To determine this the height of the ramp must first be measured. The height of the ramp will be multiplied by the weight of the cart. Remember, the height must be in meters and the weight must be in newtons.

Work equals force times distance
Work equals weight of cart times height of ramp
$W = F \times d$

The amount of work done by lifting the cart straight up can be compared with the amount done by pulling the cart up the ramp. Suppose the spring scale registered 0.7 N when the cart was supported from it. The ramp measured 1.1 m. To pull the cart up the ramp the following work was done.

Work equals force times distance
$W = F \times d$
$W = 0.7 \text{ N} \times 1.1 \text{ m}$
$W = 0.77 \text{ N} \cdot \text{m}$

The Lever, Another System

What is a lever?

Name three kinds of levers.

The use of a ramp enables you to lift objects using less force. There are other systems that make it easier to do work. The **lever** (lev'ər) is one such system.

You may already know that when you use a lever there is a relationship between distance and force. Now you will explore some other things that can be done with a lever.

A lever is a simple machine. Generally, a lever is any kind of a bar or rod that does not bend. It turns on a point called a **fulcrum** (ful'krəm). There are several kinds of levers. One type is called the **first class lever**. The first class lever consists of the fulcrum located between two forces. The force put into the system is called the **effort**. The force that must be overcome is called the **resistance** (ri zis'təns). For example, if you wanted to use a lever to move a large rock, the rock would be the resistance. A simple seesaw is an example of a first class lever.

A **second class lever** has the resistance located between the effort and the fulcrum. A nutcracker is a second class lever. A **third class lever** has the effort located between the resistance and the fulcrum. The forearm is an example of a third class lever. A shovel is another example of a third class lever.

Shown here are examples of the three classes of levers. The hammer (left) is a first class lever. The nutcracker (center) is a second class lever. The ice tongs (right) are a third class lever.

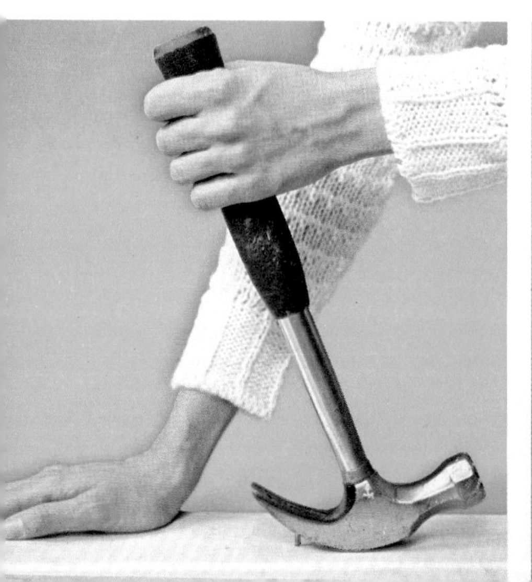

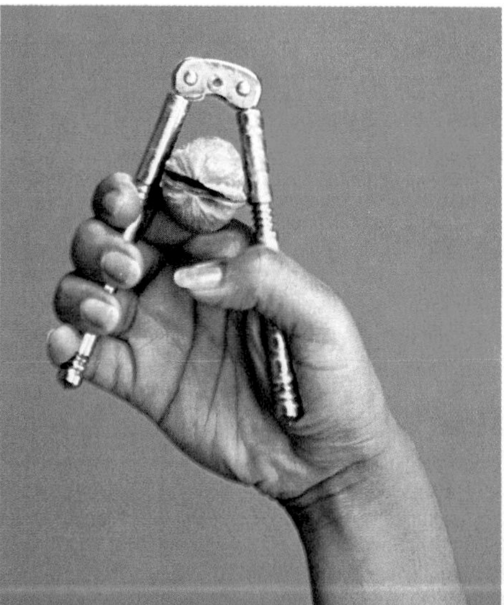

Activity 31 A Lever System

PURPOSE

To explore the relationship between force and distance in one type of lever

MATERIALS

500-g mass	Meterstick lever
String	Lever support
Scissors	Spring scale calibrated in newtons

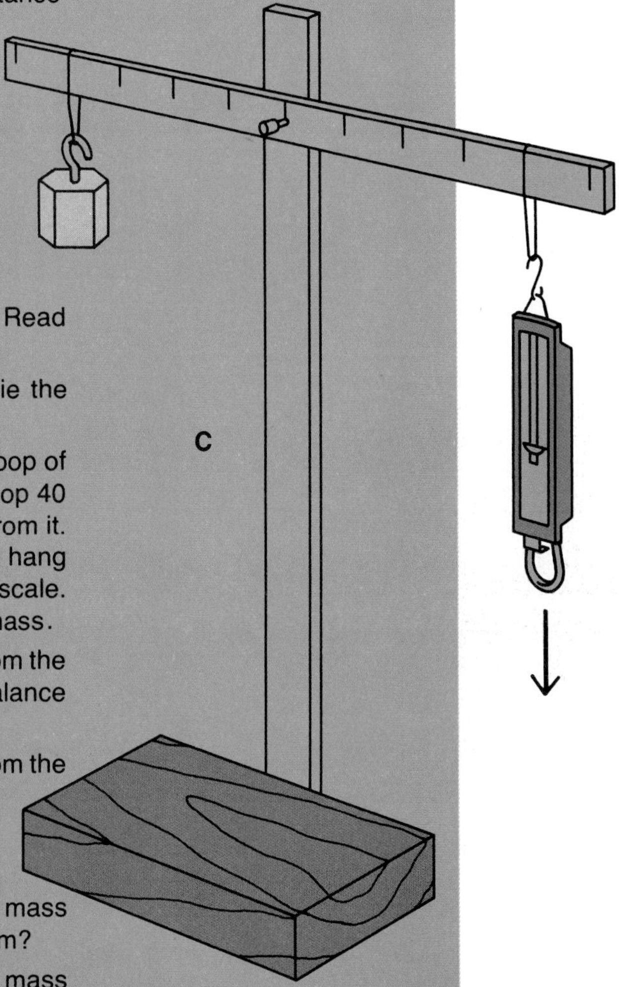

DO THIS

A. Hang the 500-g mass from the spring scale. Read and record the force registered on the scale.

B. Cut two pieces of string 15 cm in length. Tie the string to make two loops.

C. Set up the lever system as shown. Slip one loop of string onto the lever from each end. Move one loop 40 cm from the fulcrum and hang the 500-g mass from it. Move the other loop 40 cm from the fulcrum and hang the spring scale from it. Pull down on the spring scale. Record the force needed to balance the 500-g mass.

D. Move the loop with the spring scale 30 cm from the fulcrum. Read and record the force needed to balance the 500-g mass.

E. Repeat step D with the spring scale 20 cm from the fulcrum.

C

REPORT

1. What force was needed to balance the 500-g mass when the force was applied 40 cm from the fulcrum?

2. What force was needed to balance the 500-g mass when the force was applied 30 cm from the fulcrum?

3. What force was needed to balance the 500-g mass when the force was applied 20 cm from the fulcrum?

4. Where would you apply force on the lever so that the least force possible balances the 500-g mass?

EXCURSION 7

In Excursion 7, "Exploring Circles," you can prove an interesting relationship that exists between the circumference and the diameter of a circle.

Pulleys

You may have found that you can lift a greater load if several people help share the weight. Suppose four people lift a box that weighs 1000 N. Each person lifts 250 N—one fourth the weight of the box. Thus four people can lift the box more easily than one person can. The same result can be obtained if one person uses a **pulley** (pu̇l′ē) system to lift the box. Activity 32 may help you understand how a pulley system can make your work easier.

Certain disks or wheels are called pulleys. Pulleys are found in many machines. They are often connected to each other by belts or chains. Some pulleys have teeth that interlock with notches of other pulleys. The teeth and notches take the place of a belt or chain. These pulleys are called **gears**. Gears are important in many machines, such as automobiles, typewriters, and bicycles. You will investigate the operation of gears in Activity 33.

Gears are as important to the operation of the can opener (left) and the pencil sharpener (right) as they are to the operation of more complicated machines.

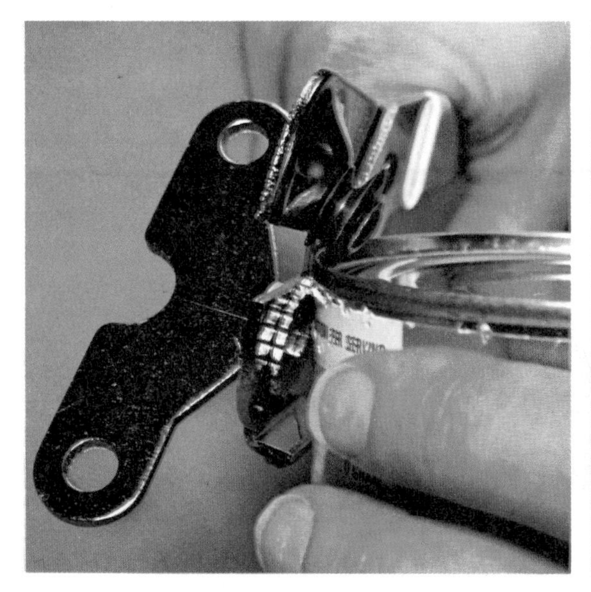

Activity 32 A Pulley System

PURPOSE

To investigate the operation of a pulley system

MATERIALS

Pulley support
2 pulleys of the same kind and size
Spring scale calibrated in newtons
Meterstick
250-g mass
String
2 paper clips

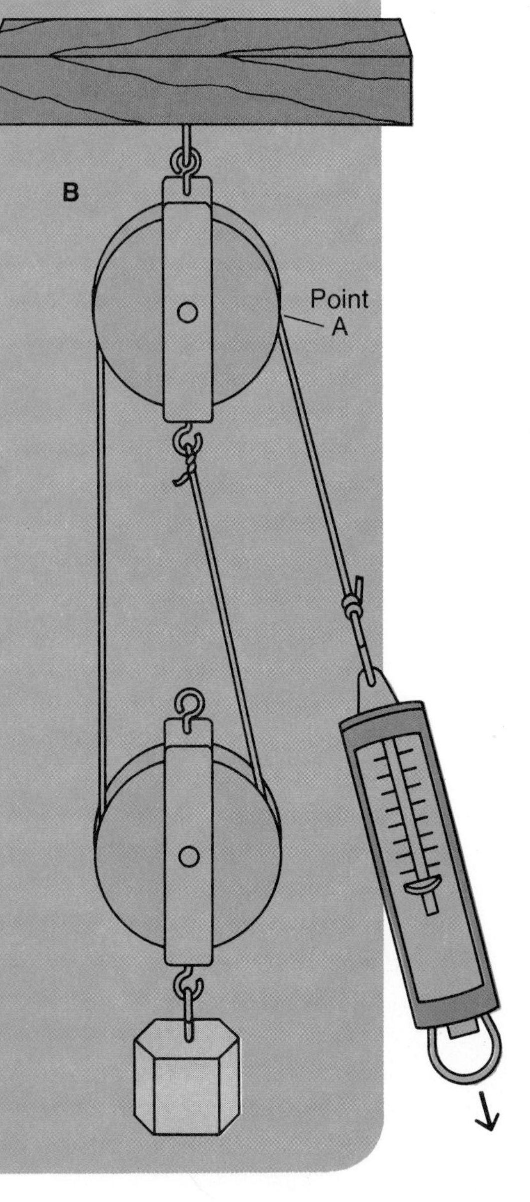

DO THIS

A. Hang the 250-g mass from a pulley, then hang the pulley from the spring scale. Read and record the force.

B. Set up the pulley system as shown.

C. Read and record the force when the spring scale is used to support the moveable pulley and the 250-g mass. As you support the moveable pulley and mass, have your partner put a paper clip on the string at point A.

D. Have your partner hold a meterstick vertically alongside the mass. Then pull the spring scale until the mass is raised 10 cm. Hold the scale steady while your partner places another paper clip on the string at point A. Measure the distance between the two paper clips. This is the distance you pulled the string to raise the mass 10 cm.

REPORT

1. Was more force needed to support the mass with, or without, the pulley system? How much more?

2. Was the distance you pulled the string greater, or less, than the distance the mass was raised? How many times greater, or less?

3. How much work was done using the pulley system to raise the mass 10 cm?

4. How much work was done to raise the mass 10 cm without using the pulley system?

Activity 33 A Gear System

PURPOSE

To investigate the operation of a gear system

Materials

2 pieces corrugated cardboard,
each about 30 cm × 30 cm
Scissors
3 roofing nails
String
Drawing compass
Masking tape
Metric ruler

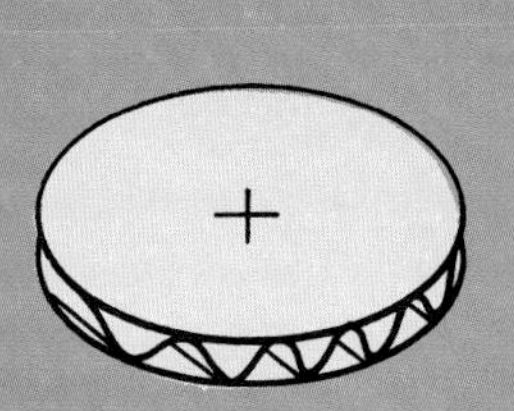

C

DO THIS

A. Use the compass to draw two circles of different diameters. One circle should have a diameter at least one third larger than that of the other circle. Draw both circles on the same piece of cardboard.

B. Cut out the cardboard disks with the scissors.

C. Make a groove along the circumference of each disk. Do this by scoring the edge of the cardboard with the pointed end of a nail.

D. Place the two disks about 9 cm apart on the second piece of cardboard. Push the point of the drawing compass through both pieces of cardboard at the exact center of each disk. Then remove the disks.

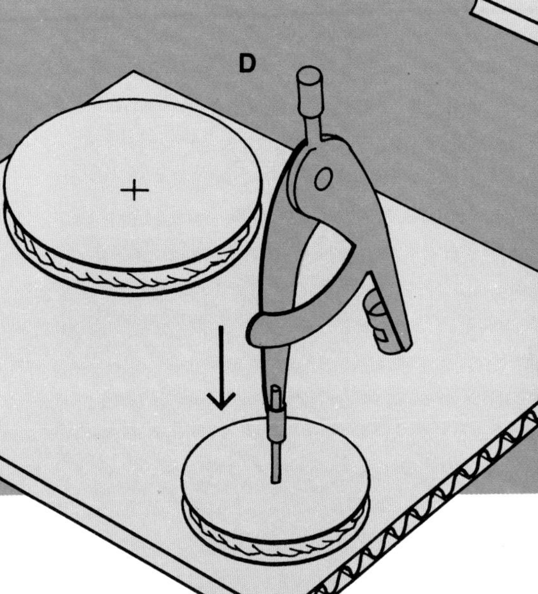

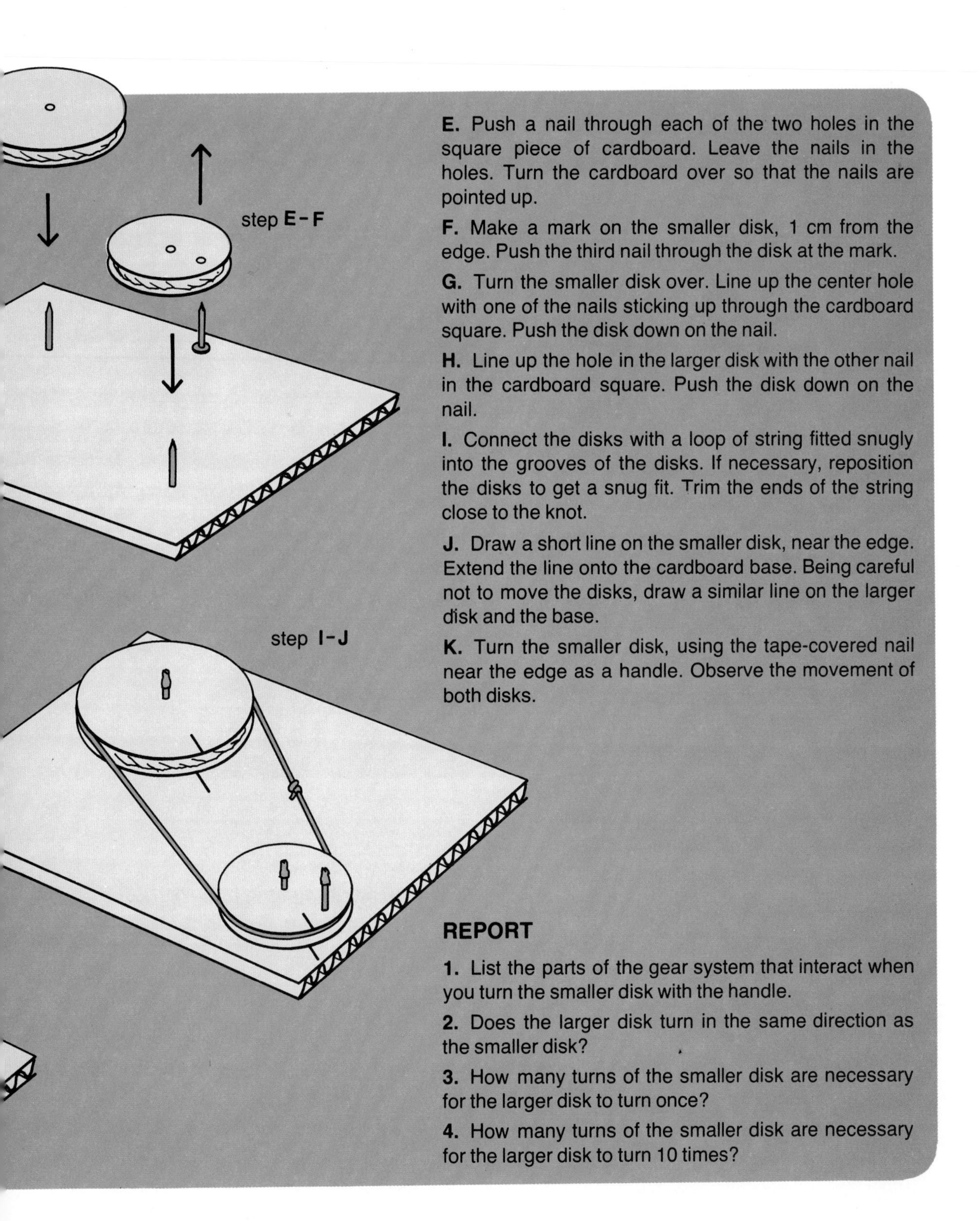

E. Push a nail through each of the two holes in the square piece of cardboard. Leave the nails in the holes. Turn the cardboard over so that the nails are pointed up.

F. Make a mark on the smaller disk, 1 cm from the edge. Push the third nail through the disk at the mark.

G. Turn the smaller disk over. Line up the center hole with one of the nails sticking up through the cardboard square. Push the disk down on the nail.

H. Line up the hole in the larger disk with the other nail in the cardboard square. Push the disk down on the nail.

I. Connect the disks with a loop of string fitted snugly into the grooves of the disks. If necessary, reposition the disks to get a snug fit. Trim the ends of the string close to the knot.

J. Draw a short line on the smaller disk, near the edge. Extend the line onto the cardboard base. Being careful not to move the disks, draw a similar line on the larger disk and the base.

K. Turn the smaller disk, using the tape-covered nail near the edge as a handle. Observe the movement of both disks.

REPORT

1. List the parts of the gear system that interact when you turn the smaller disk with the handle.

2. Does the larger disk turn in the same direction as the smaller disk?

3. How many turns of the smaller disk are necessary for the larger disk to turn once?

4. How many turns of the smaller disk are necessary for the larger disk to turn 10 times?

The pulley system on these cranes makes it easier to do work. Large objects can be moved quickly and with relative ease.

SCIENCE WORDS

system
force
friction
static friction
sliding friction
mass
weight
work
lever
fulcrum
first class lever
effort
resistance
second class lever
third class lever
pulley
gears

SUMMARY To make things move, a force must be used. A force is a push or a pull. Sometimes when a force is applied, two objects come in contact with one another. A force that opposes the motion of two objects is called friction. Friction can be reduced by using a lubricating material. The larger the mass of the object, the greater the force needed to move it. The force of gravity on a mass is called weight. The unit of force used to measure weight is the newton. When a force is used to move an object, work is being done. Work can be made easier by using machines such as ramps, pulleys and gears, and levers. The amount of work can be determined by multiplying force times distance.

REVIEW QUESTIONS

Fill in the blanks with the correct terms.

1. The friction between two objects that are in contact but are not moving is called ____________ friction.
2. Disks and wheels are types of ____________.
3. A nutcracker is a kind of ____________.
4. A ____________ is a push or a pull.
5. Friction between one object sliding across another is ____________ friction.

APPLYING WHAT YOU LEARNED

1. How does a pulley system help you do work?
2. An object weighing 7 N was lifted a distance of 4 m. How much work was done?
3. An object was pushed up a ramp with a force of 30 N. If the ramp was 15 m long, how much work was done?
4. An object weighs 40 N. What is its mass?
5. Four students lift a crate weighing 1000 N to a height of 1 m. One student is at each corner of the crate. How much work does each student do?

This corkscrew roller coaster is a system. When in operation this system demonstrates the laws of motion, velocity, inertia, and energy.

Systems Operate Predictably

In the last chapter you learned to analyze systems. Now you can use this skill to predict what systems will do. People frequently make predictions. Sometimes they make them without trying to analyze a situation. Predictions can be based on analysis or on feelings. Those based on a careful analysis of a system are much more likely to be correct than predictions based on feelings. How often have you made a hasty judgment? It is usually better to take the time required to base your prediction on careful analysis.

Pendulums

You have probably used a **pendulum** (pen′jə ləm) sometime in your life. If you haven't used one, you have probably seen one or more. Some types of clocks have pendulums. A plumb line, an instrument used by surveyors and plumbers, is a type of pendulum. Playground swings are also pendulums.

Pendulums operate in a series of swings. The time it takes to complete one back-and-forth swing of a pendulum is called a **period.** Activity 34 will help you understand how a pendulum works. Also, you will determine the period of the pendulum.

Some clocks have pendulums. The grandfather clock (right) depends on the swing of the pendulum to keep accurate time. The Foucault pendulum (left) appears to change the direction of its swing as it responds to gravity and the rotation on the earth.

What is the time it takes to complete one back-and-forth movement of a pendulum called?

Activity 34 A Pendulum System

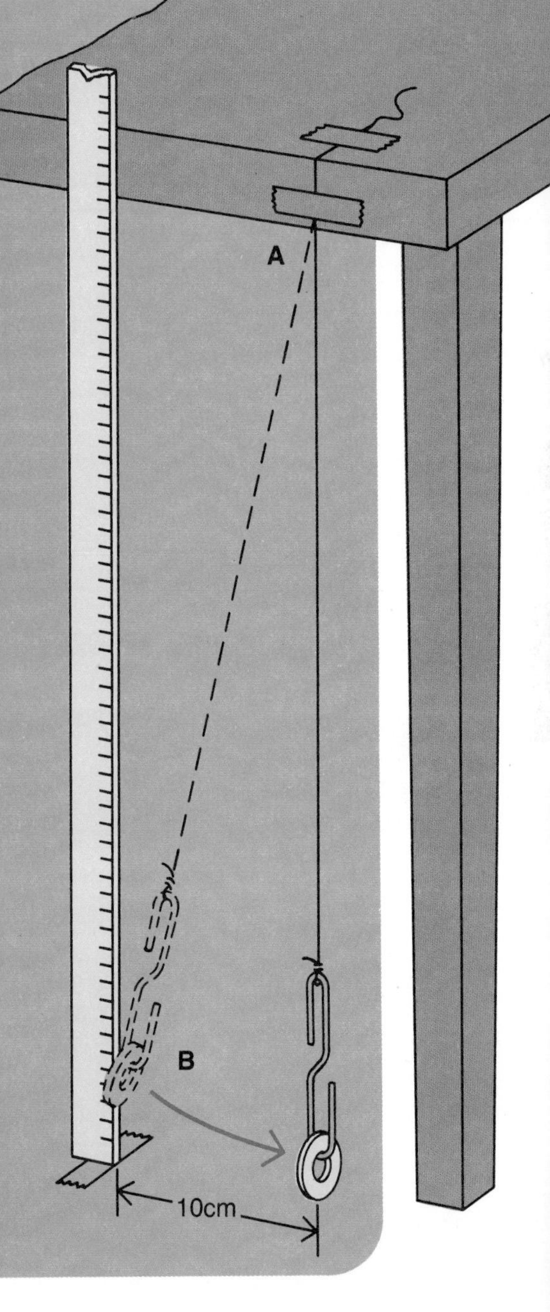

PURPOSE

To determine the relationship between the mass of a pendulum and the pendulum's period

MATERIALS

Meterstick	3 metal washers of equal mass
String	Clock or watch with a second hand
Masking tape	Scissors
Paper clip	

DO THIS

A. Bend a paper clip into an S. Tie a 50-cm length of string to the clip. Then set up the pendulum as shown.

B. Measure 10 cm along the floor from a point directly underneath the pendulum. Place a small piece of tape at the 10-cm mark. Hold the meterstick on the mark. Set the pendulum in motion by pulling the washer to the side until it touches the meterstick, then release it. At the same time remove the meterstick. Observe the movement of the pendulum.

C. Now work with a partner. Set the pendulum in motion as described in step **B** and count out loud 50 periods. Your partner should measure in seconds the time for 50 periods. Record the time.

D. Repeat step **C** with two washers and then with three washers.

REPORT

1. What are the parts of the pendulum system?

2. Calculate the period of the pendulum when the mass is one, two, and three washers. Use the following formula.

$$\text{Period} = \frac{\text{Number of seconds}}{\text{Number of periods}}$$

3. Round off each period to the nearer tenth of a second. Does the mass (number of washers) affect the period of the pendulum? Explain your answer.

The data from Activity 34 is of limited value. What could you do to make the data more useful? How could you use the data to predict how other pendulum systems would operate?

Suppose you had found the period of the pendulum to be 0.70 second (s). The period remained the same when you changed the mass at the end of the pendulum from one to two to three washers. Can you predict from this data what the period would be if a mass of one and one-half washers were used? If a mass of five washers were used? You could make both predictions if the data were presented as shown in Figure 11–1.

FIGURE 11–1

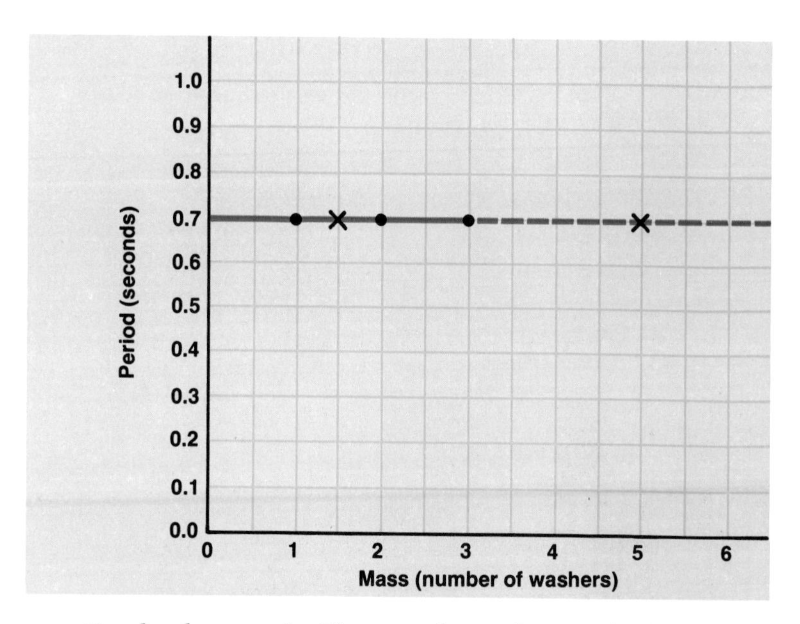

Study the graph. The graph is a horizontal straight line. This resulted because the period of the pendulum remained about the same for masses of one, two, and three washers. Notice that there are three known data points. These are indicated by dots. To predict the period for a mass of one and one-half washers you must read the graph midway between the known data points for one washer and two washers. Since the graph is a horizontal straight line between these data points, the predicted period would be the same as the measured periods. The data point for the predicted period is indicated by an X in Figure 11–1. Predicting in this manner is called **interpolation** (in tėr pə lā'shən). You interpolate whenever you make a prediction between two known data points.

What is interpolation?

Now think about the period of the pendulum when the mass is five washers. A mass of five washers falls outside, or beyond, the known data. Therefore the graph must be extended to predict the pendulum's period for that mass. Remember, the graph of the known data is a horizontal straight line. So the extension of the graph must also be a horizontal straight line. The extension of the graph is indicated by the dashed line in Figure 11–1. The point for the predicted period is indicated by an X. Reading the graph, the predicted period for the pendulum with a mass of five washers is the same as the

Many types of data can be graphed. Sales figures can be displayed on a graph for easier interpretation. Interpolations can be made, using the graphed data.

What is extrapolation?

measured periods—0.70 s. Predicting in this manner is called **extrapolation** (ek strap ə lā′shən). You extrapolate when you make a prediction outside, or beyond, your data. Predictions made by extrapolation are usually less accurate than those made by interpolation.

Figure 11–2 shows another straight-line graph. The known data points are indicated by dots. Study the graph. Interpolate the volume when the mass is 1 kg. What is the mass when the volume is 0.1 L?

Now extrapolate using the dashed portion of the graph. What would be the volume when the mass is 5 kg? What would be the mass when the volume is 1 L?

FIGURE 11–2

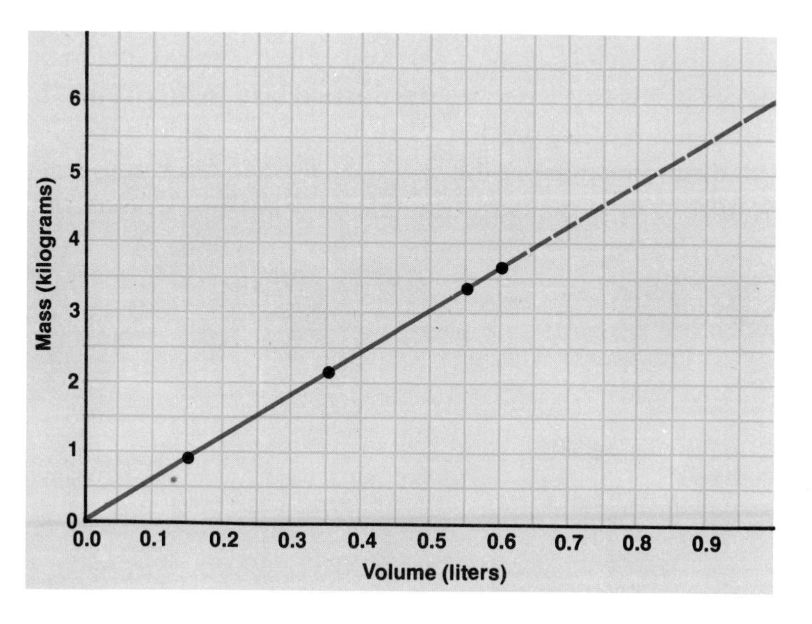

You can interpolate and extrapolate from a curved-line graph. Study the graph in Figure 11–3. The data points for this graph are deliberately not shown. First interpolate to find the length when the time is 1 s. Then interpolate to find the time when the length is 40 cm. Now extrapolate. Find the time when the length is 90 cm. Extrapolate again to find the length when the time is 1.75 s.

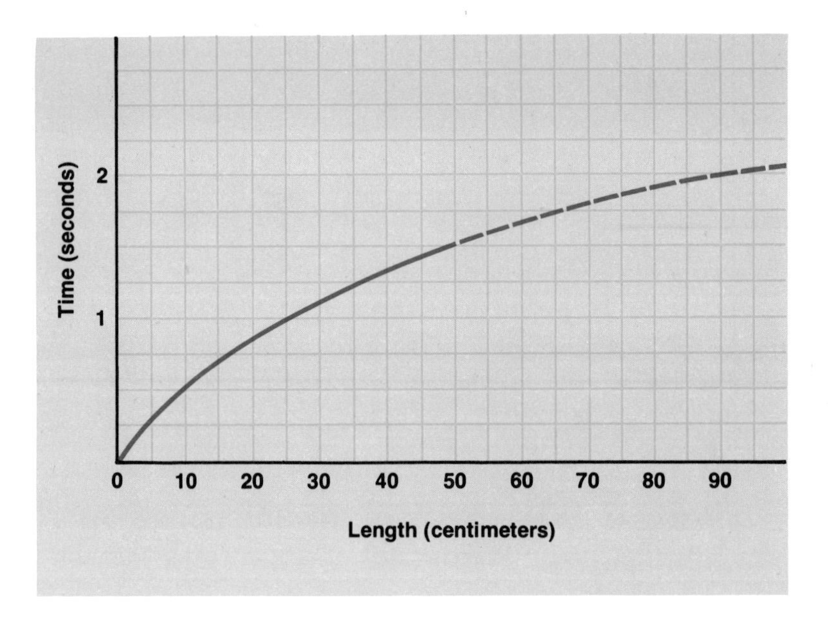

FIGURE 11–3

A curved-line graph is harder to draw than a straight-line graph. This is especially true when you must extend a curved-line graph to extrapolate. For example, consider the following data.

Length (cm)	*Time* (s)
180	2.60
170	2.62
160	2.54
153	2.45
122	2.20
70	1.68
40	1.26
5	0.45

The graph of this data is shown by the solid line in Figure 11–4. The dashed lines show how the graph might be extended for extrapolation. But which dashed line shows the proper curve for the graph? It is easier to extrapolate if the graph is a straight line. How can a curved line be changed to a straight line? This can be

FIGURE 11–4

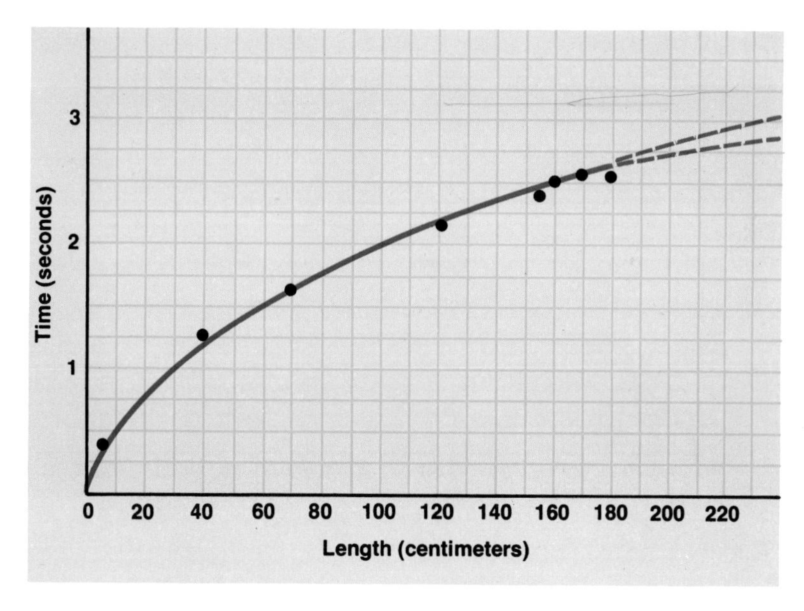

done mathematically by changing time (t) to time squared (t^2). Carrying out the necessary multiplications, the data would look like this.

Length (cm)	*Time* (s)	*Time*^{2} ($s \times s = s^2$)
180	2.60	$2.60 \times 2.60 = 6.76$
170	2.62	$2.62 \times 2.62 = 6.86$
160	2.54	$2.54 \times 2.54 = 6.45$
153	2.45	$2.45 \times 2.45 = 6.00$
122	2.20	$2.20 \times 2.20 = 4.84$
70	1.68	$1.68 \times 1.68 = 2.82$
40	1.26	$1.26 \times 1.26 = 1.59$
5	0.45	$0.45 \times 0.45 = 0.20$

The graph of this data is shown in Figure 11–5. Graphing the data this way also points out a possible error in measurement. For example, the data point for time squared at a length of 180 cm does not agree with the other measurements. Why is this so? Perhaps an error was made in the measurement. Suppose the time of the 180-cm length were remeasured and found to be

2.70 s instead of 2.60 s. When 2.70 s is squared and entered on the graph, the new value agrees with the other data. This confirms that an error was made in the original measurement.

Sometimes just looking at a graph can suggest mistakes in measuring.

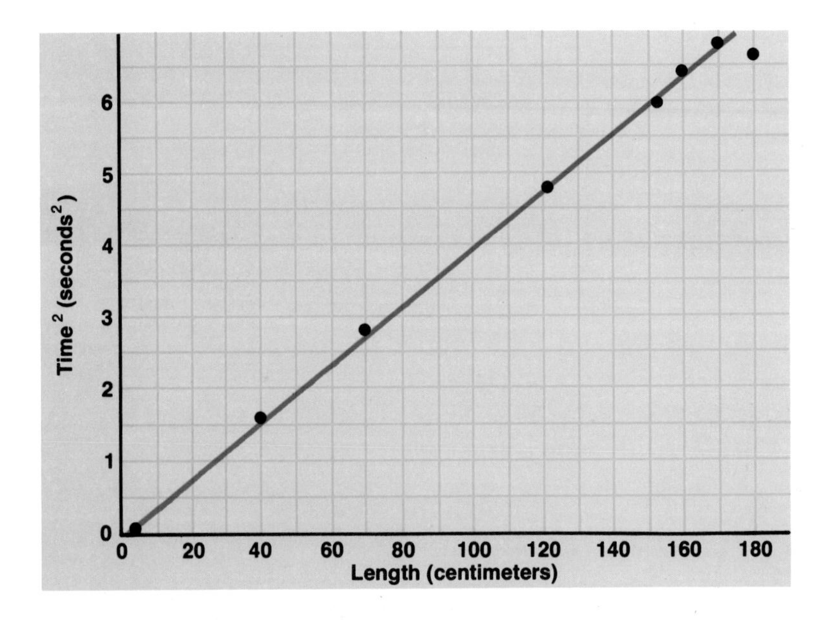

FIGURE 11–5

In Activity 34 you examined one part of the pendulum system. You were concerned only with the mass at the end of the pendulum. What about the length of the pendulum? How does changing the length affect the pendulum's period?

You probably noticed that, as the pendulum swings back and forth, the distance it travels decreases. This means that some of the energy you put into the system to start the pendulum swinging is leaving the system. Where does this energy go? Some of the energy is lost from the pendulum system in the form of heat. Much of this heat energy is the result of friction. There is friction between the pendulum and the air. There is also friction at the point where the pendulum is suspended.

Activity 35 Another Pendulum System

PURPOSE

To determine the relationship between pendulum length and period.

MATERIALS

Meterstick
Metal washer
Clock or watch with a second hand
String
Masking tape
Paper clip
Scissors

PENDULUM LENGTH	TIME FOR 50 PERIODS	PENDULUM PERIOD

TABLE 1 • Pendulum Length and Period

DO THIS

A. Set up the pendulum system as in steps **A** and **B** of Activity 34. Start with a pendulum length of at least 70 cm. Measure the length from the center of the washer to the pendulum support. Record the length in a table like Table 1.

B. Work with a partner. Set the pendulum in motion as in Activity 34. Measure and record the time for 50 periods.

C. Gather data for five different pendulum lengths. Record the length of the pendulum each time.

REPORT

1. Calculate the period for each pendulum length. Record these data in the table.

2. Construct a graph of your data. Plot the pendulum period versus the pendulum length. How does the length of a pendulum affect the pendulum's period?

3. Using the graph from question 2, predict the period for a pendulum length of exactly 10 cm. Did you interpolate or extrapolate to make this prediction?

4. Using the graph from question 2, predict the length of the pendulum when the period is one second. Did you interpolate or extrapolate to make this prediction?

Efficiency

All systems lose energy. This means that the amount of work that comes out of a system does not equal the amount of work put into the system. Systems can be compared on the basis of how efficient they are. Efficiency is the ratio of work put out to work put in. Efficiency is expressed as a percentage. Since energy is always lost, the efficiency is less than 100 percent. This relationship can be expressed as follows.

How would you describe the efficiency of a system?

$$\textit{Efficiency (\%)} = \frac{\textit{work out}}{\textit{work in}} \times 100$$

Efficiency of a Ramp System

When you studied Chapter 10 you worked with a ramp. Several measurements of force and distance are required to determine the efficiency of the ramp system. Look again at the formula for determining efficiency. Remember that work is force times distance. However, the force must act in the same direction as the movement of the object. In the ramp system, the work out (output) is the work required to lift the object the height of the ramp. The work in (input) is the work required to drag the object up the ramp.

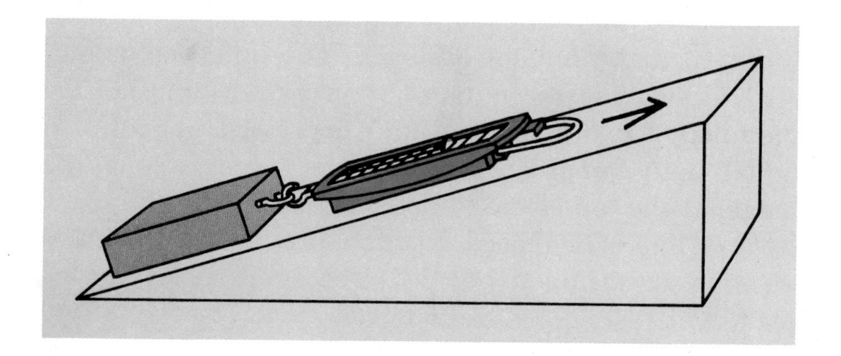

FIGURE 11–6
A simple ramp system.

Suppose the object weighs 10.0 N and the height of the ramp is 0.233 m. Output is figured as follows.

$$\begin{aligned} W_{out} &= F \times d \\ &= 10.0 \text{ N} \times 0.233 \text{ m} \\ &= 2.33 \text{ N·m} \end{aligned}$$

To determine input, the force needed to drag the object up the ramp must first be measured. The instrument used to measure this force is the spring scale. The object must be pulled at a constant speed. The length of the ramp must also be measured.

Suppose the spring scale reads 4.25 N and the ramp length is 1.185 m. Input is figured as follows.

$$\begin{aligned} W_{in} &= F \times d \\ &= 4.25 \text{ N} \times 1.185 \text{ m} \\ &= 5.04 \text{ N·m} \end{aligned}$$

What is another name for a newton meter?

A newton meter of work is also called a **joule** (J). Therefore, work out can be expressed as 2.33 J. Work in can be expressed as 5.04 J. Now that work out and work in have been determined, the efficiency of the ramp system can be determined.

$$\begin{aligned} Efficiency\ (\%) &= \frac{work\ out}{work\ in} \times 100 \\ &= \frac{2.33 \text{ J}}{5.04 \text{ J}} \times 100 \\ &= 46.2\% \end{aligned}$$

What could be used to improve the efficiency of a system?

Notice that efficiency is a pure number with no units of measurement attached. The units factor out. This is because the numerator (work out) and the denominator (work in) are both expressed in joules. A great many things affect the efficiency of a system. If the angle at the top of the ramp is increased, the efficiency of the ramp is increased. Friction also affects efficiency. Putting wheels on an object increases efficiency. Lubricants will also increase efficiency.

There is one important point to remember when figuring out efficiency. If your calculation gives you an answer greater than 100 percent, you have probably made an error. Recheck your measurement or your calculations. If a machine had an efficiency of 100 percent, it would be a perpetual motion machine.

What would a calculated efficiency of greater than 100 percent tell you?

Efficiency of a Pulley System

The efficiency of a pulley system is found in a manner similar to that used with a ramp system.

If an apparatus is set up similar to that found in Figure 11–7, it is possible to find the efficiency of the pulley system. The spring scale must be attached to the cord as shown in the figure. The weight is lifted when you pull on the spring scale. While the weight is moving, the force (F) can be found by looking at the spring scale. The work in is the product of the spring scale reading (F) and the distance (d) the cord is pulled.

$$\begin{aligned} \textit{Work in} &= \textit{force} \times \textit{distance} \\ &= \mathrm{F} \times \mathrm{d} \end{aligned}$$

The work out is just the weight of the object (w) times the distance the object was lifted (h).

$$\begin{aligned} \textit{Work out} &= \textit{weight} \times \textit{distance lifted} \\ &= \mathrm{w} \times \mathrm{h} \end{aligned}$$

Suppose a group of students used the apparatus in Figure 11–7. They pulled on the spring scale until 0.4 m of cord had been removed from the pulley apparatus (d = 0.4 m). As they were pulling, the scale showed 4 N (F = 4 N). The work in can now be calculated.

$$\begin{aligned} \textit{Work in} &= F \times d \\ &= 4\ \mathrm{N} \times 0.4\ \mathrm{m} \\ &= 1.6\ \mathrm{N{\cdot}m} = 1.6\ \mathrm{J} \end{aligned}$$

FIGURE 11–7

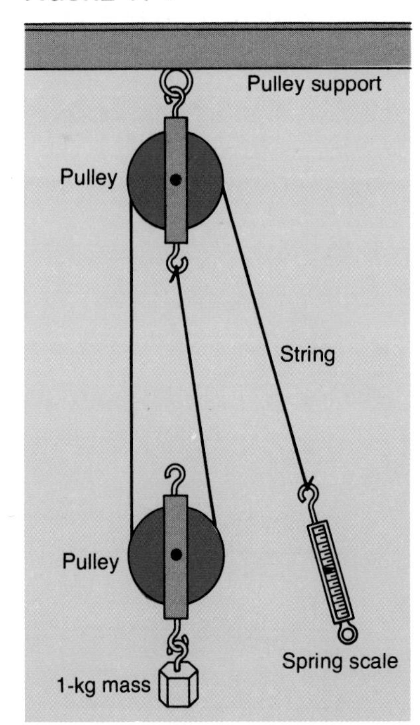

Oil is used as a lubricant in many industrial processes. The efficiency of this lathe is increased by using oil as a lubricant and as a coolant.

The students also found that while 0.4 m of cord was being removed from the pulley apparatus, the object was being lifted 0.2 m (h = 0.2 m). The weight of the object was 7.2 N (w = 7.2 N). The work out can now be calculated.

$$\begin{aligned} \textit{Work out} &= w \times h \\ &= (7.2)\ \text{N} \times (0.2)\ \text{m} \\ &= 1.44\ \text{N·m} = 1.44\ \text{J} \end{aligned}$$

After the work in and work out were calculated, the students could proceed to the next step. The efficiency of the pulley system can be calculated.

$$\begin{aligned} \textit{Efficiency} &= \frac{\textit{work out}}{\textit{work in}} \times \textit{100} \\ &= \frac{1.44\ \text{J}}{1.6\ \ \text{J}} \times 100 \\ &= 0.9 \times 100 \\ &= 90\% \end{aligned}$$

Using Scientific Laws to Predict the Operation of a System

Newton's first law of motion states that a body in motion will continue to move at the same speed and in the same direction unless acted on by an outside force. A body at rest stays at rest unless acted on by an outside force. This tendency of objects to remain in a state of motion or at rest is called **inertia** (in ėr′shə).

Objects that move on the surface of the earth are acted on by many forces. Two common forces with which you are familiar are friction and gravity. If an object is thrown straight up, it does not keep moving at a constant speed. It goes up, stops, and returns. It has changed speed and direction because of the earth's gravitational force.

Newton's second law of motion is a little more specific than the first. The second law deals with change in **velocity** (və los′ə tē) of a body. Velocity is a measure of distance with respect to time. Change in velocity during a specific time period is called **acceleration** (ak sel ə rā′shən). The second law states that the acceleration of a body is directly proportional to the force applied. This means that the more force you apply, the greater the acceleration. If you apply twice as much force, the acceleration will be twice as great. (See Figure 11–8.) The second law has a second part. It states that acceleration is inversely proportional to the mass of the body. A larger mass will be accelerated less than a smaller mass if both receive the same force. For instance, suppose there are two objects. One has twice the mass of the other. Equal forces are applied to both objects. The more massive object will accelerate half as much as the less massive object. (See Figure 11–9.)

Many ideas and laws in science can be expressed mathematically. Velocity (v) is a measure of the change

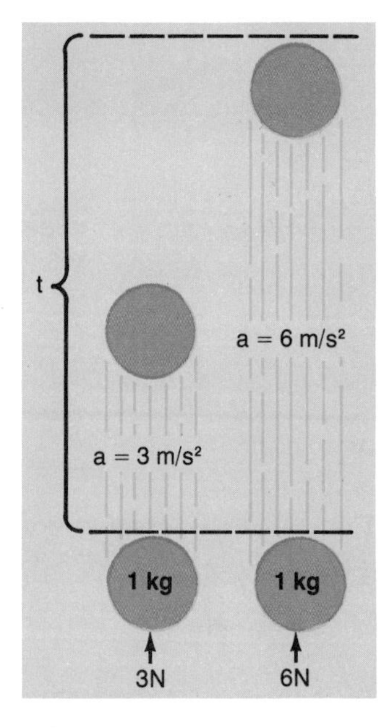

FIGURE 11–8

FIGURE 11–9

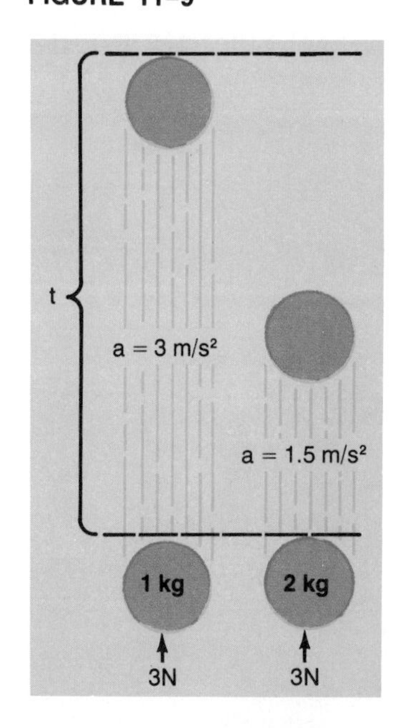

Due to inertia the forward motion of the baseball player continues as the player slides into base.

in distance (d) with respect to time (t). This is expressed in the following formula.

$$v = \frac{d}{t}$$

How would you describe acceleration?

Acceleration (a) is defined as change in velocity with respect to time. This is expressed in the following formula.

$$a = \frac{\text{change in } v}{\text{change in } t}$$

You have seen that acceleration is directly proportional to the force (F) applied. Acceleration is also inversely proportional to the mass (m) of the body. This is the second part of Newton's second law of motion. It is expressed in the following formula.

$$a = \frac{F}{m}$$

By rearranging the formula, the following is obtained.

$$F = m \times a$$

This is the mathematical form in which Newton's second law is usually stated.

Newton's second law of motion has a practical application in the design of automobiles. If you want a greater acceleration for your car, you can either install a more powerful engine (increase the force) or decrease the mass of the car. One reason why small cars get good gas mileage is their small mass. Everything else being equal, a 100 horsepower engine will accelerate a 1000 kg car up to 48 km/h in half the time that the same engine could accelerate a 2000 kg car to the same speed. You can calculate acceleration by using the formula for the second law of motion.

Newton's third law of motion states that when two bodies push on each other, equal forces are exerted in opposite directions. You may have heard this expressed as follows: For every action there is an equal and opposite reaction.

A rocket launch is an example of Newton's third law of motion. Expanding gases generated by burning fuel in the engines exert force against the rocket. An opposite reaction is produced as the rocket exerts force against the gases.

Energy

What is energy?

You have already learned that work is equal to force times distance. **Energy** (en′ər je) is the ability to do work. Energy is usually classified as either potential energy or kinetic energy.

What is potential energy?

There are many different kinds of **potential** (pə ten′shəl) **energy.** Potential energy is the energy of position or condition. Chemical, nuclear, gravitational, electrical, and magnetic energy are examples of potential energy. You will be concerned here with gravitational potential energy. Gravitational potential energy is dependent on two things. One is the position of an object. The second is the weight of the object. Gravitational potential energy can be expressed as weight times distance, or elevation (h). Using symbols the formula is as follows.

$$GPE = w \times h.$$

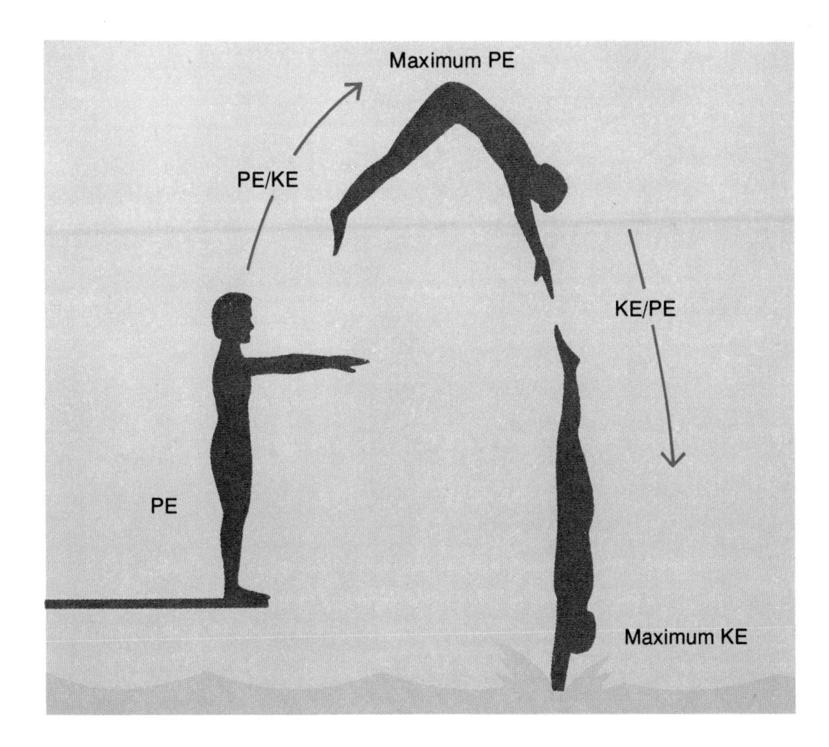

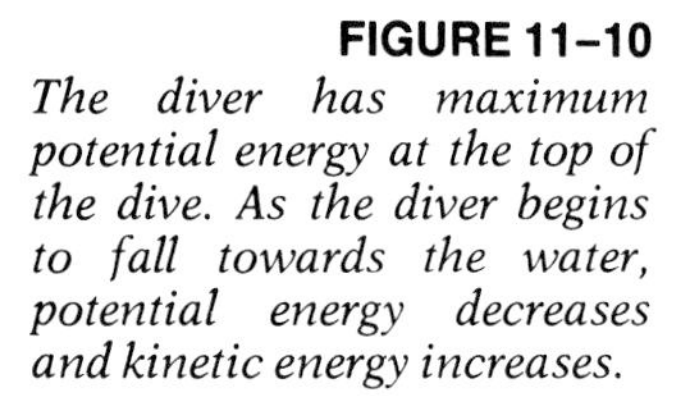

FIGURE 11–10
The diver has maximum potential energy at the top of the dive. As the diver begins to fall towards the water, potential energy decreases and kinetic energy increases.

Potential energy is stored as the arrow and string are pulled back in the bow. When the string is released, the potential energy is converted into kinetic energy of the arrow.

What is the energy of motion called?

Kinetic (ki net′ik) **energy** is the energy of motion. When an object is pushed off a shelf its potential energy is changed into kinetic energy. This is expressed as follows: The kinetic energy of a body with mass (m) moving with a speed (v) is $\frac{1}{2}mv^2$. It can be shown that $w \times h$ is equal to $\frac{1}{2}mv^2$. This relationship can be shown as follows.

Gravitational potential energy = weight times distance

$$GPE = wh$$

Kinetic energy = one-half mass times speed squared

$$KE = \frac{1}{2}mv^2$$

Gravitational potential energy = kinetic energy

$$GPE = KE \text{ or } wh = \frac{1}{2}mv^2$$

Suppose you had a 10-kg mass weighing 98 N on a shelf 6 m off the ground. If the shelf collapses, how fast will the mass be traveling when it hits the ground?

$$wh = \tfrac{1}{2}mv^2$$

$$(98)\,6 = \left(\frac{1}{2}\right) 10\,\mathrm{v}^2$$

$$\mathrm{v}^2 = 118$$
$$\mathrm{v} = 10.8\ \mathrm{m/s}$$

SUMMARY The operations of a system are predictable. The period of a pendulum is the time to complete one back-and-forth swing. This period remains the same no matter how much energy is lost. The efficiency of a system is a measurable quantity. Efficiency is affected by many factors including friction. Newton stated three laws that govern all types of motion. Energy, which is the ability to do work, can be either potential or kinetic.

SCIENCE WORDS

pendulums
period
interpolation
extrapolation
efficiency
joule
inertia
velocity
acceleration
energy
potential energy
kinetic energy

REVIEW QUESTIONS

Fill in the blanks with the correct terms.

1. You would use ____________ to predict information between points that are within a graph.
2. You would use ____________ to predict information outside the limits of the graph.
3. The ____________ of a system is always less than 100 percent.
4. Work is described by the formula ____________.
5. The curved-line graph can be changed to a straight-line graph by converting time (t) to ____________.
6. Energy is the ability to do ____________.

Mark each statement true (T) or false (F).

1. _____ The period of a pendulum is the time it takes to make a complete motion in one direction.
2. _____ The work put out of a system does not equal the work put in.
3. _____ The tendency of objects to remain in a state of motion is called velocity.
4. _____ Chemical, nuclear, gravitational, electrical, and magnetic energy, are all examples of kinetic energy.
5. _____ Predictions made by interpolation are usually more accurate than those made by extrapolation.
6. _____ Efficiency can be increased if wheels are added to a system.

APPLYING WHAT YOU LEARNED

1. Why are pendulums used as the timing device in clocks?
2. Why is it considered impossible to develop a perpetual motion machine?
3. How do lubricants improve efficiency?
4. List five things to which you can apply Newton's third law.

Lightning, a form of electrical energy produced in nature, flashes above a city lighted by electrical energy generated in power plants.

12

Supersystems

In previous chapters you investigated various systems and how they operate. In this chapter you will investigate combinations of systems. You will see how they interact. These combinations of systems are called supersystems.

In Unit 3 you constructed electrical systems. These systems were used to test materials. You will begin this chapter by constructing several electrical supersystems.

Activity 36 Electrical Supersystems

PURPOSE

To investigate different ways of constructing electrical circuits

MATERIALS

3 dry cells (D type)
3 miniature screw-base bulbs (1.5V)
3 bulb holders
Insulated copper bell wire (#22)
Wire cutters
3 battery holders

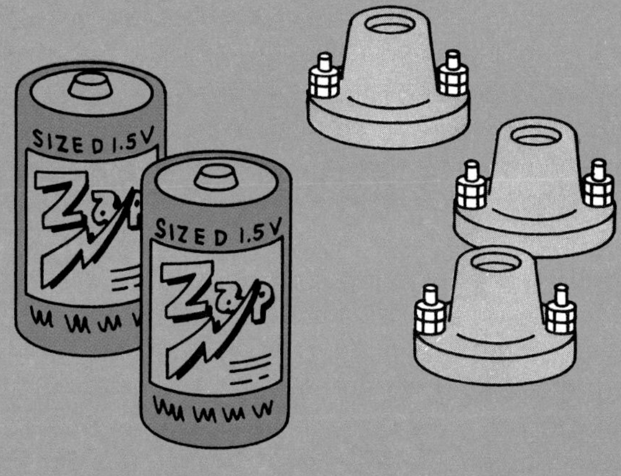

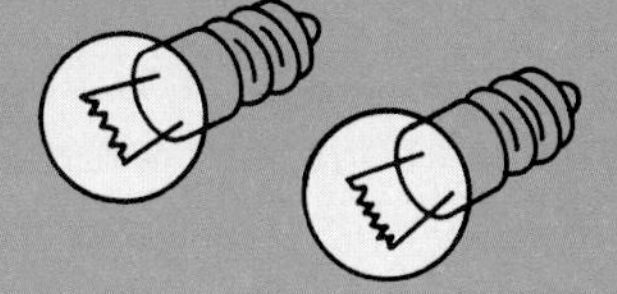

DO THIS

A. Construct a supersystem in which one D cell can light two bulbs as brightly as one bulb. Sketch the supersystem.

B. Construct a supersystem in which one bulb is lighted no brighter with two D cells than with one D cell. Sketch the supersystem.

C. Construct a supersystem in which one bulb is lighted brighter with two D cells than with one D cell. Sketch the supersystem.

D. Construct a supersystem in which one D cell lights two bulbs less brightly than one bulb. Sketch the supersystem.

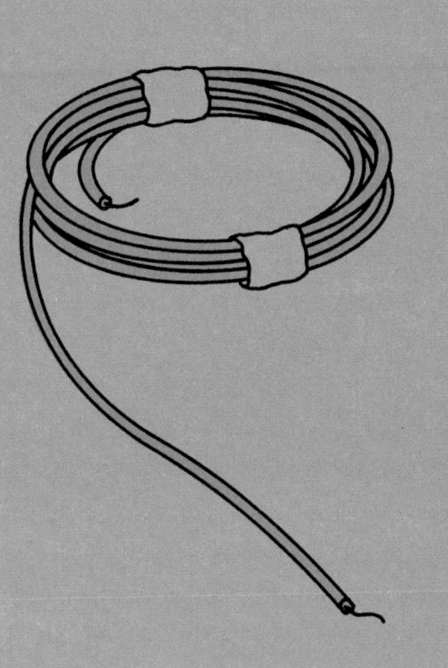

REPORT

Label your sketches.

Electric Circuits

Supersystems are combinations of several systems. In Activity 36 you combined systems or parts of systems to form larger supersystems. You found that there are many different ways to put supersystems together. You also found that different combinations of systems may interact in different ways. Electrical circuits are examples of supersystems. A continuous connection of conductors from one end of a dry cell to the other produces a **closed circuit** (sėr′kit). An **open circuit** is the result of a break in the continuous connection. This break can be anywhere between one terminal, or pole, of the dry cell and the other terminal. Perhaps your investigations gave you some idea of the different effects caused by open and closed circuits.

What is a closed circuit?

What is an open circuit?

A model can be used to examine the four supersystems that you made. This model shows what happens in a closed circuit. Examine the terminals of a dry cell. Near the terminals you may see + and − symbols. Some dry cells don't have these markings. Dry cells made in the United States always have a positive center pole and a negative outer pole. When a closed circuit exists, electrical energy can move along the conductors to make a bulb light. If you have ever touched a light bulb, you know it also gives off heat.

In an open circuit (left) the bulb does not light. The closed circuit (right) provides a continuous path for the flow of electricity and the bulb lights.

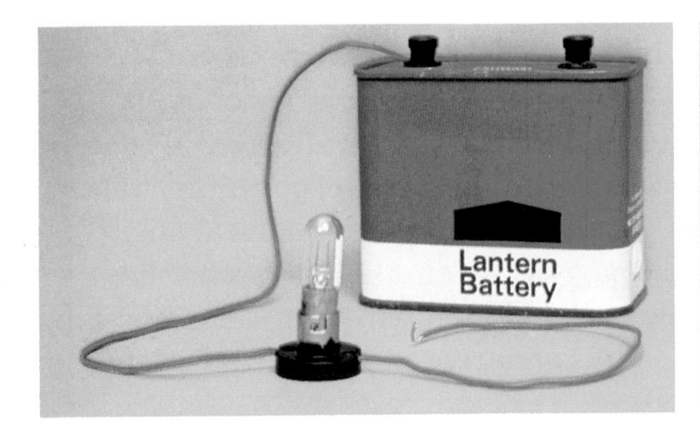

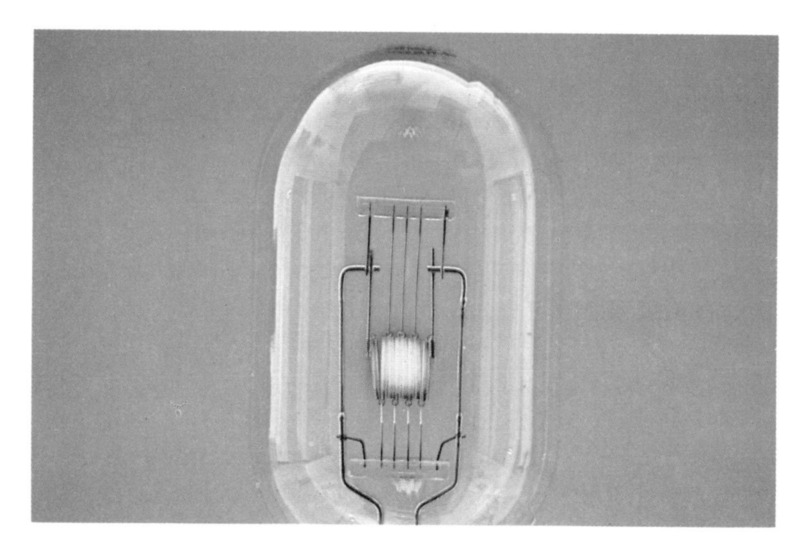

Electrical energy is conducted through the filament in this bulb, and is converted to light energy and heat energy.

Have you ever carefully examined a light bulb? If you have, you know that it is made of a number of parts. The small, fine wire inside the bulb is called the **filament** (fil′ə mənt). The filament gives off light when electricity moves along it. The model of electrical energy moving in a circuit can be used to analyze your supersystems. The electrical energy moves out of the dry cell. It moves along the conducting wires, into the bulb, and along the filament. It then moves back along conducting wires to the dry cell. Using this model, try to answer the following question. Refer to your drawings of the supersystems in Activity 36. Why is it that supersystem B and supersystem C do not light the bulb in the same way?

Define parallel circuit?

When you built the four supersystems in Activity 36, you actually made two different kinds of closed circuits. Supersystems A and B are **parallel** (par′ə lel) **circuits.** Compare them with the parallel circuits shown in Figure 12–1. In parallel circuits the electrical energy is the same in each part of the circuit. It does not have to pass through one bulb before it can get to the next bulb. Dry cells can also be connected in parallel, as you found in supersystem B.

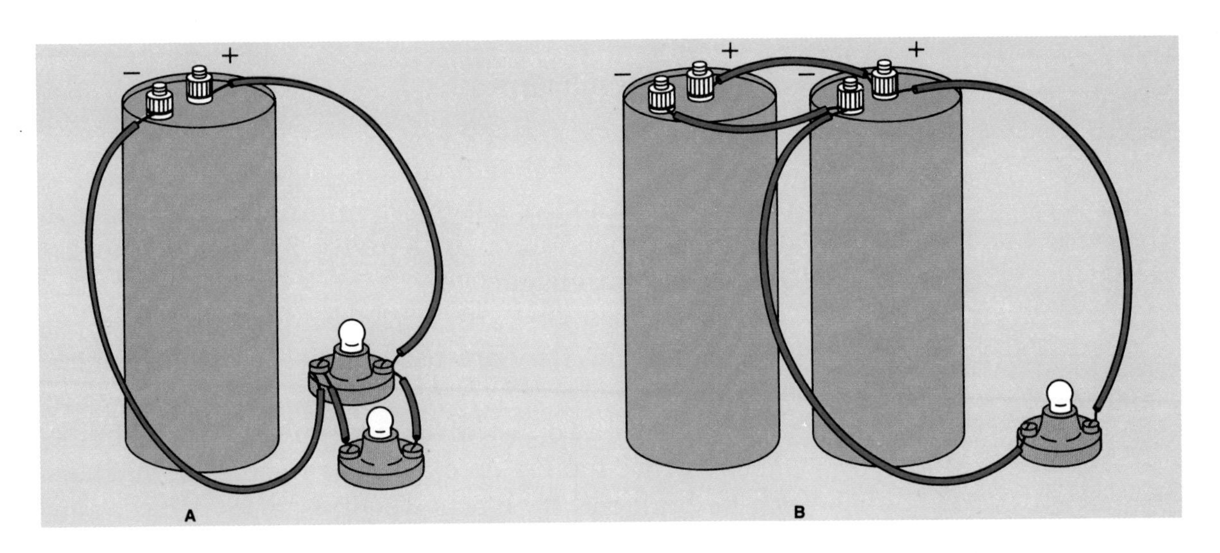

Supersystems C and D are another kind of closed circuit. This kind of closed circuit is called a **series circuit.** Figure 12–2 shows series circuits similar to supersystems C and D. In a series circuit electrical energy passes through one bulb before passing through the next bulb. Dry cells can also be placed in series. In a series arrangement of dry cells, the electrical energy in the circuit is increased. This is the arrangement of dry cells in a flashlight.

FIGURE 12–1
Parallel circuits

FIGURE 12–2
Series circuits

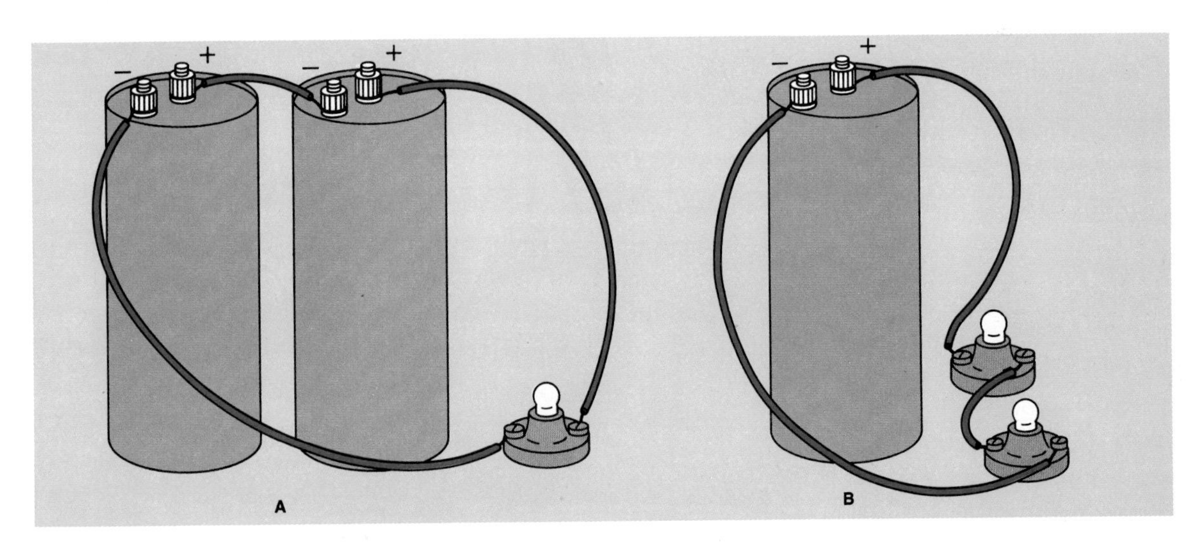

Electromagnets

Sometimes the behavior of one supersystem can be imitated by another supersystem. An electromagnet is one such supersystem. In Activity 37 you will investigate an electromagnet.

Electromagnets are fairly common devices. In modified forms they are used in electric transformers and radio speakers. In home heating systems they are used to open and close valves. They are also found in the small electric motors used to start cars. Electromagnets can be built to lift objects weighing many times their own weight. Large electromagnets are used in junkyards to move scrap metal.

Since electromagnets can be turned on and off, they are useful in picking up heavy pieces of metal and moving them to another location.

Activity 37 Electromagnets

PURPOSE

To investigate the ability of an electric current to produce magnetism

MATERIALS

Large iron nail
2 1.5-volt dry cells
Insulated copper bell wire (#22)
Finishing nails
Wire cutter

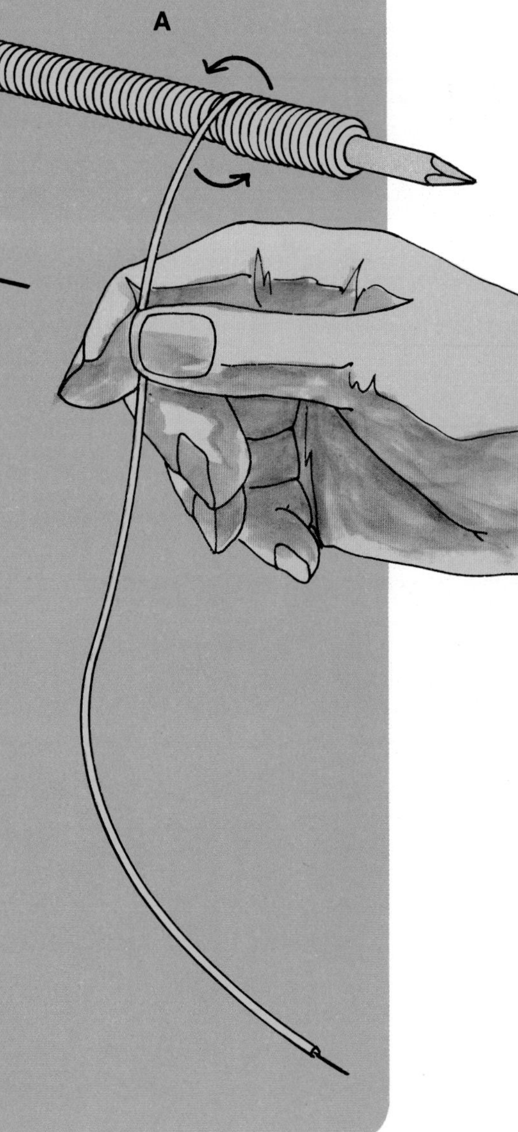

DO THIS

A. Strip about 3 cm of insulation from each end of a long piece of copper wire. Wrap 100 turns of the wire around the large iron nail. Leave about 1 cm of the nail exposed at the pointed end. Be sure to allow at least 15 cm of wire at each end of the nail for making connections to the dry cell.

B. Connect the ends of the wire to the terminals of a dry cell. Touch the end of the wrapped nail to a pile of finishing nails.

C. Disconnect one end of the wire from the dry cell. Again touch the large nail to the finishing nails.

D. Connect a second dry cell in series to the supersystem. Touch the iron nail to the finishing nails.

E. Put aside the electromagnet for use in a later activity.

REPORT

1. What, do you think, causes your supersystem to operate the way it does?

2. Does the supersystem operate with an open circuit? What is your evidence?

3. What is the effect of adding a second dry cell to the supersystem?

While exploring the behavior of the electromagnet, you probably learned that this supersystem operates much the same as a common magnet. Electromagnetism was discovered early in the nineteenth century. The reverse process was discovered when Michael Faraday produced electricity by wrapping a wire around a magnet. Electromagnets and generators were developed as a result of these discoveries.

You found that an electromagnet can be turned on and off. This gives the electromagnet an important advantage over a natural iron magnet. Also, adding more electrical energy or more turns of wire will increase the strength of an electromagnet. Does the electromagnet you made have all the other properties of an iron magnet? Activity 38 will help you to find the answer.

Electrical Units

You have now explored several electrical supersystems. These supersystems produced light and heat. You have also investigated how electricity powers supersystems and where electricity comes from.

You probably realize that the systems with which you have been working are powered by dry cells. These cells are used to produce electricity. Recall that another kind of system was used to produce electricity in Activity 18. This system is called a **wet cell.** Wet cells are different from dry cells, although both types work in basically the same way. In both dry and wet cells electrons move within the system because of chemical interaction. As the electrons move, they can do work. Lighting a bulb is one example of this work.

You have seen previously the importance of careful observation. One of the best ways to make careful observations is to take measurements. Suppose you

Activity 38 Magnetism and Electromagnetism

PURPOSE

To investigate the similarity between natural magnetism and electromagnetism

MATERIALS

Dry cell (1.5V)
Finishing nails
2 iron bar magnets
Directional compass
String
Electromagnet from Activity 37
Scissors

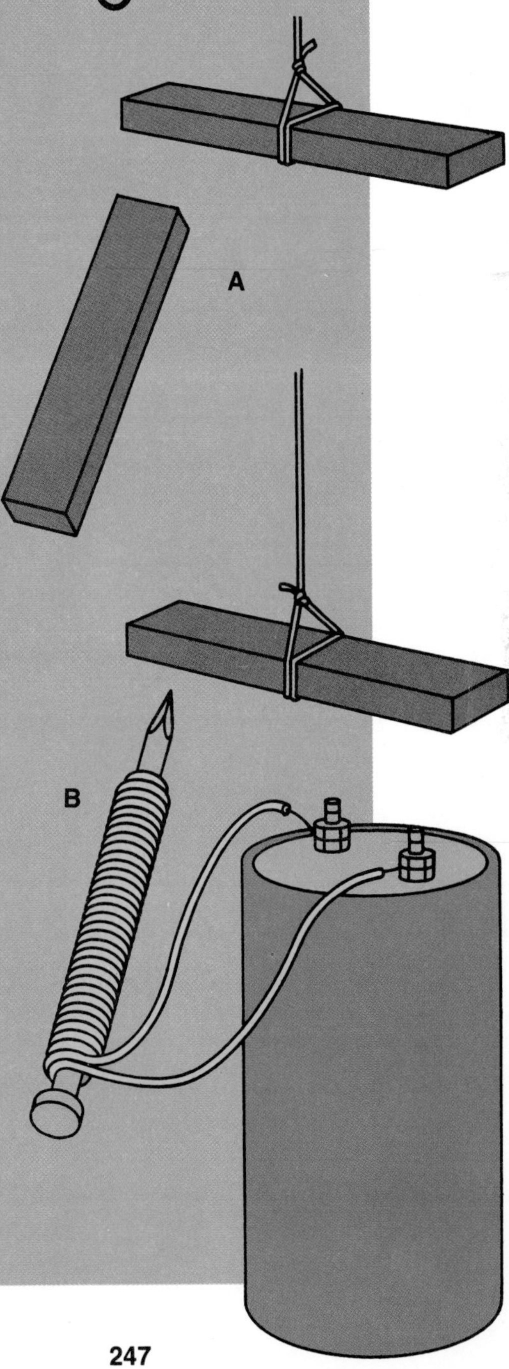

DO THIS

A. Examine the two bar magnets. If the poles aren't marked, determine which is the north-seeking pole and which is the south-seeking pole. Do this by hanging the magnet from a string tied to the center of the magnet. Allow the magnet to swing freely until it comes to rest. The end of the magnet that points north, as indicated by the directional compass, is the north-seeking pole. The opposite pole is the south-seeking pole. Using the two magnets, test to see which poles are attracted and which are repelled.

B. Connect the electromagnet to the dry cell. Using one of the bar magnets, determine if the electromagnet has a north and a south pole.

C. Reverse the wires connecting the electromagnet to the dry cell. Determine the effect this has on the electromagnet.

REPORT

1. What evidence is there that the bar magnets have two poles?

2. Does the electromagnet have two poles? What is your evidence?

3. How did reversing the wires connecting the electromagnet to the dry cell affect the electromagnet? What is your evidence?

FIGURE 12–3
A wet cell will generate electricity.

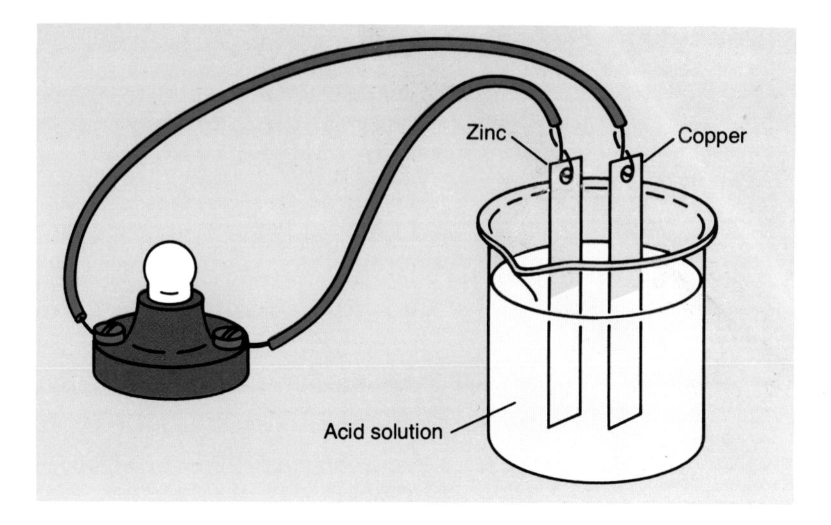

were going to build a birdhouse. Would you build a better one if you measured the wood parts or if you guessed the measurements? As you continue to explore electricity, you will need to take measurements. There is one problem with measuring electricity, however. It cannot be weighed with a balance or measured with a meterstick. Electricity is a form of energy. It does not have the properties of matter. Therefore you will need special tools to measure electricity. Scientists use the following concepts to understand electricity.

1. Matter is made of many tiny particles.
2. An electron is the smallest common particle of which matter is made.
3. The electron has a property called an electrical charge.
4. The electrical charge of an electron is negative.
5. The movement of electrons through materials or from one material to another is called electricity.
6. Electrons may be moved by physical or chemical changes involving the interaction of materials.

What is electricity?

While your senses have certain capabilities, they cannot detect all the properties of a system. It is often necessary to find new methods to measure the properties of supersystems. Sometimes another supersystem might be used for this purpose. The **voltmeter** (vōlt′mē tər), for example, is a supersystem based on the principle of the electromagnet supersystem. The voltmeter measures a property of electricity called **voltage** (vōl′tij). Voltage may be thought of as the "push" applied to electrons as they move in a circuit. Voltage is measured in units called **volts.**

What is voltage?

Another measurable property of electricity is **current** (kėr′ənt). Current is the rate of flow of electrons in a circuit. The basic unit of measurement of current is an **ampere** (am′pir) or **amp.** One ampere is about 6 million, million, million electrons flowing past a point in the circuit every second! The supersystem used to measure this property of electricity is called an **ammeter** (am′mē tər). In Activity 39 you will investigate both voltage and current.

What is current?

A voltmeter is used to measure the voltage between two points in a circuit.

EXCURSION 8
If you would like to learn a shorthand method of working with very large numbers, now would be a good time to do Excursion 8, "Powers of Ten Notation."

Activity 39 Measuring Electric Circuits

PURPOSE

To investigate how a voltmeter and an ammeter are used as measuring devices in an electric circuit

MATERIALS

2 dry cells (D type)
Insulated copper bell wire
Miniature screw base bulb (1.5V)
Bulb holder
Ammeter
Voltmeter
Wire cutter
2 battery holders

DO THIS

A. Construct the circuit shown in *A.* **CAUTION:** *Be sure the positive side of the circuit is connected to the + post on the voltmeter.* The voltmeter can be easily damaged if hooked up improperly. Read the voltage and record it in a table like Table 1.

B. Construct the circuit shown in *B.* **CAUTION:** *Be sure the positive side of the circuit is connected to the + post on the ammeter.* The ammeter can be easily damaged if hooked up improperly. Read the amperage and record it in the table.

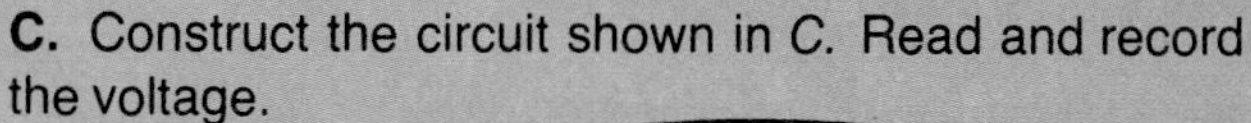

C. Construct the circuit shown in *C.* Read and record the voltage.

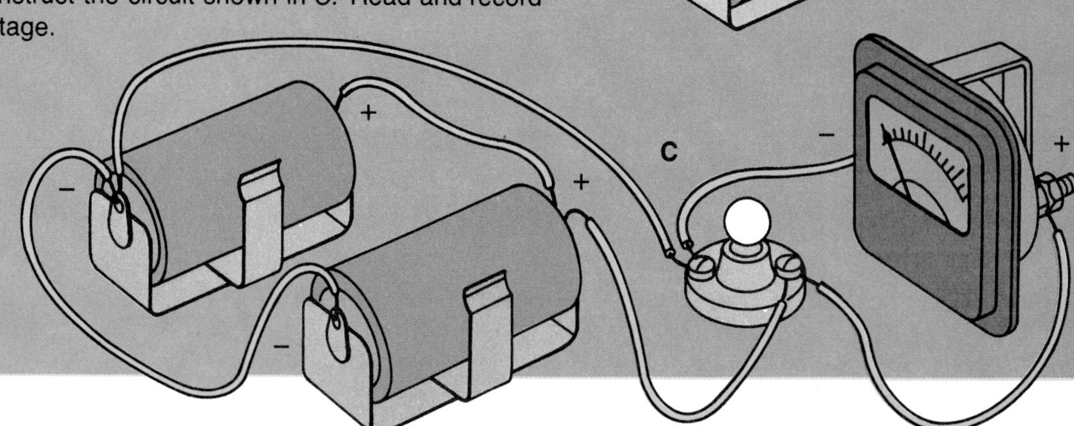

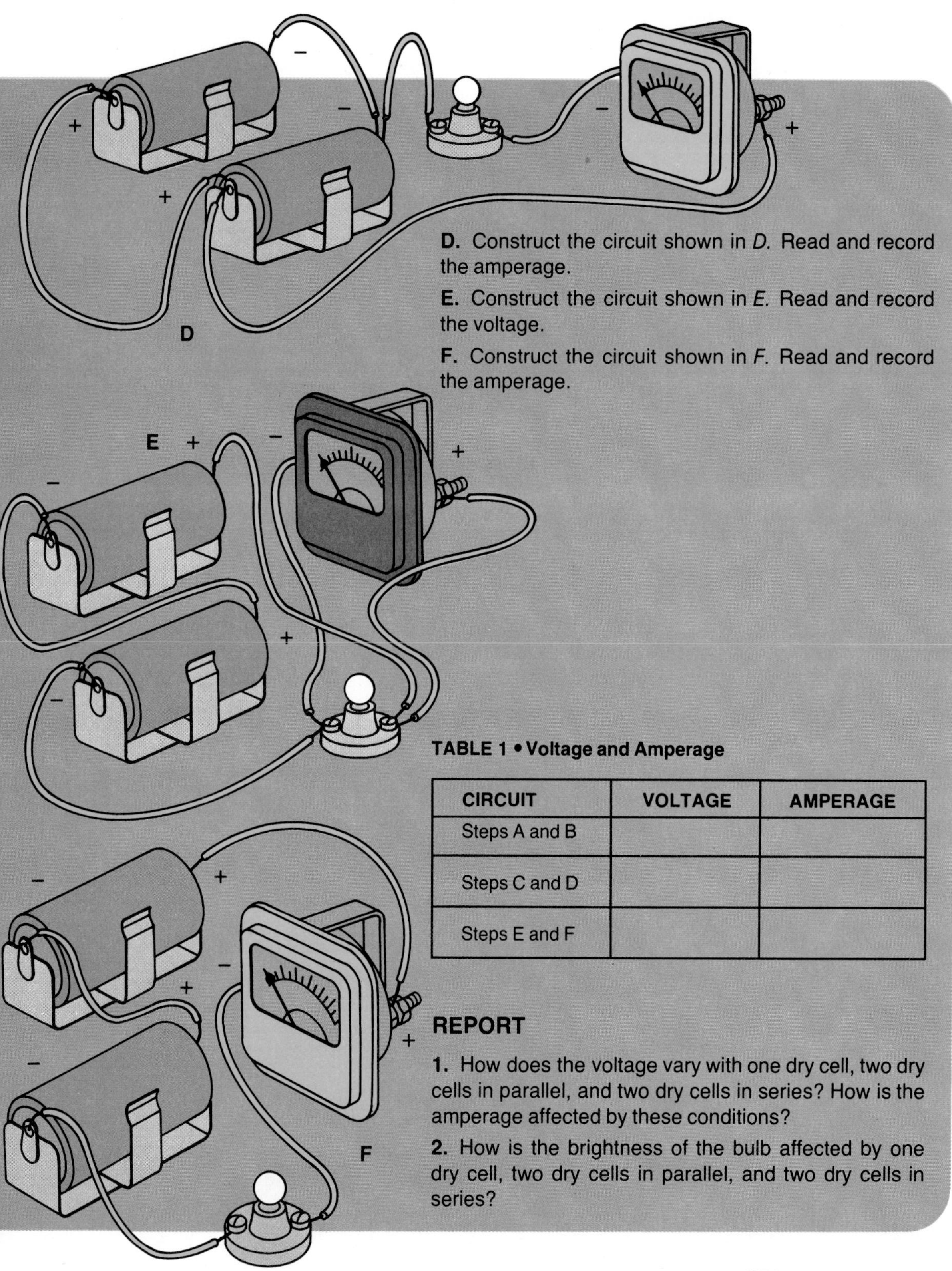

D. Construct the circuit shown in *D.* Read and record the amperage.

E. Construct the circuit shown in *E.* Read and record the voltage.

F. Construct the circuit shown in *F.* Read and record the amperage.

TABLE 1 • Voltage and Amperage

CIRCUIT	VOLTAGE	AMPERAGE
Steps A and B		
Steps C and D		
Steps E and F		

REPORT

1. How does the voltage vary with one dry cell, two dry cells in parallel, and two dry cells in series? How is the amperage affected by these conditions?

2. How is the brightness of the bulb affected by one dry cell, two dry cells in parallel, and two dry cells in series?

You may have found some interesting facts about electrical energy in Activity 39. It appears that voltage stays fairly constant if cells are connected in parallel. Voltage increases if the cells are connected in series. A decrease in voltage indicates that there is something wrong with the dry cells. Amperage increases as more cells are added to the circuit in series.

Electricity flowing in a circuit can do work. You have seen that power is the rate of doing work. Electrical power is measured in **watts** (wotz). Watts can be measured with a **wattmeter** (wot′mē tər). The power in an electrical supersystem can also be determined mathematically. The formula is

In what unit is electrical power measured?

$$\text{watts (power)} = \text{volts (voltage)} \times \text{amps (current)}.$$

This formula shows how volts and amps are related to the power in the supersystem.

Have you ever examined any of the electrical appliances in your home? You may have noticed that the number of watts an appliance uses is recorded on it. Dry cells cannot supply enough energy to operate most appliances. Your household electricity is produced at a generating plant some distance from your home. It comes into your home at a relatively constant 115 volts.

The amount of electrical power used by an electrical appliance or device is measured in watts.

A meter reader from the power company records, in kilowatt-hours, the amount of electrical energy used.

The amount of electrical energy an appliance uses depends on how long it operates. Power companies charge for electricity according to the amount used each hour. For instance, suppose you have an electric heater that is rated at 1000 watts. You operate it for 1 hour. The power company would charge you for 1000 watt-hours of electricity. If the appliance runs for 2 hours, it would use 2000 watt-hours of electricity. The amount of electrical energy used in the home is measured by an electric meter. This meter is often mounted on the outside of the house.

How is the electric supply to your home measured?

A household requires many watt-hours of electricity each day. Therefore the meter records the energy used in thousands of watt-hours, or **kilowatt-hours.** Suppose you had only one 100-watt light bulb operating at home for 24 hours. No other electricity was being used. It would use 100 watts times 24 hours, or 2400 watt-hours of electricity. The meter would record 2.4 kilowatt-hours of electricity for that day.

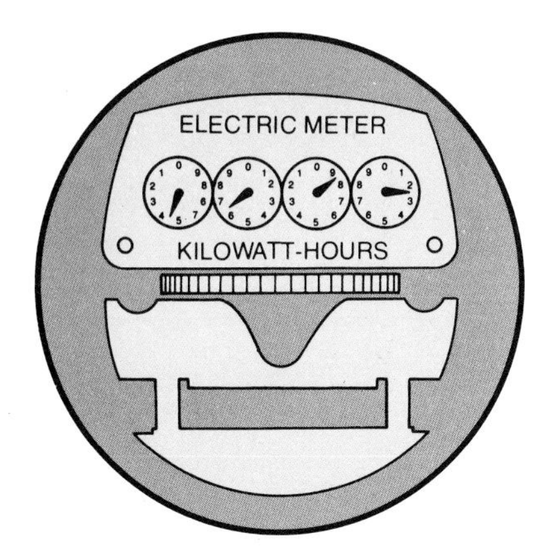

FIGURE 12–4
An electric meter

Reading an Electric Meter

As electricity flows from the power company into your home, it passes through an electric meter. The meter is enclosed in a glass case and has a series of dials on it. Figure 12–4 shows a typical electric meter. To read this meter start with the dial at the far right. The pointer is halfway between 2 and 3. Therefore you record a 2. The pointer in the next dial is between 8 and 9. You record an 8. The pointer on the second dial from the left is between 6 and 7. You record a 6. The pointer on the dial on the far left is between 4 and 5. You record a 4. When you put the numbers in the same order as the dials they read 4682. The meter has recorded that there was a flow of 4682 kilowatt-hours of electricity into your household. The meter dials read in thousands, hundreds, tens, and units from left to right.

Conserving electricity is not as easy as you might think. Electricity is a very convenient form of energy. The use of electricity by American families has been growing for the past 70 years. Sometimes the demand for electricity exceeds the supply. As electricity usage increases, new power plants may have to be built to meet the demand. In the future you may be forced to budget your use of electricity. Careful consumption of electricity may help to prevent a future energy crisis.

SCIENCE WORDS

closed circuit
open circuit
filament
parallel circuit
series circuit
wet cell
voltmeter
voltage
volts
ampere
amp
ammeter
current
watts
wattmeter
kilowatt-hours

SUMMARY Electricity is the flow of electrons from one material to another. Electrons have a negative charge. They can be moved through a circuit by either physical or chemical activity. Voltage and amperage are properties of electrical energy that can be measured. Voltage multiplied by amperage gives the power of the electrical energy in watts. The amount of electricity used in a household is measured by an electric meter. The meter measures the electricity used, in kilowatt-hours.

REVIEW QUESTIONS

Match the term in Column A with the correct answer in Column B.

A	B
1. Watt___	**a.** A break in a continuous circuit
2. Voltage___	**b.** Used to measure amperes
3. Electricity___	**c.** Movement of electrons from one material to another
4. Ammeter___	**d.** Fine wire inside light bulbs
5. Open circuit___	**e.** The rate of flow of electrons
6. Current___	**f.** Electrical power
7. Closed circuit___	**g.** Used to pick up objects much heavier than itself
8. Electromagnet___	**h.** A complete connection of conductors
9. Filament___	**i.** The "push" applied to electrons as they move in a circuit
10. Parallel circuit___	**j.** Energy is the same in each part of the circuit

APPLYING WHAT YOU LEARNED

1. Try to obtain a copy of one month's electric bill for your home. How many kilowatt-hours were used in one month? Assuming this is an average usage, estimate the kilowatt-hour usage for your home for one year.
2. Make a list of the things you can do to conserve electricity at home.
3. Make a list of the ways you can conserve electricity in school.

Chemical reactions can produce heat energy. In this photo heat produced from combustion is interacting with metal solder causing the solder to melt. As the solder resolidifies it will fuse the two pieces of copper tubing together.

13

The Products of Systems

In Chapter 12 you observed that simple physical systems can be combined to form supersystems. Systems and supersystems can interact to produce heat and light. How is heat produced by interacting systems? Try this simple experiment. Rub your hands together for 30 seconds. How do your hands feel after rubbing them? The interaction of your hands (two systems) produced heat. In this chapter you will investigate why heat is produced during system interactions.

Friction and Heat

Heat is produced when systems interact. When you rubbed your hands together, they became warm. This heat is produced by friction. Friction results when one material moves against another material. In this case your right hand, a solid, was moving against your left hand, another solid. The motion of your hands required energy. Contact between your hands produced a resistance to this motion. Scientists define friction as a force that resists motion. Friction results in some of the energy of motion being converted to heat energy.

Friction is also present when a solid moves against a gas or a liquid. When you ride a bicycle, the motion of the bicycle is resisted by the air, a gas. When you swim, the motion of your body is resisted by the water, a liquid. Therefore bicycle riding and swimming result in friction. Friction is always accompanied by some heat. In these two examples the amount of heat produced is very small.

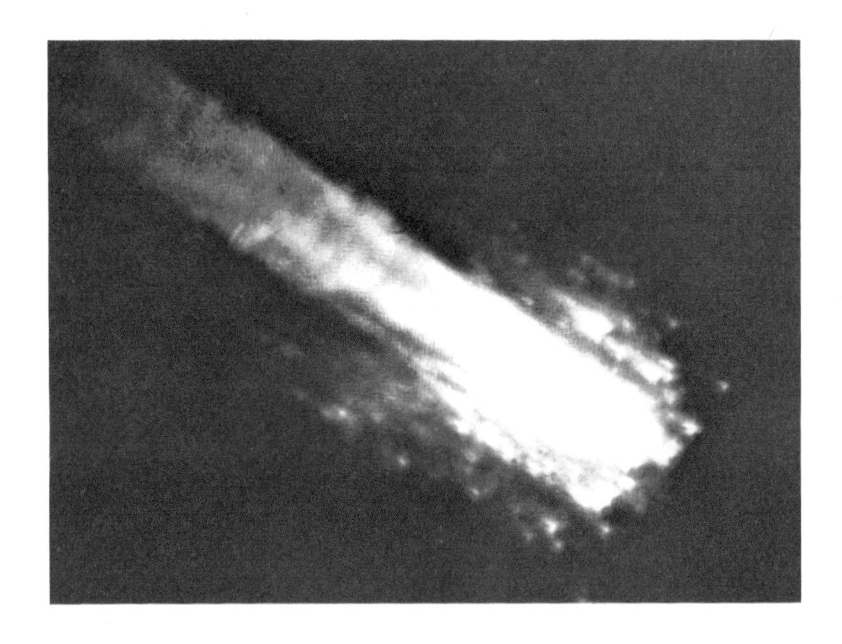

Friction between the atmosphere and the heat shield of this spacecraft causes the heat shield to char and partially disintegrate during reentry. The partial disintegration of the heat shield protects the spacecraft by carrying away the excess heat.

Friction is often very useful. The heat produced as a result of friction between the matchhead and the matchbox causes the flammable chemicals in the match to ignite.

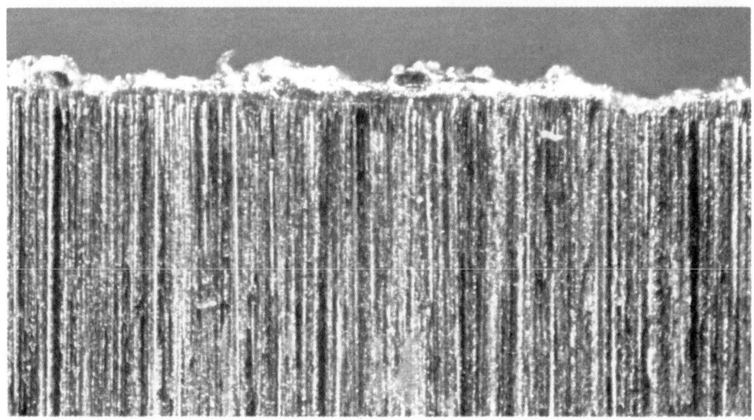

This photo shows the edge of a razor blade magnified several times. The supposedly smooth surface of the blade is actually very jagged. This results in friction between the razor blade and the skin during shaving.

Why does the motion of one material against another produce friction? You know that matter is composed of molecules and atoms. These molecules and atoms are always in motion. They can also be attracted to each other. When two materials move against each other their molecules and atoms collide. The molecules in one material may attract molecules in the second material. These collisions and attractions cause resistance to the motion of the materials. Some of the molecules and atoms pick up kinetic energy from the collisions. This increase in kinetic energy is observed as heat.

Why does friction produce heat?

The interaction of systems can produce heat. Systems can also trap heat. In Activity 40 you will investigate how a system can absorb and trap heat.

Activity 40 Heat Absorption

PURPOSE

To investigate the absorption of heat energy by matter

MATERIALS

5 Styrofoam cups
5 Celsius thermometers
Single-edge razor blade
Clip lamp with a 150– or 200–W bulb
Meterstick
Water
Dry sand
Finely crushed charcoal
Ringstand and ring
String

DO THIS

A. Using a single-edge razor blade, cut down each Styrofoam cup to a height of 3 cm. **CAUTION:** *Be very careful working with the razor blade.*

B. Fill each cup with a different material: water, dry sand, wet sand, dry crushed charcoal, wet crushed charcoal.

C. Arrange the cups in a circle under the ring of the ringstand. Put a thermometer in each cup. Tie the thermometers to the ring, suspending them so that each thermometer bulb is no more than 0.5 cm under the surface of the material in the cup.

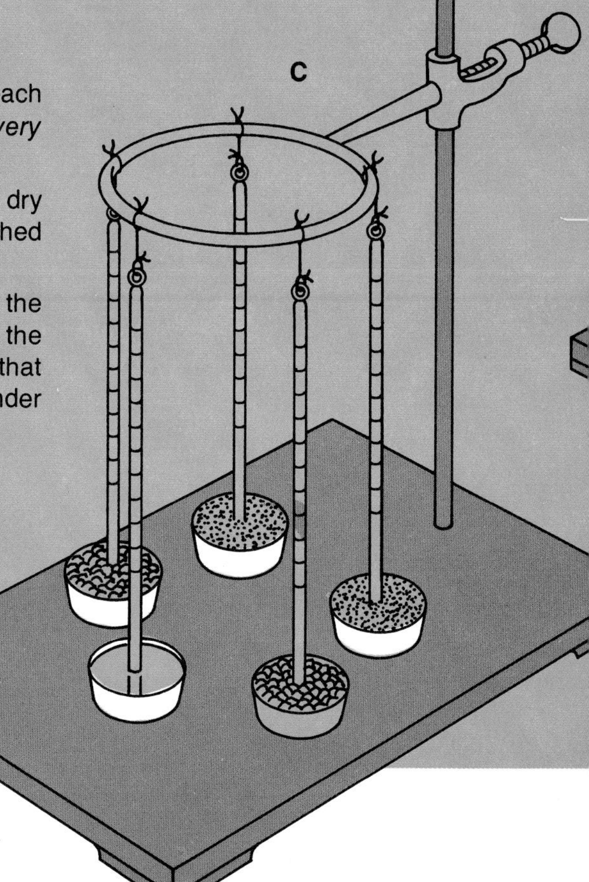

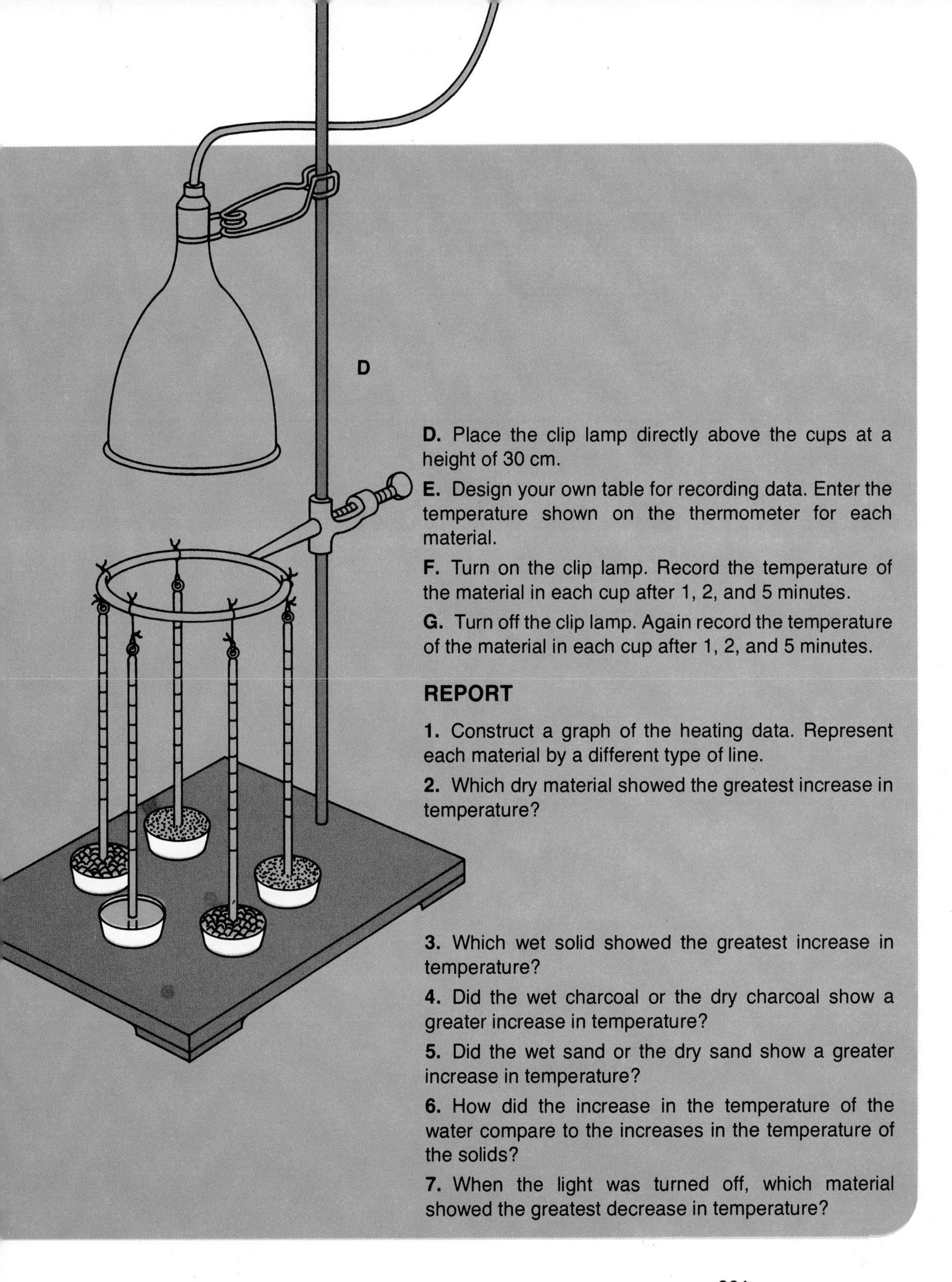

D. Place the clip lamp directly above the cups at a height of 30 cm.

E. Design your own table for recording data. Enter the temperature shown on the thermometer for each material.

F. Turn on the clip lamp. Record the temperature of the material in each cup after 1, 2, and 5 minutes.

G. Turn off the clip lamp. Again record the temperature of the material in each cup after 1, 2, and 5 minutes.

REPORT

1. Construct a graph of the heating data. Represent each material by a different type of line.

2. Which dry material showed the greatest increase in temperature?

3. Which wet solid showed the greatest increase in temperature?

4. Did the wet charcoal or the dry charcoal show a greater increase in temperature?

5. Did the wet sand or the dry sand show a greater increase in temperature?

6. How did the increase in the temperature of the water compare to the increases in the temperature of the solids?

7. When the light was turned off, which material showed the greatest decrease in temperature?

In Activity 40 you observed light interacting with the surfaces of certain materials. Light caused an increase in the surface temperatures of these materials. It would seem that light energy is closely related to heat energy. Therefore the energy from the bulb system can be called light/heat energy. The light/heat energy was absorbed by the surfaces. You observed that different types of surfaces heat and cool at different rates. Dark surfaces heat up more quickly than light surfaces. **Absorption** (ab sôrp′shən) is one way in which systems can trap heat. In Activity 41 you will investigate another method of trapping heat.

Since reptiles cannot maintain a high body temperature, they spend part of their time basking in sunlight. The light energy they absorb is converted to heat energy, which helps to raise their body temperature.

Activity 41 A Miniature Greenhouse

PURPOSE

To investigate the conversion of light to heat energy

MATERIALS

Shoe box	Cellophane tape
Clear plastic wrap	Clip lamp with 150–200 W bulb
2 Celsius thermometers	Scissors
Meterstick	Graph paper

DO THIS

A. Tape a thermometer to the inside bottom of the box. Be sure the thermometer is centered.

B. Turn the box so that the open top becomes the side. Tape another thermometer to the outside of the box.

C. Cut a piece of plastic wrap slightly larger than the opening to the box. Tape it in place over the opening.

D. Arrange the clip lamp so that the bulb is 50 cm from the plastic wrap.

E. Design your own table for recording data. Enter the temperature recorded on each thermometer. Then turn on the clip lamp. Record the temperature inside and outside of the box every 30 seconds for 5 minutes.

F. Turn off the lamp. Record the temperature inside and outside of the box every 30 seconds for 5 minutes.

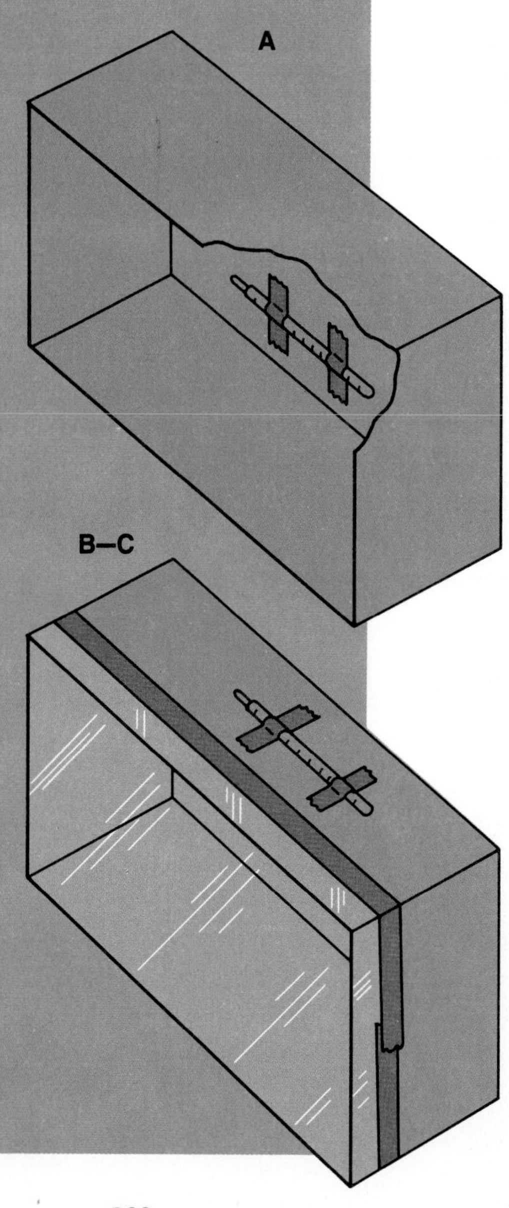

REPORT

1. What is the dependent variable in your data? What is the independent variable?

2. Construct a line graph of the heating data collected in Step **E.** Show temperature on the vertical axis and time on the horizontal axis. Use a solid line for temperature inside; dotted line for temperature outside.

3. Construct a line graph of the cooling data collected in step **F.** Follow the procedure in question **2.**

4. How did the temperature changes inside the box compare with those outside the box?

In Activity 41 you used a box as a model of a greenhouse. The model showed how heat was trapped inside the box. The light/heat energy moved through the air. It interacted with the air around the thermometers. It was also absorbed by the surfaces of the box. This produced an increase in temperature both inside and outside the box. When the light/heat energy was turned off, the temperature outside the box decreased. The temperature inside the box also decreased slightly. Yet much of the heat remained inside the box. The heat was trapped by the plastic wrap on one end of the box. This caused the temperature to decrease slowly.

How does a greenhouse trap heat?

A greenhouse traps light/heat energy in a similar way. The sun's light/heat energy passes through the glass of the greenhouse. This energy warms the air inside. Much of the light/heat energy is trapped inside the greenhouse by the glass. The glass acts like the plastic wrap in Activity 41. It prevents heat from escaping from the greenhouse.

Transferring Heat

You have seen that systems can produce heat. Systems can also absorb and trap heat. It is also possible for one system to transfer heat to another system. Sometimes heat is transferred to other parts of the same system. For example, heat produced in your furnace must be transferred to the air throughout your house. Heat produced on the stove must be transferred to the food for cooking. There are several ways in which systems can transfer heat. In Activity 42 you will investigate one of these methods.

In Activity 42 you observed a crystal of $KMnO_4$ [*potassium permanganate*] dissolve in water. As the water was heated, the warmer water at the bottom of the

Activity 42 Heat Transfer in Liquids

PURPOSE

To investigate heat transfer in a liquid

MATERIALS

250-mL beaker
$KMnO_4$ [*potassium permanganate*] crystal (about the size of a grain of rice)
Safety goggles
Heat source
Tripod
Wire gauze
Forceps
Matches

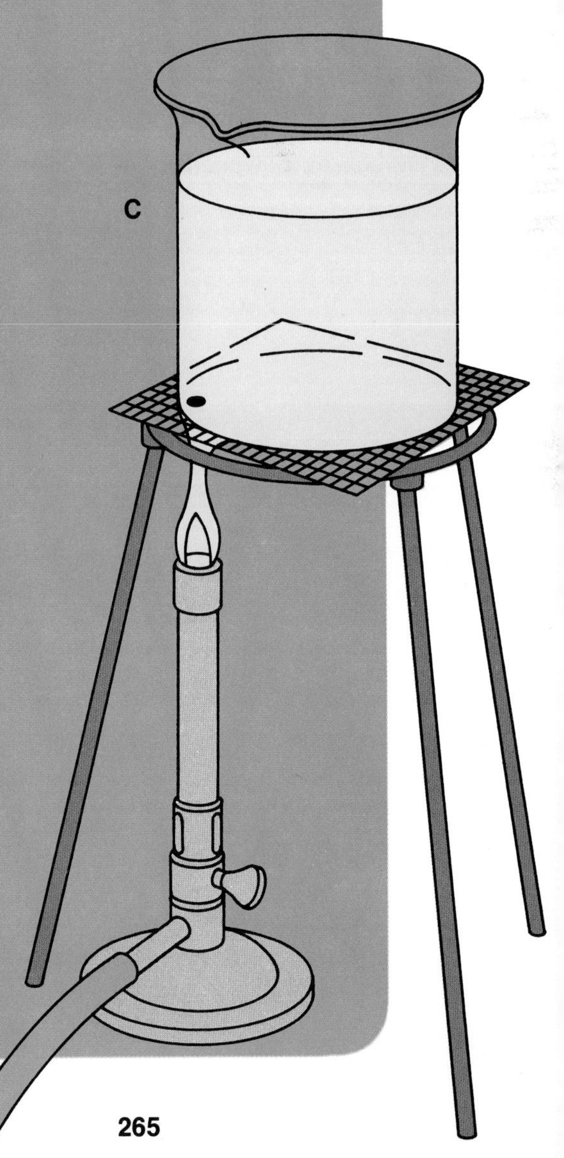

DO THIS

A. Fill the beaker with about 200 mL of tap water.

B. Use forceps to pick up a small crystal of $KMnO_4$. Drop the crystal into the water as close to the side of the beaker as possible. Observe what happens.

C. Set up the beaker and tripod as shown. **CAUTION:** *Be sure that you are wearing safety goggles*. Arrange the heat source so that the flame will be under the crystal. Then light the heat source.

D. Gently heat the water in the beaker for about 5 minutes. Observe the beaker continuously during this time. After completing your observations, turn off the heat source.

REPORT

1. Sketch or write a description of the way the water appeared shortly after you dropped the $KMnO_4$ crystal in it.

2. Sketch or write a description of how the colored water moved when heat was applied. Use arrows to indicate the direction of flow.

The heat radiated from this electric heater will be distributed throughout the air in the room by convection.

beaker moved to the surface. The cooler surface water moved to the bottom and was then heated. The $KMnO_4$ was carried by the moving water. Eventually the $KMnO_4$ was distributed throughout the beaker. In a similar manner heat was distributed throughout the beaker. The movement of the water in the beaker allowed all of it to be heated. This movement of heated molecules in a liquid or gas is called **convection** (kən vek′shən). Convection is the transfer of heat throughout a liquid or a gas by the movement of the molecules or atoms.

What is convection?

Convection does not occur in solids. In liquids and gases, molecules are free to move about. When a liquid or gas is heated, the density usually decreases. You have probably heard the saying, Warm air rises. Warm, less dense regions of liquids and gases tend to move upward. Cooler, denser regions sink. This movement allows heat to be transferred throughout the liquid or gas.

Water does not behave as do most other liquids. The density of water increases as it cools toward 4°C. However, at this point water begins to expand. As the temperature decreases from 4°C to 0°C, the density of the water decreases. At the freezing point, when liquid water changes to solid ice, there is a further expansion. This results in the ice becoming less dense than liquid water. The ice will then float in water.

Why does ice float in water?

This unusual property of water is important to living things. As the water at the surface of a lake cools to 4°C, it sinks to the bottom. Warmer water rises and cools. Eventually, all the water in the lake is 4°C. At this point, water on the surface is cooled to 0°C. The water on top of the lake is the first to freeze. It floats on the denser water below. This protects the lake from a great deal of convective heat loss.

If water continued to increase in density as it cooled, lakes would freeze from the bottom to the top. Some lakes might have a thin layer of ice on the bottom all year round. Fish and other living things would not be able to live in them.

Convection is the way heat is transferred in liquids and gases. In Activity 43 you will investigate heat transfer in solids.

Ice floats because water is less dense as a solid than as a liquid.

Activity 43 Heat Transfer in Solids

PURPOSE

To investigate heat transfer in a solid

MATERIALS

Copper strip
Heat source
Matches
Aluminum foil
Ringstand and ring
3 birthday candles
Safety goggles
Metric ruler

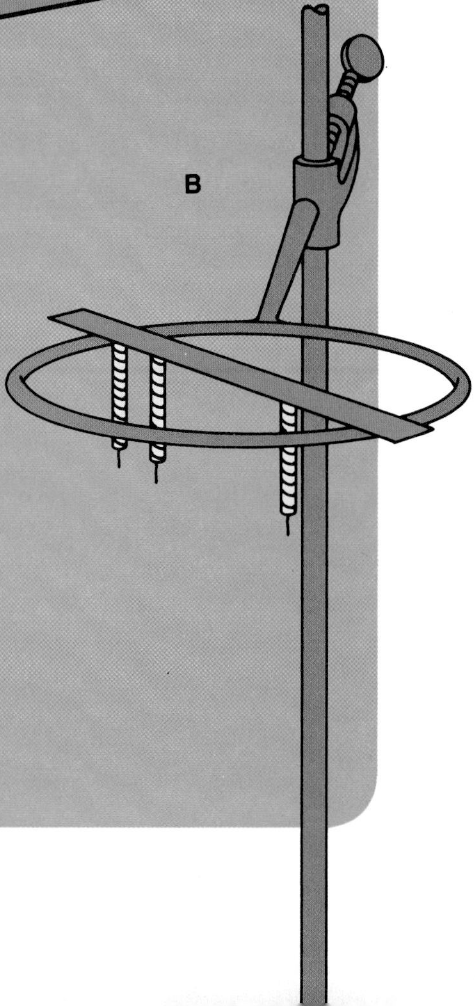

DO THIS

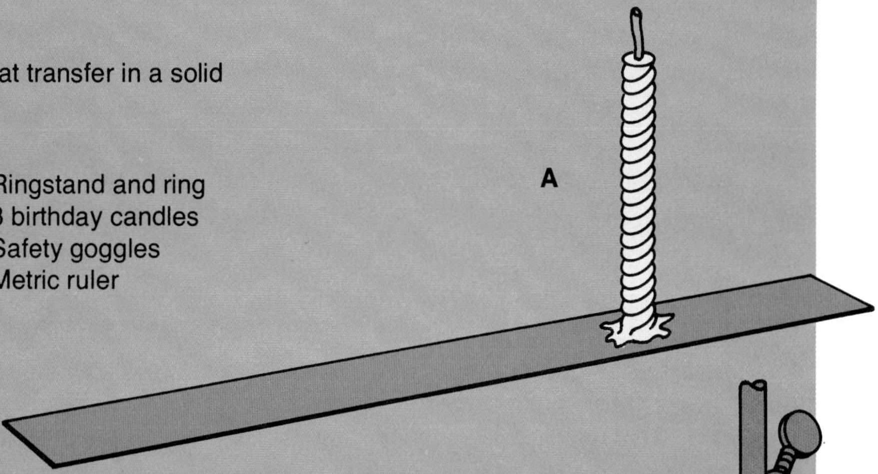

A. CAUTION: *Be sure to wear safety goggles.* Heat the base of a birthday candle until it melts. While the wax is still liquid, stand the candle on the copper strip 4 cm from one end. Do the same with two more candles, placing them at 8 cm and at 10 cm from the same end of the copper strip.

B. Place the copper strip upside down on the ring of the ringstand as shown.

C. Place a piece of aluminum foil on the table under the candles.

D. Heat the end of the copper strip farthest from the candles. Observe what happens.

REPORT

1. What happens to the candles when the copper strip is heated?

2. Explain how you think heat is transferred in a solid.

In Activity 43 the wax at the base of the candles melted even though the heat source was some distance away. Somehow, heat was transferred along the copper strip to the candles. Scientists use the term **conduction** (kən duk′shən) to describe the transfer of heat through a solid.

What is conduction?

How does conduction work? You learned that atoms and molecules in a solid are not free to move around. Yet they are constantly vibrating. When a solid is heated the molecules pick up kinetic energy. The molecules vibrate faster and move farther apart. The heated molecules collide with nearby molecules. The collisions cause them to pick up energy. These molecules vibrate faster and collide with other molecules. In this way the heat energy is passed throughout the solid. Different solids conduct heat at different rates. Usually, good conductors of electricity are good conductors of heat. Copper, aluminum, and silver are examples of good conductors of heat. Asbestos, wood, wool, paper, Styrofoam, and cork are poor conductors of heat. Poor conductors of heat are called **insulators** (in′sə lā tərz).

Name three metals that are good conductors of heat.

What are insulators?

Homes are insulated to slow down heat loss. Heat escapes mainly by conduction and convection. Materials such as Styrofoam and glass wool are used for insulation because they are poor conductors. In addition they help to prevent convection.

Heat conducted through the frying pan to the egg causes the protein in the egg to solidify.

Radiation

What is radiation?

How do electromagnetic waves generate heat?

You have already observed a third method of heat transfer. In Activity 41 light/heat energy was transferred from a light bulb to a model of a greenhouse. The transfer of heat through space without the transfer of matter is called **radiation** (rā dē ā'shən). Radiation does not involve the transfer of heat from molecule to molecule as in conduction. When heat is radiated, it travels through space in the form of **electromagnetic** (i lek tro mag net'ik) **waves.** Many forms of energy travel through space as electromagnetic waves. Light, radio waves, X rays, and ultraviolet (UV) light are all electromagnetic waves.

How do electromagnetic waves generate heat? Earlier you learned that friction was caused by one material interacting with another. This interaction produced heat energy. A similar model will help you to understand how heat is generated by electromagnetic waves. As electromagnetic waves move they interact with the air and the surface of the earth. This interaction produces heat energy. This is why electromagnetic waves can be referred to as light/heat energy.

SUMMARY Friction results when one system moves against another system. Heat is produced in the process. Systems can absorb and trap heat. Certain systems and materials absorb heat better than others. Heat can be transferred from one system to another by convection, conduction, and radiation. Materials that are good conductors of heat are considered to be poor insulators.

SCIENCE WORDS

absorption
convection
conduction
insulators
radiation
electromagnetic waves

REVIEW QUESTIONS

Fill in the blanks with the correct terms.

1. Three ways heat can be transferred are ____________, ____________, and ____________.
2. Two materials that are good insulators are ____________ and ____________.
3. Light, radio waves, and X rays are examples of ____________ waves.
4. Heat moves through a solid by ____________.
5. ____________ is a force that resists motion.
6. Energy from a bulb system is in the form of ____________ and ____________.

Mark each statement true (T) or false (F).

1. _____ Dark surfaces heat more quickly than light surfaces.
2. _____ Movement of heat in a gas is called conduction.
3. _____ Water in a lake freezes from the bottom up.
4. _____ Molecules move faster as they are heated.
5. _____ Many forms of energy travel through space as electromagnetic waves.

APPLYING WHAT YOU LEARNED

1. Describe how water in a lake freezes. Why is this important to living things in the lake?
2. Describe how a greenhouse works.
3. Why should homeowners be encouraged to insulate their homes?

Energy can be transferred as a disturbance in matter, known as wave motion.

14

Interaction and Wave Motion

In previous chapters you have investigated many interactions. Most of these interactions took place between systems in direct physical contact. For example, the interaction of a seltzer tablet and water causes a gas to be released. When water and a heat source interact, the temperature of the water increases. You are familiar with these types of interactions. In this chapter you will investigate interactions that do not require physical contact.

Wave Motion

Can you think of examples of interactions that do not require direct contact between systems? The transfer of energy from the sun to the earth is one example. Other examples are the transfer of light from a light bulb and the transfer of sound from a passing truck. In each of these cases systems interact but there is no direct contact.

What is wave motion?

There are other examples of interactions that do not require direct contact between systems. Many of these interactions are the result of **wave motion.** Wave motion is the transfer of energy from place to place without the transfer of matter. A wave can be thought of as a disturbance that transfers energy through matter. The matter through which the wave moves is called the **medium** (mē′dē əm). When the disturbance moves through matter, the matter itself does not move from one place to another. Sound is a wave motion that moves through matter. Ripples on the surface of a pond are waves that are produced by a disturbance of the water.

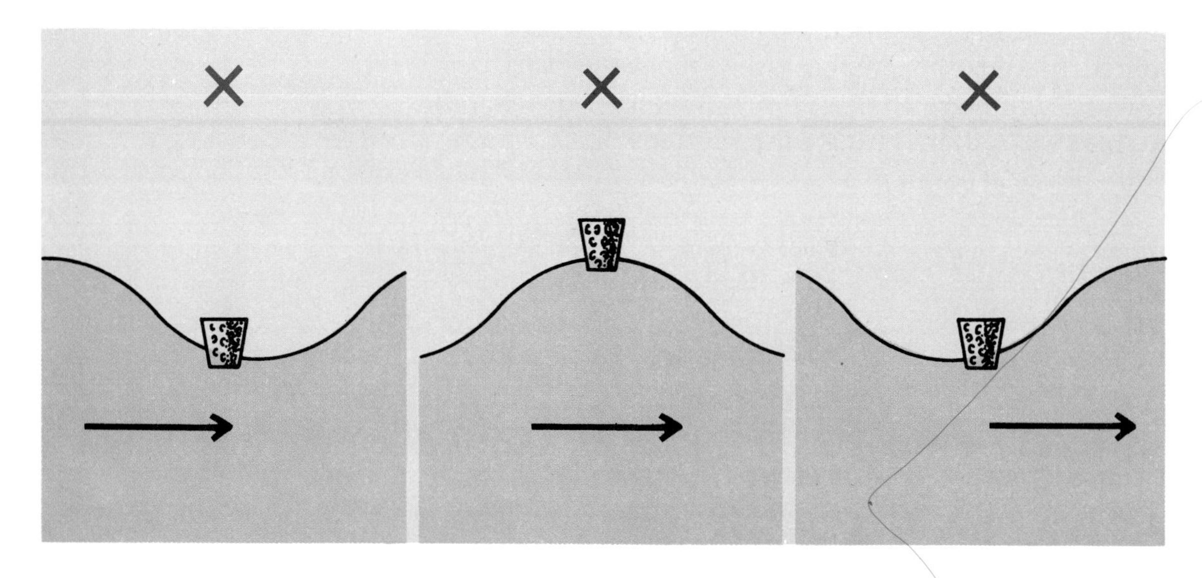

FIGURE 14–1
In wave motion, energy is transferred from place to place without the transfer of matter. Notice that the position of the cork relative to the stationary background point has not changed.

How can a simple wave be produced? Figure 14–2 shows two people, each holding one end of a rope. The person on the left has flicked the end of the rope up and down. A disturbance has been produced in the rope. The disturbance, called a **pulse** (puls), is part of a wave. The pulse moves down the rope. It transfers energy to the second person. This transfer occurs without the transfer of matter. The rope does not move from one person to the other. Only the energy is transferred. As the energy arrives, the second person's hands may move up and down. If the disturbance were strong enough, it could knock the second person down.

FIGURE 14–2
Flicking the rope produces a disturbance, or pulse, in the rope.

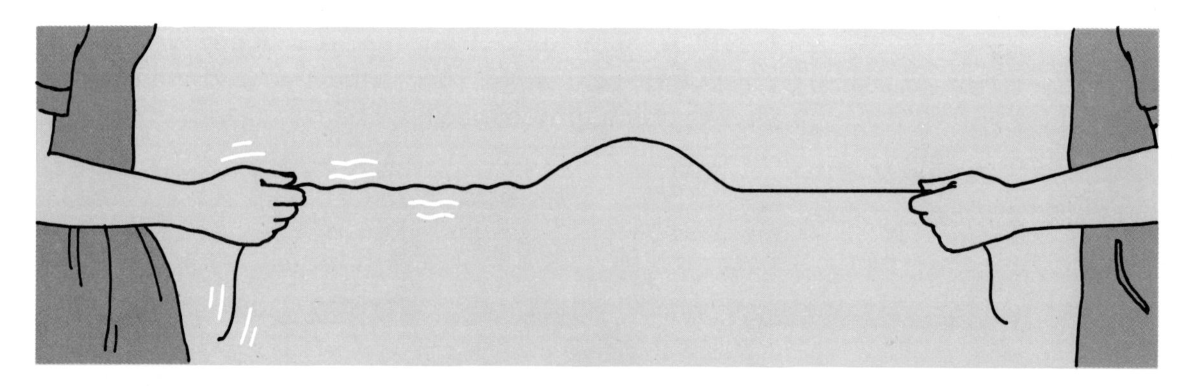

A series of waves can be produced by shaking the rope up and down at a certain speed. Figure 14–3 shows the wave pattern that might develop. Using rope, try to produce a similar wave pattern.

FIGURE 14–3
A series of waves

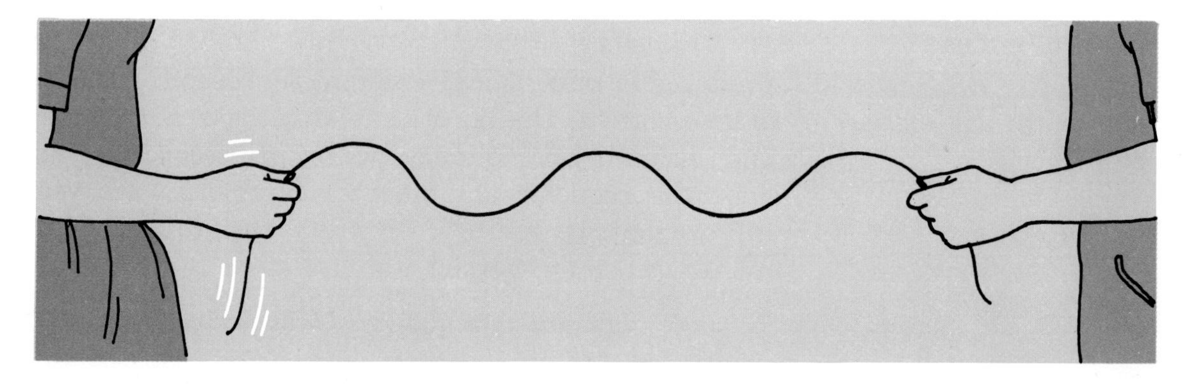

It is difficult to draw something that is constantly changing its shape. However, there is a device that can stop motion photographically. This device is called a **stroboscope** (strob′ə skōp). A stroboscope is a light source that flashes bright light at very short time intervals. The brightness and the short time intervals freeze the motion. The stroboscope is used with a camera. The photographs capture the nature of wave motion. In this way, wave motion can be analyzed in more detail.

What is amplitude?

Some of the important properties of waves are shown in Figure 14–4. **Amplitude** (am′plə tüd) is the maximum height reached by a wave from its rest position. The **crest** is the highest point on a wave. **Wavelength** is the distance from the crest of one wave to the crest of the next wave. The symbol for wavelength is the Greek letter λ, pronounced lambda.

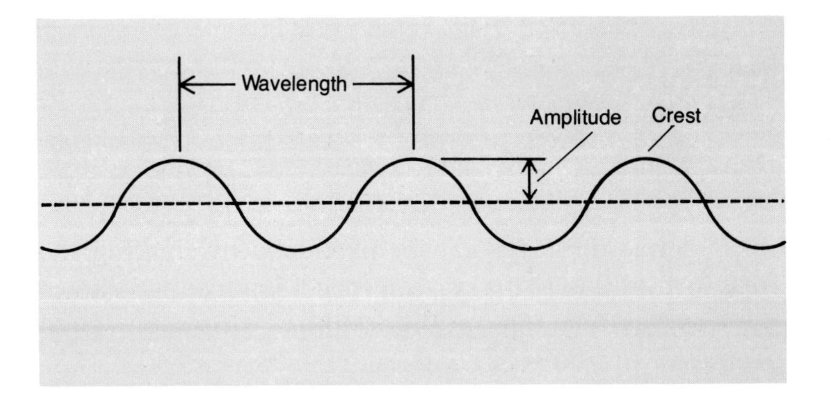

FIGURE 14–4
The properties of a wave

What is the unit for frequency?

Frequency (frē′kwən sē) is the number of waves produced or passing a given point per second. The unit of frequency is the **hertz** (Hz). One hertz is equal to one cycle, or one complete wave, per second. If you know the frequency and the wavelength of a wave, you can calculate its velocity. Velocity is the product of the frequency and the wavelength.

$$\text{velocity} = \text{frequency} \times \text{wavelength}$$
$$v = f \times \lambda$$

With this equation you can find any of the quantities (v, f, or λ) if you know the other two.

Suppose a wave had a wavelength of 33 m. Its frequency was 10 Hz. What was its velocity?

$$
\begin{aligned}
v &= f \times \lambda \\
&= 10\ \text{Hz} \times 33\ \text{m} \\
&= 330\ \text{m/s}
\end{aligned}
$$

Measure the wavelength of the wave shown in Figure 14–5. If the frequency of this wave is 25 Hz, what is the velocity of the wave?

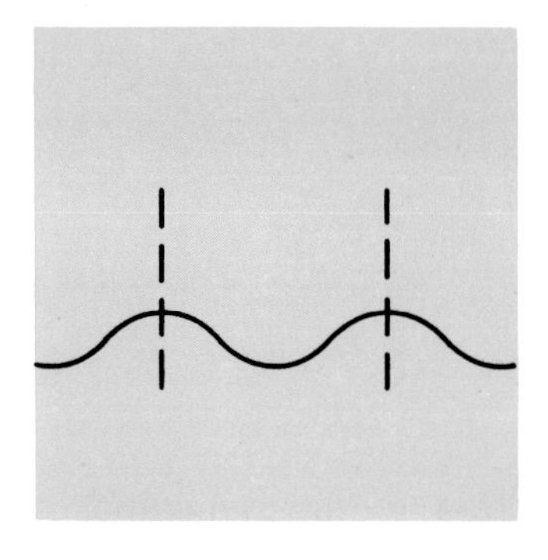

FIGURE 14–5

Sound

Sound is wave motion that can be detected by the human ear. Sound can travel through the medium of air. The disturbance created by the sound wave travels as a change in air pressure. Sound waves are compression waves. Figure 14–6 illustrates a model of a compression wave. The coils of the spring act as the medium for the wave. As the wave travels through the spring, areas of compression alternate with areas of expansion. As a sound wave travels, the air does not travel forward with the sound. Remember, in wave motion energy is transferred without the transfer of matter. Sound can also travel through solids and liquids.

What kind of wave motion is sound?

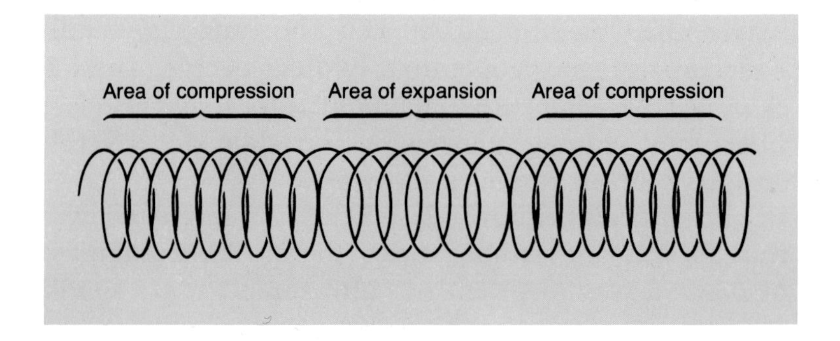

FIGURE 14–6
A compression wave

Sounds of musical instruments are produced by the vibrations of reeds, strings, air columns, and membranes. A string on a guitar can vibrate in several different ways, as shown in Figure 14–7. The main frequency of vibrations of the guitar string is called the **fundamental** (fun də men′təl) **tone. Overtones** (ō′vər tōnz) are whole-number multiples of the main frequency of vibrations. If a string vibrates at a main frequency of 210 Hz, the first overtone will be 420 Hz. The second overtone will be 630 Hz. The third overtone will be 840 Hz and so on. The strength of the different overtones gives a fundamental sound a particular tone quality. The string vibrating by itself cannot move many molecules of gas. Therefore the body of the guitar is added to help amplify the sound.

If a guitar string has a main frequency of 210 Hz, what will its third overtone be?

FIGURE 14–7

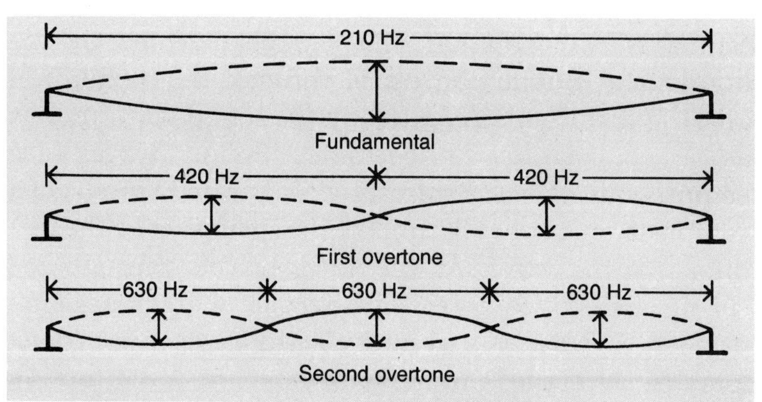

Human beings cannot hear all frequencies. Usually the human ear is sensitive to vibrations that range between 20 Hz and 20 000 Hz. The range is usually wider in younger people than in older people. There is evidence that exposure to loud music for long periods of time may damage hearing. The damage severely curtails hearing in ranges above 5000 Hz.

To what range of vibrations is the human ear sensitive?

Frequencies above 20 000 Hz are useful even though humans cannot hear them. These high-frequency waves are called **ultrasonic** (ul trə son′ik)

Bats use ultrasonic waves to locate their prey. Humans cannot hear these high-frequency waves. The bat's ability to produce and detect ultrasonic waves is essential for its survival.

waves. Ultrasonic waves are used in dentistry and in many medical laboratories. Instruments that cannot be heated to high temperatures are cleaned by the high-frequency vibrations. The U.S. Navy uses ultrasonic waves in the form of **sonar** (sō′när). A narrow beam of ultrasonic waves is sent through the water and is reflected back to a receiver. Sonar is used in navigation, communication, and detection of objects and surfaces.

What are high-frequency waves called?

All sound waves moving through the same medium travel at the same speed. This is so, even though there may be many waves with different frequencies. This is why all notes played at the same time by a band reach your ear together. However, the speed of sound changes with varying conditions in the medium. The density and temperature of the medium will affect the speed of sound moving through it. The speed of sound in air is 330 m/s at 0°C at the earth's surface.

What is the speed of sound in air?

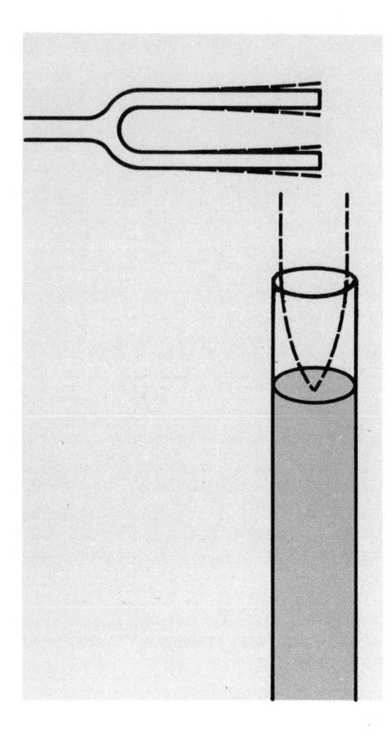

FIGURE 14–8
The sound waves from the tuning fork are reinforced by reflected waves in the column of air.

EXCURSION 13
You can become more familiar with sound by doing Excursion 13, "Sound."

Finding the Speed of Sound

Different shapes of musical instruments emphasize different wavelengths or notes. The same principle can be used to calculate the speed of sound. Sound of a particular wavelength is transmitted through a hollow tube and reflected back. When the tube is the right length for the particular wavelength, the sound waves reinforce each other. The sound becomes louder. Figure 14–8 shows that waves reinforce each other when the increase in loudness is heard.

Suppose a tuning fork is placed at the top of a tube. The tube is filled with water. The tuning fork, which vibrates with a frequency of 250 Hz, is struck. At the same time the water level inside the tube is slowly lowered. The sound travels down the air column to the surface of the water. The sound is then reflected back up the tube. When the length of the air column is $\frac{1}{4}$ the wavelength of the sound, the sound will be reinforced. The ear detects this as an increase in loudness. The same thing will occur when the length of the air column is $\frac{3}{4}$, $\frac{5}{4}$, and $\frac{7}{4}$ the wavelength of the sound. The first increase in loudness occurs when the air column is 0.33 m long. Therefore the wavelength of the sound must be four times 0.33 m, or 1.32 m.

$$\begin{aligned} v &= f \times \lambda \\ &= 250\ \text{Hz} \times 1.32\ \text{m} \\ &= 330\ \text{m/s} \end{aligned}$$

As the water is lowered further, there will be an increase in loudness at 0.99 m. Increases in loudness will also occur at 1.65 m and 2.31 m.

What might be better than fingerprints as a means of identification in the future?

Sound is a valuable part of our lives. It may become even more important in the future. Someday people may be more easily identified by their voiceprints than by their fingerprints. Using voiceprints and computer

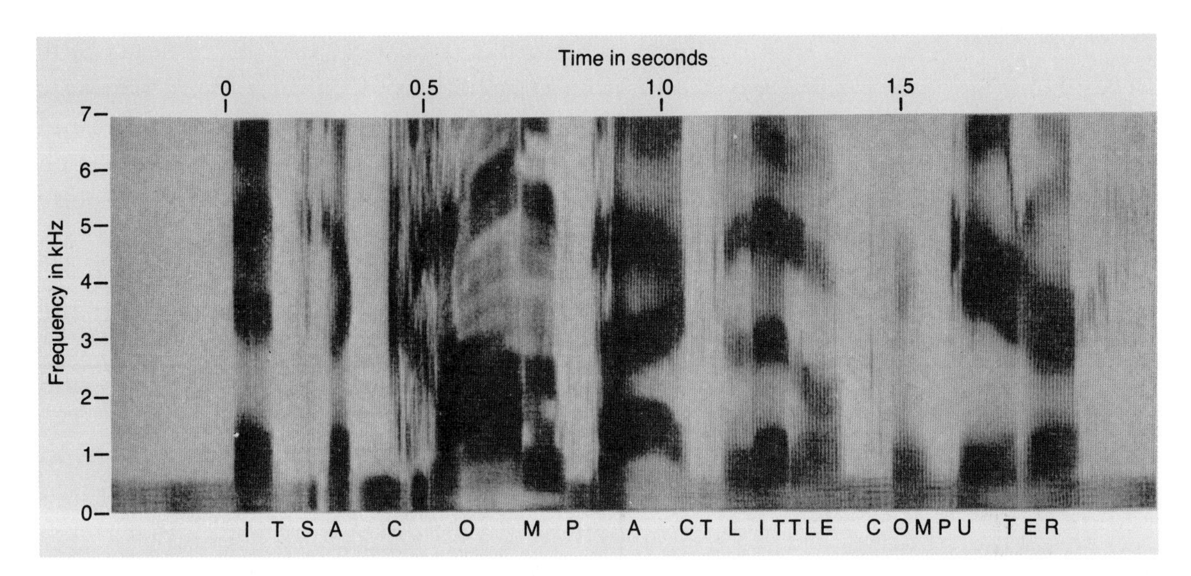

technology, most business could be done by telephone. There would be a permanent record of what was said and who said it.

This is a voiceprint of the phrase "It's a compact little computer." You can see how the voiceprint varies for each letter in the phrase. Another person speaking the same phrase would produce a similar but distinctly different voiceprint.

The Electromagnetic Waves

In Chapter 13 you learned that heat could be transferred by electromagnetic waves. There are similarities and differences between electromagnetic waves and the other wave motions you have studied in this chapter.

Electromagnetic waves do not require a medium in which to travel. They can travel through the vacuum of space. Electromagnetic waves travel at a speed of 300 000 000 m/s in a vacuum. This is much faster than the speed of the sound or other waves you have investigated. The origin of these waves is different from that of all other waves. Some electromagnetic waves are produced by energy changes in electrons in atoms. Nuclear disintegration processes also produce electromagnetic waves.

Name two sources of electromagnetic waves.

There are similarities between electromagnetic waves and other types of wave motion. Electromagnetic waves may be described in terms of frequency and wavelength. Other characteristics of wave motion, such as reflection, are also characteristics of electromagnetic waves.

There are many different kinds of electromagnetic waves. Together they make up the **electromagnetic spectrum.** Included in this spectrum are X rays, radio waves, visible light, ultraviolet light, gamma rays, and infrared rays.

List four types of electromagnetic waves.

The major parts of the electromagnetic spectrum are shown in Figure 14–9. Notice how the various types of electromagnetic waves differ from each other. Each type has a different frequency, wavelength, and energy content. The shorter the wavelength, the greater the energy content of the wave.

The spectrum diagram in Figure 14–9 shows some of the sources of electromagnetic radiation in the environment. Even in your own home you cannot avoid exposure to waves given off by electrical wiring, television, and radio. With increased usage of microwave

FIGURE 14–9
The electromagnetic spectrum

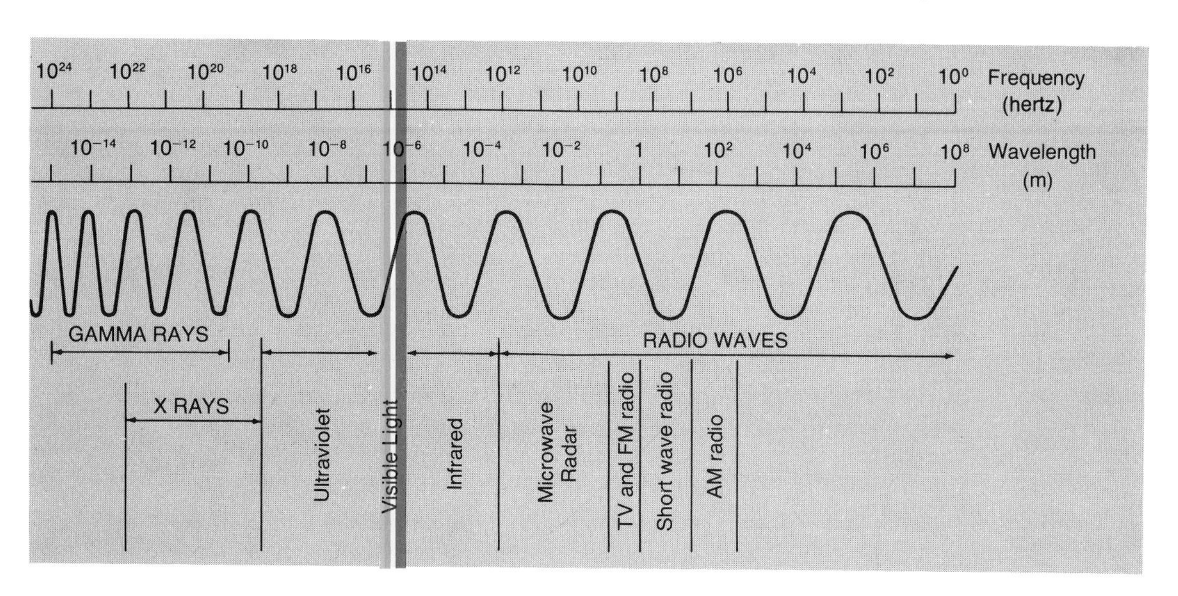

The antennas on these towers are used to pick up and retransmit low-frequency electromagnetic waves called microwaves. Microwaves are used to carry telephone, telegraph, and television signals.

EXCURSION 14
In Excursion 14, "Light," you will be introduced to the characteristics of light and become familiar with some optics.

ovens, people are exposed to yet another source of this energy. Something as simple as heat from a radiator is a source of infrared waves. Outside the home, almost the entire electromagnetic spectrum is radiated by the sun. It is almost impossible to escape exposure to this form of radiation. In Chapter 13 the terms *heat* and *light* were used to describe the energy given off by a light bulb. This indicates that most of the waves given off are in the infrared and visible parts of the spectrum.

SUMMARY Wave motion is the transfer of energy from place to place without the transfer of matter. Many types of waves require a medium in which to travel. Wavelength is the distance between the crests of two successive waves. The number of waves produced each second is the frequency of the wave motion. Wavelength and frequency can be used to calculate the speed of the wave: $v = f \times \lambda$. Sound is a compression wave. Humans can usually hear sounds with frequencies between 20 Hz and 20 000 Hz. Frequencies above this are called ultrasonic waves. Electromagnetic waves do not require a medium in which to travel. These waves are produced by nuclear and atomic changes.

SCIENCE WORDS

wave motion
medium
pulse
stroboscope
amplitude
crest
wavelength
frequency
hertz
fundamental tone
overtones
ultrasonic waves
sonar
electromagnetic spectrum

REVIEW QUESTIONS

Match the term in Column A with the correct answer in Column B.

A	B
1. Wave motion ___	**a.** The maximum height reached by a wave from its rest position
2. Amplitude ___	**b.** High-frequency waves
3. Frequency ___	**c.** Highest point on a wave
4. Overtone ___	**d.** Transfer of energy without the transfer of matter
5. Ultrasonic waves ___	**e.** Multiple of the main frequency of vibration
6. Crest ___	**f.** Distance from the crest of one wave to the crest of the next wave
7. Wavelength ___	**g.** The number of waves produced or passing a given point per second

Fill in the blanks with the correct terms.

1. The human ear is sensitive to vibrations between ____________ Hz and ____________ Hz.
2. The U.S. Navy uses ultrasonic waves in the form of ____________.
3. The ____________ and ____________ of the medium will affect the speed of sound that is moving through it.
4. Sound is a ____________ wave.
5. All electromagnetic waves together make up the electromagnetic ____________.

APPLYING WHAT YOU LEARNED

1. Suppose you observed a wave that had a wavelength of 27 m. Its frequency was 12 Hz. What was its velocity?
2. If a string vibrates at 186 Hz, what are the first, second, and third overtones?

UNIT REVIEW

1. Look up the following information about X rays: How are X rays used in medicine and dentistry? How is the dosage determined? What safety precautions must be followed? Write a report including the above information. Try to get additional information from an X-ray technician. If possible, include some X-ray pictures in your report.
2. List five examples of kinetic energy and five examples of potential energy. Show how each source of potential energy may yield kinetic energy. Identify the potential energy that is related to each example of kinetic energy given.
3. There are energy changes taking place along the entire path of a ball thrown into the air. Diagram the path that a ball follows from the time it is thrown into the air until it hits the ground. Label the type of energy the ball has in the following positions.

   a. In the hand before being thrown
   b. Just after being thrown
   c. When the ball has reached the highest point in its path
   d. Just before hitting the ground
   e. After the ball has come to rest on the ground

   Does the ball have the same amount of energy at any two points in its path? List the similarities between this situation and the pendulum activity.
4. *Speed* and *velocity* are terms that are often misused. Using reference books, write a short explanation of each term. Use specific examples.
5. Collect at least ten pictures of simple machines. Label each one and make a collage or a bulletin board display.
6. You are given two similar metal rods. You are told that one is a magnet, the other is not. Explain how you could determine which rod is the magnet, using no other materials.
7. Collect pictures and news articles that report new discoveries in physics. Make a bulletin board display and discuss the items.
8. Using reference books in the library or your classroom, write a short report on two of the following topics.
   a. Black holes in space
   b. Quarks
   c. Nuclear fusion reactors
   d. Gravitational wave theory
   e. Transistors and integrated circuits

Careers

Physics is the study of the properties and behavior of matter and energy and the laws that relate to the interactions of matter and energy. Physics is a very exact science, founded on mathematics. A scientist who specializes in physics is called a physicist.

About 50 percent of all physicists are engaged in research and development. Their work may lead to new discoveries. Often research and development improves methods and products already in use.

All R&D physicists must have completed at least four years of college with a major in physics. In most cases a physicist continues to study beyond college. Most physicists specialize in one or more subfields. Some specialize in fluid mechanics. This field deals with such phenomena as supersonic flow and shock waves. A thermal physicist studies heat, including both high and low temperature properties of matter. Cryogenics is the study of extremely low temperatures and the changes in the properties of matter and energy at these temperatures.

Nuclear and high energy physics are concerned with the basic particles that make up matter. Physicists in these fields develop nuclear power plants and the reactor designs for those plants. The study of the particles that make up the atom may lead to new sources of energy.

You are probably familiar with transistors. Transistors were invented by physicists specializing in solid-state physics. Miniature electronic devices found in television sets, radios, and computers were developed by solid-state physicists. These miniature components are also used for navigation and guidance systems here on earth and out in space.

Physicists are crossing into other fields of science. Geophysics, biophysics, oceanography, astrophysics, and chemical physics are examples of these mergers. Perhaps you will be a pioneer in one of these exciting new subfields.

Many physicists are involved in teaching and writing about the subject of physics or its subfields. Still others work for local, state, or federal government agencies. Do you see a career in physics that interests you?

Dr. Stephen Hawking (right) is an astrophysicist noted for his research concerning the possible existence of black holes in space.

Research

We take for granted most of the events that occur in the world around us. The physicist is constantly seeking to explain the behavior of the physical world in a logical way. As with other scientists, there are two basic groups of physicists, the theorists and the experimentalists. Both groups are involved in research and development. An experimental physicist usually works in a laboratory. He or she may be attempting to produce a new product or to improve an existing one. The data collected may be studied by a theorist. The theorist may propose an explanation or develop a mathematical relationship to explain the data. The experimentalist may then become involved again by testing the theory in the laboratory.

Physicists may be involved in either basic or applied research. Basic research is study carried out on the frontiers of scientific knowledge. New discoveries and theories usually result from basic research. Most basic research is carried out in university or industrial laboratories. Applied research is concerned with developing new or improved products or processes. Applied research has a more immediate goal than basic research. That goal is the development of practical uses for discoveries made in basic research. For example, basic research in solid-state physics led to the invention of semiconductor materials and transistors. Applied research made use of these discoveries with the development of the integrated circuit. Today we see the evidence of these developments in calculators, smaller TVs, and radios.

Today research is going on in all the fields of physics. Cryogenics is the study of the behavior of matter and energy at extremely low temperatures. It has been discovered that when the temperatures of certain materials are reduced to near absolute zero (−273°C), these materials become super-conductors. This means that the materials offer no resistance to the flow of electrical energy. The extremely low temperatures involved prevent practical use of this property. Therefore physicists are now looking for super-conducting materials at temperatures more realistic for everyday usage.

Astrophysicists are investigating the possible existence of black holes in space. Black holes seem to be stars that burn out and then collapse into very small dense points. They are so dense that they produce extreme gravitational fields. Light can't escape from black holes because of this.

Particle physics deals with the question of what makes up an atom. Scientists are investigating theoretical building blocks of atoms called *quarks*. Some scientists believe that a few fundamental types of particles may account for all of the more complex particles that are discovered.

The questions continue as long as humans are going to progress in their study of the physical nature of matter. Do you enjoy asking these questions, and, more important, trying to answer puzzles? If so, a branch of physics could be the place for you.

Cryogenics has applications in the fields of medicine and biology as well as in physics.

UNIT FIVE

A CHANGING WORLD

Oil is an important natural resource. Much of the oil found under land masses has been used up. Scientists are looking for new oil deposits under the oceans. This oil well is off the coast of Santa Barbara, California.

15

Our Limited Resources

Today, just as in the past, people are dependent on the earth's **resources** (ri sôr′siz). Resources are natural wealth such as land, mineral deposits, and forests. Materials such as gold, copper, and iron have always been important to people. Today oil, coal, and natural gas are equally important. In many countries these materials are the major sources of energy.

The earth's natural resources are limited. The availability of any resource depends on the existing amount of the resource. It also depends on the number of people using the resource and on how fast the resource is used. Nothing can be done to change the existing amount of most resources. It is also difficult to control the number of people using a particular resource. It may be possible, however, to control the rate of use of that resource. In this chapter you will investigate some problems related to the limited supply of natural resources.

Fossil Fuels

Name the fossil fuels.

Name the four elements found in large amounts in plants.

A **fossil** (fos′əl) **fuel** is a fuel that formed from the bodies of plants and animals that died millions of years ago. Coal, oil, and natural gas are fossil fuels.

Plants contain large amounts of hydrogen, oxygen, carbon, and nitrogen. When plants die, these elements are released into the air or ground. Most of the hydrogen and oxygen escapes in the form of water or water vapor. Nitrogen usually is released as ammonia gas, and carbon as carbon dioxide gas. During the formation of coal, dead plants became covered with rocks, soil, and water. This pressed the plants tightly together, slowing the release of the elements. In the process, much of the hydrogen and oxygen was still lost. However, almost all the carbon remained trapped. Continued pressure over many years gradually changed this remaining plant material into coal.

Coal is the most plentiful of the three fossil fuels. The largest coal reserves, about 60 percent of the world's supply, are in the Soviet Union. The United States has about 20 percent of the world's supply of coal.

The miner at the left in the photograph is operating a small electric locomotive. It is used in deep mines to move coal cars along a tunnel called a haulageway.

Coal beds close to the earth's surface are usually strip-mined. Although strip mining is fast and efficient, it may damage the land beyond repair.

Oil and natural gas usually occur together. Scientists believe that these fuels formed from deposits of dead plants and animals in the sea. These deposits are believed to have formed in places where the water contained little oxygen. There, **bacteria** (bak tir′ē ə) broke down the bodies of the plants and animals, releasing the oxygen and nitrogen. The material remaining—composed chiefly of hydrogen and carbon—gradually became covered with sand and rocks. Pressure built up as the material was buried deeper and deeper. Over many years and under great pressure, the material gradually was changed into oil and natural gas.

Sometimes natural gas is burned off from an oil well. It is a waste of a valuable and limited natural resource.

Oil and natural gas are found in many parts of the world, but in varying amounts. The United States has about 10 percent of the world's total supply of oil. The Middle East has about 30 percent of the world's oil; China and the Soviet Union together have about 25 percent.

What is a nonrenewable resource?

Fossil fuels are **nonrenewable resources.** A nonrenewable resource is one whose quantity is limited. Once the resource is used up, it cannot be renewed. Fossil fuels account for 95 percent of the energy used in the United States. Table 15–1 shows how long our fossil fuels are expected to last if they continue to be used at the present rate.

TABLE 15–1 • United States Fossil Fuel Supply

FOSSIL FUEL	SUPPLY REMAINING (years)
Coal	350–400
Natural gas	15
Oil	30–35

Activity 44 Fossil Fuel Use

PURPOSE

To determine some of the uses of fossil fuels

MATERIALS

Paper and pencil

DO THIS

A. List ten mechanical devices that require the use of a fossil fuel as their source of energy.

B. After each device listed, name the fossil fuel used.

C. Combine your data with the data of your classmates. If the same mechanical device was listed by more than one person, use it only once in making up the class list.

REPORT

1. According to your class list, which fossil fuel appears to be used the most? Which appears to be used the least?

2. What possible problems could be caused by the present use of fossil fuels in the United States?

3. Suggest some ways these problems might be solved.

Which method of mining results in the greater loss of coal?

In addition to the limited supply of fossil fuels, much of these fuels is lost during mining and drilling operations. For example, consider one metric ton (1000 kg) of coal in the ground. If that coal is strip-mined, 200 kg of it is lost when the coal is taken out of the ground. If the coal is deep-mined, 420 kg is lost. An additional 80 kg is lost when the coal is processed. Another 10 kg is

FIGURE 15–1

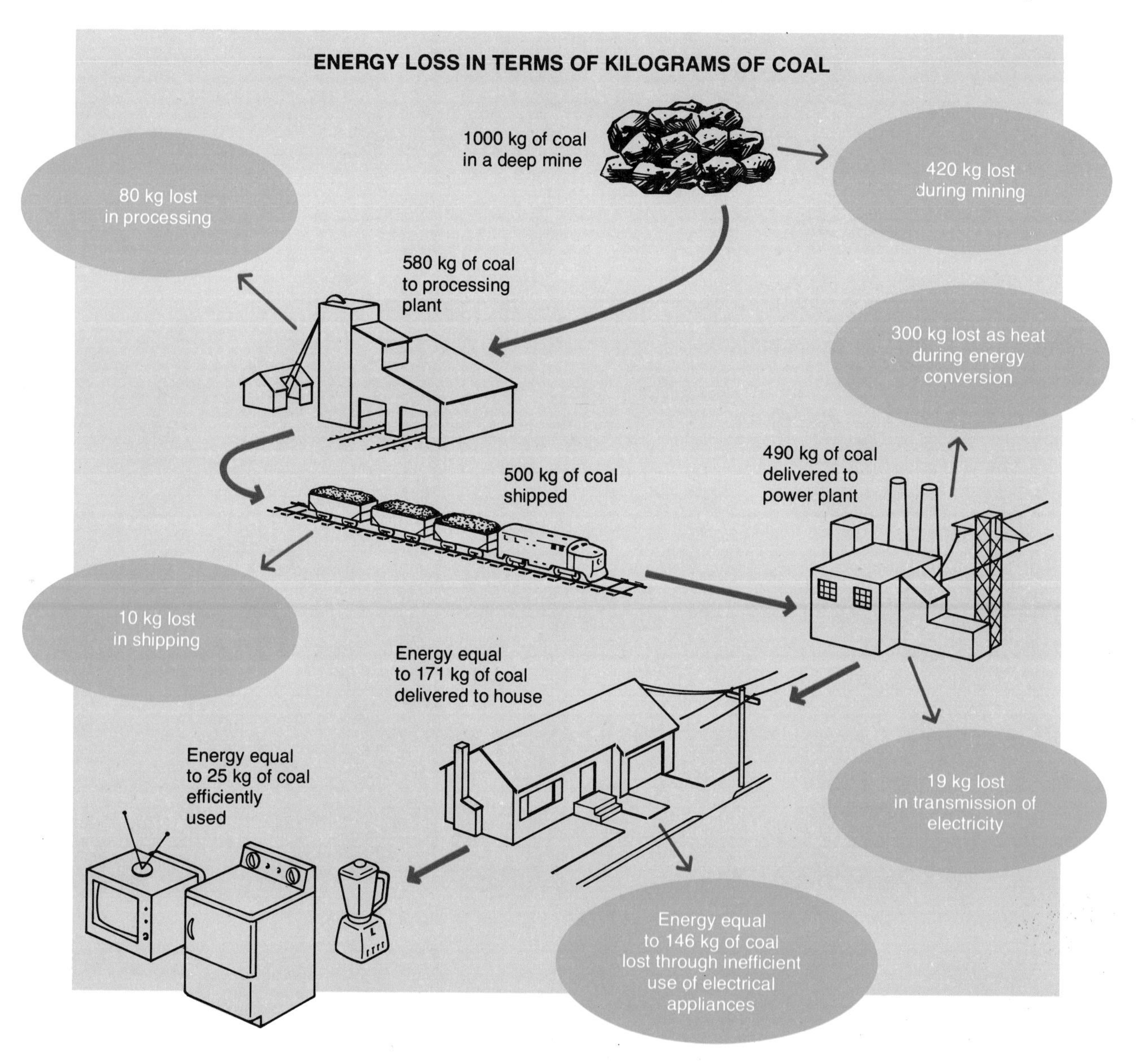

lost when the coal is shipped from the mine site to the place where it will be used. In other words, only 710 kg of the original 1000 kg of coal can be used if the coal is strip-mined. Only 490 kg can be used if the coal is taken from a deep mine.

Now assume that the coal is deep-mined and delivered to a power plant. There the coal is burned to generate **electricity.** During this process, about 300 kg of the original 490 kg of coal delivered to the power plant is lost as heat energy. About 10 percent of the remaining energy (19 kg of coal) is lost in the transmission of electricity to your home. Even more energy (146 kg of coal) is lost through the inefficient operation of electrical devices. Less than 10 percent of the remaining energy is efficiently used. This amounts to only about 25 kg of the original 1000 kg of coal.

The situation is no better with oil or gas. No matter which fuel is used, energy is lost in the process of producing useful energy.

Energy and Food Production

Food production in the United States uses a large amount of energy. Most food is shipped by truck from farmer to processor to packager to supermarket. Often, people drive many kilometers to buy their food. In addition, farmers have become dependent on fossil fuels. They need oil or oil products to run their tractors and other equipment. They also rely on oil products used in the production of artificial fertilizers, **pesticides** (pes′tə sīds), and **herbicides** (hėr′bə sīds). Pesticides and herbicides are chemical substances used to destroy pests, such as insects and weeds. Activity 45 will give you an idea of how food production is dependent on fossil fuels.

Name three things used in farming that are produced from oil products.

These photographs show contrasting farming methods. More food can be produced per unit of energy by non-mechanized farming (bottom left and right). However, mechanized farming (top) results in a greater total yield of food.

Some people in the United States believe that other countries should use our methods to produce food. If every country used our methods, there would not be enough fossil fuels to go around. In the United States, five to ten units of energy are used to produce one unit of food. Some underdeveloped countries produce five to ten units of food for every unit of energy used in food production. In terms of efficient food production, these countries produce one hundred times more food per unit of energy than we do.

Our dependence on artificial fertilizers developed from fossil fuels is wasteful. Using natural fertilizers would save energy and may be better for the soil. Practicing better crop rotation would also help to produce more food. It would decrease to some extent our reliance on fertilizers. Rotating crops regularly would help return needed minerals to the soil.

Activity 45 Fossil Fuel and Food

PURPOSE

To show how food production depends on fossil fuels

MATERIALS

Paper and pencil

DO THIS

A. Go to a supermarket in your neighborhood.

B. List ten food items found in the store. Make sure that these are edible food items.

C. Next to each item on your list, write the name of the city in which the item was produced.

REPORT

1. What fossil fuels were used to grow, process, and deliver each of the ten items on your list? Table 1 will help you to determine this.

2. Compare the fossil fuels used for each item on your list with the remaining fuel supply as shown in Table 15-1. What possible problems may we face in the future? Explain your answer.

3. Suggest some ways these problems might be solved.

TABLE 1 • Fuel and Food Production

DEVICES USED IN FOOD PRODUCTION	FOSSIL FUELS USED
Tractor	Oil
Truck	Oil
Canning machine	Natural gas, or oil
Freezer	Coal, natural gas, or oil
Machines that make fertilizers, herbicides, and pesticides	Coal, natural gas, or oil
Airplane to spray herbicides and pesticides	Oil

Our dependence on fossil-fuel products to kill weeds and insects may have to be changed. Mechanical methods of controlling weeds use much less energy. New methods that do not require the use of pesticides for controlling insects are also being developed. When pesticide spraying is necessary, however, the pesticide might be applied in a manner other than from an airplane. Spraying from an airplane wastes pesticide and creates a large amount of pollution. Spraying pesticides by hand or by mechanical means uses approximately 83 percent less energy than spraying by airplane.

After the food crops have been grown and harvested, a great deal of energy is wasted in the processing and packaging of the food. Food is usually transported in trucks. In terms of energy conservation, truck transportation is less efficient than transportation by train. Additional energy is used when we drive to the supermarket to shop. We must find more efficient methods of growing, processing, transporting, and shopping for food in order to conserve our energy resources.

In a cannery, automated machines process and package food. The canning methods are efficient and timesaving, but they use a great deal of energy.

Reusing Our Resources

Minerals are important compounds and elements scattered in pockets in the earth's crust. These mineral deposits are usually formed by slow, **geologic** (jē ə loj′ik) **processes.** Since there is a limited amount of each mineral, every available deposit may be found at some time in the future. Unfortunately, we live in a throw-away society. We junk our old automobiles and refrigerators. Cans, bottles, paper goods, and other materials are also thrown away as trash. Table 15–2 shows the composition of waste materials in a typical city.

This photograph was taken by a Landsat satellite from an altitude of 917 km. It shows a portion of Colorado and Utah that may contain uranium. Photographs of this type can be used to discover the location of ores and other natural resources.

TABLE 15–2 • Composition of City Waste Materials

PHYSICAL FORM	WEIGHT PERCENT
Cardboard	7
Newspaper	14
Other paper products	25
Plastic film	2
Molded plastic, rubber, leather	2
Garbage	12
Grass and dirt	10
Textiles	3
Wood	7
Glass, ceramics, stone	10
Metallics	8
Total	100

What are minerals?

What can we do to keep our supply of minerals and other resources from being used up? One solution is to find new materials that will do the same job as the resources that are in short supply. Another solution is to use each resource in a more efficient way. So far, the second solution appears easier to achieve. We could begin by recycling the mineral resources that we are presently using.

What material makes up the greatest percentage of city waste materials?

Activity 46 Recycling Paper

PURPOSE

To demonstrate the technique of recycling

MATERIALS

Mixing container
Hand eggbeater
10 g flour
Shallow pan or tray
Watch or clock
Piece of window screen
Wax paper
250-mL beaker
Newspaper
Water
Meterstick
Scissors
Balance and mass set
Jar

DO THIS

A. Cut into small pieces a sheet of newspaper 30 cm × 30 cm. Put the pieces of newspaper into the mixing container.

B. Pour about 250 mL of water into the mixing container. Let the newspaper soak in the water for 5 minutes.

C. Use the eggbeater to churn the newspaper and water until the paper looks like cooked oatmeal.

D. Add 10 g of flour, mixing it thoroughly with the churned newspaper.

E. Have someone hold the window screen over the pan. Then pour the mixture onto the screen to drain

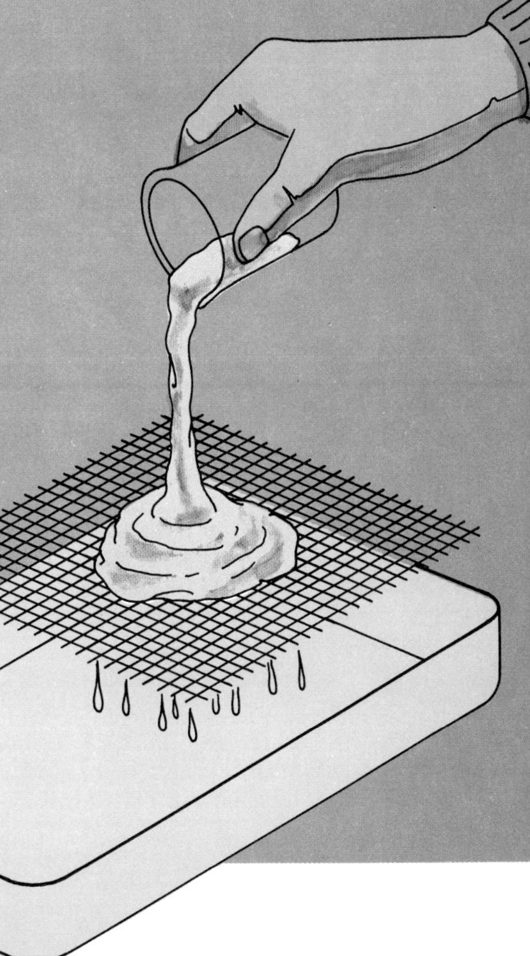

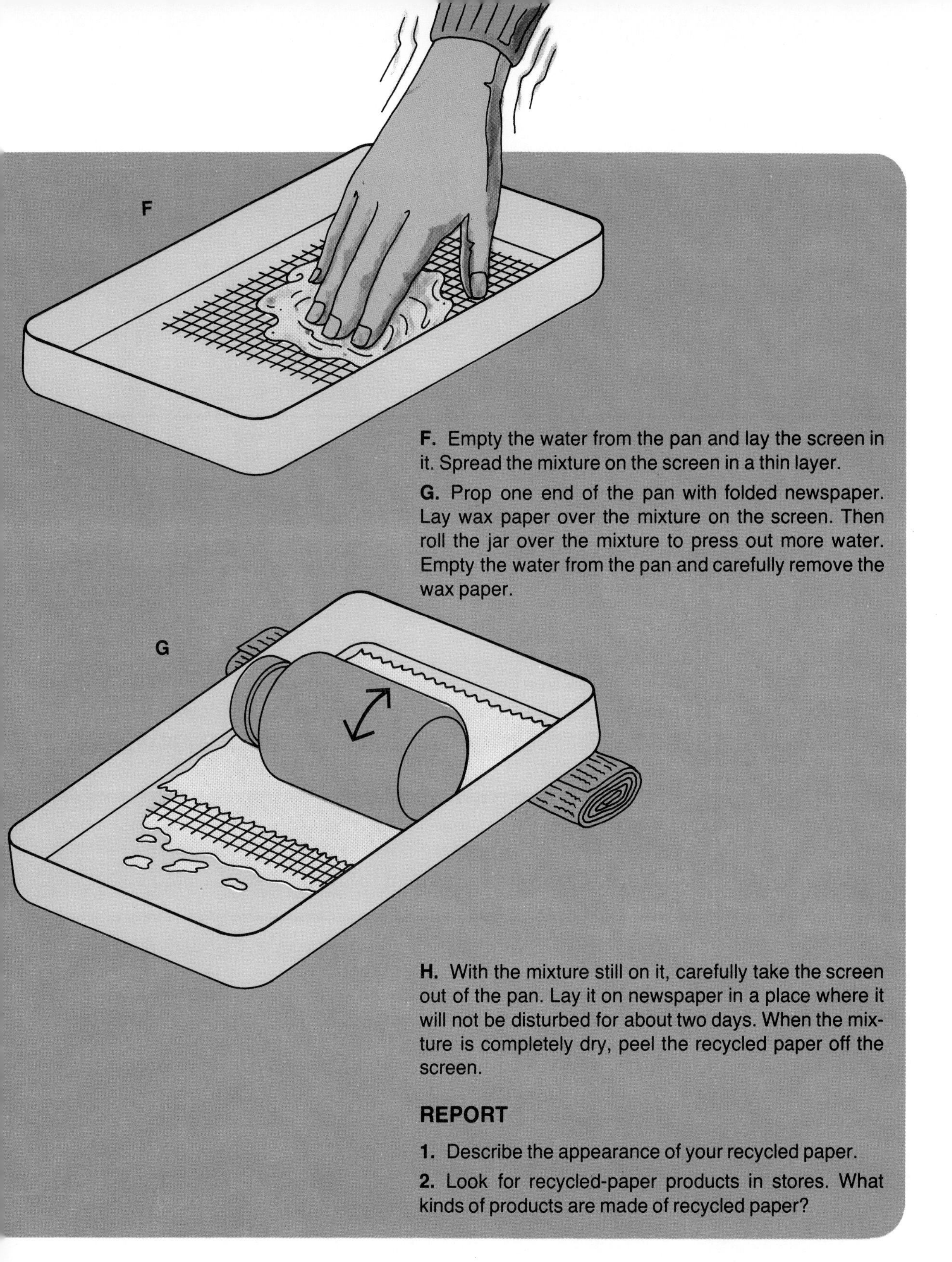

F. Empty the water from the pan and lay the screen in it. Spread the mixture on the screen in a thin layer.

G. Prop one end of the pan with folded newspaper. Lay wax paper over the mixture on the screen. Then roll the jar over the mixture to press out more water. Empty the water from the pan and carefully remove the wax paper.

H. With the mixture still on it, carefully take the screen out of the pan. Lay it on newspaper in a place where it will not be disturbed for about two days. When the mixture is completely dry, peel the recycled paper off the screen.

REPORT

1. Describe the appearance of your recycled paper.

2. Look for recycled-paper products in stores. What kinds of products are made of recycled paper?

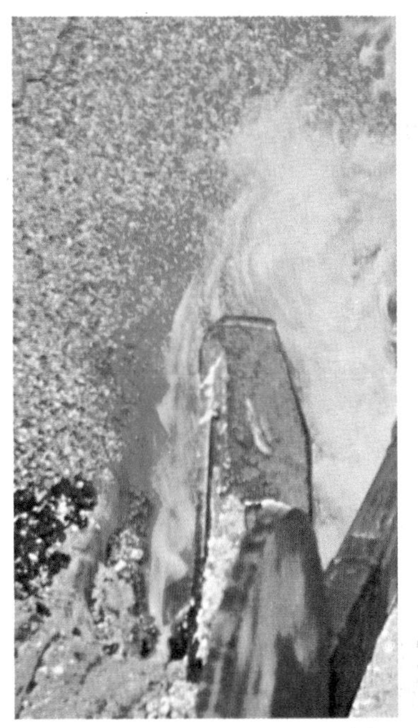

Used aluminum cans are brought to a recycling center and weighed (left); the cans are shredded and melted down at the processing plant (center); new cans are formed from the recycled aluminum (right).

Recycling can save energy as well as mineral resources. Recycling scrap metal requires only 5–20 percent of the energy needed to produce new metal from the raw material, or ore. Paper products made from recycled paper require about half the energy needed to manufacture new paper. Therefore, recycling does make good sense. It is hoped that this technique will be more widely accepted and used in the future.

SCIENCE WORDS

resources
fossil fuel
bacteria
nonrenewable resources
electricity
pesticides
herbicides
minerals
geologic processes

SUMMARY The earth's natural resources are limited. Some resources, such as oil, coal, and natural gas, can be used only once. If people continue to use fossil fuels at the present rate, there will be no oil or natural gas left by the next century. Coal will be the only fossil fuel available by the year 2050.

Food production in the United States is overly dependent on the availability of fossil fuels. New and better methods of producing food are needed. All natural resources should be used in a more efficient manner. One way this can be accomplished is by recycling as many materials as possible.

REVIEW QUESTIONS

Fill in the blanks with the correct terms.

1. The most plentiful fossil fuel is ______________.
2. Natural gas and ______________ formed from deposits of dead plants and animals in the sea.
3. Fossil fuels are called ______________ ______________ because they cannot be replaced once they are used.
4. ______________ are important compounds and elements found in scattered deposits in the earth's crust.
5. Artificial fertilizers, herbicides, and pesticides are produced from ______________.

Mark each statement true (T) or false (F).

1. ______ The United States has most of the world's oil.
2. ______ In mining coal, a large percentage of the coal is lost when it is removed from the ground.
3. ______ In terms of energy-efficient food production, the United States is more efficient than most underdeveloped countries.
4. ______ Typical city waste materials consist mostly of paper and paper products.
5. ______ Coal is composed chiefly of carbon.

APPLYING WHAT YOU LEARNED

1. Name three factors that determine the availability of any resource.
2. Explain how coal was formed.
3. All new major appliances have a label stating the energy-efficiency rating of the appliance. Make a list of the major appliances in your home. Opposite the kind of appliance, list its energy-efficiency rating. Which appliance has the highest rating? Which has the lowest rating?
4. In the library, research ways that insects and weeds can be controlled by natural means. Which of these means can be used to control insects and weeds in your home garden?

WARNING
THIS WATER IS
POLLUTED
DO NOT USE
S.F. DEPT. PUBLIC HEALTH

The sign on this rotted piling tells with stark reality the condition of the water in San Francisco Bay.

16

Pollution Supersystems

We live in a consumer society. We use huge amounts of energy for transportation, food production, recreation, and in the day-to-day operation of our homes, offices, and factories. We produce large quantities of cars, clothing, plastic materials, and other manufactured items. Our demand for these things presents two major problems: (1) we are running out of the raw materials needed to produce these products, and (2) the manufacturing of these products produces waste materials.

You have already investigated some of the problems we face because of our limited nonrenewable resources. In this chapter you will investigate some problems caused by the production of waste materials.

The Nature of Pollution

Study the photographs. They all show **pollution** (pə lü′shən). In each case, waste materials are being produced and released into the environment. List some of the effects these waste materials could have on you, your family, and the environment. Then, in your own words, develop a definition for pollution. Compare your definition with those of your classmates.

Waste materials from the jet engines (top) and the chemical plant (right) are released into the environment.

Pollution takes many forms. The waste products from the cattle in the feed lot are as much a pollutant as the trash heap and the smoke.

Did you and your classmates differ in the way you defined pollution? People often disagree about what pollution is. For example, some people feel that what is pollution in one place is not necessarily pollution someplace else. They might say that the smoke and ash produced by a fire is air pollution in the city, but not in open country. They reason that in open country the smoke and ash in the air do not directly affect anyone.

What happens to materials that interact with the environment? Eventually, waste products are formed from the interaction. These waste products are called **pollutants** (pə lü'tənts). Materials gradually change in shape and form as they interact with the environment. A car, for example, goes through a series of changes. These changes begin when a new car comes off the production line. As the car is driven, it releases pollutants into the air. Over a period of time, the metal begins to rust. Sooner or later, the car ends in the junkyard. There more rusting occurs. Unless the car is processed as scrap metal, it becomes almost totally rusted and eventually breaks apart.

What part of a material interacts with the environment?

The car underwent a series of changes. All materials undergo similar changes when they interact with the environment. In Activity 47, you will investigate **surface area**—one factor that affects how rapidly a material changes in form. The surface area is that part of a material which is exposed to the environment and therefore interacts directly with it.

Scenes like this are common in many places.

Activity 47 Surface Area and Interaction

PURPOSE

To investigate the role of surface area in physical-chemical interactions

MATERIALS

Single-edged razor blade
4 cm^3 of modeling clay
Newspaper

STEP	NUMBER OF PIECES	NUMBER OF SIDES
A		
B		
C		
D		

TABLE 1 • Surface Area

DO THIS

A. Press the clay into the shape shown. **CAUTION:** *Once the clay has been shaped, do not change its shape except as directed.* How many sides does the piece of clay have? Record this number in a table like Table 1.

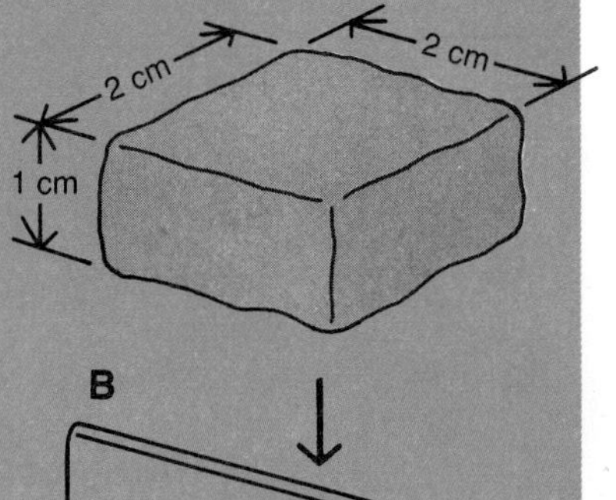

B. Place the piece of clay on newspaper, then cut the clay in half with a razor blade. **CAUTION:** *Be very careful when using the razor blade.* What is the *total* number of sides now? Record this number in the table.

C. Cut both pieces of clay in half. What is the *total* number of sides now? Record this number in the table.

D. Again, cut each piece of clay in half. What is the *total* number of sides now? Record this number in the table.

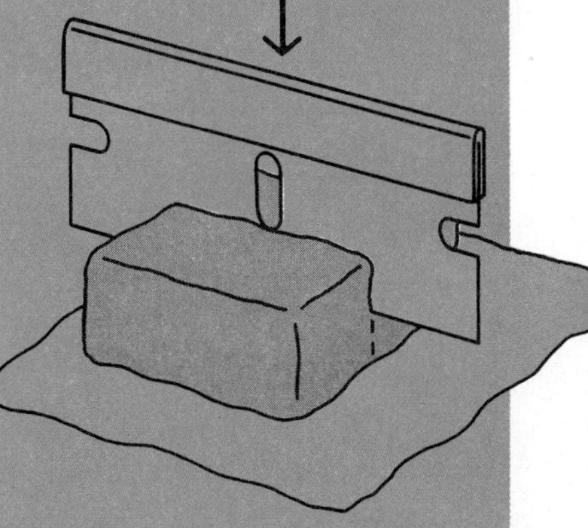

REPORT

1. Draw a line graph of the data in Table 1. Plot the number of pieces on the horizontal axis and the number of sides on the vertical axis.

2. How did cutting the clay affect the number of sides (surface area) available for interaction?

3. Is the rate of interaction increased or decreased when more surface area is in direct contact with the environment? Explain your answer.

Suppose the clay in Activity 47 represents a junked car. When you cut the clay, you demonstrated how the car would break apart. Each time the clay was divided in half, you exposed more surface area. This means that more of the car physically comes into contact with the environment. As the physical interaction increases, the amount of the chemical interaction also increases. Thus, the car would begin to rust. This physical and chemical interaction of a material with the environment is called **decomposition** (dē kom pə zish′ən). Unless interrupted, these interactions eventually result in total disintegration of the car.

What two types of interaction are necessary for decomposition of a material?

Different materials interact with the environment for varying periods of time. Some decompose slowly, while others decompose rather quickly. Materials that decompose slowly present a more serious, lasting form of pollution.

The cans littering this beach will decompose slowly. Litter such as this is unsightly and a serious pollution problem.

Invisible Pollution

So far, only examples of visible pollution have been discussed. Other forms of pollution are invisible. For example, some poisonous gases, such as **carbon monoxide** (mon ok'sīd), are odorless and colorless. Other invisible forms of pollution include certain types of insecticides, some industrial waste products, and noise.

In the 1940s, an insecticide called **DDT** was discovered. Farmers and home gardeners began using DDT to control insects that damaged their crops. Some insects died, but others built up a resistance to DDT. Several years later, scientists found that insect-eating birds were being poisoned. In addition, DDT was found in humans who had eaten plants sprayed with DDT. Later it was established that plants also contained the insecticide if they were grown in soil where DDT had been used. Similarly, evidence of DDT was found in the meat and other products of animals exposed to the insecticide. Apparently DDT remained in the environment for a very long time. This led some scientists to conclude that its continued use would produce lasting harmful effects. As a result, the use of DDT has been almost completely banned.

Why has the use of DDT been almost completely banned?

Certain industrial chemicals also seem to remain in the environment for a long time. You probably have heard of **PCBs.** They are a group of chemicals that pollute the water in certain industrial areas. Fish in rivers and lakes contaminated with PCBs have been found to contain large quantities of these chemicals. People have been warned not to eat those fish because PCBs are believed to be harmful to humans. The problem with PCBs is the same as that with DDT—they do not readily break down into harmless materials. Because of their dangerous nature, the manufacturing of these chemicals has been discontinued in the United States since 1976.

Some people feel that dumping small amounts of a pollutant into lakes and rivers does not create a problem. They feel that the pollutant will be harmless when mixed with large bodies of water. In other words, they believe a solution to pollution is dilution. Activity 48 is designed to test that idea. Think of the potassium permanganate, used in the activity, as a pollutant, like PCBs. Think of the liter of water as a lake or river. When you have completed the activity you will see that dilution is not a solution to pollution.

Scientists test for pollution levels by taking samples from different places in a body of water.

Activity 48 Is Dilution a Solution to Pollution?

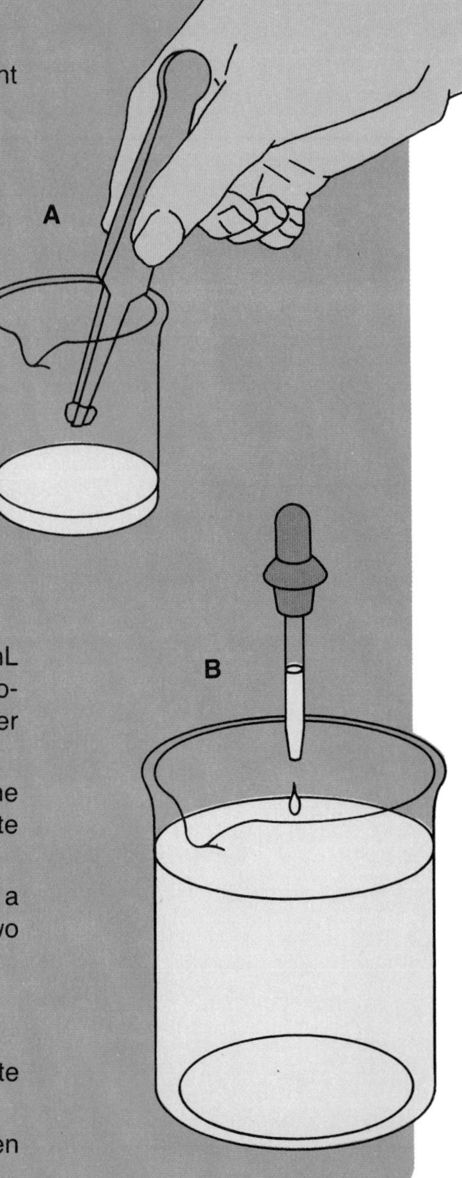

PURPOSE

To determine the effect of a small amount of pollutant on a larger body of water

MATERIALS

2 1-L beakers
100-mL beaker
Graduate
$KMnO_4$ [potassium permanganate]
Medicine dropper
Forceps
Water

DO THIS

A. Measure 10 mL of water and pour it into a 100-mL beaker. Use forceps to pick up a single crystal of potassium permanganate. Drop the crystal into the water and let it dissolve completely.

B. Fill two 1-L beakers with water. Use a medicine dropper to add 1 drop of the potassium permanganate solution from step **A** to one of the beakers.

C. Compare the water in the two 1-L beakers. Wait a few minutes and again compare the water in the two beakers.

REPORT

1. Can you see evidence of potassium permanganate in one of the two 1-L beakers?

2. Does the solute of a solution change in form when dissolved in the solvent? Explain your answer.

Why is noise considered to be more than a simple annoyance?

Noise is any undesirable sound. It is a type of pollution to which everyone contributes. It may be through the operation of a power lawnmower or even by playing a stereo set too loudly. Industrial noise is usually a by-product of the operation of machines. Noise can be more than just a simple annoyance. It can seriously affect one's hearing. Studies show that people exposed to long periods of high noise levels usually suffer hearing loss.

The intensity, or loudness, of a sound is measured in units called **decibels** (des'ə bels). The symbol, or abbreviation, for decibel is dB. Exposure to sound levels above 90 dB for long periods may damage a person's hearing. Sound levels above 140 dB may cause pain. The intensity of some common sounds is shown in Table 16–1.

TABLE 16–1 • Some Common Sound Levels

KIND OF SOUND	INTENSITY (dB)
Soft whisper	30
Quiet library	40
Average home	50
Conversational speech	60
City traffic	70
Average factory	80
Subway train	90
Boiler shop	100
Rock band with amplifiers	110
Riveting machine	120
Jet plane takeoff	140
Rocket launch	180

The period of time a person can be safely exposed to certain sound levels is shown in Table 16–2. Exposure to a specific sound level for a longer time than that shown could cause hearing damage.

TABLE 16–2 • Sound Level Exposure Time

INTENSITY (dB)	MAXIMUM HOURS PER DAY
90	8
92	6
95	4
97	3
100	2
102	1.5
105	1
110	0.5
115	0.25 or less

Which sounds listed in Table 16–1 do you encounter most often? Use Table 16–2 to determine how long these sounds can be endured before hearing damage could occur. Do you feel that you have to be concerned about a loss of hearing in the future? What things could people do to help prevent hearing loss caused by noise pollution?

You may have seen workers wearing large earmuffs at airports or in factories. These are special earmuffs designed to cut down the intensity of certain sounds. They help to protect the ears of workers who are exposed to high-intensity noise for long periods.

Thermal Pollution and Nuclear Waste

Most people think of pollutants as being in the form of solids, liquids, or gases. However, there is another form of pollution that may become a very serious problem. This is pollution in the form of heat. It is called **thermal** (thėr′məl) **pollution.** In Activity 49 you will investigate how heat acts as a pollutant.

What causes thermal pollution?

Nuclear power plants are one of the major causes of thermal pollution. The operation of nuclear power plants produces large amounts of heat. Water from a nearby lake or river is circulated through the power plant to carry the heat away. A typical nuclear power plant uses about 150 000 L of water each second. As the water circulates, it is warmed by conduction. During this process its temperature is increased about 10°C. Then the water is returned to the lake or river. This results in thermal pollution because the water is returned at higher than its original temperature. Eventually this process could permanently raise the temperature of the lake or river. It may also be harmful to animals and plants living in the water.

The hot water discharged into this lake seriously affects the living things within it.

Activity 49 Thermal Pollution

PURPOSE

To demonstrate thermal pollution in water

MATERIALS

Celsius thermometer
1-L beaker
150-mL beaker
Heat source
Matches
Tripod
Wire gauze
Stirring rod
Watch or clock
Safety goggles
Asbestos gloves

STEP	WATER	TEMP (°C)
A	Tap water	
D	Mixed water	
E	Mixed water at 1 minute	
E	Mixed water at 2 minutes	
E	Mixed water at 3 minutes	

TABLE 1 • Thermal Pollution

DO THIS

A. Prepare a data table like Table 1. Record in the table the temperature data you collect in steps **B, D,** and **E.** You may have to extend the table beyond 3 minutes.

B. Fill a 1-L beaker with tap water. Measure and record the temperature of the water.

C. Pour 125 mL of water from the 1-L beaker into a 150-mL beaker. Stand the 150-mL beaker on the tripod. **CAUTION:** *Be sure you are wearing safety goggles.* Then light the heat source and heat the water until its temperature is increased 5°C.

D. Put on asbestos gloves. Pour the heated water back into the 1-L beaker. Stir the water, then measure and record its temperature.

E. Continue to measure and record the temperature of the water each minute until it is the same as in step **B.**

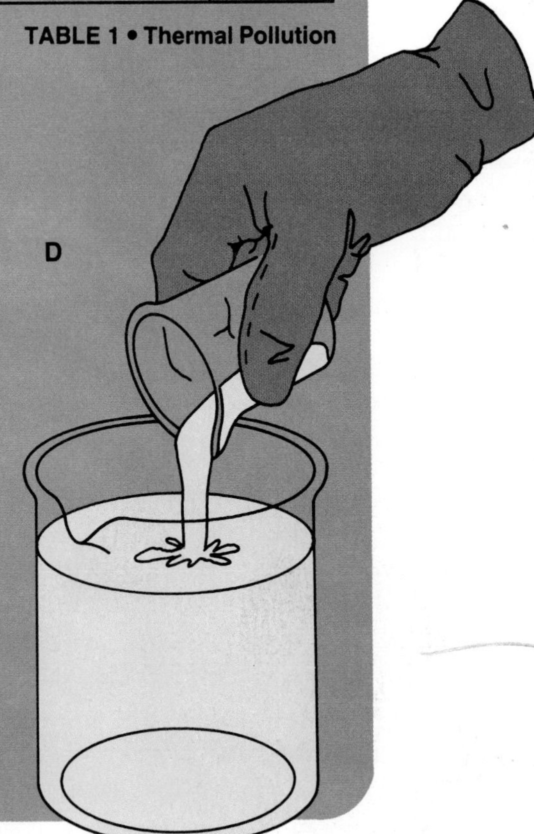

REPORT

1. What happened when the tap water was mixed with the heated water?

2. In step **E,** how long did it take for the water to cool to its original temperature?

The operation of a nuclear power plant produces radioactive waste material. Disposal of this radioactive material is a major problem. Safe, long-term storage areas must be established. Several methods of disposal are being explored. One proposed method is to store the radioactive waste in special containers. These could then be put in abandoned salt mines, and the mines filled with salt or some other material. Another proposed method is to build structures similar to the Egyptian pyramids. The Egyptian pyramids are over 5000 years old. Similar structures might be capable of storing radioactive waste safely for thousands of years. Whatever method of storage is developed, it is important that it be done soon.

SUMMARY In this chapter you developed your own definition of pollution. Most people are concerned with the effects of visible pollution, but invisible pollution is often more dangerous. Pollutants interact with the environment for different periods of time. Surface area is one factor that determines the rate of interaction. The result of the interaction is a change in form. Noise is an undesirable sound. Under certain conditions, both noise and heat are considered pollution. One of the major concerns today is the safe disposal of radioactive waste materials.

SCIENCE WORDS

pollution
pollutants
surface area
decomposition
carbon monoxide
DDT
PCBs
noise
decibels
thermal pollution

REVIEW QUESTIONS

Match the word in Column A with the correct definition in Column B.

A	B
1. PCBs ___	a. Any undesirable sound
2. Decibel ___	b. A group of chemicals sometimes found in water in certain industrial areas
3. DDT ___	c. Colorless, odorless, poisonous gas
4. Noise ___	d. Unit used to measure the intensity of sound
5. Carbon monoxide ___	e. An insecticide

Mark each statement true (T) or false (F).

1. ______ Materials that decompose quickly present a serious form of pollution.
2. ______ All forms of pollution are visible.
3. ______ People working where there is a high noise level for a long period of time may suffer hearing loss.
4. ______ A solution to pollution is dilution.
5. ______ A major problem with using nuclear power to generate electricity is the safe disposal of radioactive waste materials.

Fill in the blanks with the correct terms.

1. The rate at which a material will decompose depends on the amount of ______________ exposed to the environment.
2. The physical and chemical interaction of a material with the environment is called ______________.
3. Pollution in the form of heat is called ______________ ______________.
4. ______________ are waste products produced as a result of the interaction of materials with the environment.
5. ______________ is used to cool nuclear power plants.

APPLYING WHAT YOU LEARNED

1. Explain why people often disagree about what pollution is. Give an example different from the one used in the text.
2. Do you think any pollution occurs naturally? Explain your answer.

Baker Electric Vehicles

The Aristocrats of Motordom

**THE ELECTRIC THAT MEETS
EVERY NEED OF THE SOCIETY WOMAN**

YOU can learn to run The Baker in twenty minutes. It far exceeds all other electrics in simplicity safety, as well as mileage and speed. It is noiseless and clean— having a battery capacity of 70 to 100 miles. It is unequalled for city and suburban use.

Write for our handsome booklet. It clearly explains the many advantages of Baker Electrics, and gives full information regarding the elegant 1910 Model Coupes, Broughams, Victorias, Landaulets, Runabouts, Roadsters, etc.

THE BAKER MOTOR VEHICLE COMPANY, 33 W. 80TH STREET, CLEVELAND, OHIO.

Salesrooms in the Principal Cities.

Are electric cars vehicles of the future or vehicles of the past? This ad praising the qualities of electric cars dates back to the early 1900s.

17

Transportation Supersystems

Moving people and materials from one part of the country to another has always been a problem. Many different means of transportation have been used. Before this century, most transportation was accomplished by walking, by animal power, or by boat. Now most people walk less than ever before. The use of animal power for transportation is usually limited to sports. Today, machines move us and our merchandise faster and easier than did the older methods.

In this chapter, you will investigate the nature of transportation supersystems. You will study the automobile as a major means of transportation. You will also gain some insight into the attitudes of people regarding transportation and the way people interact with transportation systems.

Efficiency of Transportation Supersystems

Mechanical transportation supersystems have always depended on cheap, easily available energy. In the nineteenth century coal was used to make steel for the building of locomotives. The fuel for locomotives and other steam-driven engines was wood or coal. Today's more complex engines require oil and gasoline as fuel. In the United States, great quantities of oil and gasoline are used to power transportation supersystems.

What fuels are used in today's complex engines?

The fuels used in cars, trucks, planes, and buses produce air pollution. In large cities, such as Los Angeles and Chicago, air pollution is a serious problem. Evidence indicates that air pollution is a health hazard. Future transportation systems should use as little fuel and produce as little air pollution as possible.

Wood was used for fuel in these early steam-driven locomotives. As the rail transportation system expanded, coal became the preferred fuel.

Steam-powered riverboats were once used to transport passengers and cargo.

The term *efficiency* is often applied to transportation supersystems. With respect to transportation, efficiency refers to the amount of mass that can be moved one kilometer with one liter of fuel. The efficiency of various transportation supersystems (vehicles) used in the United States can be determined from Table 17–1. The average mass carried by different types of vehicles is given in kilograms. Mass, in this case, can be passengers, luggage, or other items. The average amount of fuel consumed per kilometer is given in liters.

To what does the term *efficiency* refer in respect to transportation supersystems?

TABLE 17–1 • Transportation Supersystem Efficiency

VEHICLE	AVERAGE MASS CARRIED (kg)	FUEL CONSUMED PER KILOMETER (L)
Automobile	300	0.125
Bus	4 500	0.5
Truck	35 000	0.825
Jet plane	75 000	2.5
Diesel train	4 500 000	45.0
Supertanker	90 500 000	265.0

Although not common today, interurban trolley systems, such as this one in Boston, are powered by electricity.

Efficiency is determined by dividing the mass carried by the amount of fuel consumed per kilometer. For example, assume that an automobile carried a mass of 200 kg and used 0.25 L of fuel per kilometer. To calculate its efficiency, divide 200 kg by 0.25 L/km.

$$\text{Efficiency} = \frac{200 \text{ kg}}{0.25 \text{ L/km}} = 800 \text{ kg/(L/km)}$$

In this case, the automobile can carry 800 kilograms one kilometer on one liter of fuel. The more mass carried per liter of fuel per kilometer, the more efficient the supersystem. Using Table 17–1, calculate the efficiency of each supersystem listed. Then answer the following questions.

1. Which of the supersystems is the most efficient? Which is the least efficient?
2. Which of the supersystems listed do most people use to travel from one place to another?
3. Why, do you think, a more efficient supersystem is not always used?
4. What factors should be considered in choosing to use one transportation supersystem rather than another?

A Look at the Automobile

The automobile accounts for 20 percent of all the energy used in the United States. Although other transportation systems are more efficient, the automobile is the most popular means of traveling from one place to another. For example, during the 1960s railroad passenger service in the United States decreased by 50 percent. During the same period, transportation by automobile increased by the same amount. The federal government has helped focus attention on the automobile as the primary means of transportation by developing an interstate highway system. This highway system was originally developed for national defense. However, it has been used mainly by the general public. Because of these highways, travel by automobile has been more convenient than other types of transportation.

For what purpose was the interstate highway system developed?

The automobile may have done more to change our lives than any other supersystem. America is a nation on wheels, and most of the wheels are on automobiles.

The cars on this interstate highway began as parts on an automobile assembly line like the one shown at the left.

But most people know very little about how an automobile works. The following description will help you to understand this complicated supersystem.

In an automobile potential energy (fuel) is changed into kinetic energy (motion of the auto). The most common fuel for automobiles is gasoline. Gasoline is a mixture of chemical compounds manufactured from crude oil. Gasoline is stored in a tank in the auto. It is pumped through a small metal tube to a device called a **carburetor** (kär'bə rā tər). The carburetor mixes the gasoline with air. It is controlled by the **accelerator** (ak sel'ə rā tər). Pressing down on the accelerator increases the flow of gasoline to the carburetor.

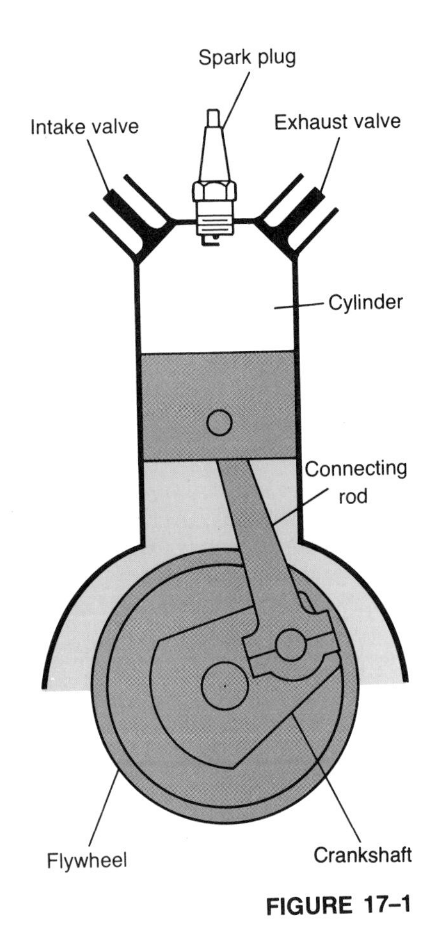

FIGURE 17–1

Name, in order, the steps in a four-stroke cylinder.

The engine is the most complicated part of an automobile. Most autos have **piston engines.** The main parts of a piston engine are shown in Figure 17–1. Automobile engines usually have 4, 6, or 8 **cylinders** (sil'ən dərs). The gasoline-air mixture is burned in the cylinders. The events taking place inside a cylinder can be broken down into four steps, or strokes. Figure 17–2 illustrates what happens in a cylinder during each stroke. As you read the description of the operation of a piston engine, refer to Figure 17–2.

During the **intake stroke,** the piston is drawn down by the **connecting rod.** As the piston moves down, the **intake valve** opens. This allows the gasoline-air mixture from the carburetor to enter the cylinder. During the **compression stroke,** the intake valve closes and the piston is pushed upward in the cylinder. This compresses the gasoline-air mixture. During the **power stroke,** a spark from the **spark plug** ignites the gasoline-air mixture. The resulting explosion pushes the piston down again with great force. In this stroke, the potential energy (fuel) is changed to kinetic energy (motion). During the **exhaust stroke,** the piston again moves upward in the cylinder and the **exhaust valve** opens. This forces the waste gases in the cylinder into the exhaust system.

When the piston reaches the top of the cylinder, the process begins again. The same process takes place in each cylinder of a 4-, 6-, or 8-cylinder engine. However, the cylinders are always at different strokes in the process. Therefore, a continuous force is produced. There may be as many as 2000 to 3000 explosions in each cylinder every minute.

FIGURE 17–2

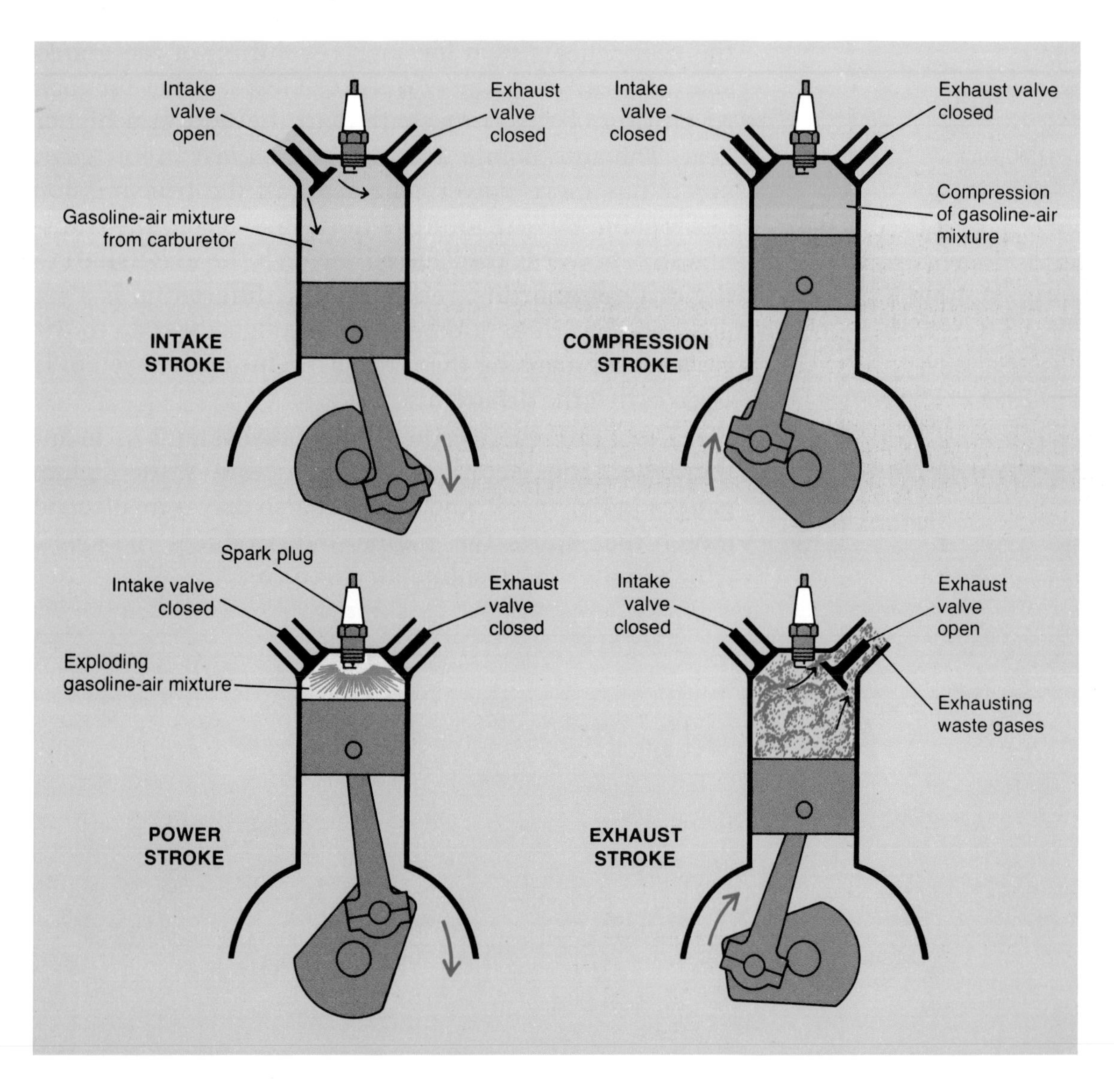

The power developed in each cylinder is transferred to the piston, producing motion. This happens when the energy from the exploding gas forces the piston downward. The piston, in turn, pushes the connecting rod downward. The connecting rod turns the **crankshaft** (krangk′shaft) which transfers the power to the **transmission.** The transmission is a complicated supersystem of gears. It determines the number of times the rear wheels turn for each revolution of the crankshaft. In low gear, the wheels turn fewer times for each revolution of the crankshaft than they do in a higher gear. The automobile doesn't move as fast in low gear, but it has more power. The gears in the transmission also enable the car to move in reverse. From the transmission, power is transferred through the **drive shaft** to the **differential** (dif ə ren′shəl). The differential is a set of gears that directs the power through the axle to the rear wheels, causing them to turn. This entire system is often called the **drive train.**

What is the name of the entire system by which power is transferred to the rear wheels of an auto?

There are several other important systems in an automobile. The electrical system operates the lights, **gauges** (gājs), clock, and radio. It also drives an electric motor that starts the engine and produces the spark which ignites the gasoline-air mixture.

FIGURE 17–3
The drive train in a typical automobile

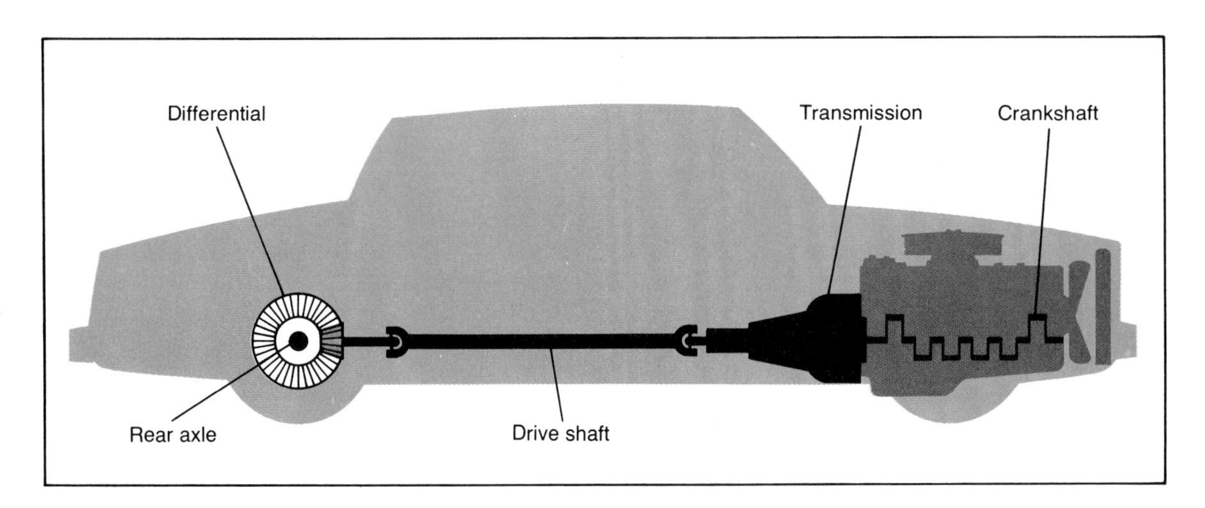

Another important system is the cooling system. Much of the energy released in the cylinders is given off as heat. If the engine were not cooled, the heat would build up and damage the engine. Therefore, water or some other heat-absorbing liquid is pumped around the engine. This liquid picks up heat from the cylinders and conducts it to the radiator. The radiator is nothing more than a tubing system. It is designed to radiate the heat from the engine into the air. A fan is attached to the engine crankshaft with a belt-and-pulley system. The fan is mounted directly behind the radiator and pulls air through the radiator. This helps the cooling process since more air comes in contact with the radiator.

In recent years, many advances have been made in automotive engineering. In some autos, the old-style carburetor has been replaced by a **fuel injection system.** With this system, a precisely measured mixture of fuel and air is sprayed directly into the cylinders. Many cars also have an **electronic ignition system.** Electronic ignition is a more refined method of igniting the fuel mixture in the cylinders.

Name two recent advances in automotive engineering.

As you can see, an automobile is a rather complicated set of supersystems. All of these supersystems must work together or the auto will not operate properly.

Perhaps you have been thinking about buying your own auto in a few years. In Activity 50 you can explore some of your ideas about autos.

EXCURSION 10

The development of a questioning, scientific attitude is discussed in Excursion 10, "A Guide to Consumer Goods."

People often buy autos without considering economic or safety factors. Yet the cost of owning an automobile and the types of safety features should be important considerations. The estimated cost of owning and operating an automobile ranges from $45 to $90 per week. The basic price of automobiles, plus the cost of fuel, maintenance, and insurance, is increasing each year. In the future, it may become more difficult for a person to own an auto.

Activity 50 Your Kind of Auto

PURPOSE

To determine why people buy certain automobiles

MATERIALS

Automotive magazines
New-car brochures
Automobile advertisements
Consumer magazines

DO THIS

A. Page through the magazines, brochures, and advertisements. Look at the pictures of automobiles and read about the various makes and models.

B. Decide which automobile you would most like to buy.

C. List five reasons for your choice of that automobile.

D. Ask your classmates what reasons they listed in step **C**. Record the make and model of each automobile they chose. Then make a class list of reasons beginning with those most frequently given.

REPORT

1. What five reasons were most frequently given by your class for choosing an automobile?

2. How many of those five reasons were economic reasons?

3. Was one make and model of automobile chosen more frequently than others?

4. What are the characteristics of the most popular automobile? (You may have to refer to a brochure, magazine, or advertisement to answer this question.)

Future Transportation Supersystems

Could you and your family live without an automobile? What changes might there be in your family's life style if you did not have an auto? To answer these questions, you will have to make some predictions about your future. Everyone has some control over his or her future. Every choice or decision you make influences what lies ahead. The choices you make about transportation are important. In Activity 51 you will make some predictions. You will determine your attitude concerning private transportation versus public transportation.

Other people have also tried to predict what future transportation supersystems will be like. There is a good chance that they also found the task difficult. The Stanford Research Institute has proposed some interesting ideas. Based on a year-long study, they have recommended new means of city transportation. They feel that these systems could be developed within 13 to 16 years. The estimated total cost of the project would be one billion dollars. In a typical city this would amount to about one thousand dollars per person.

An experimental electric car draws the attention of people passing by.

THE STANFORD RESEARCH INSTITUTE PLAN

1. *Trips of 1–3 blocks* Moving sidewalks that would carry passengers 8–21 km/h for 5 or 10 cents per ride.
2. *Slightly longer trips within the city* Small electric cars that would be used on a rental basis. The cars would be picked up at one stand and dropped off at another. These stands, located about 3 blocks apart, would store the cars and recharge their batteries. The rental cost would be 10 to 15 cents per ride.
3. *Trips similar to those in item 2 for nondrivers* A dial-a-bus system would be used. The buses would pick up passengers near their homes rather than running on a regular bus route. The cost would be 35 cents per ride.

This moving sidewalk at a Montreal airport functions like a horizontal escalator. It is a convenient means for people to get from one location to another within the airport.

In the Netherlands, one- or two-passenger electric cars are recharged at stations such as this. The cars are a highly efficient means of transportation for short trips in the city.

4. *Medium trips outside the city* A network of small, computer-controlled vehicles would be developed. The passengers would board the vehicles and push a button to indicate their destination. These vehicles would travel about 98 km/h and cost from 3 to 6 cents per ride.

These automated "people movers" in Morgantown, West Virginia, are an experiment in public mass transit.

5. *Longer trips up to 80 km* Electric trains that could reach speeds of 224 km/h would be used. Stations would be located 6–13 km apart, similar to the Bay Area Rapid Transit (BART) in San Francisco. It would cost each passenger from 3 to 5 cents per ride.

The German high-speed Supertrain *(above) and the Washington, D.C.,* Metro *(right) are efficient means of mass transit.*

Activity 51 Predicting the Future

PURPOSE

To determine your attitude concerning private transportation versus public transportation

MATERIALS

None

DO THIS

A. Assume that the government has banned the manufacturing of all automobiles. To replace automobiles, public transportation systems are being developed.

B. Read each of the following questions. Think carefully about how you would answer each one.

- What would be some advantages and disadvantages of the action taken by the government in step **A**?
- What possible bad effects might be caused by having only public transportation?
- In what ways would your life style change if there were no private transportation?
- What problems would have to be solved to improve on existing public transportation systems?

REPORT

1. What would be some advantages and disadvantages of the action taken by the government in step **A**?

2. What possible bad effects might be caused by having only public transportation?

3. In what ways would your life style change if there were no private transportation?

4. What problems would have to be solved to improve on existing public transportation systems?

High-speed monorail trains, such as this one in Tokyo, Japan, are less expensive to operate than conventional trains.

How do you feel about the Stanford Research Institute's transportation plan? Could some of the ideas in this plan be adopted where you live?

SCIENCE WORDS

carburetor
accelerator
piston engines
cylinders
intake stroke
connecting rod
intake valve
compression stroke
power stroke
spark plug
exhaust stroke
exhaust valve
crankshaft
transmission
drive shaft
differential
drive train
gauges
fuel injection system
electronic ignition system

SUMMARY Our present transportation systems are expensive to build and do not use energy efficiently. The automobile is the means of transportation most used by Americans. The automobile is a complicated set of interacting electrical, chemical, and physical supersystems. These supersystems may vary slightly from one make of automobile to another, but the basic principles of how they operate are the same. In the future, other means of transportation may be developed to replace the automobile. More efficient transportation supersystems will be needed as the supply of energy and material resources continues to decrease.

REVIEW QUESTIONS

Fill in the blanks with the correct terms.

1. The most common and popular means of transportation in the United States is the ____________.
2. During what stroke does the spark plug ignite the gasoline-air mixture in the cylinder? ____________
3. The ____________ has been replaced in newer automobiles with a fuel injection system.
4. ____________ is a mixture of chemical compounds manufactured from crude oil.
5. When an automobile is in a higher gear, the wheels turn ____________ times for each revolution of the crankshaft than when the automobile is in a lower gear.

Match the term in Column A with the correct definition in Column B.

A

1. Air pollution ___
2. Fuel ___
3. Efficiency ___
4. Exhaust stroke ___
5. Compression stroke ___

B

a. Waste gases in the cylinder are forced into the exhaust system of the auto
b. Health hazard caused by fuels used in cars, trucks, planes, and buses
c. Potential energy
d. Gasoline-air mixture trapped inside the cylinder
e. Amount of mass that can be moved one kilometer with one liter of fuel

57
82
45

The wind and sails are used mostly for recreational craft today. These sailboats use little or no fossil fuel once they are in open water.

18

Energy for the Future

The world's supply of fossil fuels and certain material resources is decreasing. As a result present-day supersystems will probably change. Most inventions go through generations of change. More recently designed models often do not resemble the original invention. In addition to this kind of change, some supersystems become **obsolete** (ob'sə lēt). This means that they are no longer useful because new supersystems replace them. Energy sources also become obsolete. The wood-burning stove was important in the nineteenth century, but it became obsolete as coal, oil, and natural gas became available. Today, however, the wood-burning stove is again being used to heat some homes.

In this chapter you will explore a number of different energy sources. Some, which were widely used in the past, are now being reintroduced into our society. Others are new sources that are still in the development stage.

Energy in the Wind

Prior to this century, wind energy was very important for transportation. Since ancient times people have used the wind to power boats and ships. Sailing ships played an important role in the political and economic history of the world. Today, however, they are primarily used for recreation. Modern cargo and passenger ships require some form of fossil fuel for power. However, the trend in the future may be to use wind-powered ships again. As fossil fuels become depleted, a new breed of sailing ships may appear. These ships would have automated equipment to raise and lower the sails. They might be similar in design to the clipper ships that sailed the oceans in the last century.

Windmills were once used to pump water on many farms in the United States. When electricity became available in rural areas, windmills became obsolete. Today national wind energy societies are promoting the

Clipper ships were the swiftest ships afloat in their time. These ships carried cargo as well as passengers on transoceanic voyages.

Wind mills, such as these, were once widely used in the Netherlands and Belgium. They pumped water and ground grain. Some of these windmills are still in operation today, and many more are being restored.

use of wind as an alternate source of energy. Modern windmills are being designed to turn generators to produce electricity. The National Aeronautics and Space Administration (NASA) is testing a large windmill of this type. This windmill has a blade diameter of 62 m. It is mounted on a tower 46 m high. With a wind speed of 29 km/h, it is estimated that the windmill will generate enough electricity for five hundred households.

One problem with using the wind to generate electricity is that wind is not always available. Some days there might not be enough wind to generate the needed electricity. The solution to this problem lies in finding a means of storing the surplus electrical energy that is produced on windy days. One method that has been

Why is the wind an unreliable source of energy?

This wind turbine generator was developed by NASA. It generates 200 kilowatts, supplying approximately 20 percent of the electricity needed on the island of Culebra, Puerto Rico.

tried involves the use of batteries. The batteries are charged on windy days when a surplus of electrical energy is being generated. They are then used to supply electrical energy on those days when there is little wind. At the present time lead-acid batteries are used for this purpose. They are the most reliable and can be charged and discharged thousands of times. One disadvantage to using lead-acid batteries is their high cost.

The wind will probably be one of several alternate energy sources used in the future.

Solar Energy

Every day the earth receives vast amounts of **solar** (sō'lər) **energy**—energy from the sun. Only a small amount of that energy is absorbed by the earth. Much of the energy that is not absorbed is wasted by being reflected back into space. The energy that is absorbed heats the earth's surface. Some is used by green plants in the food-making process **photosynthesis** (fō tə sin'thə sis). If humans could use the sun's energy directly, many energy problems could be solved. In Activity 52 you will investigate solar energy as a source of heat.

What is solar energy?

This solar collector is shaped like a parabolic dish. It focuses the rays of the sun to produce intense heat.

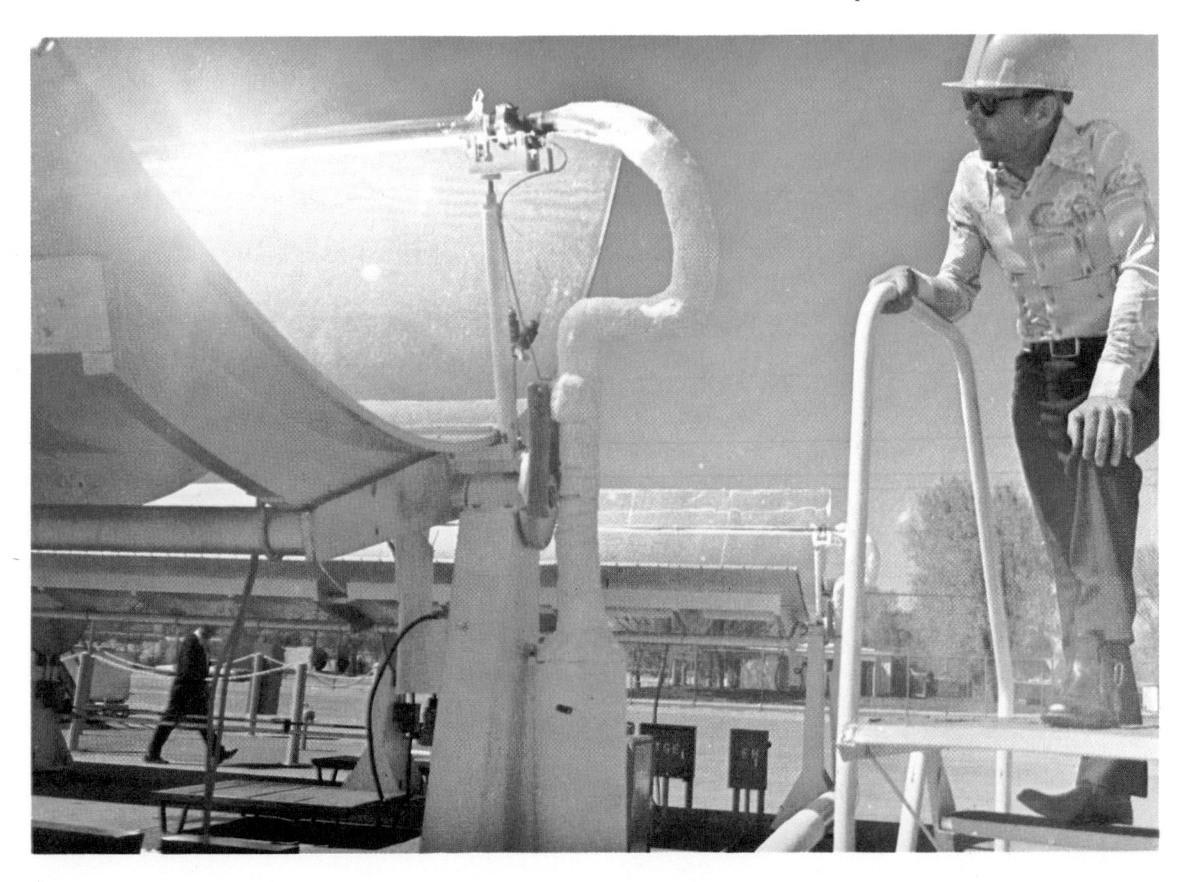

Activity 52 Concentrating Sunlight

PURPOSE

To demonstrate the effect of concentrating sunlight

MATERIALS

Double-convex lens (5 cm or more in diameter)
2 Celsius thermometers

DO THIS

A. Prepare a data table like Table 1.

B. Work either outdoors or at a window through which the sun shines. Label two thermometers *A* and *B*. Read each thermometer and record the temperatures in Table 1.

C. Place both thermometers in sunlight. Read the thermometers every 30 seconds for 5 minutes and record the temperatures. Then take the thermometers out of the sunlight and let them cool to the starting temperature.

D. Prepare a data table like Table 2.

E. Read each thermometer and record the temperatures in Table 2. Then use the lens to bring sunlight to a sharp focus. Since you will have to hold the lens in this position for some time, you may want to stack some books on which to rest your arm. Place thermometer *A* so that the bulb is in focused sunlight. Place thermometer *B* so that the bulb is in the shadow cast by the lens.

F. Read the thermometers every 30 seconds for 5 minutes and record the temperatures. **CAUTION:** *If the temperature recorded by thermometer* B *reaches 105°C, remove the thermometer from the sunlight.*

Table 1 • Temperature (°C) in Normal Sunlight

THERMOMETER	TIME (m)										
	0.0	0.5	1.0	1.5	2.0	2.5	3.0	3.5	4.0	4.5	5.0
A											
B											

Table 2 • Temperature (°C) in Shadow and Focused Sunlight

THERMOMETER	TIME (m)										
	0.0	0.5	1.0	1.5	2.0	2.5	3.0	3.5	4.0	4.5	5.0
A (shadow)											
B (focused sunlight)											

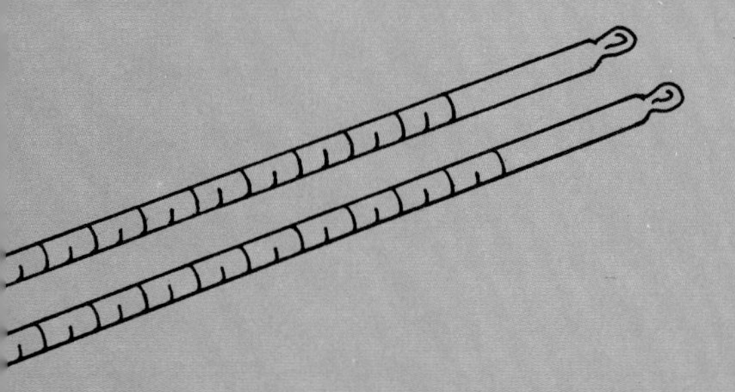

REPORT

1. Make a line graph of your data. Plot time on the horizontal axis and temperature on the vertical axis. Use a dotted line for normal sunlight temperatures, a dashed line for focused sunlight temperatures, and a solid line for shadow area temperatures.

2. Does the lens actually concentrate sunlight? Explain your answer.

3. Compare the changes in temperature in normal sunlight, focused sunlight, and shadow. How did the temperature change in the shadow area?

4. Is there evidence that the lens concentrates all the sunlight shining on it? Explain your answer.

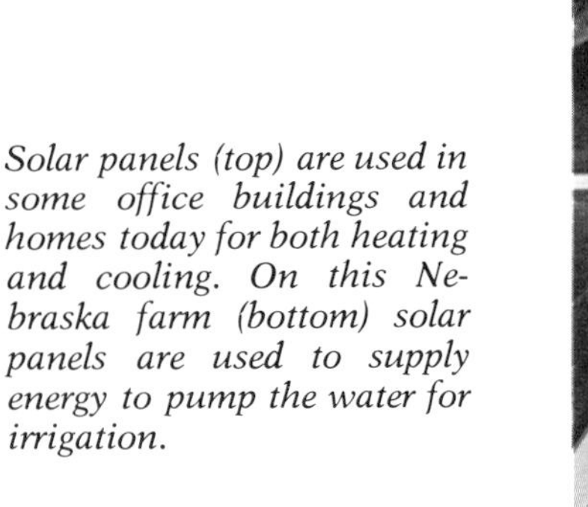

Solar panels (top) are used in some office buildings and homes today for both heating and cooling. On this Nebraska farm (bottom) solar panels are used to supply energy to pump the water for irrigation.

What happens to solar energy when it is absorbed by matter?

Lenses bend, or **refract** (ri frakt′), light rays so that they come to a **focus** (fō′kəs). However, using a lens is not the only way to concentrate sunlight. The absorption of sunlight by dark-colored materials also has that effect. Dark-colored materials absorb more sunlight than do light-colored materials. When sunlight is absorbed, light energy is changed to heat energy. This principle has a practical application in the large-scale use of solar energy as a source of heat.

The use of solar energy as a source of heat is being investigated. However, the idea of heating a house with solar energy presents special problems. Solar panels are needed. These panels have an outer covering of glass or plastic. Sunlight passes through the outer covering and is absorbed by a collecting surface called an **absorber plate.** The absorber plate is usually a rough, dark-colored material. As sunlight strikes the absorber plate, the temperature of the plate increases. A fluid, such as air or water, is pumped under the absorber plate. The fluid absorbs heat from the absorber plate by conduction and carries it to a **heat reservoir** (rez′ər vwär). The reservoir can be a large tank containing liquid or a specially designed rock pile in the basement of the house.

This solar furnace is located in France. The large concentrator turns to follow the sun across the sky. The concentrated rays of the sun heat water to produce steam, which then powers a steam engine. The resulting energy can be used to distill salt water, to grow and dry agricultural products, to heat buildings, and to supply hot water.

The circulating fluid from the absorber plate transfers heat by conduction to the heat reservoir. A large amount of heat energy can be stored in the heat reservoir. When the heat energy is needed, the heated liquid in the reservoir is pumped through a **heat exchanger** that heats the surrounding air. The heated air is then circulated throughout the house. In the case of a rock-pile reservoir, air is forced through the pile and heated by the rocks. The heated air is then circulated throughout the house.

To prevent heat in the system from radiating into space, solar panels are often covered at night. Also, the fluid under the absorber plate does not circulate at night.

The cost of installing a solar heating system in a new home may be $10 000 or more. Therefore not many people are using solar heating systems at this time. As more efficient solar heating systems are developed and

FIGURE 18–1
A solar heating system

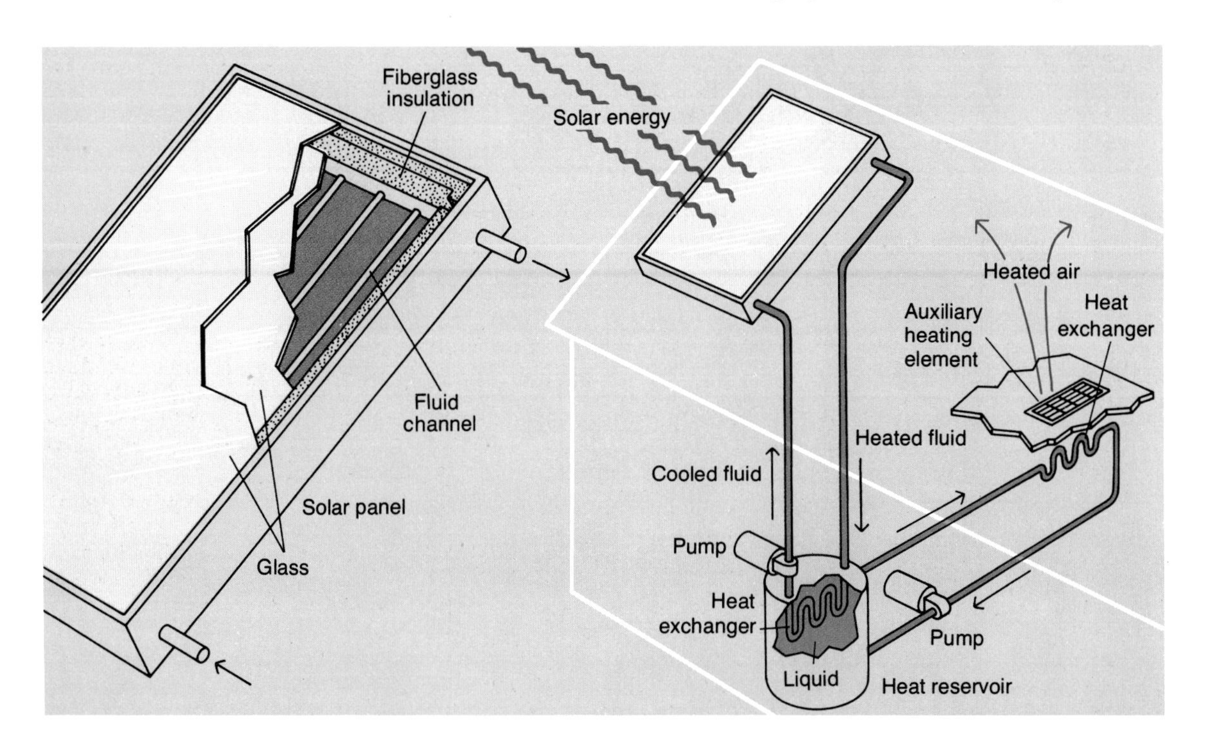

mass-produced, this form of home heating may become more practical. In the future it may cost less to heat a home with solar energy than with the energy of fossil fuels.

Some federal buildings, such as this post office in Saginaw, Michigan, use solar panels to supplement energy needs.

Any home-heating system can be made more efficient by reducing the amount of heat loss. On the average, 30 percent of the heat is lost through the roof. Another 20 percent is lost through poorly sealed windows and doors. Many homes are not sufficiently insulated. In Activity 53 you will investigate how insulation helps to reduce heat loss.

This thermogram (heat picture) shows invisible heat energy as a visible picture. Various ranges in temperature appear as different-colored spots or areas of brightness. The hotter an area is, the lighter the spot that appears on the thermogram. Thermograms can be used to detect heat loss in a building.

Activity 53 Saving Heat Energy

PURPOSE

To construct heating and cooling graphs of an insulated house

MATERIALS

Shoe box
Styrofoam insulation board, 2 cm thick
Clear plastic wrap
Single-edge razor blade
2 Celsius thermometers
Meterstick
Clip lamp with 150–200 W bulb
Glue
Cellophane tape
Graph paper
Scissors

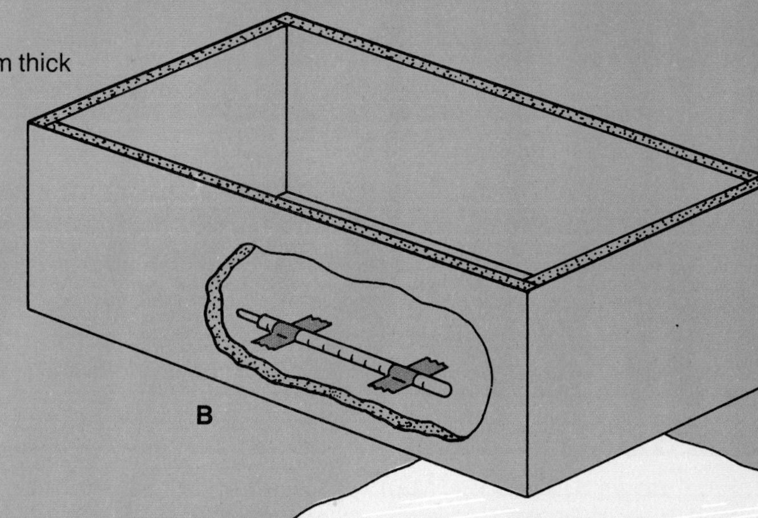

DO THIS

A. Cut pieces of Styrofoam insulation board to completely cover the sides and bottom of the box. Fit the pieces *inside* the box and glue them in place.

B. Tape a thermometer to the insulation board lining the bottom of the box. Be sure the thermometer is positioned so that it can be easily read when the box is turned on its side.

C. Cut two pieces of plastic wrap slightly larger than the opening of the box. Use the plastic wrap to make an insulated window. Do this by taping one piece *inside* the box, 2 cm from the opening. Lay the other piece over the opening and tape it to the *outside* of the box.

C

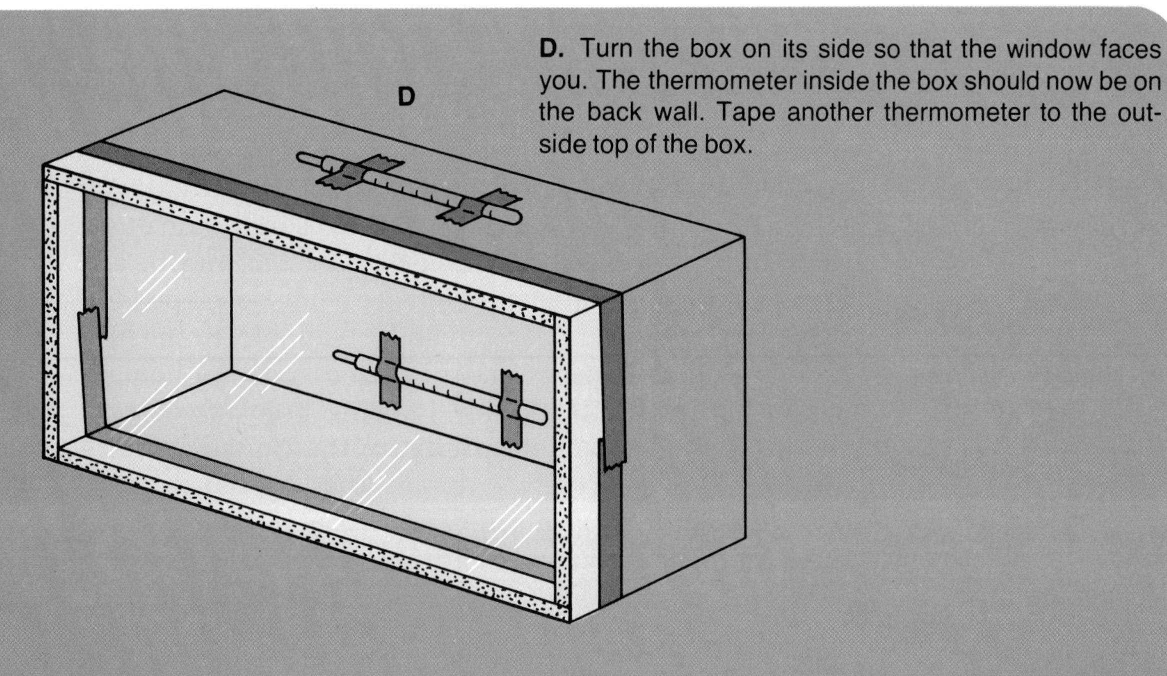

D. Turn the box on its side so that the window faces you. The thermometer inside the box should now be on the back wall. Tape another thermometer to the outside top of the box.

E. Arrange the clip lamp so that the bulb is 50 cm from the insulated window.

F. Design your own table for recording data. Enter the temperature recorded on each thermometer. Then turn on the clip lamp. Record the temperature inside and outside of the box every 30 seconds for 5 minutes.

G. Turn off the clip lamp. Again record the temperature inside and outside of the box every 30 seconds for 5 minutes.

REPORT

1. Construct a line graph of the heating data collected in step **F.** Show temperature on the vertical axis and time on the horizontal axis. Use a solid line to graph the temperatures inside the box. Use a dotted line to graph the temperature outside the box.

2. Construct a line graph of the cooling data collected in step **G.** Follow the procedure described in question **1**.

3. Compare the heating and cooling graphs in this activity with those in Activity 41. If the graphs are different, explain why.

Geothermal Energy and Tidal Power

What is geothermal energy?

An alternate to fossil fuels as an energy source is **geothermal** (jē ə thėr′məl) **energy.** Geothermal energy refers to the earth's internal heat. Research indicates that temperatures within the earth vary but may be as high as 1400°C. Drilling methods are being developed to make this untapped energy readily available. In the future, geothermal energy may be used directly for home-heating purposes. It already is being used in several countries to generate electricity. In the United States, however, it is not expected that geothermal energy will replace fossil fuels as a source of energy in the near future.

Geysers (bottom left) are natural springs or fountains that give off columns of hot water or steam. Geothermal power plants (bottom right) convert the thermal energy of geysers and hot springs into electrical energy.

The Le Rance Power station in St. Malo, France, is one of many such stations built to convert tidal energy into electricity. The turbines in these power stations can convert the energy of incoming or outgoing tides into electrical energy.

Another energy source that may be tapped more widely in the future is the oceans' tides. Tides are caused by the gravitational pull of the moon on the oceans. At various times throughout the day, water rises and falls along ocean shorelines. By building large dams across natural bays, the incoming high tide could be used to turn **hydroelectric** (hī drō i lek′trik) **turbines** (tėr′binz) to produce electricity. As the tide recedes the direction of the turbines could be reversed. Additional electricity could then be generated by using the energy of the outgoing water.

Tidal power may be an excellent alternative to fossil fuels for generating electricity. The geographic limitations, however, permit its use on a large scale only in certain areas.

Why is the use of tidal power limited?

Solar Cells and Other Sources of Energy

Solar cells are devices that can change sunlight directly into electricity. They have been used mainly as a source of electrical energy for artificial satellites. Now other applications of solar cells are being investigated. Huge banks of solar cells might some day be used as a source of electricity for an entire city.

Solar cells are too expensive to produce for large-scale use at the present time. If they can be made more cheaply, they might become important energy sources.

Solar cells have many applications. At the left is one of the newer types of solar cells. Solar cells are used to monitor and direct traffic on this interstate highway (right).

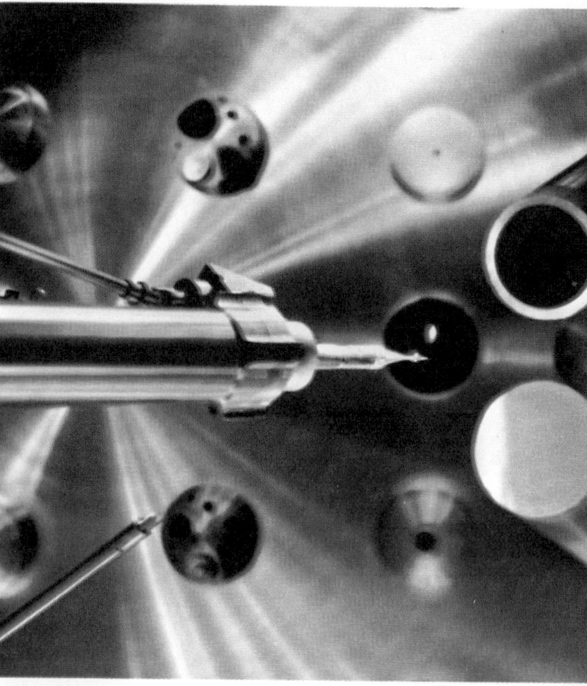

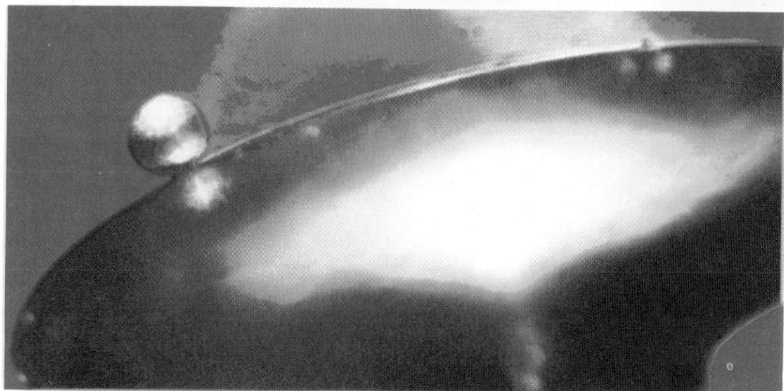

Laser fusion experiments may lead to a new energy source in the future. The Shiva laser, located at the Lawrence Livermore Laboratory at the University of California in Berkeley is shown in these three pictures. Six of the twenty amplifier chains of the laser are shown (top left). The laser fusion targets are shown being positioned in the laser (top right). These fusion targets are about the size of a grain of sand. The pellets used in the laser fusion experiments are about the size of the diameter of a human hair. One of them is shown on the head of an ordinary pin (bottom).

Other possible energy sources are being investigated. In the Midwest, experiments are being conducted in which straw is used as fuel for electrical generating plants. A **biochemical** (bī o kem′ə kəl) system for breaking down turkey manure is also being tested. The manure is decomposed by bacteria and turned into natural gas, which can then be used as fuel.

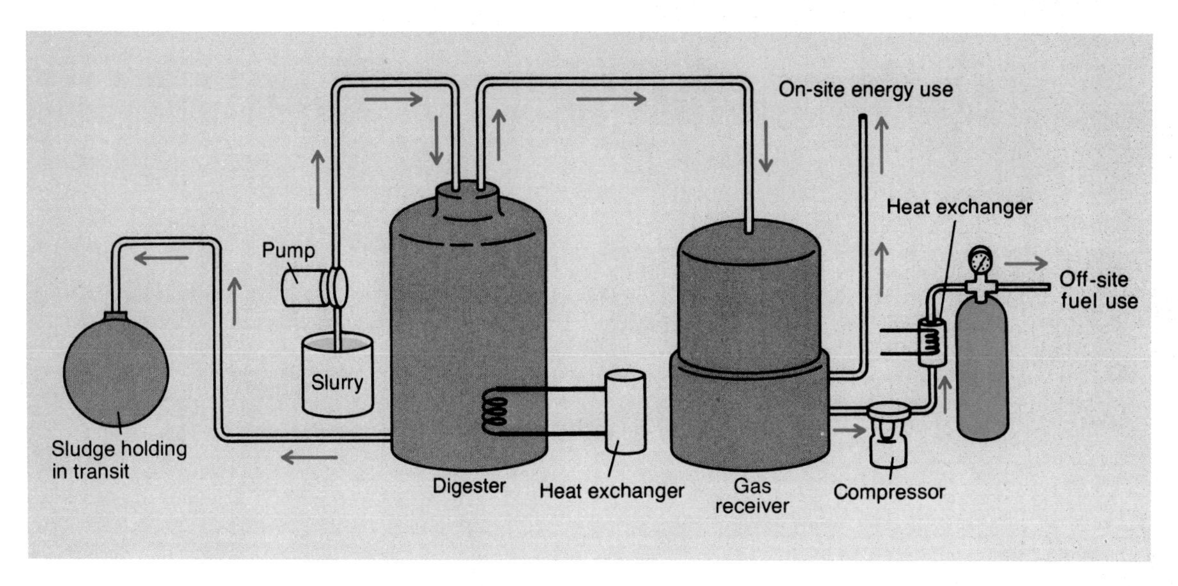

FIGURE 18–2
A biochemical system for converting manure into methane gas

It is generally agreed that new sources of energy are needed to overcome the growing energy shortage. However, exactly what those energy sources will be is still uncertain. It is quite possible that many of the proposed alternatives will be utilized to some extent in the future.

SUMMARY Energy has always been important to people. Supersystem development was made possible by the widespread use of fossil fuels. However, supersystems often waste energy. As fossil fuel supplies are depleted, alternative energy sources must be found. The need for energy demands that new ways be developed for utilizing energy sources used in the past. In addition, new and previously untapped sources of energy must be explored and developed.

SCIENCE WORDS

solar energy
photosynthesis
refract
focus
absorber plate
heat reservoir
heat exchanger
geothermal energy
hydroelectric turbines
solar cells
biochemical

REVIEW QUESTIONS

Fill in the blanks with the correct terms.

1. Solar energy is energy from the ______________.
2. In a solar heating system, heat energy is stored in a ______________ ______________.
3. The biochemical breakdown of manure produces ______________ ______________.
4. The internal heat of the earth is called ______________ energy.
5. ______________ ______________ change sunlight directly into electricity.
6. The energy of tides can be harnessed by building ______________ across natural bays.
7. In the average home ______________ percent of the heat is lost through the roof.
8. Research indicates that the temperature inside the earth may be as high as ______________°C.

Mark each statement true (T) or false (F).

1. ______ Most homes are sufficiently insulated.
2. ______ Geothermal energy is energy from the sun.
3. ______ Modern windmills are designed to turn generators to produce electricity.
4. ______ Dark-colored materials reflect sunlight.
5. ______ Solar heating systems operate on the principle of concentrating the energy of sunlight.

APPLYING WHAT YOU LEARNED

1. Make a model of a solar heating system and describe how it works.
2. Collect pictures and information about alternate energy sources reported in magazines and newspapers. Then decide which energy source or combination of energy sources would be best for meeting your future electrical and heating needs. Explain the basis for your decision.

SUN DAY
IN
NEW YORK.
MAY 3-6, 1978

These people are observing Sun Day—a day set aside to encourage solar energy research and development.

19

People and Changing Supersystems

In this unit you have investigated many different types of energy and material resources. It is clear that the United States is facing serious energy and material shortages. Newpapers, radio, and television frequently carry stories about our energy crisis. Misuse of our natural resources is an equally important topic for discussion. In this chapter you will investigate how changing supersystems may affect your life in the future.

Change Affects People

What two things may cause your life style to change?

How do you think that energy and material shortages might affect your life and the lives of your classmates? You may find that shortages of certain resources could completely alter your life style. Energy shortages could force you to look for new forms of recreation. Using motorized vehicles, such as minibikes, motorboats, and snowmobiles, could be viewed as wasting energy. Fuel for motorized vehicles might be needed exclusively for transportation. Energy and material shortages could also influence your life style by their effect on things you now take for granted. Electricity, gasoline, and the fuel used to heat your home may be in short supply. You might have to decide which electrical appliances are essential and which are not. This might mean watching less TV to ensure enough electricity to operate the refrigerator. It could mean eliminating those electrical devices you can live without. In Activity 54 you will investigate your dependence on energy and material resources.

Recreational activities, such as this snowmobile race, might be considered a nonessential use of fuel in the future.

Activity 54 How Shortages May Affect You

PURPOSE

To determine your dependence on energy and material resources

MATERIALS

Paper and pencil

DO THIS

A. Make a list of ten of your favorite activities. These can be things you do at home, at school, or outdoors.

B. Write the letter *E* in front of each activity that requires using energy other than human energy.

C. Write the letter *M* in front of each activity that requires using material resources.

REPORT

1. How many of your favorite activities require the use of energy or material resources or both?

2. Draw a bar graph of your data. Label the bars *E* (energy), *M* (material resources), *E and M* (energy and material resources), and *N* (neither energy nor material resources).

3. Combine your data with the data of your classmates. Then graph the combined data. Compare the graph of your data with the graph of the class data. In what way are the graphs similar? In what way are they different?

4. How would you be affected by an energy shortage or a shortage of material resources or both?

5. How would your classmates be affected by an energy shortage or a shortage of material resources or both?

This person is cutting blocks of peat. Peat is partially decayed plant material that is the forerunner of coal. In some parts of the world peat is used for fuel.

How else might people have to change their life styles because of possible shortages? In the future it may be necessary for people to use their cars only when no other means of transportation is available. Some people have already cut back on their use of the family car. Car pools and public transportation are becoming more widely accepted in the United States.

Define the term *renewable resource.*

Home heating practices are also changing. In many homes, thermostats are now set at a lower temperature than they were a few years ago. Some people are installing additional insulation in their homes to prevent heat loss. In places where it is plentiful, wood is used more and more as a part-time fuel for home heating. Wood is a **renewable resource.** A renewable resource is one that is replaced as it is used and therefore is always available. Using wood for fuel—even on a part-time basis—helps to conserve the remaining supply of fossil fuels.

Some material resources, such as iron and copper, are being used at tremendous rates. Eventually these materials will become scarce. This will affect the availability and size of our consumer goods. The large car may become a thing of the past. Certain appliances may no longer be manufactured. More tasks may have to be done by hand. The recycling of materials may become a necessary practice. In the future everyone may have to accept some changes in life style. Activity 55 is designed to explore the attitudes adults have regarding energy and material resource problems.

There often are differences in attitudes, thinking, and life styles between young people and adults. The young people of today will be the adults of tomorrow. It is possible that young people may have different attitudes than adults regarding energy and material resource problems. You can determine the attitudes of young people in Activity 56.

EXCURSION 10
The development of a questioning, scientific attitude is discussed in Excursion 10, "A Guide to Consumer Goods."

These people have definite ideas concerning a controversial topic. Their views may not agree with those of other people.

Activity 55 Attitude Survey—Adults

PURPOSE

To determine the attitudes of adults regarding energy and material resource problems

MATERIALS

Questionnaire
Pencil

DO THIS

A. Copy the questionnaire.

B. Interview ten adults in your neighborhood. Be sure to interview both men and women.

Read the statements on the questionnaire to each person you interview. Ask the person if he or she agrees with, disagrees with, or has no opinion concerning each statement. If the person agrees with the statement, write *A* in the column under his or her number. If the person disagrees, write *D.* If the person has no opinion, write *NO.*

C. Combine your data with the data of three classmates. Organize the combined data in a table like Table 1.

D. Collect the combined data from each group of four students. Organize these data for the entire class in a table similar to Table 1.

REPORT

1. Using the class data, determine the percentage of adults who agreed with each question. Disagreed. Had no opinion.

2. What advantage is there in interviewing a large number of people rather than just a few people?

Table 1 • Combined Questionnaire Data

STATEMENT NUMBER	TOTAL RESPONSES		
	A	D	NO
1			
2			
3			
4			
5			
6			
7			
8			
9			
10			

QUESTIONNAIRE • Attitude Survey—Adults

STATEMENT	PERSON INTERVIEWED									
	1	2	3	4	5	6	7	8	9	10
1. We are facing a serious energy crisis.										
2. Nuclear power is the answer to future energy needs.										
3. Spending tax dollars to develop ways to use wind energy to produce electricity is a wise investment.										
4. More tax dollars should be spent to develop ways to convert solar energy into heat and electrical energy.										
5. All cars sold in the U.S. should get at least 30 miles per gallon of gasoline.										
6. Production of large cars should be banned in the U.S. to help conserve materials.										
7. It is very important to insulate your home.										
8. Conserving energy and other resources is everyone's concern.										
9. Everyone can help stop pollution.										
10. Recycling cans and bottles is a good way to save material resources.										

Activity 56 Attitude Survey — Young People

PURPOSE

To determine the attitudes of young people regarding energy and material resource problems

MATERIALS

Questionnaire
Pencil

DO THIS

A. Use the same questionnaire as in Activity 55 to interview ten students who are not taking physical science. Follow the same procedure for interviewing as you used previously.

B. Combine your data with that of three classmates. Organize the combined data in a table like Table 1 in Activity 55.

C. Collect the combined data from each group of four students in your class. Organize these data in a table like the one used in Activity 55.

REPORT

1. Compare the responses of the students with the responses of the adults in Activity 55. How are the responses similar? How do they differ?

2. Using the results of both surveys, list any problems that might occur in the future. For example, what problems might occur if most of the people interviewed disagreed that we are facing an energy crisis?

3. In view of the different attitudes of people, what do you propose as solutions to the problems listed in question 2?

Everyone's Problem

Future energy and material resource shortages will affect everyone, directly or indirectly. The effect can be minimized if people recognize the problem and conserve now while planning for the future. Listed below are some things you can do to help.

How can the effect of future shortages of energy and material resources be minimized?

1. Be aware of developing energy and material resource shortages.
2. Don't waste energy or resources.
3. Work for the establishment of a recycling center in your community.
4. Recycle recyclable resources.
5. Make community leaders aware of environmental problems, such as air pollution, water pollution, littering, and so on.
6. Encourage support of legislation for environmental protection and conservation.

Bicycles are a major means of transportation in many European countries. They are economical to use, they conserve energy, and they do not harm the environment.

Paper is a recyclable material. This storage park (top) holds bales of shredded paper for reprocessing. Adding insulation (right) to the outside walls and attic of a house helps prevent heat loss.

These worn-out tires need not have become a pollutant and an eyesore. They could have been used as playground equipment, or to build artificial reefs for fish breeding and breakwaters to protect beaches. Tire manufacturers are experimenting to find other ways of recycling old tires.

SUMMARY In this chapter you have investigated people's attitudes concerning energy and material resources. You did this by conducting interviews with a number of different people. You examined your own life style to determine whether your activities depend on energy and material resources. You made some predictions concerning the future. These predictions were based on the information you collected in your interviews. Other people probably view the status of the earth's resources differently than you. Perhaps you found that some people agreed with your views and others disagreed. You should now be more aware of the difficulty in finding solutions to meet everyone's future needs.

SCIENCE WORDS

renewable resource

REVIEW QUESTIONS

Complete the following by choosing the correct answer.

1. Which fuel is a renewable resource?
   (a) coal (b) oil (c) gas (d) wood
2. Which electrical device would it be easier to live without?
   (a) TV (b) refrigerator (c) oven (d) heater
3. What would be a good way to conserve nonrenewable resources?
   (a) take cans and bottles to be recycled (b) car pool or use mass transportation (c) turn off electric lights and appliances when they are not in use (d) do all the things described in a, b, and c

Mark each statement true (T) or false (F).

1. ______ One way to save fuel used for home heating is to turn down the thermostat.
2. ______ Recycling is a good way to conserve certain resources.
3. ______ Iron and copper are renewable resources.
4. ______ Shortages of energy and materials may result in changed life styles within the next few years.
5. ______ Insulation does little to prevent heat loss from homes.
6. ______ A scarcity of material resources in the future may affect the availability and size of consumer goods.

APPLYING WHAT YOU LEARNED

1. Some people feel that shortages of energy and material resources are caused by the increasing population. Read a recent magazine article on this topic and report on it to your class. State whether you agree or disagree with the author and why.
2. Try to live for one day without one of the following: paper products, fossil fuels, electricity, plastic products, metal products. Report to the class on the difficulties you had and whether it was possible to completely do without this material. It might be best to try this on a weekend.

UNIT REVIEW

1. List at least five ways in which energy use could be reduced in your home.
2. Give five examples of how you might be exposed to noise pollution. For each example list what might be done to reduce this type of pollution.
3. Collect pictures and news articles that are concerned with pollution. Use them to create a bulletin board display.
4. Find out the location of the nearest pollution monitoring station. If it is close enough, arrange to talk with an official about the various pollutants and how they are measured. Report on your findings to the class.
5. List at least two oxides each of nitrogen and sulfur. Using reference books determine what makes these compounds so dangerous as pollutants. What are the major sources of this type of pollution? What is being done to eliminate or reduce these materials?
6. Find the location of the recycling facility nearest your home. Find what materials are recycled there and any restrictions or requirements for recycling those materials. Report your findings to the class and to your family. Encourage your family and friends to participate in recycling projects. Write a letter to your local newspaper, making people aware of the benefits of recycling.
7. What is meant by thermal pollution? How does it affect water? What causes this type of pollution?
8. List five items that are thrown away as garbage or trash. Use reference books to find out what happens to each item as it decays and returns to nature. How long does it take for each item to completely decompose? How could the changes be carried out faster?

Careers

In this unit you have investigated several types of pollution. Methods that could help to reduce or eliminate pollution and waste have also been discussed. There are many scientists involved in studying the world's pollution problems. Large corporations and government agencies employ environmental scientists to help determine the effects of pollution on the evironment. Emphasis is placed on finding the sources of pollution and ways to control the pollutants. These scientists also warn people of possible health dangers caused by pollution.

Pollution is studied by various types of environmental scientists. Climatologists are attempting to determine how pollution affects weather patterns. A climatologist may work on such problems as smoke and air pollution control. He or she may advise a company of the best location for a new plant. Oceanographers may study the effects of waste and chemical pollution on plant and animal life in the ocean. A polluted ocean affects all of us. Plant life in the ocean is an important source of the earth's oxygen. Fish and other marine animals are an important source of food for many nations. These resources may be endangered by pollution. Climatologists and oceanographers must have a college degree. However, there is always a need for technicians and laboratory assistants. In these cases, a high school diploma or a two-year technical school education is often sufficient.

Food scientists study the production, handling, and nutritive value of food. They also supervise the sanitary packaging and distribution of food to prevent contamination. A job in this field usually requires a college degree with a major in food science or biology.

The handling and disposal of nuclear waste is one of the most dangerous and challenging fields in pollution control. A sound education in science and engineering is required. Nuclear waste engineers may be needed for centuries, since nuclear waste products remain radioactive for long periods of time.

The use of pesticides presents another challenge to the environment. The chemicals used to control insects and other pests have been found in our food and water. Scientists must advise the users of pesticides about possible dangerous side effects. Modern farmers have become aware of the effects of pesticides through courses offered by various chemical companies.

There are many jobs available in the care and preservation of our environment. Check into becoming a scientist who assists nature.

Technology from many branches of science and engineering led to the development of this new type of solar collector. Instead of turning to track the sun, it uses a system of lenses to focus the sun on the collector elements.

Research

The world demand for energy is increasing every year. However, there is a limited supply of many of our energy resources. Reserves of petroleum may be exhausted early in the next century. According to some estimates, only a two- or three-decade supply of petroleum remains. With supplies of petroleum dwindling, scientists are searching for new sources of energy. Our vast coal resources offer possible alternatives. Coal supplies will probably last several centuries rather than several decades. However, a big disadvantage to the use of coal is that it causes a great deal of pollution when it is burned. If methods can be found to reduce the pollutants, coal could be an important energy resource in the future.

The use of nuclear energy also has possibilities. Vast amounts of energy can be obtained by nuclear fission. But critics argue that nuclear explosions or fatal leaks of radiation from nuclear reactors could occur. Environmentalists express concern that plants, animals, and people could be killed in a nuclear accident. In addition, the radioactive waste must be stored safely.

Nuclear physicists are working on clean forms of nuclear energy production. One answer may be the fusion reaction. Recent progress in controlling nuclear fusion has been reported by a team of physicists at Princeton University in New Jersey. However, usable energy from such a reaction will probably not be available for several more decades.

Another possible energy source is solar energy. Solar energy is nonpolluting, inexhaustible, and readily available. The big problem with solar energy is in developing inexpensive methods to capture and use it. Some physicists and space engineers want to develop huge solar satellites. These satellites would be placed in orbit around the earth. The sun's energy would be collected and transmitted back to earth in the form of microwaves. Back on earth the microwaves could be transformed into other more useful forms of energy.

Geochemists and geophysicists are presently studying geothermal energy. This is energy provided by the tremendous heat within the earth. Several facilities are currently in operation supplying energy from geothermal sources. Scientists are studying the possibility of tapping the geothermal energy near Mt. Hood, Oregon. If all goes well, Portland, Oregon, might receive some of its energy from this source. The technology being developed there might be useful in similar locations in the future.

Processing garbage and biomass into energy are also possible alternatives. Methane can be produced from animal manure. Tree plantations could someday supply wood for methanol (wood alcohol) production. Methanol could be a competitive fuel in our near future. The investigations needed to develop new energy sources are going on now.

Amplifiers for fusion lasers are assembled in the dust free environment of a clean room. The aim of laser fusion research is to develop a clean, inexhaustible source of electrical energy.

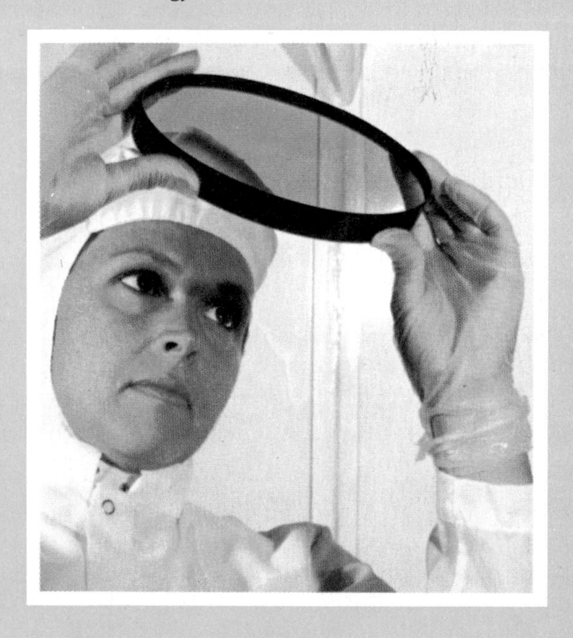

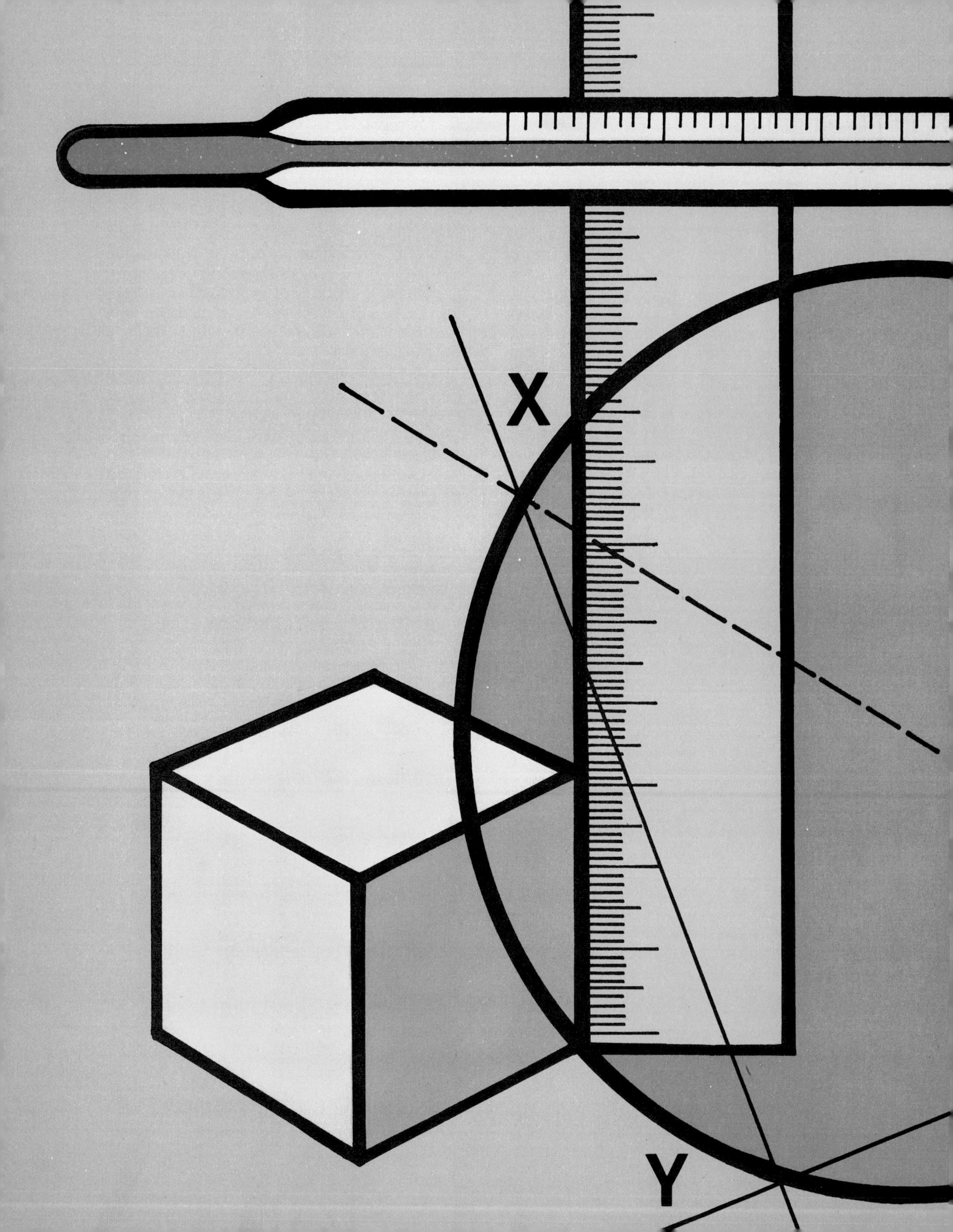
X
Y

EXCURSIONS

1 Metric Linear Measurement

You have probably heard that the United States is "going metric." The metric system is the measurement system used in science. In the future, metric measurements will be used in every aspect of daily living. Chefs, auto mechanics, construction workers, lawyers, athletes, homemakers—everyone will be using metric measurements. In some cases you may have already "gone metric" without really "thinking metric." For example, you may own, or have used, an 8-, 16-, or 35-millimeter camera. Your favorite radio station broadcasts at the frequency of a certain number of **megahertz** (meg′ə hėrtz) or **kilohertz** (kil′ə hėrtz). You tune in the station by dialing that frequency.

The dial on an AM/FM radio is calibrated in both kilohertz and megahertz units.

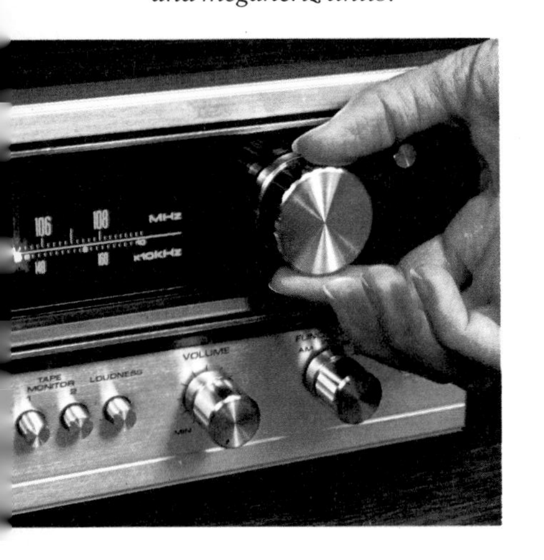

There are many reasons why you may not yet be "thinking metric." One reason is that all your life you have been exposed to the English system of measurement. The English system is the measurement system still commonly used in the United States. It measures in units such as feet, yards, pounds, and gallons. These customary units are the units with which you are most familiar. But the changeover from English to metric measurements is taking place. **Pharmaceutical** (fär mə sü′tə kəl) companies have already used metric measurements for many years. More recently, labels on food items and many other products carry both customary and metric units. Some road signs state distances in customary and metric units.

In this excursion you will "think metric" by learning to use metric units when making **linear** (lin′ē ər) **measurements.** A linear measurement is a measurement of length, such as distance or height. Other excursions deal with metric measurements of volume and mass.

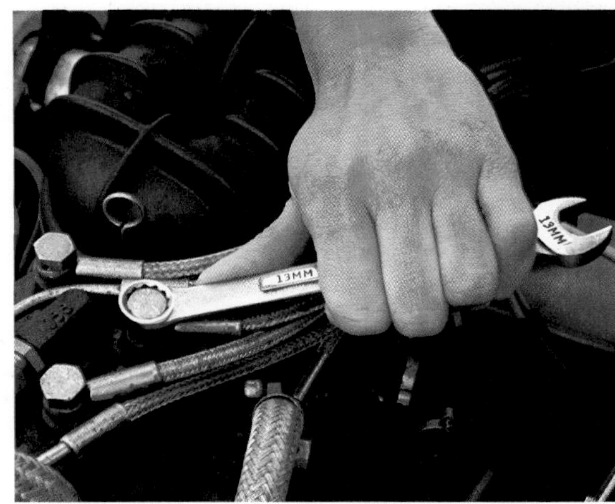

Many cameras and tools are manufactured to metric specifications.

Table E1–1 lists the common units used for linear measurement in the metric system. The basic unit of length is the **meter** (mē′tər). A meter is a little longer than a yard. For measuring long distances, the **kilometer** (kil′ə mē tər) is used. Lengths of less than one meter are usually measured in **centimeters** (sen′tə mē tərz) or **millimeters** (mil′ə mē tərz).

TABLE E1–1 • Metric Units of Linear Measurement

UNIT	SYMBOL	VALUE
Kilometer	km	1000 m
Meter	m	0.001 km or 100 cm or 1000 mm
Centimeter	cm	0.01 m or 10 mm
Millimeter	mm	0.001 m or 0.1 cm

Notice that a **prefix** (prē′fiks) is used with the word *meter* for units that are larger or smaller than the meter. The prefix tells you the size of the unit. For example, the prefix *kilo* means one thousand. Therefore a kilometer is 1000 meters. *Centi* means hundredth, so a centimeter is 0.01 meter. *Milli* means thousandth, so a millimeter is 0.001 meter.

The millimeter, centimeter, meter, and kilometer are related to each other in the following way:

10 millimeters (mm) = 1 centimeter (cm)
100 centimeters = 1 meter (m)
1000 meters = 1 kilometer (km)

If you understand the meaning of the prefixes, it is easy to change from one metric unit to another. You simply multiply or divide by ten or by a power of ten. You multiply when changing from a larger unit to a smaller unit. You divide when changing from a smaller unit to a larger unit.

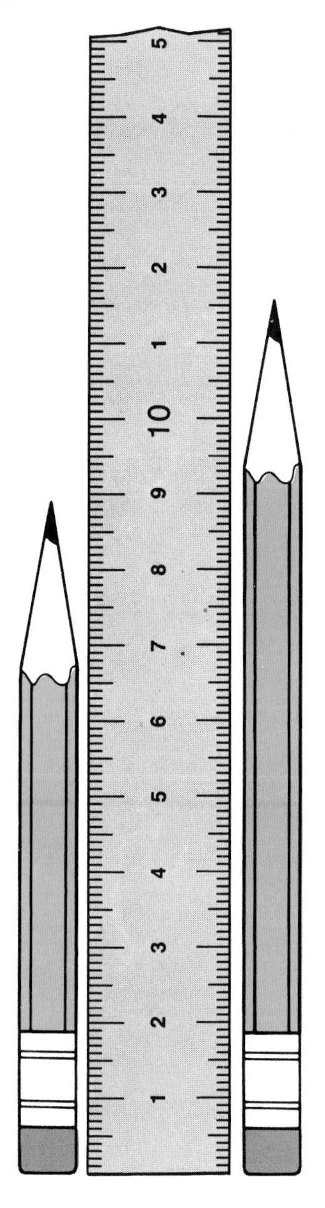

FIGURE E1–1

Measuring

Examine a meterstick and a metric ruler. Also examine a metric tape measure, if one is available. The smallest divisions on the meterstick are millimeters. Usually every fifth millimeter is shown as a slightly longer line. Every tenth millimeter marks off the next larger unit—a centimeter. The centimeter divisions are numbered.

Look at Figure E1–1. The figure shows part of a metric ruler, drawn to scale. The length of the pencil lying along the upper edge of the ruler is 9 cm. Since 1 cm equals 10 mm, the length of the pencil is also 90 mm.

Now look at the pencil lying along the lower edge of the ruler. This pencil is longer than 11 cm, but shorter than 12 cm. Its exact length is found by counting the number of millimeters beyond the 11-cm mark to the tip of the pencil. Count them. You should have counted 6 mm. The length of the pencil is 11 cm plus 6 mm. Since 1 mm is 0.1 cm, the length of the pencil is 11.6 cm.

Suppose you want to know the length in millimeters of the pencil. You could count the millimeter marks from the end of the pencil to its tip. You would count 116 mm. Instead of counting all the millimeter marks, remember that 1 cm equals 10 mm. Since 11 cm equals 110 mm, the length of the pencil is 110 mm plus 6 mm or 116 mm.

Now measure the things called for in the following activity. In each case, decide if you will use a metric ruler, or a meterstick. If you need more practice, measure other things, too.

MATERIALS

Metric ruler
Meterstick
Metric tape measure (optional)

DO THIS

A. Measure in centimeters the height, width, and depth (thickness) of a door. The door may be the classroom door, a cabinet door, or a closet door. Record the measurements in a table like Table 1.

TABLE 1 • Metric Measurements

OBJECT	MEASUREMENT
Door height	
Door width	
Door depth	
Line A	
Line B	
Line C	
Triangle perimeter	
Classroom length	
Classroom width	

B. Measure in millimeters the lengths of lines *A, B,* and *C.* Record the measurements.

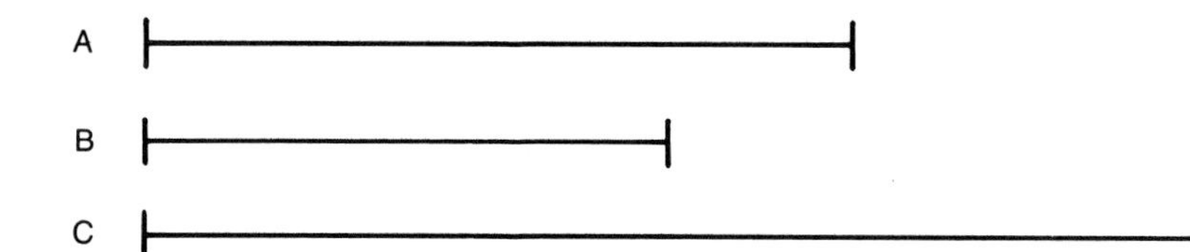

C. Measure in millimeters the perimeter of the triangle. To do this, you must measure the length of each side. Then add these lengths. Record the measurement.

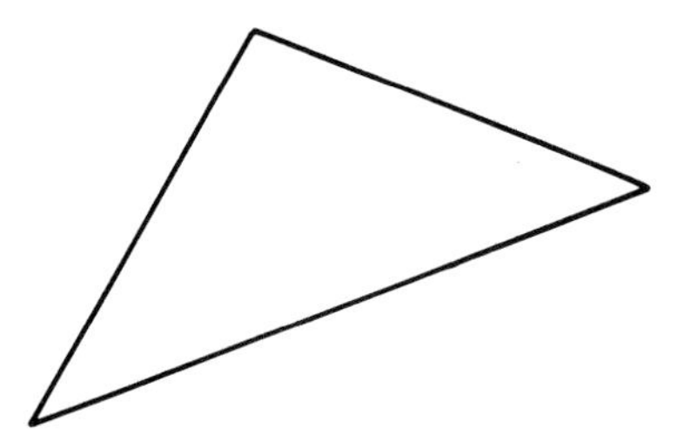

D. Measure in meters the length and width of the classroom. Record the measurements.

REPORT

1. Explain why you chose to measure some things with the metric ruler and other things with the meterstick.

2. Change each measurement in Table 1 to the next larger or smaller metric unit. For example, change millimeters to centimeters; change centimeters to millimeters or meters. Change meters to centimeters.

Measuring Mass

2

Mass is the amount of matter an object has. Table E2–1 lists the common metric units of mass. The basic unit of mass is the **kilogram.** A convenient smaller unit of mass is the **gram.** A paper clip has a mass of about one gram. There are one thousand grams in a kilogram.

TABLE E2–1 • Common Metric Units of Mass

UNIT	SYMBOL	VALUE
Metric ton	t	1000 kg
Kilogram	kg	0.001 t or 1000 g
Gram	g	0.001 kg or 1000 mg
Milligram	mg	0.001 g

In this excursion you will learn to measure mass with a balance. Look at Figure E2–1. It shows a balance that may be like those in your classroom. Study the diagram. Then examine your balance. On your balance find the parts that are similar to those labeled in the diagram.

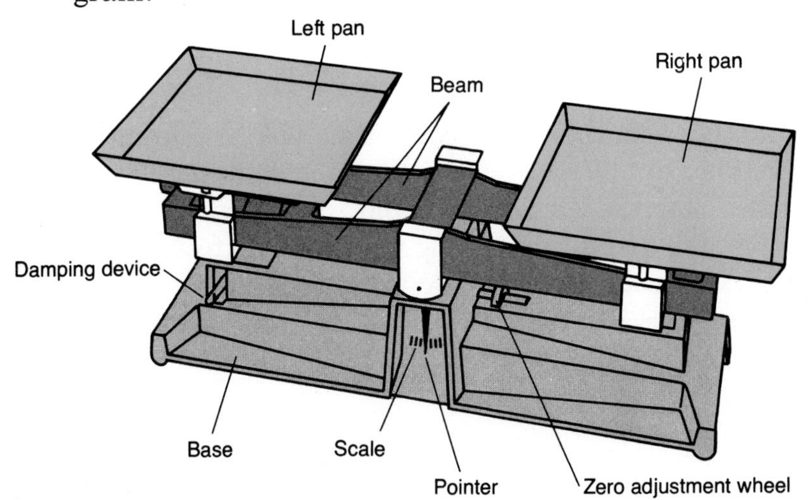

FIGURE E2–1

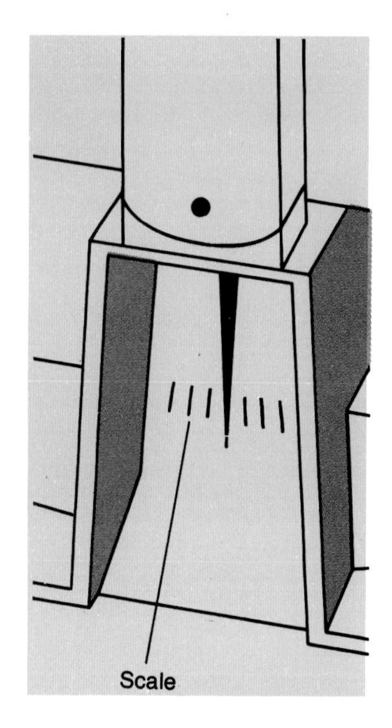

FIGURE E2–2

The balance should always be on a level surface. It should also be *zeroed.* The balance is zeroed when the pointer lines up with the center mark on the scale, as shown in Figure E2–2. If adjustment is necessary, rotate the zero adjustment wheel to line up the pointer with the mark.

Mass is measured with a balance by comparing an unknown mass with known masses. The balance works like a seesaw. The object whose mass you want to measure is placed on the left pan. This will cause the pointer to swing to the right. Known masses are then placed on the right pan until the pointer swings back to the center mark. When the pointer is on the center mark again, the mass of the object is equal to the sum of the known masses on the right pan. The known masses are marked with numbers that show how many grams each mass equals. Suppose the known masses in Figure E2–3 were needed to balance an object. The object would have a mass of 27 g.

FIGURE E2–3

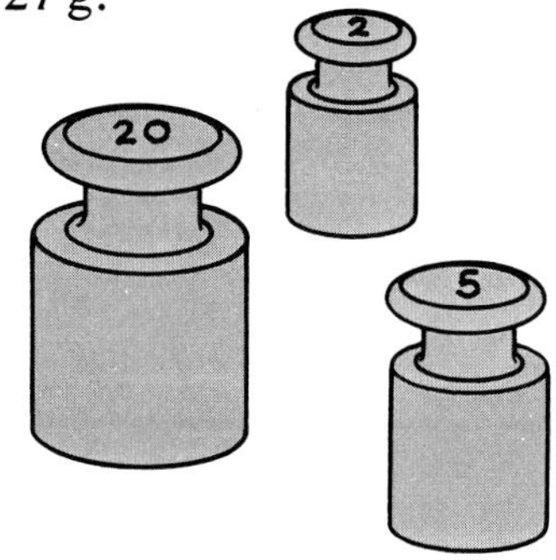

When measuring with the balance, the pointer will swing back and forth for some time before coming to rest. This can be avoided by using the damping device located near the left end of the base (see Figure E2–1). It is operated by gently pressing the wire loop from left to right with your finger. Some balances may not have a damping device. In those cases, the motion may be slowed by holding the eraser end of a pencil underneath either pan.

Now practice using the balance. Measure the amount of sand that equals 10 g. Also measure the mass of several objects.

MATERIALS

Balance
Set of metric masses
2 50-mL beakers
Supply of sand
Spoon
Pencil
Piece of chalk
Eraser

DO THIS

A. Place a 50-mL beaker on each balance pan. Then zero the balance.

B. Place a 10-g mass on the right pan.

C. Use the spoon to put sand in the beaker on the left pan. **CAUTION:** *Chemicals and similar materials should not be put directly on the balance pans.* Put sand in the beaker a little at a time until the pointer is on the center mark. When the pointer is centered, you have measured 10 g of sand.

D. Remove everything from the balance.

E. Check that the balance is zeroed. Then place a pencil on the left pan. Place known masses on the right pan until the pointer is on the center mark. The sum of the masses on the right pan is equal to the mass of the pencil. Record the mass in a table like Table 1.

TABLE 1 • Mass Measurements

OBJECT	MASS (g)
Pencil	
Eraser	
Chalk	

F. Repeat steps *D* and *E,* using an eraser and a piece of chalk in place of the pencil. Record the masses.

REPORT

1. On which balance pan should you place the object whose mass you want to measure?

2. Why, do you think, should the balance be on a level surface?

3. Why should the balance be zeroed each time before using it?

4. Ask a classmate to measure the same things you did. If the measurements do not agree with yours, explain why.

Measuring Volume

3

All materials take up space. Water, rocks, wood, plastic—even air—take up space. The space a material occupies is called its **volume.** In this excursion you will learn to measure the volume of liquids and solids in metric units.

Liquid Volume

Table E3–1 shows the relationship between the metric units most commonly used for measuring liquid volume. The basic unit of liquid volume is the **liter** (lē′tər). A liter is a little larger than a quart. A convenient smaller unit of liquid volume is the **milliliter.**

TABLE E3-1 • Metric Units of Liquid Volume

UNIT	SYMBOL	VALUE
Liter	L	1000 mL
Milliliter	mL	0.001 L

Liquid volume can be measured with several kinds of instruments. You will use a graduated cylinder, called a **graduate,** and a **graduated beaker.**

There are graduates of different sizes to measure different volumes. Figure E3–1 shows a graduate that may be used to measure volumes up to 50 mL. The scale on the graduate is marked in 1-mL divisions. Every tenth milliliter is shown by a longer line that is numbered. The graduate shown in Figure E3–2 may be used to

FIGURE E3–1

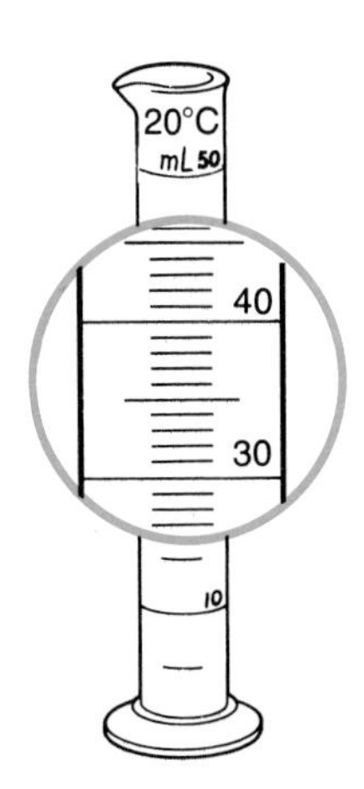

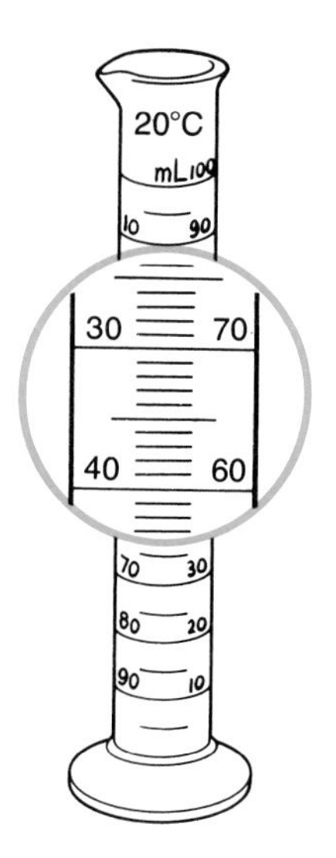

FIGURE E3–2

measure volumes up to 100 mL. This graduate has two scales. The scale on the right measures upward from 0.0 mL to 100 mL. It is marked in 1-mL divisions. Every tenth milliliter is shown by a longer line that is numbered. The scale on the right shows how many milliliters of liquid are in the graduate. The scale on the left measures downward from 0.0 mL to 100 mL. It also is marked in 1-mL divisions and every tenth milliliter is numbered. This scale tells you how much liquid can be added to the graduate before it is full.

Figure E3–3 shows sections from two graduates. The surface of the liquid in the graduates is called the **meniscus** (mə nis′kəs). The meniscus curves upward at the edges. When you read a graduate, hold it with the meniscus at eye level. Then read the volume of the liquid from the lowest point of the meniscus. The graduate at the left is filled to the 63-mL mark. The volume of the liquid in the graduate is 63 mL. What is the volume of the liquid in the graduate at the right?

FIGURE E3–3

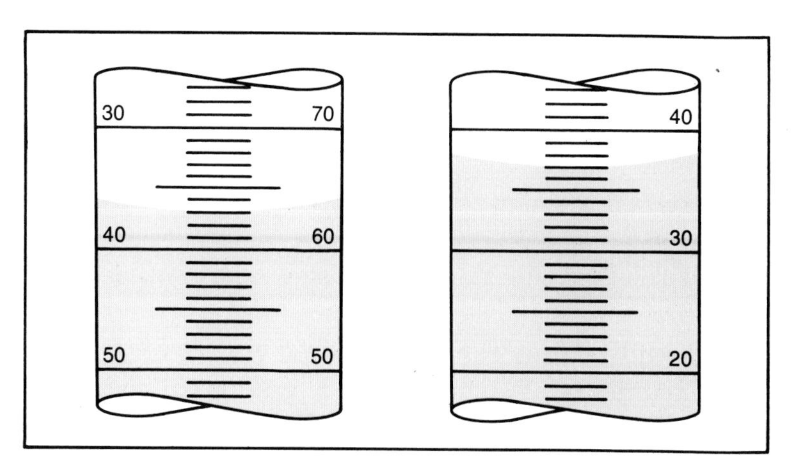

Graduated beakers are often used to measure large volumes of liquid. Also they are used when it isn't necessary to measure the volume exactly. Look at Figure E3–4. This beaker is marked in 25-mL divisions. How many milliliters of liquid are in the beaker?

Now practice measuring with a graduate and a beaker. The following activity will help you to develop your skills.

MATERIALS

100-mL graduate
2 250-mL graduated beakers
Water

DO THIS

A. Fill one of the 250-mL beakers with water. The level of the water should be above the 200-mL mark.

B. Carefully pour water from the beaker into the graduate. Measure 40 mL of water. Empty the graduate into the second beaker.

C. Use water from the first beaker to measure 50 mL in the graduate. Empty the graduate into the second beaker.

D. Use water from the first beaker to measure 67 mL in the graduate. Empty the graduate into the second beaker.

E. Use water from the first beaker to measure 18 mL in the graduate. Empty the graduate into the second beaker.

REPORT

1. What is the volume of water in the second beaker? Is this volume about the same as the total volume measured in steps **B–E?**

2. In step **D**, how much additional water would be needed to fill the graduate?

3. Ask a classmate to pour some water into a graduate. Read the volume. Do you and your classmate agree on the volume? If not, explain why.

FIGURE E3–4

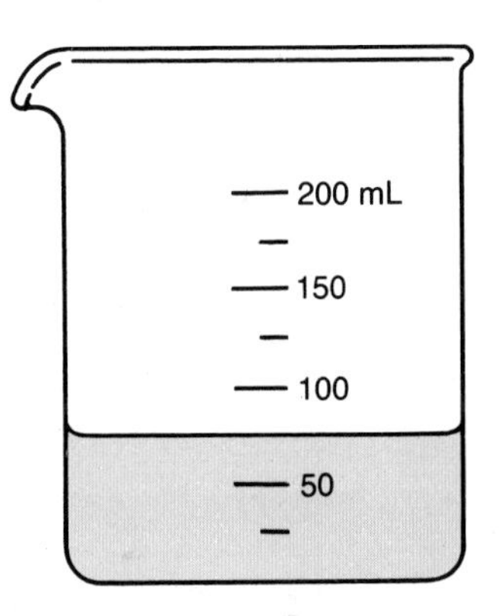

Solid Volume

When a solid has a regular shape, its volume can be found by measuring its length, width, and height. The volume of the solid is the product of the three measurements. It is always stated in cubic units. Mathematically this is shown by the equation:

$$V = l \times w \times h$$

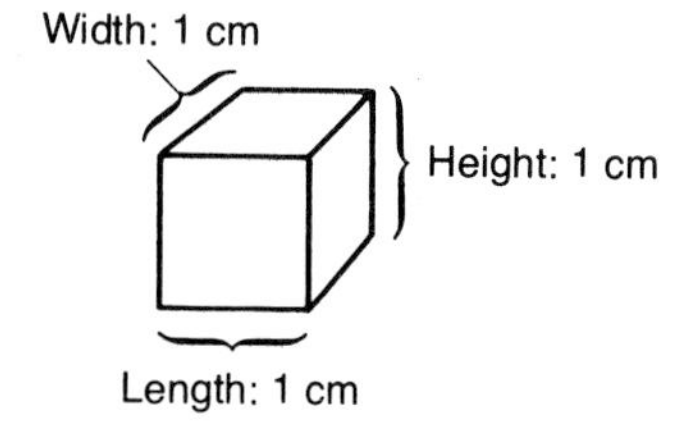

FIGURE E3–5

For example, the solid in Figure E3–5 has these measurements: length, 1 cm; width, 1 cm; height, 1 cm. Its volume is:

$$\begin{aligned} V &= l \times w \times h \\ &= 1\text{ cm} \times 1\text{ cm} \times 1\text{ cm} \\ &= 1\text{ cm}^3 \end{aligned}$$

How can you find the volume of a solid with an irregular shape? One way this can be done with small objects is to use a graduate and water. Partially fill the graduate with water. Note the volume. Then lower the solid into the water. Two things cannot occupy the same space at the same time. Therefore, the water level in the graduate will rise. The difference between the new volume and the original volume is equal to the volume of the object. In the metric system, 1 mL of water takes up 1 cm^3 of space. Therefore, if the volume of the water changed by 10 mL, the volume of the object would be 10 cm^3.

The following activity will give you practice in measuring the volume of various solids.

MATERIALS

3 regularly-shaped blocks: A, B, and C
Metric ruler
50-mL graduate
Small rock
Piece of chalk
40-cm length of thread
Water

DO THIS

A. Use the metric ruler to measure the length, width, and height of the three blocks. Record the measurements in a table like Table 1.

TABLE 1 • Volume—Solids with Regular Shapes

BLOCK	LENGTH (cm)	WIDTH (cm)	HEIGHT (cm)	VOLUME (cm^3)
A				
B				
C				

B. Now find the volume of each block by multiplying its length, width, and height. Record each volume in the table.

C. Make a table like Table 2. Record in the table the measurements you will make in steps **D** and **E.**

TABLE 2 • Volume—Solids with Irregular Shapes

OBJECT	ORIGINAL VOLUME OF WATER (mL)	NEW VOLUME OF WATER (mL)	CHANGE IN VOLUME (mL)	VOLUME OF OBJECT (cm^3)
Rock				
Chalk				

D. Fill the graduate with water to the 25-mL mark. Tie the thread to the rock. Then gently lower the rock into the water. Read the new volume of water in the graduate.

E. Repeat step **D**, but use a piece of chalk instead of the rock.

F. Using the data you collected, complete the last two columns of the table.

FURTHER ACTIVITIES

1. Find the volume of the following figures.

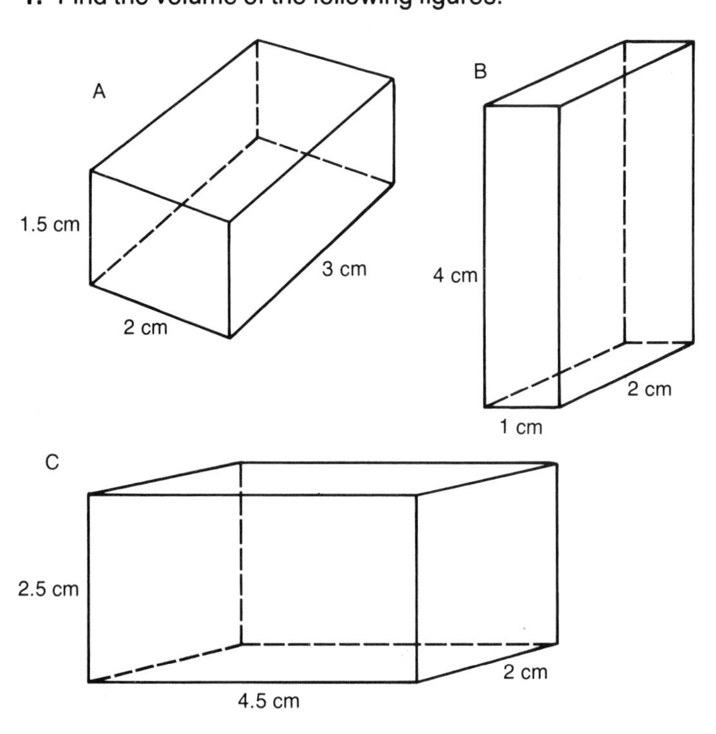

2. What is the volume in cm^3 of 5 mL of liquid water?

3. A solid object has a volume of 9.5 cm^3. It is submerged in 27 mL of water in a graduate. By how many milliliters will the water level rise in the graduate?

Measuring Temperature

4

Temperature is a measure of how hot something is. The **kinetic** (ki net′ik) **energy** of the molecules of a substance determines the temperature of the substance. Kinetic energy is the energy of motion. The warmer a substance is, the greater the kinetic energy of its molecules. As the substance cools, its molecules slow down. The kinetic energy of the molecules becomes less. In other words, the lowest possible energy results in the lowest possible temperature. This temperature is called **absolute zero.** At absolute zero, the molecules of a substance are very nearly at rest.

Temperature measurements are an important part of everyday life. The instrument used to measure temperature is the thermometer.

The thermometer you will be using is called a **Celsius** (sel′sē əs) **thermometer.** This thermometer was developed by the Swedish astronomer Anders Celsius. Celsius based the temperature scale for his thermometer on two fixed points—the freezing point and the boiling point of pure water at sea level. He called the freezing point *0 degrees* and the boiling point *100 degrees.* The Celsius thermometer in Figure E4–1 has the temperature scale marked in whole degrees. Every tenth degree is numbered. What temperature reading is shown on this thermometer?

Examine the thermometer you will be using. The temperature scale may be marked differently from the one shown in Figure E4–1. What is the highest temperature it can measure? What is the lowest temperature?

Practice using the Celsius thermometer by taking a series of temperature measurements. **CAUTION:**

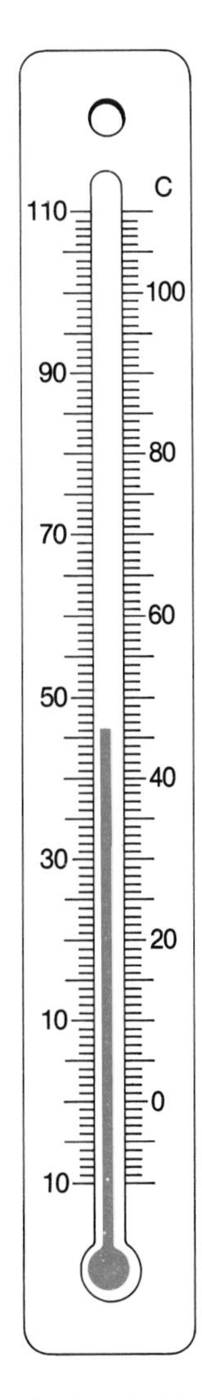

FIGURE E4–1

Handle the thermometer carefully. It is fragile and can be easily broken.

MATERIALS

Celsius thermometer
250-mL beaker
Watch or clock
Water
Ice

DO THIS

A. Half fill the beaker with water.

B. Hold the thermometer in the water. Make sure that the bulb is in the center of the water, as shown.

C. Watch the liquid in the thermometer move. When it stops, read the temperature of the water. Record the temperature in a table like Table 1.

TABLE 1 • Temperature Data

SUBSTANCE	TEMPERATURE (°C)
Water	
Water/ice cube (1 min)	
Water/ice cube (2 min)	
Water/ice cube (3 min)	
Water/ice cube (4 min)	

D. Add an ice cube to the water in the beaker. Wait one minute. Then measure and record the temperature.

E. Measure the temperature three more times. Wait one minute between each measurement. Record the temperatures.

FURTHER ACTIVITIES

1. Find the temperature of two different places in your classroom. Were the temperatures the same in both places? If not, try to explain why they were different.

2. Look around your home and school for thermometers. Make a list of the different kinds you find. Examine the temperature scales. In what ways are they different? Why, do you suppose, are they different?

Another kind of thermometer is the familiar **Fahrenheit** (far′ən hīt) **thermometer.** Like the Celsius thermometer, it also has a temperature scale based on the freezing and boiling points of water. However, one degree Fahrenheit is not the same temperature as one degree Celsius. In the United States, most temperatures have always been measured in degrees Fahrenheit (°F). Now that the United States is "going metric," temperatures are being measured in degrees Celsius (°C). The following may help you to "think metric" with regard to temperatures you normally encounter.

−20°C	Bitter cold (−4°F)
0°C	Freezing point of water (32°F)
20°C	Room temperature (68°F)
30°C	Quite warm, almost hot (86°F)
37°C	Normal body temperature (98.6°F)
40°C	Very hot (104°F)
100°C	Boiling point of water (212°F)

5 ESP—Fact, or Fiction?

Have you ever "had a feeling" that something was about to happen—and then it did happen? Has this happened more than once? If so, you may have what some people call **ESP.** ESP, or **extrasensory perception** (eks trə sen′sər ē pər sep′shən), is defined as perception by other than normal means. Such perception is often described as a **psychic** (sī′kik) **event.** A psychic event is one that cannot be explained in a purely physical way. Scientific and public opinion are both sharply divided concerning ESP. In this excursion you will have the chance to explore your own feelings regarding ESP.

The idea of ESP is not new. It dates back to Ancient Greece. A scientific study of an ESP-type activity was done by Michael Faraday in 1853. Faraday conducted experiments to test whether a person's thought could affect the movement of an object. He concluded that it was impossible to move an object by thought alone. In a later investigation, Sir William Crookes used a different technique to test the same idea. He, too, was unsuccessful in demonstrating that a person's thought could move an object.

Investigators of ESP have identified five types of activity considered to be extrasensory. **Telepathy** (tə lep′ə thē) is probably the most familiar type of ESP. Telepathy is the ability of one mind to communicate with another by means other than the five senses. Telepathy may also be called **mind reading.** Being able to tell what another person is thinking is an example of telepathy.

Clairvoyance (klār voi′əns) is the ability to know about things that are out of sight. It has also been called

second sight. An example of clairvoyance is being able to describe an object in a box when the object has not been seen previously and the box is in another room.

A third type of ESP is **precognition** (prē kog nish′ən). Precognition is the ability to sense what is going to happen before it takes place. An example of precognition is sensing that tomorrow there will be an earthquake where you live, and an earthquake does occur.

Psychokinesis (sī kō ki nē′sis) is the ability of a person to influence the movement of an object by thinking about it. It may also be called **levitation** (lev′ə tā′shən). Making a leaf curl up by thinking about it is an example of psychokinesis. The experiments performed by Faraday and Crookes dealt with this type of ESP.

Extraocular (eks trə ok′yə lər) **vision** is the ability to perceive visual sensations without the use of the eyes. Being able while blindfolded to name the colors on cards by touching the colors is an example of extraocular vision.

Many thousands of ESP experiences have been reported. Some of the experiences appear to be valid; others do not. "My Aunt Maude knows someone who has a friend who can tell you when and where a disaster will occur before it happens" is not scientific evidence of ESP. In recent years investigators have experimented with ESP in the laboratory. Some of the test results were positive. This suggests there may be such a thing as ESP. But ESP defies explanation in any normal scientific way. What we have always known to be "true" we have perceived with our five senses. Scientific fact is based on what can be measured and observed.

Those who believe in ESP claim that everyone has ESP to some degree. But they quickly add that the "power" has not begun to surface in most people. Believers in ESP offer as proof the apparent success investigators have had in testing certain people. They say

ESP works even though it is not known exactly what ESP is or how it works. They predict ESP will be widely used in the future. It will be used in locating hidden resources, in health work, and in police work.

A great many people do not believe in ESP. Many scientists are included in this group. They say that the experiments conducted to prove ESP are not valid. They say that in many cases only the so-called "positive" results are reported. People who do not believe in ESP raise some interesting questions. For example, if ESP exists, why do only some people display it? If certain people do have ESP, why, in tests, are they not 100% accurate in their perceptions? If even a few people had the power of precognition and psychokinesis, they would win at every game of chance. That has not happened.

In this short discussion of ESP you have been exposed to two points of view. Before making up your own mind, you may want to do the following activity. The activity is an example of one test that has been used to investigate ESP.

MATERIALS

25 blank white note cards, 3 in. x 5 in.
Black wide-tip marking pen

DO THIS

A. Make 5 cards like each of those shown in Figure E5–1. Use the symbols *star, square, wavy lines, circle,* and *plus sign.* Draw the symbols only on one side of the cards. Check each card to be sure the ink did not "bleed" through to the other side.

B. Wait until the ink is completely dry. Then stack the cards in a deck and shuffle them, mixing the cards thoroughly. Place the deck face down on your desk.

C. Now work with a partner. Ask your partner to guess the symbol on each card in the deck, one card at a time. Start with the top card. After each guess, remove the card and check if the guess was correct. **CAUTION:** *Do not let your partner see the symbols on the cards as you remove them from the deck. Do not let your partner know if the guess was correct.* Record the guesses in a table like Table 1.

D. Reshuffle the cards and have your partner repeat the guessing procedure. Do this ten times.

E. Change places with your partner and repeat steps **C** and **D**. Your guesses should be recorded in Table 1, next to those of your partner.

TABLE 1 • Guessing Data

Trial	Correct Guesses		Incorrect Guesses	
	Partner	Mine	Partner	Mine
1	𝍸 ||||		𝍸 𝍸 𝍸 |	
2				
3				
4				
5				
6				
7				
8				
9				
10				

REPORT

1. What percent of your guesses were correct in each trial? What percent of your partner's guesses were correct?

2. What percent of your guesses were correct in ten trials? What percent of your partner's guesses were correct in ten trials?

3. Did you, or your partner, have a higher percentage of correct guesses in some trials than in others?

4. How would you evaluate these guessing data in terms of clairvoyance?

According to the laws of mathematics, anyone should have guessed correctly 5 out of 25 times, purely by chance. Believers in ESP claim that more than chance is involved if a higher score is gotten for a number of trials. People who do not believe in ESP claim that if there is such a thing as ESP, all the guesses should be correct. What is *your* feeling concerning ESP?

Telemetry

6

Have you ever wondered how satellites or space probes can take pictures deep in space and then transmit those pictures back to earth? Scientists don't bring the satellites back to develop rolls of film. Therefore they must have some method of transmitting all those pictures. Scientists use a method known as **telemetry** (tə lem′ə trē) to receive these messages from space. *Telemetry* comes from the Greek words tele meaning "far off" and metron meaning "measure."

You can demonstrate how telemetry works by using two reel-to-reel variable-speed tape recorders, a cricket clicker, and graph paper.

The tape recorders will be called A (the satellite) and B (the ground station).

One student should plot a simple design, such as the one shown in Figure E6–1, by shading squares on graph paper. (Do not let the other students see the design.)

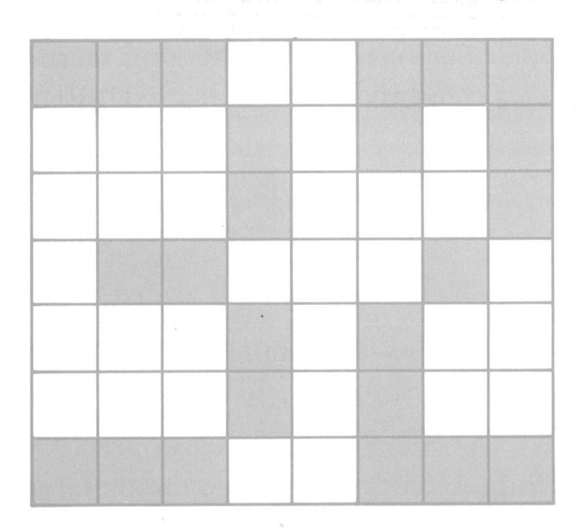

FIGURE E6–1

Fill in each blank square on the graph paper with an x. Fill in each shaded square with an xx (Figure E6–2).

FIGURE E6–2

xx	xx	xx	x	x	xx	xx	xx
x	x	x	xx	x	xx	x	xx
x	x	x	xx	x	x	x	xx
x	xx	xx	x	x	x	xx	x
x	x	x	xx	x	xx	x	x
x	x	x	xx	x	xx	x	x
xx	xx	xx	x	x	xx	xx	xx

Now prepare the satellite (tape recorder A).

1. Set the tape recorder at its slowest speed.
2. Use the clicker to read the message to the satellite. A single click represents a single x. A double click represents a double x. Make sure you space the message for each square with a one-second pause between clicks. Starting at the top of the graph, read the message from left to right and then move down to the next row.
3. After coding the design on the graph paper into the satellite, stop the tape recorder. Rewind the tape.
4. Now reset the tape recorder at its fastest speed.
5. When the ground station is ready to receive the transmission, turn on the tape recorder.

Another student should prepare the ground station (tape recorder B). The ground station should be across the room from the satellite.

1. Set the ground station tape recorder at its fastest speed.

2. Turn on the tape recorder and indicate that the ground station is ready. The code can now be transmitted from the satellite to the ground station.

3. When the transmission is completed, rewind the taped message.

4. Set the ground station tape recorder at its slowest speed.

5. Play back the tape and plot the coded message on graph paper. (This graph paper should have the same number of horizontal and vertical lines as the one on which the design was plotted.) Remember, a single click represents a single x and a double click represents a double x.

If done correctly, the ground crew's design should look like the original design.

Scientists use a telemetry system similar to this to receive pictures from satellites. A satellite may take an hour (half an orbit) to shoot sixteen TV pictures and store them on tape. When the satellite passes over the ground station, however, it may have only three minutes to transfer all the information. To do this, the satellite must transmit at a much faster rate all that had been recorded at a normal rate.

7 Exploring Circles

A **circle** is a plane figure with all of its points the same distance from a point called the center. Many objects that you use every day are circular or have parts that are circular. The distance around a circle is called the **circumference** (sər kum′fər əns). The longest distance through the center of a circle is called the **diameter** (dī am′ə tər). In the activity that follows, you will measure the circumference and the diameter of each of several circular objects. Then you will determine if there is a mathematical relationship between the circumference and the diameter of a circle.

MATERIALS

10 different circular objects
Metric tape measure
Protractor
Metric ruler or meterstick

DO THIS

A. Measure the circumference of one object. Do this with the tape measure. Record the measurement in a table like Table 1.

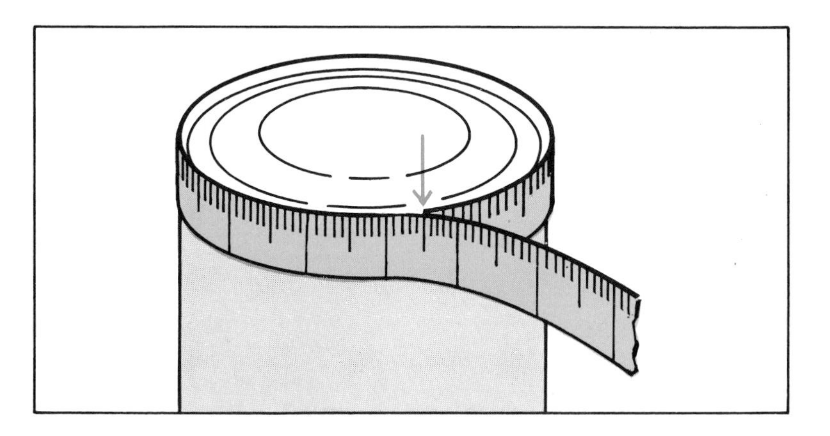

TABLE 1 • Circle Data

OBJECT	CIRCUMFERENCE (cm)	DIAMETER (cm)	$\frac{\text{CIRCUMFERENCE}}{\text{DIAMETER}}$
1			
2			
3			
4			
5			
6			
7			
8			
9			
10			

B. Place the object on a sheet of paper and trace the circumference. **CAUTION:** *Be sure to keep the pencil as close to the object as you can.*

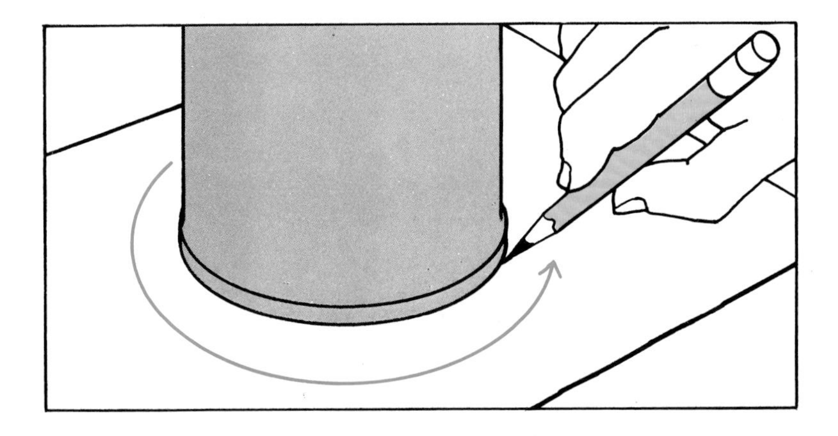

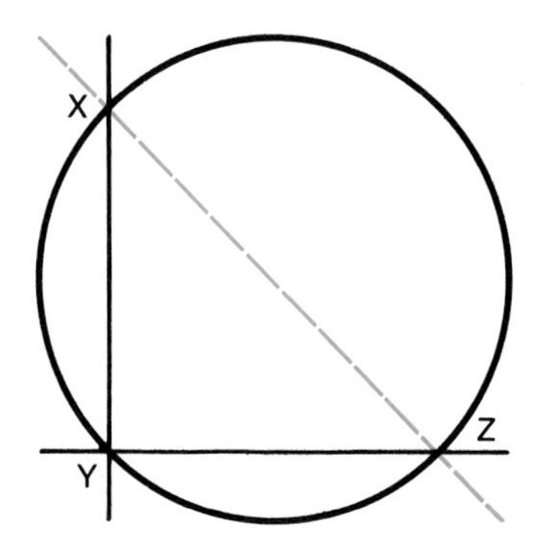

C. Draw a straight line that intersects this circle at two points, *X* and *Y*.

D. Draw a straight line that forms a right angle with line segment *XY* at point *Y*. This line must intersect the circle at point *Z*. Measure the right angle with a protractor.

E. Connect points *X* and *Z* with a straight line. Line segment *XZ* is the diameter of the circle. Measure the diameter and record it in Table 1.

F. Repeat steps **A** through **E** with each of the other objects. Be sure to record all measurements.

G. For each object, divide the circumference by the diameter. Carry the division to three decimal places. Record these data in the last column of the table.

REPORT

1. Study the data obtained for the different circles. What do you notice about the values in the last column of the table? What is the average of these values?

2. Compare your data with the data of several classmates. What do you notice?

3. Write a statement that describes the mathematical relationship between the circumference and the diameter of a circle.

You probably noticed that the relationship between the circumference and the diameter of a circle is constant. That is, each time you divide the circumference by the diameter of any circle, you get the same number. This number is called **pi.** The symbol for pi is the Greek letter π. The value of pi is 3.141592653589793. . . . This value never changes. However, in common usage the value of pi is usually accepted as 3.14.

Powers of Ten Notation

8

Sometimes a scientist must work with very large or very small numbers. For example, the distance that light travels in one year is known as a **light-year.** A light-year is approximately 9 461 000 000 000 000 m. Light travels at a speed of about 310 000 000 m/s. The diameter of the **virus** (vī′rəs) that causes polio is approximately 0.000 000 025 m. The mass of an electron is about 0.000 000 000 000 000 000 000 000 000 91 g. Numbers such as these are awkward to write and difficult to read. The numbers would be more meaningful and easier to use if they were written in a mathematical shorthand called **powers of ten notation.**

In this excursion you will learn how to express numbers in powers of ten notation. You will also learn to add, subtract, multiply, and divide numbers written in this mathematical shorthand.

Powers of Ten Notation with Positive Exponents

The number 1000 can be expressed as $10 \times 10 \times 10$. It can also be written as 10^3. The number 3 in the last expression is called an **exponent** (ek spō′nənt). An exponent is a number or symbol placed above and to the right of another number or symbol called the **base.** The expression 10^3 is shorthand for the multiplication sentence $10^3 = 10 \times 10 \times 10$. The exponent, 3, tells how many times the base, 10, is used as a multiplier in the sentence.

Copy Table E8–1 and fill in the blanks.

TABLE E8–1 • Positive Exponents

NUMBER	POWER OF TEN	NUMBER EXPRESSED ANOTHER WAY
100	10^2	10×10
1 000	10^3	$10 \times 10 \times 10$
10 000	10^4	$10 \times 10 \times 10 \times 10$
100 000	10^5	?
1 000 000	?	$10 \times 10 \times 10 \times 10 \times 10 \times 10$
10 000 000	?	?
100 000 000	?	?

Powers of Ten Notation with Negative Exponents

Powers of ten notation can also be written with negative exponents such as 10^{-2}. In this case, the number that is expressed in a power of ten is a decimal less than 1.

$$10^{-2} = \frac{1}{10 \times 10} \quad \text{or} \quad \frac{1}{100} \quad \text{or} \quad 0.01$$

Copy Table E8–2 and fill in the blanks.

TABLE E8–2 • Negative Exponents

DECIMAL	POWER OF TEN	DECIMAL EXPRESSED ANOTHER WAY
0.01	10^{-2}	$\frac{1}{10 \times 10}$ or $\frac{1}{100}$
0.001	10^{-3}	$\frac{1}{10 \times 10 \times 10}$ or $\frac{1}{1\ 000}$
0.000 1	10^{-4}	? or $\frac{1}{10\ 000}$
0.000 01	?	$\frac{1}{10 \times 10 \times 10 \times 10 \times 10}$ or ?
0.000 001	?	? or ?

Scientific Notation

So far the numbers you have worked with were easily expressed in powers of ten. But what about a number like 356 000? This number could be expressed in many ways as the product of a number and a power of ten. For example, it could be written as

$35\ 600 \times 10$	35.6×10^4
$3\ 560 \times 10^2$	3.56×10^5
356×10^3	

The power of ten notation 3.56×10^5 is also called **scientific notation.** Scientific notation is always written as one number multiplied by another number. The first number is always expressed as a number between 1 and 10; the second number is expressed as a power of ten.

To write a number that is greater than 1 in scientific notation, do the following:

1. Move the decimal point to the *left* until a number between 1 and 10 is obtained.

$$356\ 000 = 3.56 \times 10^5$$

first number

2. Write the second number as ten to some power. The exponent is determined by the number of places the decimal point is moved. In the example, the decimal point was moved five places to the left. Therefore, the exponent is 5.

$$356\ 000 = 3.56 \times 10^5$$

5 4 3 2 1 second number

Copy Table E8–3. Apply what you have learned by converting the numbers in the table to scientific notation.

TABLE E8–3 • Numbers Greater Than One

NUMBER	SCIENTIFIC NOTATION
565 000	
1 960	
8 356 000	
21 000 000	
958 000	

To write a number that is less than 1 in scientific notation, do the following:

1. Move the decimal point to the *right* until a number between 1 and 10 is obtained.

$$0.005\ 68 = 5.68 \times 10^{-3}$$

first number

2. Write the second number as ten to some power. The exponent is determined by the number of places the decimal point is moved. In the example, the decimal point was moved three places to the right. Therefore, the exponent is -3.

$$0.005\ 68 = 5.68 \times 10^{-3}$$

1 2 3

second number

Copy Table E8–4. Then apply what you have learned by converting the numbers to scientific notation.

TABLE E8–4 • Numbers Less Than One

NUMBER	SCIENTIFIC NOTATION
0.005 6	
0.013 45	
0.000 08	
0.034 689 1	
0.001 3	

Addition and Subtraction

Adding and subtracting numbers written in scientific notation is done in the following way:

1. Make all exponents the *same.* For example, $6.32 \times 10^4 \pm 3.1 \times 10^3$ cannot be accomplished because the exponents are different. However, the exponents can be made the same by rewriting both 6.32×10^4 and 3.1×10^3 as follows:

$$\begin{array}{r} 6.32 \times 10^4 \\ \pm\ 3.1 \quad \times 10^3 \\ \hline \end{array} \quad \textit{becomes} \quad \begin{array}{r} 6.32 \times 10^4 \\ \pm\ 0.31 \times 10^4 \\ \hline \end{array} \quad \textit{or} \quad \begin{array}{r} 63.2 \times 10^3 \\ \pm\ \ 3.1 \times 10^3 \\ \hline \end{array}$$

Note that the decimal point in one of the numbers was moved either to the left or to the right. This had the effect of increasing or decreasing the exponent (power of ten). For each place the decimal point was moved, the exponent changed by 1. The same rule applies when the exponent has a negative value.

2. Add or subtract only the numbers appearing to the left of the multiplication sign. The exponent for the base 10 remains the same.

$$\begin{array}{r} 6.32 \times 10^4 \\ +\ 0.31 \times 10^4 \\ \hline 6.63 \times 10^4 \end{array} \quad \textit{or} \quad \begin{array}{r} 63.2 \times 10^3 \\ +\ \ 3.1 \times 10^3 \\ \hline 66.3 \times 10^3 \end{array} \quad = 6.63 \times 10^4$$

$$\begin{array}{r} 6.32 \times 10^4 \\ -\ 0.31 \times 10^4 \\ \hline 6.01 \times 10^4 \end{array} \quad \textit{or} \quad \begin{array}{r} 63.2 \times 10^3 \\ -\ \ 3.1 \times 10^3 \\ \hline 60.1 \times 10^3 \end{array} \quad = 6.01 \times 10^4$$

Copy and solve these problems:

a. $\begin{array}{r} 5.35 \times 10^4 \\ +\ 6.10 \times 10^5 \\ \hline \end{array}$ **b.** $\begin{array}{r} 5.10 \times 10^3 \\ -\ 3.18 \times 10^3 \\ \hline \end{array}$ **c.** $\begin{array}{r} 4.62 \times 10^4 \\ -\ 3.32 \times 10^3 \\ \hline \end{array}$

d. $\begin{array}{r} 3.65 \times 10^{-5} \\ +\ 1.62 \times 10^{-4} \\ \hline \end{array}$ **e.** $\begin{array}{r} 8.36 \times 10^{-6} \\ -\ 1.50 \times 10^{-7} \\ \hline \end{array}$ **f.** $\begin{array}{r} 1.19 \times 10^2 \\ +\ 2.35 \times 10^3 \\ \hline \end{array}$

Multiplication

To multiply numbers written in scientific notation, follow these rules.

1. Multiply only the numbers appearing to the *left* of the multiplication sign.
2. *Add* the exponents.

multiply

$(3 \times 10^3) \times (6 \times 10^5) = 18 \times 10^8 = 1.8 \times 10^9$

add

Copy and solve these problems.

$(3.1 \times 10^5) \times (2.5 \times 10^3) =$
$(6.5 \times 10^4) \times (3.2 \times 10^{-2}) =$
$(8.5 \times 10^3) \times (2.1 \times 10^5) =$

Division

To divide numbers written in scientific notation, follow these rules.

1. Divide only the numbers appearing to the *left* of the multiplication sign.
2. *Subtract* the exponents.

divide

$(6 \times 10^5) \div (3 \times 10^3) = 2 \times 10^2$

subtract

Copy and solve these problems.

$(6 \times 10^6) \div (3 \times 10^3) =$
$(3.5 \times 10^5) \div (1.5 \times 10^3) =$
$(4 \times 10^{-4}) \div (2 \times 10^6) =$

Qualitative Analysis

9

When American astronauts first landed on the moon, they collected samples of moon rocks. The rock samples were brought back to Earth to be analyzed. Scientists wanted to know what elements the rocks contained. Your city's water supply is tested regularly. The water is analyzed for the presence of bacteria, harmful chemicals, and other impurities. The process of testing to determine what substances are present in a specific material is called **qualitative analysis.**

In the following activity, you will qualitatively analyze six liquid solutions. Some dye has been added to the liquids to give them all the same appearance. To identify the solutions, you must conduct specific tests on each one. Remember, you will be testing only *what* substances are present—not *how much* of the substances are present. A test to determine how much of each substance is present in a specific sample of material is called **quantitative analysis**.

MATERIALS

6 Pyrex test tubes
6 small pieces of aluminum foil
6 pieces of red litmus paper
6 pieces of blue litmus paper
3 g $BaCl_2 \cdot 2H_2O$ [*barium chloride*]
Balance
Set of metric masses
Benedict's solution
Unknown solutions A, B, C, D, E, and F
Distilled water
Tap water
Safety goggles
Watch or clock
250-mL beaker
600-mL beaker
Masking tape
Tripod
Wire gauze
Heat source
Matches
Test tube rack
Graduate
Forceps

DO THIS

A. Prepare a table like Table 1. The procedures for the five tests are described later in the activity. As you complete each test, record the results in the table. Write Yes or No to indicate whether the solution has the specific property for which it is being tested.

TABLE 1 • Test Data

TEST	Solution A ____	Solution B ____	Solution C ____	Solution D ____	Solution E ____	Solution F ____
Test 1 Acid						
Test 2 Base						
Test 3 Reaction with Aluminum Foil						
Test 4 Reaction with Barium Chloride						
Test 5 Presence of Sugar						

B. Using masking tape, label six test tubes *A, B, C, D, E,* and *F,* respectively. Place the tubes in the test tube rack.

C. Fill each test tube with 5 mL of the corresponding unknown solution—solution A in tube *A*, solution B in tube *B*, and so on. Be sure to clean the graduate before measuring each solution.

D. Now conduct the following tests. As you complete each test, save the unknown solutions unless you are specifically told to discard them. They will be used for more than one test.

***Test 1* Acid**

1A. Use forceps to hold a piece of blue litmus paper by one end. Dip the other end into the solution in test tube *A*. If the blue litmus paper turns red, the solution is an acid.

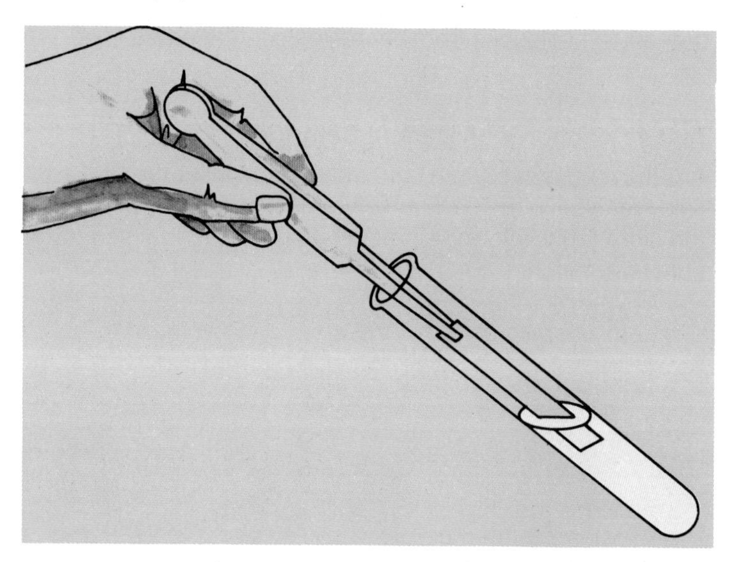

1B. Test the other unknown solutions in the same way. Use a different piece of blue litmus paper for each solution.

***Test 2* Base**

2A. Use forceps to hold a piece of red litmus paper by one end. Dip the other end into the solution in test tube *A*. If the red litmus paper turns blue, the solution is a base.

2B. Test the other unknown solutions in the same way. Use a different piece of red litmus paper for each solution.

***Test 3* Reaction with Aluminum Foil**

3A. Use forceps to place a small piece of aluminum foil in each unknown solution. Be careful that the forceps does not come into contact with the solutions. If it does, rinse the forceps in distilled water before proceeding.

3B. Wait five minutes. Then look for any change or reaction that may have occurred between the aluminum and the solutions.

3C. Discard any solution that reacted with the aluminum and replace it with 5 mL of fresh solution. The solutions that did not react may be used again after the aluminum has been removed. Remove the aluminum with forceps. Be sure to rinse the forceps in distilled water after each use to prevent the solutions from becoming contaminated.

Test 4 Reaction with Barium Chloride

4A. Put 0.5 g of barium chloride in each test tube. If a solution reacts with barium chloride, a white precipitate (pri sip′a tāt) will form. A precipitate is a solid that separates out of a solution.

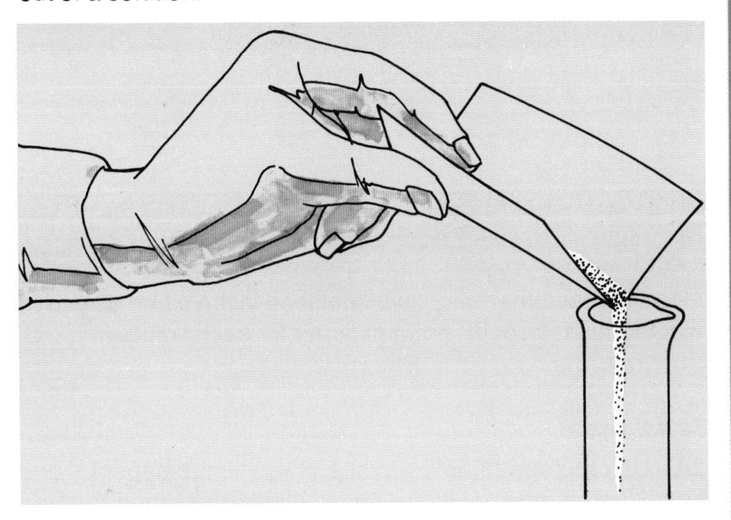

4B. Empty the test tubes. Rinse them in tap water and then in distilled water.

Test 5 Presence of Sugar

5A. Fill each test tube with 5 mL of the corresponding unknown solution.

5B. Add 5 mL of Benedict's solution to each tube. **CAUTION:** *If you get Benedict's solution on your skin, wash it off with water immediately.*

5C. Stand the six test tubes in a 600-mL beaker. Fill one-third of the beaker with water. Then stand the beaker on the tripod as shown.

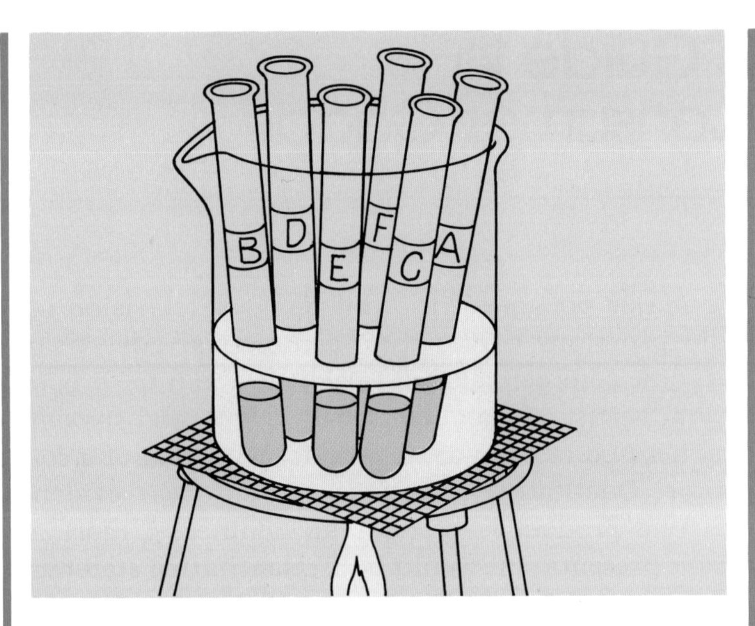

5D. CAUTION: *Be sure you are wearing safety goggles.* Then light the heat source. Heat the water until it almost boils. If it does begin to boil, remove the heat source for a short time. Leave the test tubes in the heated water for about 5 minutes. If any of the solutions turn yellow, green, or orange, sugar is present in those solutions.

REPORT

1. Study the data in Table 1. Which solutions have similar properties? What are those properties?

2. The solutions can be crudely classified on the basis of similar properties. However, the solutions still cannot be identified. If you knew that the solutions were hydrochloric acid, sodium sulfate, copper (II) chloride, sodium hydroxide, and sugar, which can you now identify?

3. Knowing the names of the solutions does not always help in identifying them. Use the following additional information to fill in the names of the unknown solutions under the column heads in Table 1. Sodium sulfate and sodium hydroxide react with barium chloride to form a while precipitate. Copper (II) chloride reacts with aluminum to give a brownish color and turns blue litmus red. Distilled water is neutral and will not give a positive reaction in any of the tests.

10 A Guide to Consumer Goods

The major portion of the financing of television and radio programs comes from commercial advertising. But some commercials tell very little about the product they advertise. Terms like *softer, lighter,* and *smoother* may be used to compare a product with that of a competitor. Qualitative adjectives give no clear evidence that one product is better than another. A more accurate presentation would be a quantitative statement of *how much* softer, lighter, or smoother the product is.

Some commercials use a catchy slogan or song, or have a famous person endorsing the product. Frequently the slogan or song gives no indication of the worth of the product being advertised. People who endorse a product are paid well to say only good things about it. Describe some other selling methods used in commercials that fail to inform the buyer of the true worth of the products.

A questioning mind is one of the characteristics of a scientist. A questioning mind can be important for everyone when deciding which products to buy. If people carefully examine and question information about a specific product, it is possible that they may buy more wisely. They would be able to distinguish real evidence from meaningless words.

This excursion is designed to assist you in examining some advertisements on radio or TV. You will investigate whether these ads provide valid information about the products. This may help you to develop a more questioning mind regarding the consumer goods you buy.

MATERIALS

None

DO THIS

A. Select five commercials from radio, TV, or both.

B. Study each commercial by using the Consumer Goods Guide in Figure E10–1. The four categories of the guide are explained below. You may not need to use all the categories for each commercial. This will depend on the design of the commercials you select.

FIGURE E10–1

COMMERCIAL	a	b	c
1. Situation	Realistic	Semi-realistic	Unrealistic
2. Presentation	Endorsed by famous person	Designed to make viewer/listener laugh	Other
3. Theme	Slogan	Song	Other
4. Facts presented	Sound facts presented	A mixture of facts and nonfacts	No facts presented

1. *Situation*
   Is the situation in the commercial realistic, or unrealistic, with characters such as talking animals or miniature people? Realistic situations give more accurate information.
2. *Presentation*
   Is the product endorsed by a famous person? Is the commercial designed only to make people laugh? Neither tells much about the true quality or effectiveness of the product.
3. *Theme*
   Is there a song or a slogan used in the commercial? Neither gives much information about a product.

4. *Facts presented*
   Does the commercial present factual evidence such as cost, weight, or other measurable facts to show that the product is better than another? Or are words such as *softer, lighter,* or *smoother* used to describe the product?

C. Make a table like Table 1. Use the letters *a, b,* and *c* from the Consumer Goods Guide to record the situation, presentation, theme, and facts presented for each commercial.

TABLE 1 • Commercial Study

PRODUCT ADVERTISED	SITUATION	PRESENTATION	THEME	FACTS PRESENTED
1.				
2.				
3.				
4.				
5.				

REPORT

1. Based on the commercials, which products might you decide to buy? What was it about the commercials that convinced you?

2. Which commercial gave the most factual information?

3. Which commercial did you like the most? Why?

4. Were the answers to questions 2 and 3 the same or different? Explain.

5. Make a general statement about the effectiveness of the commercials you studied.

The Language of Science

11

Some words in science, such as *force* or *work*, are easy to say and understand. Others, such as *thermodynamics* and *magnetohydrodynamics*, may seem more difficult. If some of these more complex words were broken down, they would not seem nearly as difficult. This excursion will help you understand the origin and meanings of complex words.

Look at the terms in the table below and study their meaning. These are parts of words that can be combined to make more complex words.

TABLE E11–1 • Word Parts and Meanings

WORD PART	MEANING	WORD PART	MEANING	WORD PART	MEANING
alter	change	*helio*	sun	*nona*	nine
ar	relating to	*hepta*	seven	*octa*	eight
astr	star	*hetero*	other, another, different	*ortho*	straight, regular, upright
aud	hear	*hexa*	six	*pan*	all
auto	self	*homo*	the same	*penta*	five
bi	two	*hydr*	water	*phon*	sound
cent	hundred	*hydro*	fluid	*photo*	light
chrom	color	*hyper*	over, above	*poly*	many
chron	time	*hypo*	less than	*scope*	see
dec	ten	*iso*	equal	*son*	sound
dyna	power	*logy*	study of	*stella*	star
geo	earth	*luna*	moon	*tele*	far
graph	record	*magneto*	magnetic force	*tetra*	four
gyro	to turn	*meter*	measurer	*thermo*	heat
hedron	a three-dimensional form with sides	*micr*	small	*tri*	three
		mono	one		

You can use these word parts to understand the meaning of many complex words. For example, using the terms in the table, you can determine that *geology* means "the study of the earth." The table cannot be used to positively identify all science words, but it can give you a basic idea of what some words mean. You may have seen the word *thermodynamics* in a science book. Using the table, you might guess that its meaning is related to heat and power. If you look in a dictionary you will find that thermodynamics is, in fact, a branch of physics that deals with heat and energy changes. Without a dictionary you would have had at least some idea of the word's meaning by using the table.

Using the word parts in Table E11–1, try to determine the meanings of the words below.

microphotometer	photometer	panchromatic
microscope	magnetohydrodynamics	photograph
stellar	isotherm	monophonic
telephone	monochromatic	isohedron
chronometer	dynamometer	hydrology
geothermal	tetrahedron	telescope
sonar	geochronology	heterochromatic
polygraph		

These words and their meanings have been accepted by scientists in all parts of the world. Use of standardized words makes it easier for scientists from different countries to communicate.

The roots of most science words originate from Latin or Greek. A few come from European or African languages. No country in the world uses Latin as a conversational language. Because of this, Latin never changes, and it is therefore the ideal language for scientific communication.

These scientific words, as well as symbols and mathematics, make up the language of science.

Exploring the Periodic Table

12

The periodic table of the elements is a useful way of classifying and organizing the elements. It can be used to quickly identify those elements with similar chemical properties. It can also be used by chemists to make predictions about the properties and the behavior of elements in chemical reactions.

In the periodic table each element is represented by a box containing information about that element. Usually this information consists of the element's name, chemical symbol, atomic number, and atomic mass. Figure E12–1 shows the element iron the way it appears in the periodic table.

FIGURE E12–1

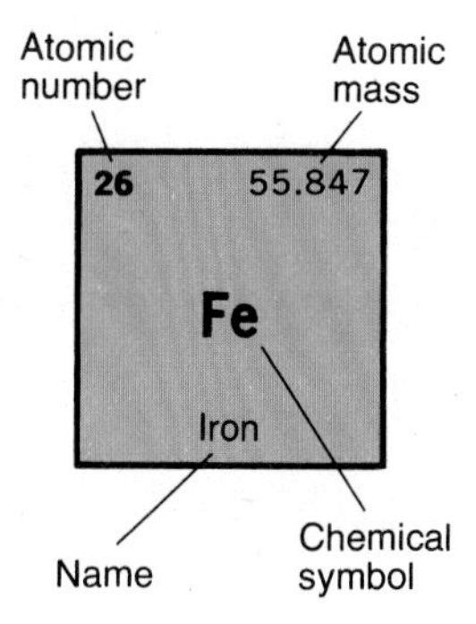

The first periodic tables were developed in the 1860s. Since that time a number of changes have been made in the table. For example, the element *hydrogen* is now placed in two separate groups because of its unique behavior. Under some circumstances hydrogen has the properties of the group I elements, the alkali metals. Under other circumstances it behaves much like the group VII elements, the halogen family.

In the early periodic tables, the elements were placed according to their atomic masses. The atomic masses were originally determined with respect to the element *hydrogen*. Hydrogen was given the atomic mass value 1.000. Later it was found oxygen (atomic mass 16.000) was a more accurate base value. More recently isotopes of many elements have been discovered. Since the isotopes of an element may vary by one or more neutrons, none of the elements are likely to have an atomic mass that is a whole number. The listed atomic mass for an element is an average of the atomic masses of all the isotopes that would be found in a common sample of that element. The present value of atomic masses is based on the standard of an isotope of carbon with an atomic mass of 12.000.

In 1869 Dmitri Mendeleev, a Russian scientist, developed a periodic table. When he first proposed his table, Mendeleev purposely left gaps. He predicted that these gaps would be filled by elements that had not yet been discovered. Mendeleev even predicted some of the chemical properties of these mystery elements. Other

FIGURE E12–2
The modern periodic table

TRANSITION ELEMENTS

PERIODS / GROUPS	I	II							
1	1 1.00797 **H** Hydrogen								
2	3 6.939 **Li** Lithium	4 9.0122 **Be** Beryllium							
3	11 22.9898 **Na** Sodium	12 24.312 **Mg** Magnesium							
4	19 39.102 **K** Potassium	20 40.08 **Ca** Calcium	21 44.956 **Sc** Scandium	22 47.90 **Ti** Titanium	23 50.942 **V** Vanadium	24 51.996 **Cr** Chromium	25 54.9380 **Mn** Manganese	26 55.847 **Fe** Iron	27 58.9332 **Co** Cobalt
5	37 85.47 **Rb** Rubidium	38 87.62 **Sr** Strontium	39 88.905 **Y** Yttrium	40 91.22 **Zr** Zirconium	41 92.906 **Nb** Niobium	42 95.94 **Mo** Molybdenum	43 (99)* **Tc** Technetium	44 101.07 **Ru** Ruthenium	45 102.905 **Rh** Rhodium
6	55 132.905 **Cs** Cesium	56 137.34 **Ba** Barium	57 138.91 **La** Lanthanum †	72 178.49 **Hf** Hafnium	73 180.948 **Ta** Tantalum	74 183.85 **W** Tungsten	75 186.2 **Re** Rhenium	76 190.2 **Os** Osmium	77 192.2 **Ir** Iridium
7	87 (223)* **Fr** Francium	88 (226)* **Ra** Radium	89 (227)* **Ac** Actinium ‡	104 (259)* **Rf** ** Rutherfordium	105 **Ha** Hahnium**	106 ***	107	108 ***	
† LANTHANIDE SERIES		58 140.12 **Ce** Cerium	59 140.907 **Pr** Praseodymium	60 144.24 **Nd** Neodymium	61 (147)* **Pm** Promethium	62 150.35 **Sm** Samarium	63 151.96 **Eu** Europium	64 157.25 **Gd** Gadolinium	65 158.924 **Tb** Terbium
‡ ACTINIDE SERIES		90 232.038 **Th** Thorium	91 (231)* **Pa** Protactinium	92 238.03 **U** Uranium	93 (237)* **Np** Neptunium	94 (242)* **Pu** Plutonium	95 (243)* **Am** Americium	96 (247)* **Cm** Curium	97 (247)* **Bk** Berkelium

*Atomic masses appearing in parentheses are those of the most stable known isotopes.

**Names are unofficial.

elements were discovered later and were found to possess many of the properties he had predicted. In 1913 Henry Moseley, an English scientist, proposed the ordering of the elements by atomic number rather than by atomic mass. He gave each element an atomic number and arranged the elements in sequence.

Following the discovery of radioactivity, physicists began to experiment with elements by bombarding them with high energy particles. In this way new elements, which did not exist naturally on earth, were

NONMETALS

			III	IV	V	VI	VII	0
							1 1.00797 H Hydrogen	2 4.0026 He Helium
			5 10.811 B Boron	6 12.01115 C Carbon	7 14.0067 N Nitrogen	8 15.9994 O Oxygen	9 18.9984 F Fluorine	10 20.183 Ne Neon
			13 26.9815 Al Aluminum	14 28.086 Si Silicon	15 30.9738 P Phosphorus	16 32.064 S Sulfur	17 35.453 Cl Chlorine	18 39.948 Ar Argon
28 58.71 Ni Nickel	29 63.54 Cu Copper	30 65.37 Zn Zinc	31 69.72 Ga Gallium	32 72.59 Ge Germanium	33 74.9216 As Arsenic	34 78.96 Se Selenium	35 79.909 Br Bromine	36 83.80 Kr Krypton
46 106.4 Pd Palladium	47 107.870 Ag Silver	48 112.40 Cd Cadmium	49 114.82 In Indium	50 118.69 Sn Tin	51 121.75 Sb Antimony	52 127.60 Te Tellurium	53 126.9044 I Iodine	54 131.30 Xe Xenon
78 195.09 Pt Platinum	79 196.967 Au Gold	80 200.59 Hg Mercury	81 204.37 Tl Thallium	82 207.19 Pb Lead	83 208.980 Bi Bismuth	84 (210)* Po Polonium	85 (210)* At Astatine	86 (222)* Rn Radon

66 162.50 Dy Dysprosium	67 164.930 Ho Holmium	68 167.26 Er Erbium	69 168.934 Tm Thulium	70 173.04 Yb Ytterbium	71 174.97 Lu Lutetium
98 (251)* Cf Californium	99 (254)* Es Einsteinium	100 (257)* Fm Fermium	101 (258)* Md Mendelevium	102 (255)* No Nobelium	103 (256)* Lw Lawrencium

KEY

Atomic Number	6
Atomic Mass	12.01115
Symbol of Element	C
Element Name	Carbon

***No names have been given and no mass data is available.

Atomic masses based on C-12 = 12.0000

produced. These elements are often referred to as the transuranium elements because they all have atomic numbers larger than that of uranium. Uranium (atomic number 92) has the largest atomic number of any naturally occurring element. The transuranium elements are all radioactive. They spontaneously break apart into other elements with smaller atomic numbers, giving off energy in the form of particles. This spontaneous breakdown often occurs very rapidly. The lifetime of these elements is only a few seconds or less, and therefore their chemical properties and atomic masses are not well known. The elements break down into simpler elements faster than they can be investigated.

The names of the transuranium elements are quite interesting. Table E12–1 shows the origins of some of these names.

At this time, elements 104 and 105 have not been officially named. Both American and Russian scientists have proposed names for these elements. However, the international committee of chemists that names elements has not yet made a decision. It is likely that other

TABLE E12–1 • Transuranium Elements

ATOMIC NUMBER	ELEMENT	ORIGIN OF NAME
93	Neptunium	the planet Neptune (following Uranium, planet Uranus)
94	Plutonium	the planet Pluto
95	Americium	America, the continent on which it was first made
96	Curium	Marie Curie, investigator of radioactivity
97	Berkelium	Berkeley, California, the city in which it was first made
98	Californium	California, the state in which it was first made
99	Einsteinium	Albert Einstein
100	Fermium	Enrico Fermi, a famous nuclear physicist
101	Mendelevium	Mendeleev, developer of the periodic table
102	Nobelium	Alfred Nobel, inventor of dynamite and institutor of the Nobel Prizes
103	Lawrencium	Ernest Lawrence, a famous physicist

elements will be made in the future. Some physicists and chemists predict that some of these elements may be more stable than those that have been synthesized so far.

The real significance of the periodic table is its usefulness to scientists. Many properties of the elements are charted on the periodic table, and predictions can be made, based on these properties. The eight vertical groups labeled with roman numerals represent **chemical families.** The horizontal rows are called **periods.** The elements in a chemical family have similar chemical properties. The elements in a period change from metallic to nonmetallic as you move from left to right. Groups I and II are characterized by their chemical reactivity and by the fact that they are all metals. The elements in the middle of the table are referred to as transition elements. They are also metals and have some similar chemical properties. The lanthanide and actinide series are special components of the transition elements. Starting with group III and working downward in a stepwise arrangement through group VII are the nonmetals. While some of these elements exist as solids, others such as nitrogen, oxygen, fluorine, chlorine, and bromine are gases under normal conditions. Group 0, at the far right of the table, is composed of elements that are gases. These gases are similar to one another in that they do not react with other chemicals under most conditions. They are known as the inert gases, although some of them, such as xenon, have been successfully combined with other elements.

To better understand the relationships among the elements, you will perform an activity similar to the one that enabled Mendeleev to predict the properties of unknown elements. Figure E12–3 shows a periodic table that contains the elements in groups I through 0. The transition elements, including the lanthanide and

I	II	III	IV	V	VI	VII	0
3 179 Li 1.52 0.53 Li_2O 1.0 5.39	4 1278 Be 1.11 1.85 BeO 1.5 9.32	5 2300 B 0.79 2.34 B_2O_3 2.0 8.30	6 3550 C 0.77 2.25 CO_2 2.5 11.3	7 −209.86 N 0.74 1.25×10^{-3} N_2O_3 3.0 14.5	8 −218.4 O 0.73 1.4×10^{-3} 3.5 13.6	9 −219.62 F 0.71 1.8×10^{-3} 4.0 17.4	10 −248.67 Ne 0.9×10^{-3} 21.6
11 97.81 Na 1.86 0.97 Na_2O 0.9 5.14	12 651 Mg 1.60 1.74 MgO 1.2 7.64	13 660 Al 1.43 2.70 Al_2O_3 1.5 5.98	14 Mystery element B	15 44 P 1.10 1.8 P_2O_3 2.1 11.0	16 119 S 1.02 2.07 SO_2 2.5 10.4	17 −101 Cl 0.99 3.2×10^{-3} Cl_2O 3.0 13.0	18 −189 Ar 1.7×10^{-3} 15.8
19 Mystery Element A	20 850 Ca 1.97 1.55 CaO 1.0 6.11	31 30 Ga 1.22 5.89 Ga_2O_3 1.6 6.00	32 937.4 Ge 1.22 5.32 GeO_2 1.8 7.88	33 817 As 1.21 5.72 As_2O_3 2.0 9.81	34 217 Se 1.16 4.79 SeO_2 2.4 9.75	35 −7.2 Br 1.14 3.1 Br_2O 2.8 11.8	36 −157 Kr 3.7×10^{-3} 14.0
37 38.89 Rb 2.48 1.53 Rb_2O 0.8 4.18	38 769 Sr 2.15 2.6 SrO 1.0 5.69	49 157 In 1.62 7.3 In_2O_3 1.7 5.79	50 232 Sn 1.41 7.3 SnO_2 1.8 7.34	51 Mystery element C	52 449.5 Te 1.3 6.2 TeO_2 2.1 9.01	53 113.5 I 1.33 4.9 2.5 10.5	54 −112 Xe 5.9×10^{-3} 12.1
55 28.5 Cs 2.65 1.93 Cs_2O 0.7 3.89	56 725 Ba 2.17 3.5 BaO 0.9 5.21	81 304 Tl 1.71 11.9 Tl_2O_3 1.8 6.11	82 327 Pb 1.75 11.4 PbO_2 1.8 7.42	83 271 Bi 1.55 9.8 Bi_2O_3 1.9 7.29	84 254 Po 1.4 9.2 2.0 8.43	85 At 1.4 2.2	86 −71 Rn 9.9×10^{-3} 10.8

FIGURE E12–3

actinide series, have been omitted. Figure E12–4 shows which properties are given for each element in the table. Although you may not be familiar with all the properties given, you should be able to predict their value for the unknown elements. These predictions can be made by carefully examining the properties of the other elements in the table.

FIGURE E12–4

atomic number		melting point °C
	symbol	
atomic radius		density (g/mL)
formula of oxide	electro-negativity	ionization energy

DO THIS

A. Carefully study the properties of the elements in the periodic table, Figure E12–3. Be sure to examine both the groups and the periods.

B. Predict the values of the properties for three mystery elements.

C. Make a table like Table 1 and record your predictions.

TABLE 1 • Properties of Mystery Elements

MYSTERY ELEMENT	A	B	C
Atomic number	19	14	51
Symbol			
Melting point			
Atomic radius			
Density (g/mL)			
Formula of oxide			
Ionization energy			
Electronegativity			

13 Sound

The study of sound appropriately begins with the study of vibrating matter. All sound originates in matter and is transmitted by matter. Some vibrations, or disturbances, cause a slow displacement of matter. These can be seen or felt. Other disturbances are repeated many times per second. This class of repeated disturbances is usually referred to as sound.

Any disturbance that travels through a medium by the periodic motion of its particles is a wave motion. The nature of waves and wave motion is discussed in Chapter 14. If a series of disturbances move at right angles to the motion of the disturbed particles in the medium, a transverse wave is produced. If the series of disturbances move parallel to the motion of the disturbed particles in the medium, a longitudinal wave is produced. Sound is a longitudinal, or compression, wave.

The manner in which a longitudinal wave is produced can be shown with a tuning fork. When the fork is struck, it is set into vibration. The tines of the fork move back and forth. Figure E13–1 shows what hap-

FIGURE E13–1

pens to the molecules in air as a tine vibrates. Molecule A receives energy from the left when it is struck by the tine. It moves toward molecule B. As A approaches B, it is repulsed and bounces back toward the tine while B moves toward molecule C. The repulsion between B and C sends B to the left and C to the right. In the meantime, the vibrating tine strikes A again and the process repeats. Thus as energy is transferred from molecule to molecule, a series of compressions and rarefactions are created. These spread out in all directions. However, energy is transmitted to more than one molecule by the tuning fork. Therefore, the compressions and rarefactions produced might be better shown as in Figure E13–2.

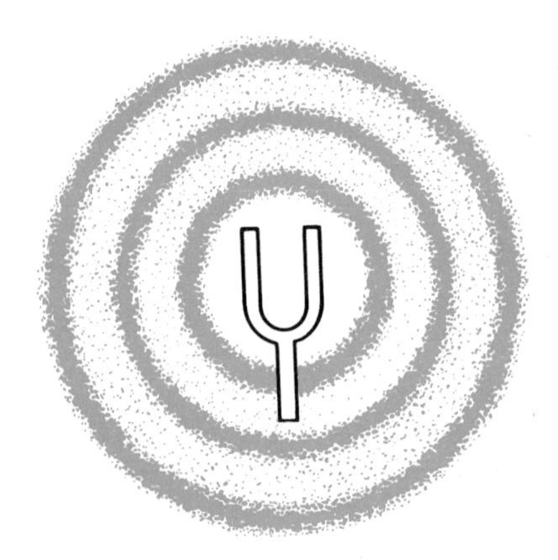

FIGURE E13–2
Areas of compression and rarefaction resulting in a sound wave

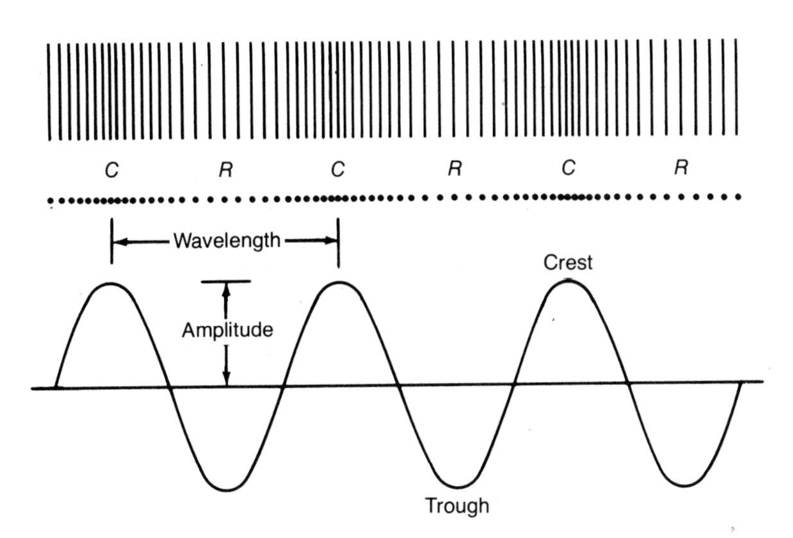

FIGURE E13–3
Comparison of a longitudinal wave (top) and a transverse wave (bottom); C represents an area of compression, R an area of rarefaction.

An oscilloscope is often used to analyze sound waves. If a microphone is attached to an oscilloscope, longitudinal sound waves can be converted into electrical impulses. These impulses are projected on the oscilloscope screen as a transverse wave. Figure E13–3 shows the relationship of a longitudinal wave to a transverse wave. It also identifies specific characteristics of the waves.

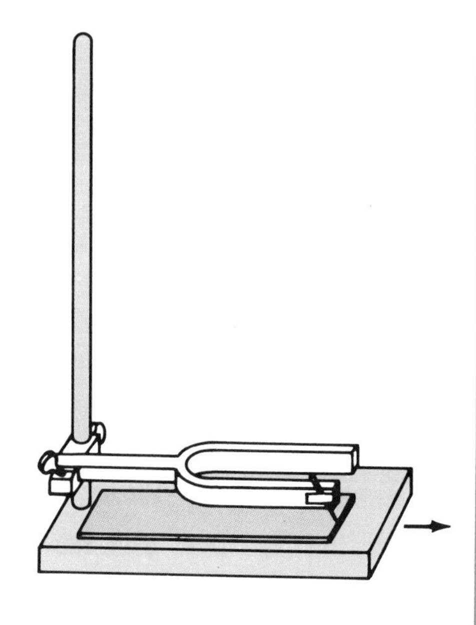

MATERIALS

2 tuning forks with different frequencies
Rubber mallet
2 microscope slides
Ring stand with clamp
Pointer (broom straw or sewing needle)
Cellophane tape
Candle
Matches
Safety goggles

DO THIS

A. Light the candle. Then smoke one surface of each slide by repeatedly passing it over the candle flame. Do this until there is an even deposit of soot over the entire surface. **CAUTION:** *Be sure you are wearing safety goggles. Also be sure the slides do not become hot enough to burn you or crack.* Lay the soot-covered slides aside until step **C.**

B. Using tape, attach the pointer to one tine of a tuning fork.

C. Lay a soot-covered slide on the base of the ring stand. Then clamp the tuning fork to the ring stand so that the pointer just touches the sooty surface.

D. Strike the tuning fork to make it vibrate.

E. With a steady motion, pull the slide toward you at constant speed.

F. Repeat steps **B–E** with the other tuning fork and slide.

REPORT

1. Are the tracings on the slides transverse waves, or longitudinal waves?
2. Compare the patterns of the two waves. Which tuning fork vibrated at the higher frequency? How can you tell?

The Speed of Sound

Unlike light and other forms of electromagnetic radiation, sound is transmitted only through some medium. A ringing alarm clock in a vacuum produces no sound. The speed of sound depends on the density and the elasticity of the medium. The speed of sound in air at 0°C is about 331 m/s. In other kinds of matter, the speed is different. In water, sound travels about 1440 m/s; in steel, about 5000 m/s. The speed of sound in air increases about 0.5 m/s for each degree Celsius increase in temperature. At a track meet, you see the smoke from the starter's gun before you hear the report. Similarly, you usually see lightning before you hear thunder. This happens because light travels much faster than sound—about 299 792 km/s.

At some time in your life, you probably have heard a sonic boom. A sonic boom is produced when an airplane is flying faster than the speed of sound. An airplane flying at a relatively low speed pushes the air in front of it, compressing the air. This creates a wave that moves forward from the airplane at the speed of sound. If an airplane is flying at the speed of sound or a greater speed, the molecules in the air cannot move away fast enough. This results in the air in front of the airplane being further compressed, creating a shock wave. If you are in the path of the shock wave, you hear a sonic boom. The sound produced is caused by the great difference in pressure from compression to rarefaction as the wave passes.

Characteristic Properties of Sound

The characteristic properties of sounds make it possible to distinguish one kind of sound from another. Many people may disagree as to whether a certain sound is music or noise. What, then, is the difference between sounds that are music and sounds that are noise? Scientifically, a musical sound is one that has a definite frequency caused by a regular vibration. Musical sounds do not necessarily have to be produced by a musical instrument. The sound of a chain saw or a fire whistle might be a musical sound. Noise, on the other hand, is caused by irregular vibration. An example is the sound produced by a squeaking door. The difference between these two wave forms is shown in Figure E13–4.

FIGURE E13–4
The wave on the left has a regular frequency and could represent a musical sound. The wave on the right has an irregular frequency and would represent noise.

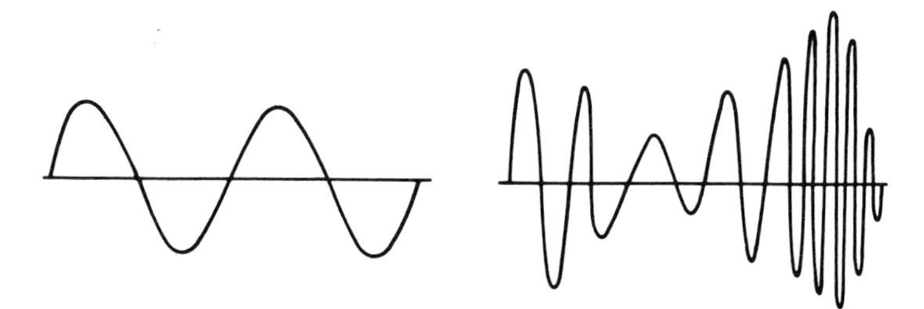

Pitch is another characteristic of sound. Pitch may be defined as how high or how low a sound is on the musical scale. It is determined by the frequency. A high-frequency sound has a high pitch; a low-frequency sound has a low pitch. As the frequency, or pitch, of a sound increases, the length of the sound wave decreases. The waves of two sounds differing in pitch are shown in Figure E13–5.

FIGURE E13–5
These two waves have the same amplitude, but the wave on the right represents a sound with a higher pitch.

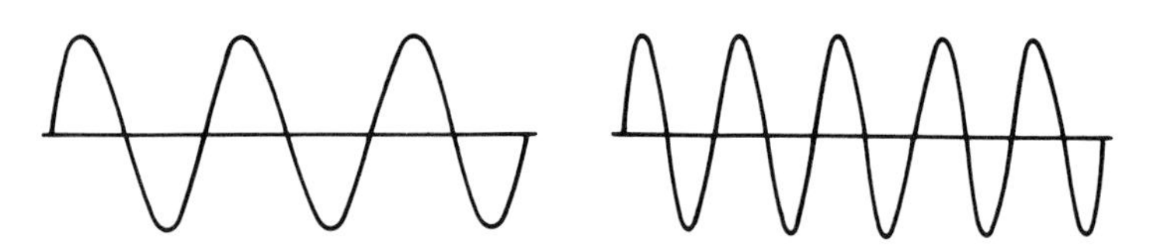

The loudness, or intensity, of a sound is determined by its amplitude. The waves of two sounds with the same pitch but differing in loudness are shown in Figure E13–6. Loudness is a characteristic of sound that depends on the initial strength of the vibration producing the wave. It also depends on the distance one is from the source of the sound.

Quality is another characteristic property that describes sounds. It can be defined as the product of blending the fundamental tone and the overtones produced by the vibrating body. Quality is the property of sound that enables one to recognize who among several friends is speaking by merely listening to their voices. Similarly, one can tell the difference between various instruments by the quality of the sounds produced when the same note is played on each. The sound waves in Figure E13–7 each have the same wavelength and therefore the same pitch. The waves each have a different shape, however, because of the different number of overtones and the relative amplitude of the overtones.

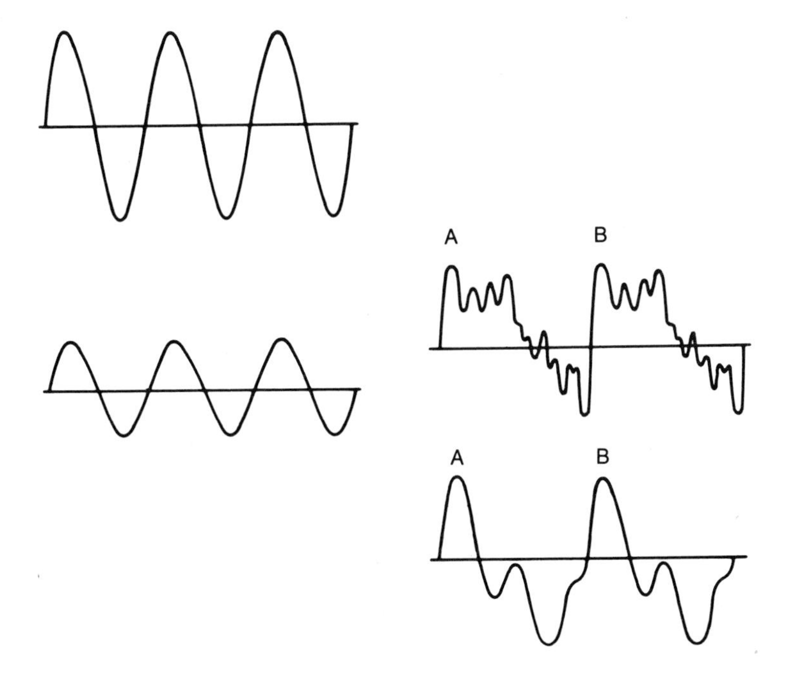

FIGURE E13–6
Of the two waves shown at far left, the top one would represent a sound of greater intensity.

FIGURE E13–7
The waves at left represent sounds of different qualities resulting from different overtones.

Echoes

Sound can be reflected. When a sound wave strikes a surface with a density different from the medium through which it was transmitted, the wave bounces back. A reflected sound wave is called an **echo.** Relatively hard, smooth surfaces are good reflectors of sound. In order to hear an echo, the reflected sound must reach our ears more than 0.1 second later than the original sound. If the time interval is less than 0.1 second, the two sounds blend together and only one sound is heard.

In a large room, sound waves may be reflected back and forth many times. You may have experienced this in a large auditorium or gymnasium. Usually sound-absorbing materials are placed on the walls and ceilings in such places to deaden the sound. In homes carpets, stuffed furniture, and curtains or draperies help to deaden sound.

Doppler Effect

You know that the pitch of a sound depends on the frequency. But have you ever thought about why the sound of a train whistle seems to change pitch as the train speeds past you? The same is true for the sound of a high-speed racing car or an automobile horn. As the source of the sound approaches you, the pitch increases; as it passes you and moves away, the pitch decreases. This seeming change in pitch is called the **Doppler effect.** Figure E13–8 shows why this happens. The number of sound waves reaching your ear increases as the source of the sound approaches. The pitch of the sound becomes higher because the sound waves are being crowded closer together. When the source of the sound passes and begins to move away from you, the pitch becomes lower again as the sound waves spread apart.

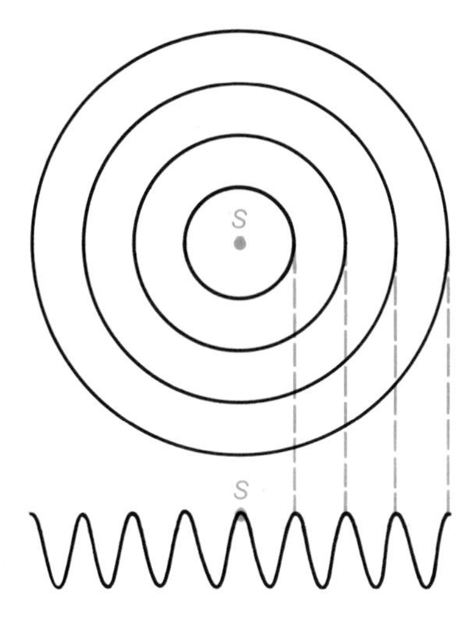

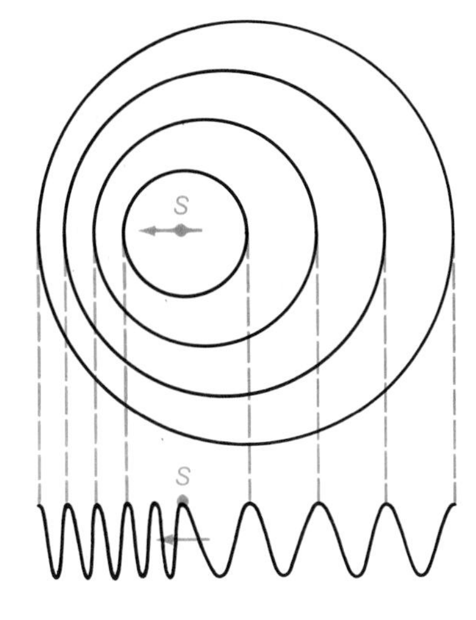

FIGURE E13–8
The number of sound waves per second reaching a person's increases as the source of the sound approaches (right). This results in an increase in frequency that is heard as a higher pitch.

Ultrasonics

Under certain conditions, some matter can be made to produce waves having frequencies above 20 000 Hz. These waves are called **ultrasonic waves.** Ultrasonic waves are compression waves, like ordinary sound. They require a medium for transmission. The high frequencies of ultrasonic waves are beyond the audible range of human hearing.

Ultrasonic waves are used in a variety of applications. They are used to measure ocean depth, pasteurize milk, kill insects, sterilize surgical instruments, and detect flaws in metals and other materials. In medicine, they are used to treat such diseases as arthritis, and in certain types of nerve surgery. The usefulness of these high-frequency waves stems from two factors: they can be readily focused, and they are strongly reflected by objects. The most commonly used ultrasonic waves have frequencies as high as 500 000 000 Hz.

14 Light

Sufficient light is needed for you to be able to see the words on this page. In a totally darkened room you would not be able to see anything. Your brain is able to register a "picture," or an "image," of the world because your eyes can detect light. But what is light? People frequently use the term "light rays" and "light beams" when describing light. However, these terms do not tell anything about the nature of light. To understand light, it is necessary to investigate the behavior of light. It will also be useful to determine whether light is similar in any ways to other things in nature.

Light as Energy

If you did Activity 40 in Chapter 13, you exposed several materials to light. The temperature of each material was noted over a period of five minutes. An increase in temperature occurred for each material. Apparently the materials absorbed some of the light. In the process, the materials were heated. Heat is a form of energy. When light is absorbed by a material, some of the light seems to be changed into heat energy. Therefore, light seems to be related to heat.

Electricity is a form of energy. When electricity passes through the filament of a bulb, light is produced. Heat may also be produced. Light seems to be related to electrical energy in some manner.

What can you infer about light, based on its relationship to both heat energy and electrical energy? It appears that light is a form of energy. It differs from other forms of energy, such as heat and electricity. However, it seems that one form of energy can be converted into another form. Thus, light energy that is absorbed by a material does not disappear. The light energy is converted into heat energy.

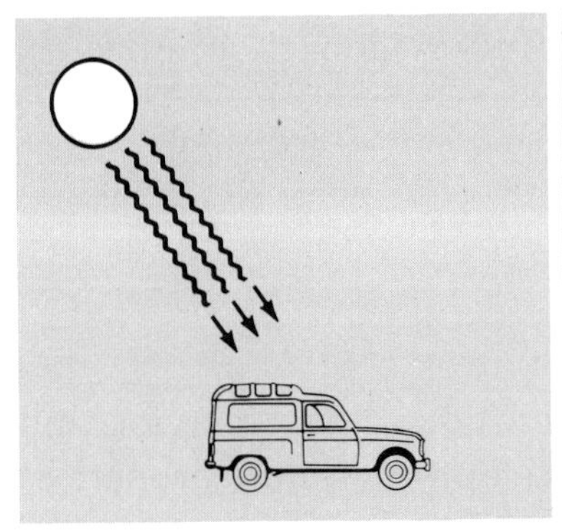
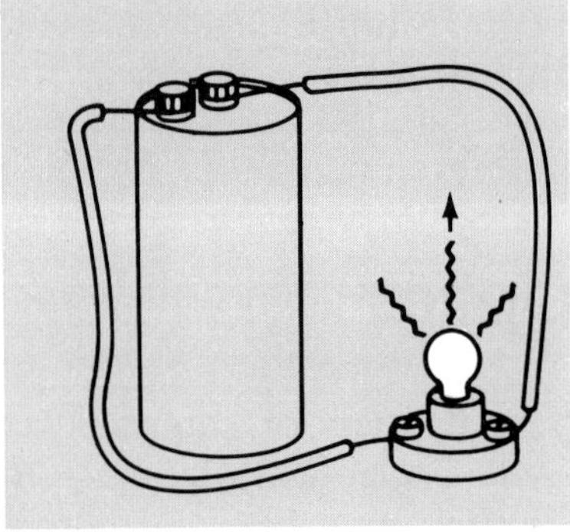

FIGURE E14–1
One form of energy may be converted to another form.

Scientists have investigated many types of energy conversions. It has been found that in all cases in which energy is converted from one form to another no energy is lost. This means that a certain amount of light energy is equal to a certain amount of heat energy (or any other form of energy). Energy is neither created nor destroyed when it is converted from one form to another. This statement is known as the **law of conservation of energy**.

Wave motion is discussed in Chapter 14. A wave can be described as a disturbance in matter. Energy can be transferred from place to place as a result of wave motion. Sound is a type of energy that is transferred in the form of waves. Scientists have found much evidence indicating that light travels in the form of waves. However, light waves seem to differ from sound waves. Light waves can travel through a vacuum.

Since a vacuum is the absence of matter, a light wave is not a disturbance in matter. Other forms of energy, such as X rays and radio waves, are related to light energy. In Chapter 14 these related forms of energy are called electromagnetic waves. Thus, it seems that we can describe light as energy that travels as an electromagnetic wave. This model has proved useful in explaining the behavior of light in many circumstances. However, as you will see, the wave model of light has been modified as a result of evidence obtained in this century.

Optics

The branch of science that studies the behavior and properties of light is called **optics**. Some properties of light have been recognized for thousands of years. One of these properties is that light travels in straight lines. This statement is often misunderstood. Light rays (or waves) can change direction, as when they bounce off an object. However, the path of light to and away from the object is a straight line. The following activity can provide some evidence for the statement that light travels in straight lines.

MATERIALS

Small cardboard box with lid (e.g., shoe box)
Scissors
Sharp needle
Aluminum foil
Waxed paper
Tape
Candle
Dish
Metric ruler
Matches

DO THIS

A. Cut an opening 5 cm by 5 cm at one end of the box.

B. Tape a square piece of aluminum foil over this opening.

C. Puncture the center of the foil with a needle, making a small hole.

D. Cut an opening 7 cm by 7 cm at the other end of the box.

E. Tape a square piece of waxed paper over this opening.

F. Place a candle on a dish about 15 cm in front of the end of the box with the pinhole. Light the candle and darken the room.

G. By adjusting the distance between the box and the candle, an image of the candle should be visible through the waxed paper. Observe the image.

H. Make a sketch of the candle and the image of the candle side by side on a piece of paper.

REPORT

1. How did the image of the candle differ from the candle?

2. On your sketch, draw lines to show the path of light from the tip of the flame to the flame tip on the image. Do the same for the bottom edge of the candle and candle image. How do these lines indicate that light travels in straight lines?

3. What does the intersection of these lines represent?

You can see an image of yourself on smooth, shiny surfaces, such as a mirror or polished metal. How is this image produced? All objects reflect back at least some of the light that falls upon them. Therefore, **reflection** is one of the properties of light. Smooth, shiny surfaces reflect a great deal of the light that falls upon them. In addition, the light is reflected in a regular pattern. You can investigate this pattern of reflection in the following activity.

MATERIALS

Plane mirror (at least 20 cm by 20 cm)
Metric ruler
Pencil

DO THIS

A. Hold the mirror on your work table, perpendicular to the surface of the table.

B. Place the narrow edge of the metric ruler against the mirror. The ruler should be flat on the table as shown.

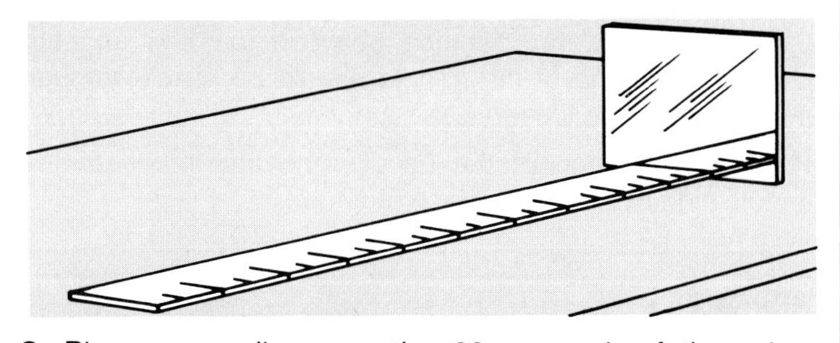

C. Place a pencil across the 20-cm mark of the ruler. Observe the image of the ruler and pencil in the mirror. Record what you see.

D. Have your partner hold the mirror in front of you.

E. Hold up your right hand, palm toward the mirror, so that you can see the image of your hand in the mirror.

F. Compare the *image* of your right hand with your left hand. Record your observations.

REPORT

1. Where does the image of the pencil appear in the mirror?

2. How does the image of your right hand compare with your left hand?

As was mentioned, vision depends on light. You can see objects either because they emit light or reflect light. Objects that have rough, dull surfaces reflect light, just as a mirror does. Yet no image can be seen on such surfaces. How does the reflection of light

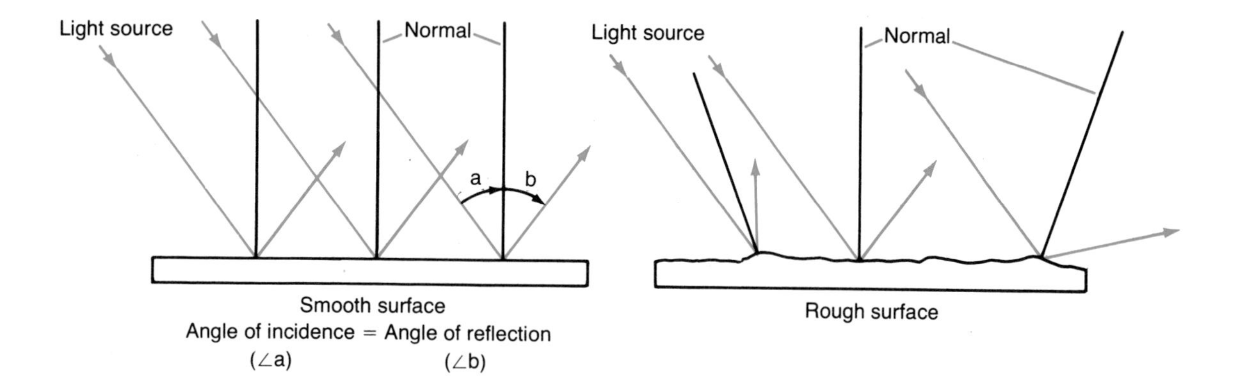

FIGURE E14–2
Angle of incidence equals angle of reflection.

from a rough surface differ from the reflection of light from a smooth surface? Remember, light rays travel in straight lines. The angle at which a light ray strikes the surface of an object is called the **angle of incidence**. This angle is measured from an imaginary line perpendicular to the surface at the point where the light ray strikes. This line is called the **normal**. The light ray is reflected from the surface at a certain angle called the **angle of reflection**. This angle is also measured from the normal. For all light rays reflecting off a surface, the angle of incidence equals the angle of reflection. Figure E14–2 illustrates light rays being reflected off a smooth surface and a rough surface. As you can see, the light rays striking the smooth surface have the same pattern before and after being reflected. This consistent pattern allows you to see an image of the object from which the light was originally reflected (or emitted). Light rays striking the rough surface are reflected in many directions. On a rough surface, not all light rays have the same angle of incidence. Therefore, the angles of reflection of the light rays differ. Instead of being reflected in a regular pattern, the light rays are scattered. Thus, no image is produced.

Clear, undistorted images are produced in smooth, flat mirrors. Such a mirror is called a **plane mirror**.

Images can also be produced in curved mirrors. However, the image will be distorted. This distortion occurs because the pattern of reflected light rays differs somewhat from the pattern of light rays striking the curved mirror.

FIGURE E14–3

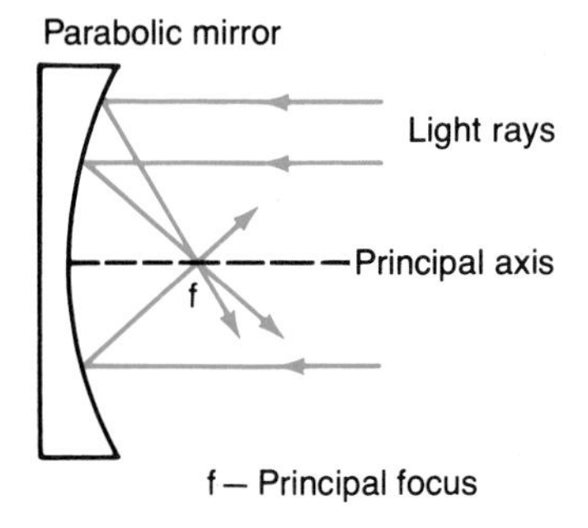

Curved mirrors can be made in the shape of a parabola. A **parabolic mirror** would have a shape similar to that shown in Figure E14–3. A parabolic mirror has reflective properties that make it useful in searchlights and some other devices. Refer to Figure E14–3 as we discuss these properties.

A straight line drawn out from the center of a parabolic mirror is called the **principal axis**. All light rays parallel to this axis that strike the mirror are reflected through a point in front of the mirror. This point is called the **principal focus**. Solar ovens have a parabolic mirror with the "oven" located at the principal focus. Thus, light rays are concentrated on the oven.

If a light source is placed at the principal focus of a parabolic mirror, an intense beam of light can be produced. Refer to Figure E14–4 to understand how this beam is produced. Light rays from a source at the principal focus that strike the parabolic mirror are reflected parallel to the principal axis. A small mirror in front of the light source reflects additional light rays back through the principal focus. These rays are also reflected off the parabolic mirror parallel to the principal axis. Thus, an intense beam of light is produced. Searchlights and the high beam of an automobile headlight are based on this principle.

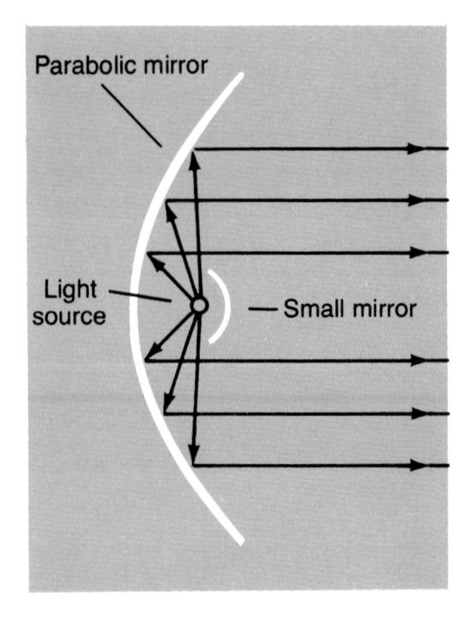

FIGURE E14–4

Some materials reflect most of the light that falls upon them. Other materials absorb most of the light that falls upon them. However, certain materials permit most of the light that falls upon them to pass through. A material that permits light to pass through it is said to be **transparent**.

A light ray that passes from one transparent material

to another at an angle other than 90° changes direction. (See Figure E14–5.) The change of direction occurs at the boundary between the two materials. It is sometimes said that the path of light is bent when it passes from one transparent material to another. The bending of light under these conditions is called **refraction**. You can investigate refraction in the following activity.

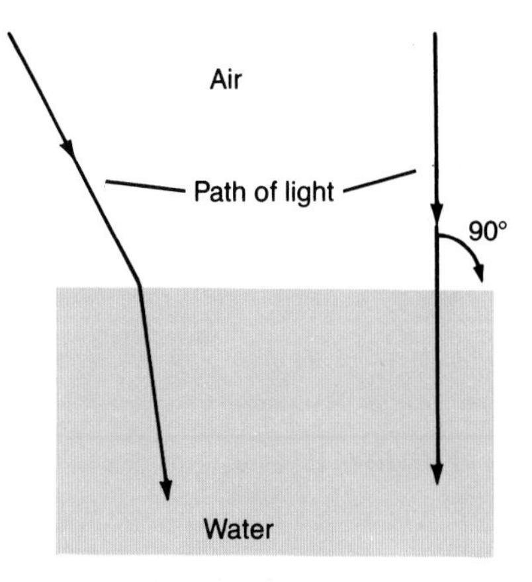

FIGURE E14–5
Light passing from one medium to another at an angle other than 90° is refracted.

MATERIALS

250-mL beaker
Glass rod
Can (coffee can)
Coin

DO THIS

A. Add about 200 mL of water to the beaker.

B. Place the glass rod in the beaker. Observe what happens. Record your observations.

C. Place a coin in the bottom of the can, near the side of the can.

D. Stand (or sit) on the same side of the can as the coin. Adjust your position backward until the coin just disappears.

E. Have your partner *slowly* add water to the can. Observe what happens. Record your observations.

REPORT

1. Describe the appearance of the glass rod in the breaker.
2. What happened as your partner added water to the can containing the coin? Explain your observations.

Refraction is due to a change in the speed of light as it passes from one medium to another. Light travels at a constant speed in a vacuum. Light travels at a

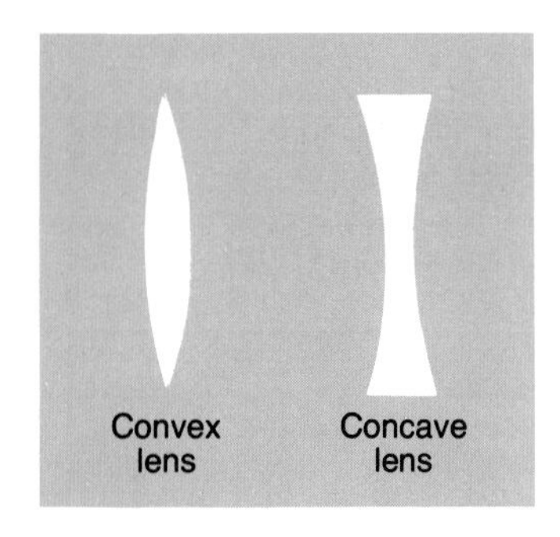

FIGURE E14–6

slower but constant speed in different materials. However, the speed of light in one material differs from the speed of light in another material. Thus, light bends as it passes from one transparent material to another.

A **lens** is a transparent material, usually glass or plastic, that has at least one curved surface. Instruments such as cameras, projectors, microscopes, and telescopes contain lenses. The lenses in these items refract light. This refraction may be useful for forming images or magnifying objects.

There are two basic types of lenses. A **convex lens** is thicker at the center than at the edges. A **concave lens** is thinner at the center than at the edges. Figure E14–6 illustrates both types of lens.

A convex lens can be used to form an image of an object on a screen. Such an image is called a **real image**. The image that is formed is inverted. As with a parabolic mirror, a convex lens has a principal focus, called f_1. The distance from the center of the lens to f_1 is called the **focal length** of the lens. The lens also has a principal axis defined as a line passing through the center of the lens horizontally. All light rays that are parallel to the principal axis and strike the lens will pass through f_1. A secondary focus, f_2, is defined as a point located in front of the lens at a distance equal to the focal length. All light rays pass-

FIGURE E14–7
Image formation by a convex lens

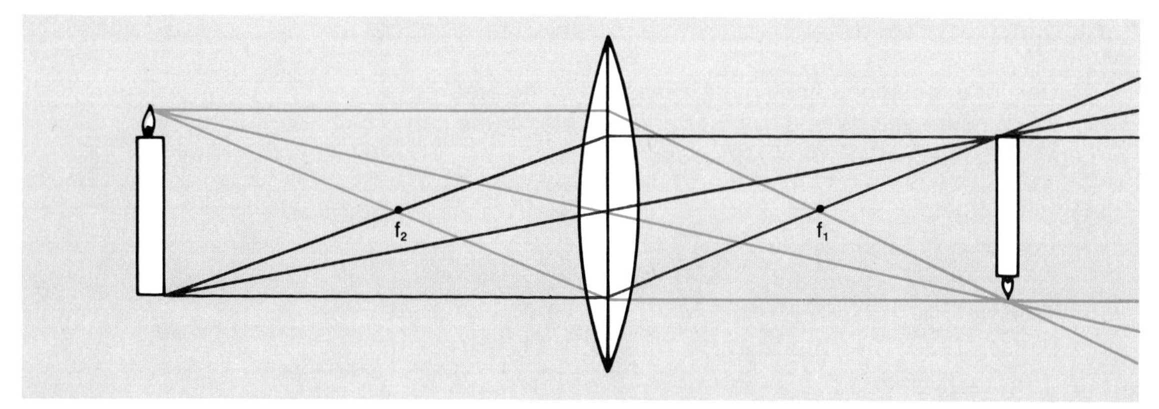

ing through f_2 that strike the lens will be bent so that they leave the lens parallel to the principal axis. Any light ray that passes through the center of the lens will not be bent. Figure E14–7 illustrates image formation by a convex lens for an object located more than two focal lengths in front of the lens. Figure E14–8 illustrates image formation by a convex lens for an object located between one and two focal lengths in front of the lens. If an object is placed between f_2 and the lens, no real image will form. However, a **virtual image** will form. A virtual image is an image that cannot be projected onto a screen. The virtual image will be on the same side of the lens as the object. It will be larger than the object and right side up.

FIGURE E14–8
Image formation by a convex lens

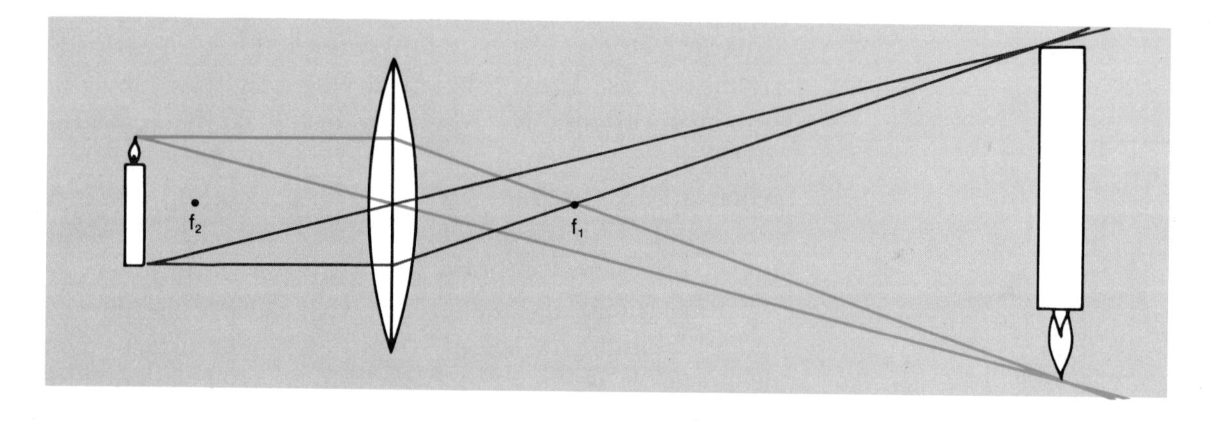

The upright, magnified image seen through a magnifying glass is a virtual image.

A concave lens bends light rays toward the edges of the lens, as shown in Figure E14–9. A concave lens will not produce a real image. However, it will produce an erect, virtual image of an object. The image will be smaller than the object and located on the same side of the lens as the object. Concave lenses are used in eyeglasses to correct nearsightedness. In this vision defect, the person is unable to see distant objects clearly.

FIGURE E14–9

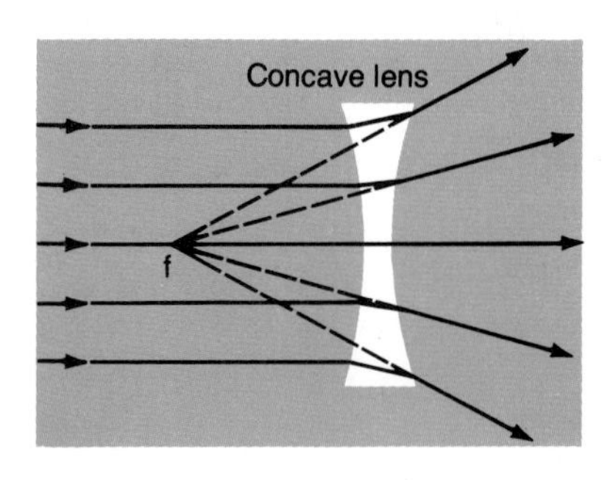

Models of Light

As was mentioned earlier, a model of light as energy in the form of electromagnetic waves has proved to be very useful. However, the first scientific model of light held that light was made up of particles. This model was proposed by Isaac Newton in the seventeenth century. By passing a beam of white light through a prism, Newton was able to produce a band of colors called the **spectrum**. This band of colors consists of red, orange, yellow, green, blue, and violet light. According to Newton's model, light consists of a stream of tiny particles. The particles of one color of light differ slightly from the particles of any other color. In passing through a prism, the particles of different colors are bent, or refracted, at slightly different angles. Thus, a beam of white light is separated into a spectrum. Newton also felt that the reflection of light from a surface was similar to what happens when a ball strikes a surface. The ball rebounds at an angle equal to its angle of incidence with the wall. Light reflects, or "rebounds," in the same manner.

Some scientists disagreed with Newton's particle model of light. A scientist named Christian Huygens proposed a wave model of light in the seventeenth century. Huygens compared the spreading out of light from a source to waves spreading out on a liquid from the point of a disturbance. Different colors of light could be explained by different wavelengths, according to the wave model.

In the nineteenth century a scientist named Thomas Young found that two beams of light could interfere with each other. Young allowed two beams of light to strike a screen. In some areas of the screen, dark bands appeared. Young explained these dark bands as areas where light waves arrived out of phase. Figure E14–10 illustrates how two waves that are out of phase cancel each other out. The particle model of light could not explain this "interference" pattern.

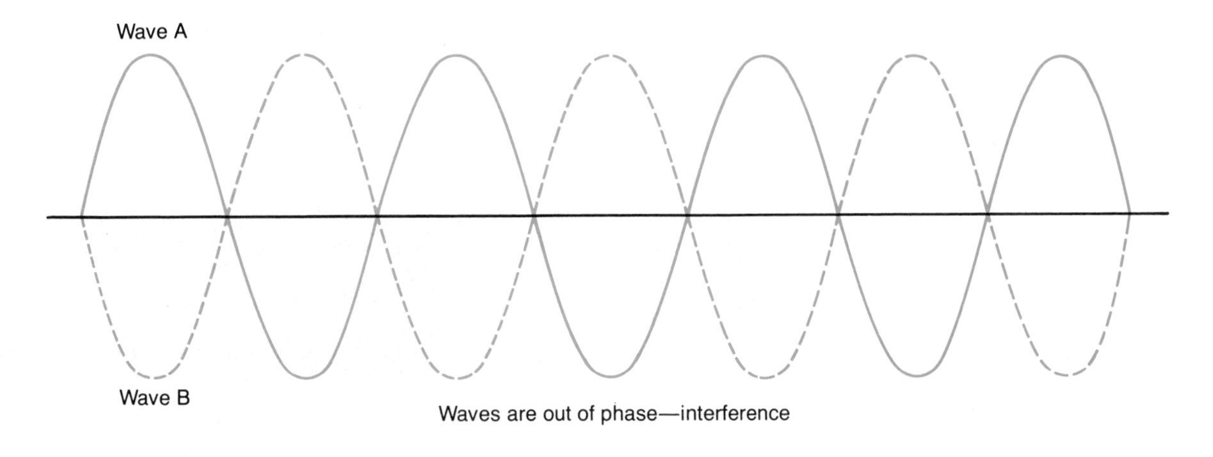

Waves cancel each other out, eliminating the light pattern

FIGURE E14–10

By the end of the nineteenth century the wave model of light had gained wide acceptance. Light was considered to be energy in the form of electromagnetic waves. As similar but invisible forms of energy were detected, the idea of an electromagnetic spectrum was developed. Gamma rays, X rays, radio waves, and other forms of energy are included in the electromagnetic spectrum.

The wave model of light ran into difficulties in the first part of the twentieth century. It had been discovered that an electric current could be produced by shining light on certain metals. This was called the **photoelectric effect**. Apparently light was able to knock electrons out of the metals, producing a current. However, each metal had to be struck with light of a minimum energy content before it would release electrons. The minimum differed for different metals but was constant for a particular metal.

The wave model predicted that different colors of light had different energy values. Violet light had the most energy. Energy value decreased from blue to green to yellow to orange. Red light had the least amount of energy. As an example of the photelectric effect, let us assume that shining yellow light on a certain metal causes it to release electrons. Light of greater energy value, such as green, blue, and violet, would also cause electrons to be released. Even very dim yellow light would release some electrons from the metal. However, neither orange nor red light would release energy from the metal. No matter how bright or intense you made the red light, it would not knock electrons from the metal. Yet increasing the intensity of the light meant that more energy was falling on the metal. According to the wave theory, the electrons should absorb more and more energy from the incoming red light. Eventually, some electrons should have enough energy to be released. But light below a certain energy value just would not release electrons, no matter how great its intensity. The wave theory could not explain this photoelectric effect.

In the early twentieth century, a scientist named Max Planck proposed a new particle model of light. In Planck's model, light (and all other forms of electromagnetic energy) travels as tiny bundles of energy called **quanta** or **photons**. Planck proposed this model to help explain how objects at high temperatures give off energy. Albert Einstein used this particle model of light to explain the photoelectric effect. In the particle model, photons of yellow light have more energy than photons of red (or orange) light. For the metal in our example, yellow light will release electrons but red will not. According to Einstein's explanation, a photon of yellow light can be absorbed by an electron in the metal. The electron then obtains just enough energy to be freed from the metal. An electron that absorbs a photon of red light also obtains energy. However, the energy is not great enough to knock the electron out of the metal. The electron will rapidly lose this energy. No matter how many photons of red light strike the electron, it is not freed from the metal. The electron absorbs the photon's energy but loses it before it is struck by another photon. Thus, the particle model explains the photoelectric effect.

Now you are probably asking, "Which model is correct? Is light a wave, or a particle?" Scientists accept both models together. Light behaves both as a wave and as a particle, depending on the circumstances. This "dual nature of light" may seem incredible, but taken together the two models are very useful. As scientists continue to study light, modifications in these models may occur in the future.

Glossary

Key to Pronunciation

a hat, cap	e let, best	ō open, go	th thin, both	ə represents
ā age, face	ē equal, see	ô order, all	ŦH then, smooth	a in about
ã care, air	ėr term, learn	oi oil, voice	u cup, butter	e in taken
ä father, far	i it, pin	ou house, out	u̇ full, put	i in pencil
ch child, much	ī ice, five	o hot, rock	ü rule, move	o in lemon
	ng long, bring	sh she, rush	zh measure, seizure	u in circus

absolute zero The temperature at which the molecules of a substance are considered to be very nearly at rest.
absorber plate A collecting surface on a solar panel that absorbs sunlight.
absorption (ab sôrp'shən) The conversion of light energy (or other electromagnetic radiation) into heat energy as the light energy interacts with the surface of a material.
acceleration (ak sel ə rā'shən) A change in velocity during a specific time period.
accelerator (ak sel'ə rā tər) The pedal in an automobile that controls the flow of gasoline to the carburetor.
acid-base indicator (in'də kā tər) An organic chemical compound used to measure the concentration of an acid or a base.
acids (as'idz) Compounds that, dissolved in water, increase the number of hydronium ions in the solution.
actinide (ak'tə nīd) **series** The period of elements beginning with actinium (atomic number 89) and ending with lawrencium (atomic number 103). Elements in the actinide series are classified as metals.
aerosol (ãr'ə sol) A liquid-in-gas colloid.
alchemists (al'kə mists) Magicians in the Middle Ages who tried to change different kinds of metals into gold.
alkali (al'kə lī) **metals** The first group or family of the periodic table. The elements in this group are, for the most part, reactive metals.
alloy (al'oi) A metal that is combined with metallic or nonmetallic elements to form a mixture having metallic properties.
alpha (al'fə) **rays** Positively charged particles given off by radioactive substances.
ammeter (am'mē tər) An instrument for measuring electric current.
ampere (am'pir) The basic unit of electric current in the metric system; abbreviated A.
amplitude (am'plə tüd) The maximum height reached by a wave from its rest position.
analogy (ə nal'ə jē) A familiar or simple model that can be used to explain or clarify a difficult concept because of some limited similarities between the two.
anion (an'ī ən) An ion with a negative electrical charge.
atomic number The number of protons in an atom of an element.
atom The smallest particle of an element that has all the properties of the element and can enter into a chemical combination.
axis (ak'sis) On a line graph, one of two number lines that intersect at zero.

bar graph The type of graph on which straight lines, or bars, are used to present a picture of the data.
base (bās) A number or symbol placed below and to the left of another number or symbol called the exponent; a compound that, dissolved in water, increases the number of hydroxide ions in the solution.
best fit line A line on a graph that connects some but not all the points and has half the points on either side.
beta (bā'tə) **rays** Rays consisting of negative particles identical in charge and mass to the electron. Beta rays are given off by radioactive substances.
binary (bī'nər ē) **classification** Grouping objects on the basis of whether or not they have a certain property.
boiling point Temperature at which a liquid changes into a gas.
bond The attractive force between two atoms or ions, based on either the transfer or sharing of electrons. The bond permits the atoms or ions to act as a unit or molecule.
Brownian (brou'nē ən) **movement** The random movement of suspended particles.
bubble chamber A device used to measure the paths made by radioactive particles.
buffer solution A solution of a weak acid and weak base that can be used to keep the pH of a second solution fairly constant.

carbon monoxide (mon ok'sīd) An odorless, colorless, poisonous gas; formula, CO.
carburetor (kär'bə rā tər) The device in an automobile that mixes gasoline with air.
cation (kat'ī ən) An ion with a positive electrical charge.
Celsius (sel'sē əs) **thermometer** A thermometer that uses 0 degrees as the freezing point of water and 100 degrees as the boiling point.
centimeter (sen'tə mē tər) A metric unit of length equal to 0.01 meter; abbreviated cm.
chemical change Change in a material that results in the formation of new and different materials.
circumference (sər kum'fər əns) The distance around a circle.
clairvoyance (klăr voi'əns) The ability to know about things that are out of sight.
classification (klas ə fə kā'shən) A method of grouping objects based on their properties.
classified (klas'ə fīd) Grouped on the basis of given properties.
closed circuit (sėr'kit) A continuous connection of conductors from one end of an electrical source to the other.
cloud chamber A device used to measure the paths made by radioactive particles.
colloid (kol'oid) A mixture made up of tiny, suspended particles of one material distributed evenly in another material
compound A chemical combination of two or more elements.
compression stroke Second in a series of four strokes in a piston engine; the stroke during which the intake valve closes and the piston is pushed upward in the cylinder, compressing the fuel-air mixture.
concentration (kon sən trā'shən) A measure of the amount of a particular substance in a given quantity of a mixture or solution.
condensation A change from the gaseous state into the liquid state.
conduction (kən duk'shən) The transfer of heat through a solid; also, the transmission of electricity through a material.
connecting rod A bar connecting two or more moving parts in a piston engine.
convection (kən vek'shən) The transfer of heat throughout a liquid or a gas by the movement of the molecules or atoms.

coordinates (kō ôr'də nits) The *X* and *Y* values on a line graph.
covalent (kō vā'lənt) **bond** A bond between atoms in which electrons are shared.
crankshaft (krangk'shaft) The shaft in an automobile that transfers power to the transmission.
crest The highest point on a wave.
crystalline (kris'tə lin) Made or composed of crystals.
crystal (kris'təl) The special shape or form produced by the arrangement of particles in a solid.
current (kėr'ənt) The rate of flow of electrons in a circuit.
cylinders (sil'ən dərs) The parts of a piston engine in which the air-gasoline mixture is burned.

data (dā'tə) Measurements and observations used to solve a problem.
data table An arrangement of data in rows or columns for easy reference.
DDT An insecticide, the use of which is greatly restricted because of its harmful effects on higher forms of life.
decibel (des'ə bel) A unit of sound intensity, or loudness, in the metric system; abbreviated dB.
decomposition (dē kom pə zish'ən) The physical and chemical interaction of a material with the environment that results in the formation of altered and often simpler materials.
decomposition reaction A chemical reaction that involves breaking a compound apart into simpler compounds or elements.
density (den'sə tē) The amount of mass contained in a given volume of a material.
destructive distillation (dis tə lā'shən) A process by which wood is changed physically and chemically to form new materials.
diameter (dī am'ə tər) The distance across a circle measured through the center.
differential (dif ə ren'shəl) A set of gears in an automobile that directs the power through the axle to the rear wheels, causing them to turn.
dipolar molecule A molecule that has a positively charged pole and a negatively charged pole.
double replacement reaction A chemical reaction that takes place when two compounds react to form two new compounds.
drive shaft The shaft in an automobile that transfers power from the transmission to the differential.
drive train The entire system by which power is transferred to the rear wheels of an automobile.
dynamic equilibrium (ē kwə lib'rē əm) Balance between two opposing and continuing processes.

effort The force put into a system
electricity Energy in the form of electrons that can move along a path or conductor and can be changed into heat, light, mechanical, and chemical energy.
electromagnetic (i lek trō mag net'ik) **spectrum** The entire range of electromagnetic energy.
electromagnetic waves The form in which electromagnetic energy is transmitted.
electrons (i lek'trons) The negatively charged particles in an atom.
element A primary material that cannot be chemically broken down into simpler materials.
emulsion (i mul'shən) A liquid-in-liquid colloid.
energy (en'ər jē) The ability to do work.
energy levels The shells around the nucleus of an atom where electrons are located.

equilibrium (ē kwə lib rē əm) Balance.
evaporation A change from the liquid state into the gaseous state.
exhaust stroke Fourth in a series of four strokes in a piston engine; the stroke in which the piston is pushed upward by the connecting rod, forcing the waste gases out of the cylinder.
exhaust valve A device in a piston engine that permits the waste gases in the cylinder to be released into the exhaust system.
expansion joints Devices used in the construction of large bridges or buildings to allow for expansion and contraction as the temperature changes.
exponent (ek spō′nənt) A number or symbol placed above and to the right of another number or symbol called the base.
extraocular (eks trə ok′yə lər) **vision** The ability to perceive visual sensations without the use of the eyes.
extrapolation (ek strap ə lāshən) Predicting information beyond known data points on a graph.
extrasensory perception (eks trə sen′sər ē pər sep′shən) Perception by other than normal means. Also known as ESP.

Fahrenheit (fər′en hīt) **thermometer** A thermometer that uses 32 degrees as the freezing point of water and 212 degrees as the boiling point.
filament (fil′ə mənt) The small, fine wire inside a light bulb.
first class lever A lever that consists of the fulcrum located between two forces.
fluorescence (flü ə res′əns) The property of certain materials of giving off light when struck by radiation.
foam A gas-in-liquid colloid.
focus (fō′kəs) A point at which rays of light, heat, and so forth, meet after being reflected or refracted.
force Something that can make things move; a push or a pull.
fossil (fos′əl) **fuels** Coal, oil, and natural gas, which were formed from the bodies of plants and animals that died millions of years ago.
frequency (frē′kwən sē) The number of waves produced or passing a given point per second.
friction (frik′shən) A force that opposes motion between two objects in contact.
fuel injection system A system in which a precisely measured mixture of fuel and air is sprayed directly into the cylinders of an engine. It has replaced the carburetor in some automobiles.
fulcrum (ful′krəm) The point about which a lever turns.
fundamental (fun də men′təl) **tone** The main frequency of vibrations.

gamma (gam′ə) **rays** Rays given off by the nucleus of an atom of a radioactive substance. Gamma rays are similar to X rays but are more penetrating.
gaseous (gas′ē əs) **state** A state of matter in which a substance is without definite shape or volume.
gauges (gā js) Measuring instruments.
gears Devices in a machine that transmit motion by means of teeth or friction wheels.
geiger (gī′gər) **counter** An instrument used to detect or measure radiation.
general properties Properties that may be the same for two or more objects.
geologic (jē ə loj′ik) **processes** Operation of physical forces in and on the earth, causing changes in structure and appearance.
geothermal (jē ə thėr′məl) **energy** The earth's internal heat.
graduate A scaled cylinder used to measure liquid volume.

graduated beaker A calibrated flat-bottomed container with a pouring lip.
gram A metric unit of mass equal to 0.001 kilogram; abbreviated g.
graph (graf) A picture of data.
grouping Numerical ordering of data.

half-life The period of time necessary for half the atoms of a radioactive substance to decay into another element.
heat exchanger A solar-heating-system device through which heated liquid from the heat reservoir is pumped to warm the surrounding air.
heat reservoir (rez′ər vwär) A storage place for heat energy in a solar heating system.
herbicide (hėr′bə sīd) A chemical substance used to destroy harmful weeds.
hertz (hėrtz) The basic unit of frequency in the metric system, equal to one cycle per second; abbreviated Hz.
heterogeneous (het ər ə jē′nē əs) **mixture** A mixture in which the materials are unevenly distributed.
histogram (his′tə gram) Another name for a bar graph.
homogeneous (hō mə jē′nē əs) **mixture** A mixture in which the materials are evenly or uniformly dispersed.
horizontal (hôr ə zon′təl) **bar graph** A type of bar graph on which the bars run horizontally.
horizontal coordinate The *X* value on a line graph.
hydrochloric acid A solution of hydrogen chloride in water.
hydroelectric turbine (hī drō i lek′trik tėr′bin) A device for producing electricity by waterpower.
hydrogen bond The special bond between a proton and the negative side of a water dipole that forms a hydronium ion.

identifying properties Specific properties that make one object different from all the other objects to which it is similar.
inertia (in ėr′shə) The tendency of objects in motion to remain in motion or of objects at rest to remain at rest.
inference (in′fər əns) An interpretation of an observation.
insulator (in′sə lā tər) A poor conductor of heat or electricity.
intake stroke First in a series of four strokes in a piston engine; the stroke in which the piston is drawn down by the connecting rod, enabling the cylinder to fill with a gasoline-air mixture.
intake valve In a piston engine, a device which allows the gasoline-air mixture from the carburetor to enter the cylinder.
interpolation (in tėr pə lā′shən) Predicting or estimating data between known points on a graph.
ion (ī′ən) An atom that does not have a neutral electrical charge.
ionic (ī on′ik) **bond** The bond formed when electrons are transferred from the outer shell of one atom to the outer shell of another atom.
isotopes (ī′sə tōps) Atoms of the same element with different mass numbers.

joule A basic unit of energy, work, or heat in the metric system; abbreviated J.

kilogram The basic unit of mass in the metric system; abbreviated kg.
kilohertz (kil′e hėrtz) A metric unit of frequency; 1000 hertz; abbreviated kHz.
kilometer (kil′ə mē tər) A metric unit of length equal to 1000 meters; abbreviated km.
kilowatt-hour A metric unit of electrical energy equal to 1000 watt-hours; abbreviated kW·h.

kinetic (ki net′ik) **energy** Energy of motion.
kinetic particle theory The model used to explain changes of state of materials and the motion of particles.
kinetic (ki net′ik) **theory of matter** The model that states all materials are made up of particles that are in constant motion.

lanthanide (lan thə′nīd) **series** The period of elements beginning with lanthanum (atomic number 57) and ending with lutetium (atomic number 71). Elements in the lanthanide series are classified as metals.
law of conservation of matter The law that states that matter cannot be created nor destroyed in physical and chemical changes.
law of definite composition A law that states that the elements in a compound always combine in definite proportions by mass.
lever (lev′ər) Any kind of bar or rod that does not bend and that turns on a fulcrum.
levitation (lev′ə tā′shən) Another term for *psychokinesis*, or the ability of a person to influence the movement of an object by thinking about it.
light-year The distance that light travels in one year.
line graph A graph drawn on a rectangular grid, with number lines drawn at right angles to each other.
linear (lin′ē ər) **measurement** A measurement of length, such as distance or height.
liter (lē′tər) The basic unit of liquid volume in the metric system; abbreviated L.

mass The amount of material in an object, expressed in grams or kilograms.
mass number The sum of the protons and neutrons in the nucleus of an atom.
medium (mē′dē əm) The matter through which a wave moves.
megahertz (meg′ə hėrtz) A metric unit of frequency equal to 1 million hertz; abbreviated MHz.
melting point The temperature at which a material changes from a solid into a liquid.
meniscus (mə nis′kəs) The curved surface of a liquid in a narrow container.
metallic (mə tal′ik) **bond** The result of metal atoms combining to form solid crystals, with the electrons able to move freely from one atom to the next in the metallic crystals.
metallurgy (met′ə lėr jē) The study of the chemistry of metallic bonds and of the properties of metals and alloys.
meter (mē′tər) The basic unit of length in the metric system; abbreviated m.
milliliter A metric unit of liquid volume equal to 0.001 liter; abbreviated mL.
millimeter (mil′ə mē tər) A metric unit of length equal to 0.001 meter; abbreviated mm.
mineral An important chemical compound or element deposited by slow, geologic processes and scattered in pockets in the earth's crust.
mixture (miks′chər) A substance composed of two or more materials not chemically bonded.
molecule (mol′ə kyül) The smallest unit of a substance that retains the chemical properties of the substance.

negative pole An area of a molecule which becomes negatively charged because of an excess or proximity of electrons.
neutral (nü′trəl) Not being positively or negatively charged.
neutrons (nü′tronz) Atomic particles that have no electrical charge and are therefore electrically neutral.

newton (nü'tən) The basic unit of force in the metric system; abbreviated N.
newton meter A basic unit of work in the metric system; abbreviated N·m. A newton meter of work is also called a joule.
noise Any undesirable sound.
nonrenewable resources Resources whose quantity is limited and, once used, cannot be renewed.
nucleus (nü'klē əs) The central, positively charged, dense portion of the atom.

open circuit An incomplete circuit due to a break in the continuous connection of conductors from one end of an electrical source to the other.
organic (ôr gan'ik) **chemistry** The study of carbon compounds.
overtones (ō'vər tōnz) Multiples of the main frequency of vibrations.
oxide A compound formed by an element combining with oxygen.

parallel (par'ə lel) **circuit** A circuit having two or more paths through which electricity can flow.
particle theory of matter The model that states that all materials are composed of small particles.
PCBs A group of chemicals that pollute the water in certain industrial areas.
pendulum (pen'jə ləm) A weight so suspended from a fixed point as to swing freely under the combined action of gravity and momentum.
period One complete back-and-forth swing of a pendulum.
periodic (pir ē od'ik) **law** The grouping of elements so that there is a periodic repetition of their chemical and physical properties.
periodic (pir ē od'ik) **table** A table of chemical elements arranged according to increasing atomic number and grouped according to the periodic changes that occur in their chemical properties.
pesticide (pes'tə sīd) A chemical substance used to destroy pests such as insects.
pH A scale for expressing the relative concentration of hydronium ions.
photosynthesis (fō tə sin'thə sis) The food-making process in green plants.
physical change A change that results in a different physical shape or form of a material but not in the material itself.
piston A sliding cylindrical part that moves back and forth within a cylinder.
piston engine An engine that converts heat energy to mechanical energy by means of pistons that move back and forth in a cylinder.
pollutant (pə lü'tənt) Anything that contaminates the environment.
pollution (pə lü'shən) Contamination resulting from the physical and chemical interaction of a material (or energy) with the environment.
positive pole An area of a molecule which becomes positively charged because of a deficiency of electrons.
power stroke Third in a series of four strokes in a piston engine; the stroke in which a spark from the sparkplug ignites the gasoline-air mixture.
powers of ten notation A mathematical shorthand. (See **scientific notation.)**
precipitate (pri sip'ə tat) A solid substance that forms from a chemical reaction in a liquid or a gas. It separates out of a solution.
precognition (prē kog nish'ən) The ability to sense what is going to happen before it takes place.
prefix (prē'fiks) One or more letters or syllables added to the beginning of a word to modify its meaning.

product The material formed in a chemical action.
properties Features that describe an object.
proton (prō'ton) **acceptors** Bases that form hydroxide ions by taking protons away from water molecules.
proton donors Another name for acids.
protons (prō'tonz) Atomic particles that have a positive electrical charge.
psychic (sī'kik) **event** An event perceived by other than normal means.
psychokinesis (sī kō ki nē'sis) The ability of a person to influence the movement of an object by thinking about it.
pulley (pu̇l'ē) A wheel with a grooved rim in which a belt, rope, or chain runs. Used in running a machine or in lifting.
pulse (puls) A disturbance in matter that transfers energy without transferring matter; part of a wave.

qualitative (kwol'ə tā tiv) **analysis** The process of testing to determine what substances are in a specific material.
qualitative observations Observations that describe the quality of an object but not the value or amount of that quality.
quantitative (kwon'tə tā tiv) **analysis** A test to determine how much of each substance is present in a specific sample of material.
quantitative (kwon'tə tā tiv) **observation** An observation involving measurement.

radiation (rā dē ā'shən) The transfer of energy in the form of waves. The waves do not require a material medium for transmission; also, the emission from a radioactive atom.
radical (rad'ə kəl) A group of atoms having a positive or negative charge that interact as a single unit.
radioactive decay The process by which an atom of one element becomes an atom of a different element by the emission of alpha or beta particles from the nucleus.
radioactivity (rā dē o ak tiv'ə tē) The giving off of particles and rays from the nucleus of an atom.
radioisotopes The name sometimes given to radioactive elements used as tracers in scientific investigations.
reactants (rē ak'tənts) The starting materials in a chemical reaction.
refract (ri frakt') To bend, as the bending of light rays by a prism.
renewable resource A resource that can be regenerated and is therefore always available.
resistance (ri zis'təns) The force that must be overcome in a system.
resources (ri sôr'siz) Natural wealth, such as mineral deposits and forests.
responding variable The one variable in an experiment that is not controlled.
rotational (rō tā'shə nəl) **motion** The turning or movement of a molecule about its axis. It occurs in liquids and gases.

saturated (sach'ə rā tid) **solution** A solution containing the maximum amount of solute possible at that particular temperature of the solution.
scientific notation A shorthand system of writing very large or very small numbers. The very large or very small number is expressed as a number between one and ten (the base) raised to an exponential power of ten.
scintillation (sin tə lā'shən) **counter** An instrument used to measure radiation.
second class lever A lever that has the resistance located between the effort and the fulcrum.

series circuit A circuit with only one path through which electricity can flow.
shells The areas in which electrons are located around the nucleus of an atom.
single replacement reaction A chemical reaction in which an element and a compound react to form a new compound and a different element.
sliding friction The friction caused when one object moves across another.
solar (sō'lər) **cell** A device that can change sunlight directly into electricity.
solar (sō'lər) **energy** Energy from the sun.
solidify (sə lid'ə fī) To freeze, or to become solid.
solute (sol'yüt) In a solution, the material that dissolves.
solution (sə lü'shən) A homogeneous mixture.
solvent (sol'vənt) In a solution, the material in which the solute dissolves.
sonar (sō'när) An apparatus that detects the location of a submerged object by means of sonic and ultrasonic waves that are reflected back to it from the object.
spark plug A device in the cylinder of a piston engine that ignites the gasoline-air mixture by an electric spark.
specific (spi sif'ik) **gravity** The ratio of the density of a material to the density of a standard.
spectator ion An ion that remains unchanged in solution during a chemical reaction.
spherical (sfer'ə kəl) Globular, or shaped like a sphere.
static friction The friction between two objects that are in contact but not moving.
stroboscope (strob'ə skōp) A device that can stop motion of a body by periodically interrupting light.
strong acids Acids that produce many hydronium ions in solution.
strong bases Bases that produce many hydroxide ions in solution.
sulfide (sul'fīd) A compound containing sulfur combined chemically with a more metallic element. In sulfides, sulfur has a valence of −2.
sulfuric acid A solution of hydrogen sulfate in water.
supersaturated (sü pər sach'ə rāt ed) **solution** A solution that holds more solute than it should be able to hold at a certain temperature.
surface area That part of a material that is exposed to the environment and therefore interacts directly with it.
synthesis (sin'thə sis) **reaction** A chemical reaction in which two elements or compounds are chemically combined to form a new compound.
system A group of objects that work together.

telemetry (tə lem'ə trē) A method of transmitting to earth data and pictures obtained in space by satellites or space probes.
telepathy (tə lep'ə thē) The ability of one mind to communicate with another by means other than the five senses.
thermal (thėr'məl) **pollution** Pollution caused by excess heat released into the environment.
third class lever A lever with the effort located between the resistance and the fulcrum.
tracers Radioisotopes used to follow and identify certain biological, chemical, and physical processes.
transition (tran zish'ən) **elements** The center group of elements in the periodic table.
translational (trans lā'shə nəl) **motion** The motion characteristic of particles in the gaseous state. The particles change their positions with respect to each other.

transmission A complicated supersystem of gears for transmitting power to the drive shaft in an automobile.

Tyndall (tin′dəl) **effect** The scattering of a light beam as it is passed through a mixture that is not a true solution.

ultrasonic (ul trə son′ik) **waves** High-frequency waves above 20 000 Hz.

uncontrolled (un kən trōld′) **variable** The one influence, or variable, in an experiment that is not controlled.

variable (vãr′ē ə bəl) **property** A property that influences the solubility of a material.

velocity (və los′ə tē) A measure of rate of change of distance with respect to time.

vertical (vėr′tə kəl) **bar graph** A type of bar graph on which the bars extend up from the horizontal axis.

vertical coordinate The *Y* value on a line graph.

vibrational (vī brā′shə nəl) **motion** An oscillating or back-and-forth motion of a molecule. It is the only type of particle motion in the solid state of matter.

voltage (vōl′tij) The "push" (electrical pressure) applied to electrons as they move in a circuit.

voltmeter (vōlt′mē tər) An instrument for measuring voltage.

volt The basic unit of voltage in the metric system; abbreviated V.

volume The space a material occupies.

wattmeter (wot′mē tər) A device for measuring watts.

watt (wot) The basic unit of electrical power in the metric system; abbreviated W.

wavelength The distance from the crest of one wave to the crest of the next wave.

wave motion The transfer of energy from place to place without the transfer of matter.

weak acids Acids that produce relatively few hydronium ions in solution.

weak bases Bases that produce relatively few hydroxide ions in solution.

weight The effect of the force of gravity on the mass of an object.

wet cell A system used to produce electricity. A wet cell has a free-flowing electrolyte.

work A measurement of force times the distance through which the force is applied.

***X* axis** The horizontal axis on a line graph.

X rays Rays of very short wavelength. They can be generated by a stream of electrons striking against a metal surface in a vacuum tube. They also form part of the electromagnetic spectrum. X rays can penetrate various thicknesses of solids and act on photographic film like light.

***Y* axis** The vertical axis on a line graph.

Index

CREDITS

Cover: © 1978 Harald Sund
Title page: Manfred Kage from Peter Arnold
Unit divider art: Don Pulver
Graphs, Charts & Illustrations: John Lind

Chapter 1 2: Howard Sochurek from Woodfin Camp. 4: Silver Burdett. 6: *t.l.* Silver Burdett, courtesy St. Barnabas Medical Center; *t.r.* John Marmaras from Woodfin Camp; *b.l.* Werner H. Müller from Peter Arnold; *b.r.* Allied Chemical. 9: Silver Burdett. 13: *t.l.* Silver Burdett; *b.l.* Art D'Arazien from Shostal Associates; *r.* Courtesy Steuben Glass. 19: Grant Heilman.
Chapter 2 24: David Forbert from Shostal Associates. 27: Focus on Sports. 40: Leahey from Shostal Associates. 41: *l.* Silver Burdett, courtesy Carolina Biological Supply Co.; *r.* Silver Burdett, courtesy St. Barnabas Medical Center. 44: Silver Burdett. 45: Allied Chemical.
Chapter 3 48: David Overcash from Bruce Coleman. 53: Craig Aurness from Woodfin Camp. 54: Courtesy Eagle Picher Co. 55: *l.* Ralph Williams from Bruce Coleman; *r.* L. Weiner from Shostal Associates. 57: *t.* Frank Wing from Stock, Boston; *b.l.* © 1978 Shorty Wilcox; *r.* Michael Provost for Silver Burdett. 60: Silver Burdett. 61: Irwin from Shostal Associates. 62: Susan Perry from Woodfin Camp.
Chapter 4 64: Howard Brainen. 66: Culver Pictures. 68: Silver Burdett. 69: John Running for Silver Burdett. 71: Dr. E. R. Degginger for Silver Burdett. 72: *t.* Silver Burdett; *b.* Michael P. Gadomski from Bruce Coleman. 73: Reiner from Shostal Associates. 77: *t.l.* Hans D. Müller from Peter Arnold; *t.r., b.l., b.r.* Manfred Kage from Peter Arnold. 78: Richard Choi from Peter Arnold. 80: Adam Woolfitt from Woodfin Camp.
Chapter 5 82: Silver Burdett. 86: *l.* Tony Howarth from Woodfin Camp; *r.* Everett Johnson from Leo de Wys. 87: Dr. E. R. Degginger for Silver Burdett. 89: S. Jonasson from Bruce Coleman. 90: *l.* Dr. E. R. Degginger for Silver Burdett; *r.* Rhoda Sidney from Leo de Wys. 91: John Running for Silver Burdett. 95: Silver Burdett. 100: Allied Chemical. 101: Allied Chemical.
Chapter 6 104: Sygma. 107 *t., b.* Dr. E. R. Degginger for Silver Burdett. 108: Joe Barnell from Shostal Associates. 109: *t.* Courtesy Fisher Collection, Fisher Scientific Co.; *b.* Dr. E. R. Degginger for Silver Burdett. 112: *t.* Culver Pictures; *b.* Dr. E. R. Degginger for Silver Burdett. 113: Silver Burdett, courtesy St. Barnabas Medical Center. 114: Culver Pictures. 116: *l.* The Bettmann Archive, Inc.; *r.* Silver Burdett, courtesy Morris Museum of Arts & Sciences. 119: Alvis Upitis from Shostal Associates.
Chapter 7 127: Courtesy American Telephone & Telegraph. 129: The Bettmann Archive, Inc. 130: Silver Burdett. 131: Dr. E. R. Degginger for Silver Burdett. 133: Dr. E. R. Degginger for Silver Burdett. 135: William Wright from Taurus Photos. 136: Silver Burdett. 139: Courtesy Bausch & Lomb. 140: NASA. 144: Silver Burdett. 146: Tim Eagan from Woodfin Camp. 148: NASA. 149: Silver Burdett.
Chapter 8 152: Silver Burdett. 154: Jerry Howard from Stock, Boston. 155: *l.* Silver Burdett; *r.* Dr. E. R. Degginger for Silver Burdett. 157: Dr. E. R. Degginger for Silver Burdett. 159: Taurus Photos. 161: Jane Burton from Bruce Coleman. 162: Silver Burdett. 164: Silver Burdett. 165: Dr. E. R. Degginger for Silver Burdett. 171: *l.* Ellis Herwig from Stock, Boston; *r.* Silver Burdett. 172: The Bettmann Archive, Inc. 174: Dr. E. R. Degginger for Silver Burdett.
Chapter 9 178: Courtesy The Bethlehem Steel Corporation. 181: *l.* Culver Pictures; *r.* The Bettmann Archive, Inc. 182: Courtesy Brookhaven Labs. 185: Michael Collier from Stock, Boston. 186: Courtesy Brookhaven Labs. 189: *l.* William Hubbell from Woodfin Camp; *r.* Courtesy Varian Associates. 190: *l.* Donald Baird, Princeton University; *r.* Michael Collier from Stock, Boston. 194: Allied Chemical. 195: Courtesy Billings Energy Corporation.
Chapter 10 198: Shostal Associates. 200: Norman Myers from Bruce Coleman. 201: Everett Johnson from Leo de Wys. 204: *t.* Silver Burdett; *b.* NASA. 205: John S. Flannery from Bruce Coleman. 208: Silver Burdett. 210: Silver Burdett. 214: Leo de Wys.
Chapter 11 216: Morton Beebe. 218: *l.* Smithsonian Institution; *r.* Silver Burdett. 221: Silver Burdett. 230: Courtesy Motch & Merryweather. 232: Krispinsky from Shostal Associates. 233: NASA. 235: Craig Aurness from Woodfin Camp.
Chapter 12 239: Adam Woolfitt from Woodfin Camp. 241: Silver Burdett. 242: Silver Burdett. 244: Daniel S. Brody from Stock, Boston. 249: Silver Burdett. 252: Silver Burdett. 253: Silver Burdett.
Chapter 13 256: Silver Burdett. 258: NASA. 259: Silver Burdett. 262: Alan Foley from Bruce Coleman. 269: Silver Burdett.
Chapter 14 272: Malak from Shostal Associates. 279: S. C. Bisserot from Bruce Coleman. 281: Bell Labs. 283: Denny McMains. 285: General Electric. 286: Julian Calder from Woodfin Camp.
Chapter 15 290: Exxon. 292: Exxon. 293: Dan Budnik from Woodfin Camp. 294: Tony Howath from Woodfin Camp. 298: *t.* Grant Heilman; *b.l., b.r.* Marc & Evelyn Bernheim from Woodfin Camp. 300: Carl Kummels from Shostal Associates. 301: NASA. 304: Reynolds Aluminum.
Chapter 16 306: Bruce Coleman. 308: *t.* Kondrotos from Shostal Associates; *b.* Dan Budnik from Woodfin Camp. 309: *t.l.* Rick Winsor from Woodfin Camp; *t.r.* Jeffrey Foxx from Woodfin Camp; *b.* Marvin Newman from Woodfin Camp. 310: Peter Guntner from Shostal Associates. 312: Peter J. Menzel from Stock, Boston. 314: David Forbert from Shostal Associates. 317: Art D'Arazien from Shostal Associates. 318: Ellis Herwig from Stock, Boston.
Chapter 17 322: Culver Pictures. 324: Joseph Martin from Editorial Photocolor Archive. 325: The Bettmann Archive, Inc. 326: Cary Wolinsky from Stock, Boston. 327: *l.* General Motors Corporation; *r.* Silver Burdett. 333: Donald Dietz from Stock, Boston. 334: Eric Carle from Shostal Associates. 335: *t.* Daniel S. Brody from Stock, Boston; *b.* Boeing Aerospace Company. 336: *t.* Cary Wolinsky from Stock, Boston; *b.* Paul Conklin. 338: James R. Holland from Stock, Boston.
Chapter 18 340: Cary Wolinsky from Stock, Boston. 342: The Bettmann Archive, Inc. 343: *l.* L. Foster from Bruce Coleman; *r.* James Sugar from Woodfin Camp. 344: NASA. 345: Sandia Laboratories. 348: *t.* NASA; *b.* David Cupp from Woodfin Camp. 349: Peter J. Menzel from Stock, Boston. 351: *t.* John Shaw from Bruce Coleman; *b.* NASA. 354: *l.* Bruce Coleman; *r.* Nicholas de Vore III from Bruce Coleman. 355: Gontcheros from Shostal Associates. 356: *l.* RCA Labs, Princeton; *r.* Arizona Department of Transportation. 357: Lawrence Livermore Labs.
Chapter 19 360: Penny Coleman. 362: Alvis Upitis from Shostal Associates. 364: Eric Carle from Shostal Associates. 365: Mike Mazzaschi from Stock, Boston. 369: Eric Carle from Shostal Associates. 370: *t.* Art D'Arazien from Shostal Associates; *b.* Joe Barnell from Shostal Associates. 374: NASA. 375: Lawrence Livermore Labs.
Excursions 378: Silver Burdett. 379: Silver Burdett.

1 2 3 4 5 6 7 8 9 10—WAK—88 87 86 85 84 83 82 81

PERIODS	GROUPS I	II				TRANSITION ELEMENTS			
1	1 1.00797 H Hydrogen								
2	3 6.939 Li Lithium	4 9.0122 Be Beryllium							
3	11 22.9898 Na Sodium	12 24.312 Mg Magnesium							
4	19 39.102 K Potassium	20 40.08 Ca Calcium	21 44.956 Sc Scandium	22 47.90 Ti Titanium	23 50.942 V Vanadium	24 51.996 Cr Chromium	25 54.9380 Mn Manganese	26 55.847 Fe Iron	27 58.9332 Co Cobalt
5	37 85.47 Rb Rubidium	38 87.62 Sr Strontium	39 88.905 Y Yttrium	40 91.22 Zr Zirconium	41 92.906 Nb Niobium	42 95.94 Mo Molybdenum	43 (99)* Tc Technetium	44 101.07 Ru Ruthenium	45 102.905 Rh Rhodium
6	55 132.905 Cs Cesium	56 137.34 Ba Barium	57 138.91 La Lanthanum †	72 178.49 Hf Hafnium	73 180.948 Ta Tantalum	74 183.85 W Tungsten	75 186.2 Re Rhenium	76 190.2 Os Osmium	77 192.2 Ir Iridium
7	87 (223)* Fr Francium	88 (226)* Ra Radium	89 (227)* Ac Actinium ‡	104 (259)* Rf** Rutherfordium	105 Ha Hahnium**	106***	107***	108***	

† LANTHANIDE SERIES	58 140.12 Ce Cerium	59 140.907 Pr Praseodymium	60 144.24 Nd Neodymium	61 (147)* Pm Promethium	62 150.35 Sm Samarium	63 151.96 Eu Europium	64 157.25 Gd Gadolinium	65 158.924 Tb Terbium
‡ ACTINIDE SERIES	90 232.038 Th Thorium	91 (231)* Pa Protactinium	92 238.03 U Uranium	93 (237)* Np Neptunium	94 (242)* Pu Plutonium	95 (243)* Am Americium	96 (247)* Cm Curium	97 (247)* Bk Berkelium

*Atomic masses appearing in parentheses are those of the most stable known isotopes.

**Names are unofficial.